A NORTHERN SCHOOL

A NORTHERN SCHOOL

Lancashire artists of the twentieth century

PETER DAVIES

REDCLIFFE
Bristol

First published in 1989
by Redcliffe Press Ltd.,
49 Park St., Bristol

ISBN 0 948265 73 6

Typeset by The Picador Group
Printed by Biddles Ltd., Guildford

Contents

Foreword	6
Introduction	9
One – Art Across Merseyside	14
Two – Liverpool Academy	45
Three – Strands of Manchester Art: Past and Present	65
Four – Manchester Academy: 1929 - 38	93
Five – Manchester Academy: The War	114
Six – Manchester Academy: 1946 - 59	127
Seven – Margo Ingham, The Midday Studios and The Manchester Group	150
Eight – Ian Grant	169
Nine – Theodore Major	178
Ten – Alan Lowndes	185
Eleven – Kenneth Gribble	199
Twelve – Roger Hampson	210
Thirteen – Harold Riley and William Turner	218
Illustrations	232
Index	235

Foreword

Peter Davies's book takes me back to my *Guardian* years, when from 1948 to 1951 I was a foreign leader-writer on the legendary corridor in Cross Street and found myself almost by accident also going out to cover art exhibitions in and around Manchester, a city which unlike Vienna, Madrid and Cairo was quite unknown to me. It was a memorable experience, and I am deeply grateful for it, not only because of what I took away on leaving - lifelong friendships plus a number of pictures including a fine Wigan drawing by Theodore Major which was subsequently stolen in France - but also because of the special characteristics of the Mancunians, the still largely Victorian conurbation, the splendid country fringing it to the East, and the many stories and episodes which could have been situated nowhere else in the world. I loved it all; and perhaps I should have stayed.

Then in the late 1960's I became involved with the neighbouring but strangely irreconcilable city of Liverpool, about whose artists and their role in that city I wrote a report. This originated back in 1949 (I think) when I had gone to review the Manchester Academy show for the *Guardian* and found among much tedious Establishment work two very striking paintings, the one signed Le Breton, the other - a lovely view of industrial building in the Medway valley - N.Horsfield. Le Breton, who also had an excellent small street scene in the Salford municipal gallery, turned out to be neither Constant nor Louis but the landlady of a Salford pub; I wish I had found out more about her. Horsfield, who wrote to me because he liked what I said in my review, proved to be working in the local Arts Council offices. Round the corner, in the Crown Hotel, he started telling me that the Liverpool painters (among them Arthur Ballard and George Jardine) were more interesting than those in Manchester, so I was not surprised when he left the Arts Council to join them. But it was he and Hugh Scrutton of the Walker Art Gallery who got me commissioned to survey the Liverpool art scene and write what later appeared as *Art in a City*. And in the process I fell for Liverpool too.

All this is to explain how haphazardly one may come to realise that not only Venice and Barbizon but also supposedly less attractive places have a subtle power to stimulate and form the visual arts. Manchester in my time had Lowry, Ned Owens, Baskerville, Le Breton, Harry Rutherford, Emmanuel Levy and Alan Lowndes, reinforced by Major, Harold Hemingway and the Belgian-born engraver Françoise Taylor from the neighbouring towns: those were the people who most clearly reflected its particular character. The Austrian refugee Georg Eisler had just left for Vienna, and I never saw the show which Margaret Bulley arranged for him. But last year his paintings of the city of his adolescence showed that he too belonged with them; and this book has other names to add, to say nothing of those who have come along since.

Liverpool has an older and larger professional art community, whose Academy—now sadly defunct—depended, unlike Manchester's, neither on London exhibitors nor on local amateurs. I started spending two or three days a week there just as the Mersey Sound was beginning to boom, and the interaction of the pop influence with Victorian and Lancastrian tradition and the city's ethnic openness was fascinating. Broadly speaking two generations were then active: that of the Beatles themselves (who like many pop stars were in part art school products—educationists please note- and that of their College teachers; there was no Lowry. But there were Ballard, Jardine, John Hart, Arthur Dooley, Martin Bell and Roderic Bisson of the older lot; Adrian Henri, Sam Walsh, Peter Mackarell, Robin Riley and the (prematurely) late Stuart Sutcliffe of the younger; and most of these were flagrantly Liverpudlian and quite capable, as a close-knit group, of absorbing and appreciating such recruits as Horsfield, Maurice Cockrill, the non-figurative John Edkins and the Hungarian George Mayer-Marton. There was in those days a recognisable Liverpool 'art scene', largely independent of London and owing much to the *genius loci*, the character of the place.

It was this twofold experience of the North-West that made me, in my mind's eye, start enumerating the distinct centres of more or less indigenous art outside London. There were of course places like St Ives which were inherently picturesque and had been largely colonised by artists from elsewhere; there was a great tradition in East Anglia, going back to Gainsborough; there also seemed to be an active school in the North-East, where Newcastle was (and is) a notable poetry centre. Brighton too has an original character, determined for me by Jeff Keen's drawings and films; while Peter Davies in an earlier book has made a convincing case for Dorset. More clearly than any of this, yet even less consciously recognised in London, there is the semi-independent art scene in Scotland, with Glasgow as its powerhouse and Edinburgh as its metropolis; I was amazed in my *Guardian* days when I encountered the work of W.G.Gillies and realised that in England he was virtually unknown. Admittedly all this adds up to nothing so decentralised as the pattern in Italy, Germany or Austria, whose culture is regional and in some cases spills across national frontiers. But in the new supranational context into which we are moving regions, cities and even parishes will be increasingly important.

It was Adrian Henri who taught me that from the local art scene the individual can now judge the seminal influences of his time directly, without having to follow what London thinks right: he or she can feel the impact of Andy Warhol, say, for better or for worse, without worrying about how Warhol's work tastes to Ruskin or Fry or Herbert Read or Kenneth Clark. This is one thing that has changed since the 1930's. Another is the blurring of the distinction between professional and amateur status in the visual arts (in contrast to music); these are no longer practised only by an élite, and when they are they are sometimes not visual at all. A third is the erosion of national frontiers, a fourth the increase in travel. Once we recognise all this it would seem a worthwhile task for our museum and exhibition authorities to pay attention not only to art's central figures, judged nationally or worldwide, but also to establishing the individuality of the smaller centres: a series of galleries in the Tate, say, devoted separately to Glasgow, Liverpool, Manchester, St Ives etc. from their earliest artists until now. Then we would see how they differ.

In the new context parochialism will be regarded as a form of strength and originality; researches like Peter Davies's having more than purely local relevance. This book must be followed by others to illuminate a neglected area of the arts: something we certainly need in a changing world.

John Willett

Introduction

Why Lancashire? It is an inevitable question, with an equally obvious answer. Until now, scant justice has been done to a wealth of artistic activity in this neglected region. A so-called 'northern school' of urban, industrial and social realists forms a nucleus for a wider, multifarious movement in art that draws from the local peculiarities, traditions and unmistakable character of the north west. As well as echoing trends within British art as a whole in this century, the northern school evaluated here has also drawn on a number of macro-international artistic developments of our century. So it is not surprising that the waves of artists who exhibited at the Liverpool and Manchester Academies throughout the period drew on impressionist and post-impressionist styles, techniques and subjects. But more crucially they were followed by painters who often successfully adapted modernist modes.

In Liverpool, Roderick Bisson worked in a style that integrated architectural design and cubo-constructivism with a range of sea-shore surrealist imagery. Bisson, from the 1930's onwards, was a member of the Sandon Studios Society and his 1965 book on the history of that important Liverpool institution is the definitive account. According to Nicholas Horsfield, even in the context of the Sandon - a conventional society "which would have accepted Sickert as advanced" - Bisson's work appeared 'extraordinary.' Middle East war service enabled him to note desert forms that also later informed and enriched his surrealist imagery. Bisson became a critic for the *Liverpool Daily Post,*and for 25 years a consistently high level of critical appreciation for both local and national artistic figures seen on Merseyside contributed to the overall quality of criticism in the region's newspapers. My greatest immediate debt is to the rich vein of art criticism in these newspapers, which has enabled me to quote at some length the substance of many local exhibitions in the north west over 50 years.

The story of art in the north west is not, however, characterised only by a provincial or sub-national school responding to continental modernist developments. Nor is it limited to a competent topographical and impressionist recording of a changing urban scene. Many artists of exotic or expressionist flavour come into the story at regular intervals, giving Lancashire art an unexpected spice and unpredictability. The fact that the 'Beatles', as leather-clad rock and rollers, early on made Hamburg their first stomping ground indicates, I think, an expressionist tenor running through much northern art in England. In Germany, Astrid Kirchherr's stark black and white photographs of the group whose dress and hairstyle she influenced, touched a mood similar to that evoked by the black and white woodcut that was so typical a feature of the 'Brücke' phase of German Expressionist art. Max Blond's memorable woodcut 'Across the Mersey,' with its amalgam of 'Brücke' forms with Pop, confirms this link. The grey climate, brooding skies, social poverty were all factors that gave Manchester and Liverpool at least a partial temperamental kinship to the angst, melancholy or intensified feeling of German, Nordic or mid-European expressionist art. Yet artists like Adolphe Valette and Emmanuel Levy in Manchester also instilled impressionistic colour into northern art. Both Emmanuel Levy and Sam Rabin, later renowned for his boxing subjects, came from the Jewish society of Manchester, but later moved to London and Poole respectively. Sam Rabin gave me my first drawing lessons in Poole in 1978, an experience remembered less for his rigorous and somewhat rigid analytical and anatomical approach than for his warmly conveyed anecdotes about the multitude of artists-Lowry among them-who were a part of Rabin's own colourful and rich Manchester background. I was fortunate in having my portrait painted by Emmanuel Levy at his Belsize Park flat in December 1985, a month before he died at the age of 85.

An artist whom I never met, but who indirectly started me on the path towards this book was Alan Lowndes. At the request of his widow Valerie, I wrote an as yet unpublished biography on the life of this colourful and individual artist. It certainly set me on my way towards making a general investigation into Lancashire art. I was encouraged by the realisation that the study had never before been attempted. The section on Alan's early life and career in Stockport has been recycled into the chapter on him for this book, and to the following I am especially grateful for their information, encouragement and help on Alan Lowndes: Valerie Lowndes, the artist's widow, Christine Lowndes, his sister, and Andreas Kalman, Lowndes' lifelong dealer and promoter. Old Stockport friends like the school teacher Ron Hassell and Ron Thomas, a watercolourist and textile teacher at Stockport Technical College, were also extremely helpful, as were Frieda Taylor Clowes and Elizabeth Horsfield, former girlfriends of Alan Lowndes. The late Ken Kelsall of Shaw Heath, Stockport provided me with hospitality and an insight into old Stockport. Later friends in Alan's life included Jack Harris, Terry Frost and Brian Bull and all were of help, as were Christopher Hull and writers Keith Waterhouse and Bill Naughton. Both writers corresponded with me about Alan, providing affectionate memories and appreciation of his work. Lowndes represents a very obvious example of the link between Lancashire and St Ives. Fred Yates is another such artist, with similar spirit and inclination, and has been of great help.

The second stage in the construction of the text came in late 1987 with access to Margo Ingham's invaluable archive material, bequeathed to the Manchester City Art Gallery. For allowing me full access to these important sources, as well as to the huge scrapbooks of the annual Manchester Academy exhibition archives, I owe special thanks to Julian Spalding, former Director, and to Julian Treuhertz, former Keeper, then of the Manchester gallery and now of Glasgow and Liverpool museums respectively. Treuhertz's exhibition 'Hard Times,' with its scholarly text on nineteenth century northern industrial and social realist painting, is a precursor to my twentieth century study. Sandra Martin was also helpful in supervising my studies in Manchester. In Liverpool, I was able to make similar use of the rather thinner, but still enormously informative Liverpool Academy scrapbooks kept at the Walker Art Gallery. For that I am thankful to Alex Kidson, Xanthe Brooke and Edward Morris. I also owe thanks to Stephen Sartin and Caroline Simon of the Lancashire Museums Service, and to Stephen Forshaw of the Atkinson Museum, Southport, who not only provided some important illustrative material but also gave me the opportunity to arrange an exhibition, 'My Generation', of contemporary abstract art, as well as coincidentally to represent several of the Lancashire-born artists who are featured in the book.

The artist who perhaps above all others proved to be the most useful pointer and guide was Nicholas Horsfield, whom I originally went to see in the autumn of 1985 in connection with my Alan Lowndes biography. John Willett helped me a great deal with Alan Lowndes and other artists of the period, and his study *Art in a City* (1967) will remain a standard book on Merseyside art. I owe a debt to Merseyside artists George Jardine, Adrian Henri, Donald McKinlay; and to Ros McAlastair, for supplying information and photographs. As the present study unfolded, I came to seek out Theodore Major, Roger Hampson, Ian and Margaret Grant, Kenneth Gribble, William Turner, Max Blond, Dr Marion Maxwell Reekie, Donald Hewit, Brian Gordon, Harold Riley, Lesley Young, Stephen Lewis and Kevin Lewis. All gave their time and were of the utmost help with my researches. Jonathan Blond provided information on his distinguished family's contribution to art in Liverpool. Long-standing friends, whose work I knew and championed before I began the northern book, included Peter Hoida, Kay Saunders, Barbara Lander and Geoff Rigden, and all spent time patiently answering my questions. Sven Berlin and especially Frank Dodman provided some perceptive commentary on Manchester and Liverpool artists after the war. I am also grateful to Dorothy Almond and to Alex and June Simpson for much help, the latter providing hospitality and friendship. I also thank my late brother Robin Davies, and my girlfriend Pat Evans for their encouragement and inspiration. Mike Bayntun, Kay Saunders, Barbara Hunt and Valerie Lowndes helped with some of the typing.

Several exhibitions of note in the last few years have indicated the need for a full survey such as the one I have attempted. Julian Spalding's 'Forgotten Fifties' show, organised while he was Director at Sheffield, highlighted a northern working class realist 'school,' though this was more Yorkshire than Lancashire-based. But his exhibition 'Georg Eisler, Landscape of Exile' shown at Manchester City Art Gallery in 1988, presented an artist from a central European, expressionist tradition, able to draw on early memories as an Austrian war emigré in Manchester to create meaningful and powerful evocations of the spirit of Manchester's red brick and grey slate environment beneath grey skies. Eisler's paintings of Manchester were produced in the early 1980's at the suggestion of John Willett. The result was a body of work that not only emulated the realism of Lowndes and Hampson, but also fitted in to a northern school of landscape painting. Less obvious was the way Eisler, with his handling and colour sense, slots into a Jewish category of expressionist painters who have been active across the region. The greatest exhibition that in recent years anticipated this book and indeed the Pelter/Sands exhibition of Lancashire art which has been aimed to coincide with publication, was the three-part 'Lancashire South of the Sands' exhibition which was the brainchild of the Lancashire Museum Service. Reg Singh's success as an art dealer began in Manchester, where he was an apprentice at the Crane Gallery. He knew many of the artists and clients that formed an important part of Andreas Kalman's rise to prominence. He has always been a valuable source of insight into that period of Manchester art.

Other people I wish to thank for generosity and support include Ambrose Shere and Brian and Sheila Read, all of Skelmersdale. Kelvin Redford of Brecon helped with the reading of proofs. Ultimately I owe greatest thanks to my publisher John Sansom, whose enthusiasm and faith in British art generally, and in this project in particular, has helped the book materialise. With Richard Pelter of the magnificent Pelter/Sands gallery in Bristol I collaborated in the organisation of the large exhibition of artists featured in this book.

I have attempted to be comprehensive in this study, and I apologise to any artists who may have been overlooked. A number of late items came in as a result of artists contacting me after reading my article 'A Northern

School' in the January 1989 isssue of *The Artist* magazine. For the publication of that article I am grateful to a Liverpool-born art editor of long standing experience and renown in London, Bernard Denvir, and to the magazine's editor Sally Bulgin. But one or two artists, too late to include in the main text, deserve a mention. London-based Carolyn Stafford is one such painter, who still draws on northern subjects long after her remove from her native Bolton. She was taught by Ian Grant at Manchester and was a contemporary of Harold Riley at the Slade. In 1987 and 1988 she exhibited etchings depicting Bolton with the Printmakers Council in Manchester. She also exhibited, appropriately, with a group of northern women artists in 1977 - among them Helen Bradley and Sheila Fell, who became a confidante and friend of L.S. Lowry. Fell's generously handled landscape paintings are also worthy representations of northern art in a more rural and poetic mood. Stafford studied at Bolton School of Art in the early 1950's, from where she went to study at Manchester College of Art, and then from 1955 to 1957 at the Slade. While in Manchester she won a Proctor Memorial Travelling Scholarship to Paris, then a Steer Landscape Prize at the Slade. After her post-graduate studies she studied etching with the renowned printmaker S.W. Hayter in Paris. Since the 1960's she has taught and lived in south London, whilst continuing to draw on the unforgettable and formative northern subjects of her youth. Another painter resident in south London, Maurice Cockrill, also paints landscape with a feeling for paint. Cockrill studied under Arthur Ballard in Liverpool, and moved south after nearly 20 years in the north.

There will be some who question my failure to allocate a complete chapter to Lowry, the north's greatest and best loved artistic ambassador. One reason for the decision not to give him a whole chapter is that his posthumous reputation—a largely market phenomenon - has outgrown both his true artistic stature and certainly his stature at the time within a large milieu of both pre- and post-war Manchester artists. So much material, most of it of a biographical nature, has been written on Lowry that it would be facile merely to rewrite it in slightly different terms. However, an attempt has been made here, and I believe it to be a unique one, to trace Lowry's slowly growing reputation during the 1935-1955 period by setting him in the context of the wider Manchester art scene, particularly of the annual Manchester Academy exhibition. By looking at the press response to his work throughout this period one can gauge the gradual rise to national, and ultimately international, prominence. Meanwhile my conversation with younger followers helped give me a sense of his unique importance as a central figure within the myth and legend of our so-called 'northern school.'

One

Art Across Merseyside

Whatever degree of truth attaches to Liverpool's claim to being the greatest artistic mecca in the north west – and perhaps even outside London itself – on one point there can be no doubt. Art in that city went back much further than it did in Manchester. And despite the fluctuating fortunes of the longer established Liverpool Academy, the story of art in Liverpool tends to contain a greater degree of exoticism or bohemianism than does Manchester's more conventional artistic history. Perhaps the city's position as a port, attracting Welsh, Irish and international immigrant populations, added to its unpredictable cultural temperament. It is not surprising that the Tate Gallery chose the city to open its first regional branch, using a large warehouse at the Albert Dock. The Walker Art Gallery's unrivalled provincial collection is a prime testimony to the great nineteenth century shipping boom which underpinned some enlightened patronage. One of these patrons, the shipping magnate Frederick Leyland (1831-92), drew the great American artist James McNeill Whistler to his large Tudor home, Speke Hall near Liverpool. For some years, Whistler made working visits to Speke, and in the 1870's produced 18 etchings depicting the Leyland family and the grounds of Speke Hall.

The tall, thin, bearded figure of Frederick Leyland formed an ideal subject for Whistler's brand of full length portraiture which, set against a dark background, recalled the great Spanish master Velasquez. Whistler's *Arrangement in Black, Portrait of Leyland,* painted in the early 1870's, now belongs to Washington's Smithsonian Institute. Leyland's rapid rise from an obscure background led to his purchasing a Liverpool shipping firm from the Bibby family. Leyland had ambitions to become a significant connoisseur and soon collected the work of the early Italians, as well as the contemporary work of the Pre-Raphaelite Rossetti. Rossetti introduced Leyland to Whistler, and soon after Leyland was advancing money to Whistler, helping the artist finance an extravagant lifestyle in Chelsea. In the following few years Whistler made many trips north to stay with the Leylands. The artist got on particularly well with the women of the Leyland family, and made a number of portraits of them. He was also responsible for introducing Leyland to the splendours of Velasquez's painting, which the

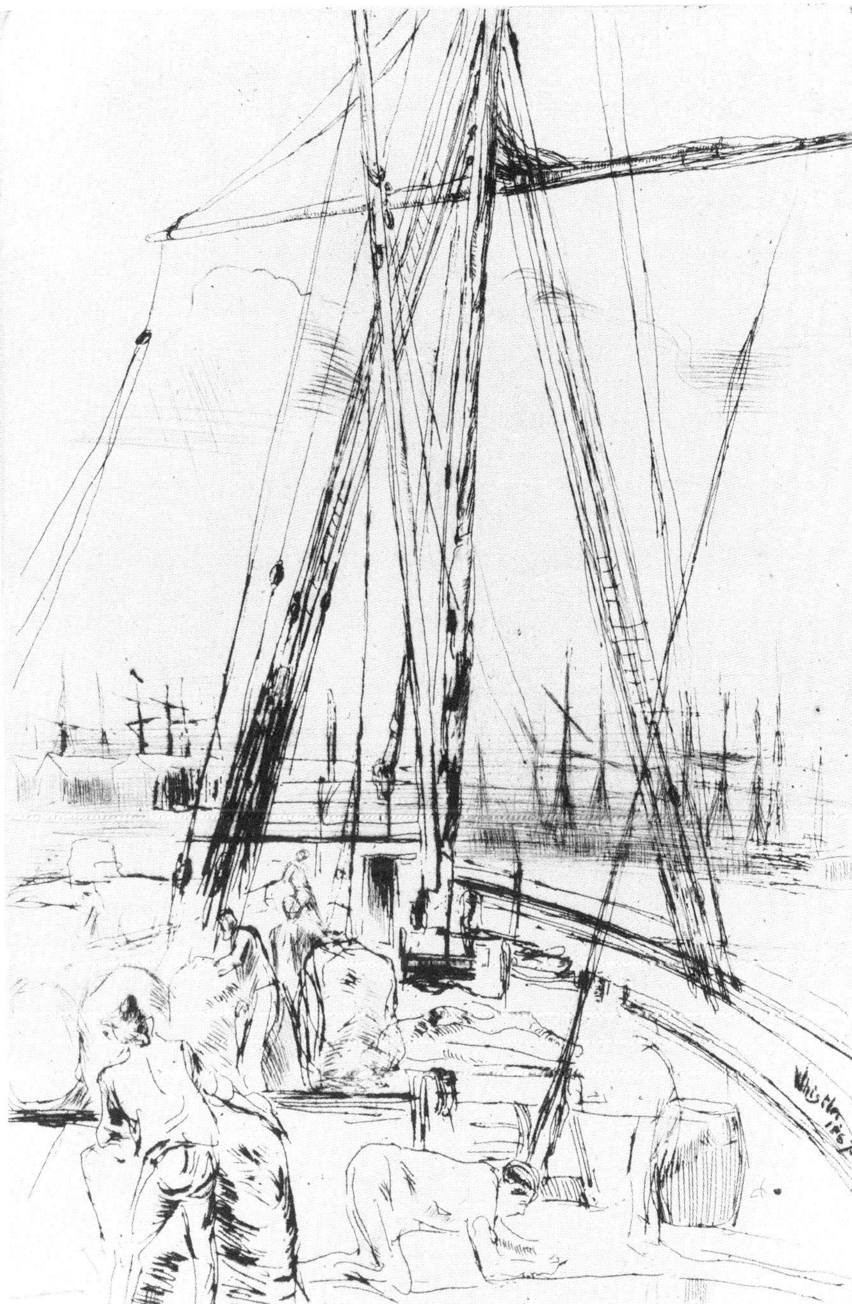

J.M. Whistler: Shipping at Liverpool, *etching 1867 (courtesy: Courtauld Institute of Art).*

Liverpool collector shortly after began acquiring. An etching, 'Speke Hall' by Whistler, not only accurately depicted the timber mansion seen from the driveway, but also indulged in the 'tilted' composition and careful placing of elements that Whistler developed out of a love of Japanese prints. The building is depicted at a distance yet assumes equal importance with the much closer foreground figure of Mrs Leyland. The exquisitely positioned objects in this composition jostle with areas of blank space.

Whistler spent Christmas 1871 at Speke, and during this visit worked on portraits of Leyland's wife and children. A group of etchings followed in 1873, depicting Mrs Leyland and the daughters Elinor, Fanny and Florence. Significantly, at Speke in 1873, Whistler first used the butterfly signature, the sign that evolved during the remaining three decades of his career as the unique personal emblem for the subtle stylistic changes borne out in the work of this precocious artist. Among local subjects near Speke Hall during the artists's final visit there in 1875, were etchings like 'Shipbuilder's Yard' and 'Speke Shore.' The following year, 1876, saw Whistler making modifications to Leyland's dining room at Princes Gate in London. It led to difficulties between artist and patron and to a permanent rift between the two egoists. Whistler took undoubted liberties when, having painted the ceiling with a decorative peacock feather pattern, he invited the press to see his work. But this piece of bold self-publicity alienated the owner of the room, who had been notified neither of this nor indeed of the original design schemes. Matters were exacerbated when rumours, spread about by Rossetti, reached Leyland's ears. These stories alleged – believably, in view of their very friendly relations – that Whistler was about to elope with Mrs Leyland. Leyland threatened Whistler, refused to pay the bill for the uncommissioned 'Peacock Room' decorations and ordered the artist to stay away from Mrs Leyland. A battle between artist and patron continued for two years, leading to Whistler's financial bankruptcy in 1879. Meanwhile, Frances Leyland left her husband, who thereafter lived in quiet seclusion at Princes Gate until his death in 1892.

A decade after Whistler's inopportune Peacock Room controversy, Maxwell Gordon Lightfoot was born in Liverpool. During his tragically short life – Lightfoot committed suicide in 1911 aged only 25 – he made a significant mark on the British arts scene, highlighted by his contributions to a Camden Town Group exhibition in the summer of 1911. Lightfoot died too young to leave behind a great body of work, which is particularly scarce because he destroyed much of his landscape and still life work. Lightfoot trained at Chester School of Art, and, after his family returned to Liverpool in 1905, attended art classes at the Sandon Terrace studios. He studied under

Gerard Chowne (1875-1911), who had a pronounced influence on his early work, and Herbert McNair (1868-1955) who was largely responsible for Liverpool Art Nouveau. In 1907, the year he moved to London and entered the Slade under Tonks, Lightfoot showed at the Liverpool autumn exhibition and later at the Sandon Studios Society. At the Slade Lightfoot became friendly with fellow students Stanley Spencer, Nevinson, Wadsworth and Gertler. He lived at Hampstead where he used the children of his landlord as models. Had Lightfoot lived a full and active career he would perhaps have been Liverpool's equivalent to Henry Lamb, a contemporary whose early background was solidly based in Manchester. The Walker Art Gallery has several of Lightfoot's paintings and drawings, and one – an elaborate pen and ink drawing of an unidentified landscape near Abergavenny, executed in 1910 – shows possible connection with Augustus John's trips to record the Welsh border country of this period. Another contemporary artist who became closely associated with Liverpool was Dundee-born James Mann (1883-1946). Trained at Liverpool School of Art, Mann lived in the Liverpool area for many years and died on the Wirral shortly after the last war. The Walker also owns a significant example of Mann's work, *Tide Time* depicting a Blue Funnel liner on the Mersey.

The next significant artist to spend a large amount of time in Liverpool was Augustus John, though the city establishment did not then accord him the respect or recognition that his later reputation commanded. His attempts to show work with the Academy there failed. Indeed, the Walker Art Gallery did not acquire its first John painting until 1938, though *Two Jamaican Girls,* the picture that the gallery did finally purchase, was an especially fine example of John's portraiture. Nevertheless, John had a marked impact on the bohemian sub-culture of Liverpool's artistic life, which in those early days centred around the University 'Art Sheds', the Applied Arts Section before its absorption into a new Liverpool Art School, and the group that would centre itself around premises on Sandon Terrace.

The Applied Arts Section was originally set up as a separate department within University College. Robert Anning Bell, another painter influenced by Pre-Raphaelitism, was director. Charles Allen, the modelling instructor, and Richard Rathbone, metalwork teacher, also taught there. Together with the book binding designs of D.S. MacColl, these artists showed work in an Art Nouveau style at the Walker Art Gallery's Spring shows during the mid-1890's. Richard Rathbone's ornate metal doors for the Unitarian church, and the Philharmonic Hotel's metal gates, are distinctive features of a Liverpool Art Nouveau style. The Applied Arts Section also benefitted from the recruitment of Herbert MacNair (brother-in-law of Charles

Rennie MacIntosh), Gerard Chowne and Augustus John. The Education Act of 1902 forced the Corporation to take over the existing design school and merge it with the Applied Arts Section. A new School of Art was thus created in Liverpool in 1905. A group of independent-minded artists broke away from this new institution which they suspected smacked of orthodoxy, and formed their own independent art school at Sandon Terrace with MacNair and Chowne as the leaders.

John, who was sympathetic to the Sandon group, painted a number of portraits at this time depicting notable Liverpool contemporaries including Kuno Meyer, John Brunner and Lord Mayor Dowdall, which after its completion in 1909 caused controversy because of its unconventional, even irreverent tone. This was due not to the picture's treatment, which remained safely, if strongly, academic, but rather to the choice of unorthodox garb and posture. The episode showed Liverpool as a solidly conservative Victorian business centre. The cult of the individual and bohemian is one that today we can easily associate with the quick-witted, proud and sometimes rebellious people of Liverpool. But at the time it was a necessary strand providing Liverpool culture with an antidote to the conservative academic hierarchy that catered for a pious business community. Nevertheless, other dangers attended the new century, which saw the establishment of centralised artistic institutions, accountable to the corporation. John Willett wrote that the "social, educational, almost philanthropic view of the arts which evolved in the nineteenth century only appealed to the brighter spirits so long as it was not bureaucratized. As soon as it became official corporation policy there was a reaction in the name of artists' exclusiveness and good taste . . . The Sandon Society, for instance, accepted the idea of the artist as gypsy, as gentleman or as scholar. It was more than doubtful about his role in civic life."[1]

Sandon Terrace was pulled down in 1907 but the new and independent Sandon group moved into Georgian premises at the Bluecoat Schools. In what was to become its permanent home, the Sandon Studios Society set up as an independent artists' exhibiting society and meeting place. The Society got off to a spectacular start in its Edwardian heyday. Its Spring show of 1908 had a Claude Monet landscape, bathed in impressionist light, depicting Etretat. The Monet was accompanied by no fewer than 21 works by Augustus John, indicating the respect accorded to John by his colleagues, contemporaries and fellow artists outside the Liverpool Academy establishment. Two Post-Impressionist exhibitions, in 1911 and 1913, were also held at the Sandon, showing Liverpool's desire to follow up on Roger Fry's momentous and pioneering exhibitions of major French modern art at

London's Grafton galleries in 1910 and 1912. The Liverpool Post-Impressionist shows had a strong local impact, even if much of the response was incredulity from an unappreciative and backward-looking audience. But the exhibition allowed the Sandon artists to show their work, albeit as a sideline in a separate section, in truly spectacular and epoch-making company. From that moment on, Liverpool artists would never decline the opportunity to show their work in a challenging or cosmopolitan context. Later, a number who regularly succeeded in showing their work in the Summer shows at Burlington House were applauded in the Liverpool press, while in the 1960's others managed to jump the selection hurdles and enter the home straight for the John Moores national painting competition at the Walker Art Gallery.

Between the wars, the Liverpool Academy once again came to the fore, and a chronological survey of the annual Academy exhibitions from the mid-1930's until its demise in 1981 is related in a separate chapter. That study makes plain the difficulties of identifying a tangible Liverpool style, though a number of discernible traits, attitudes and tendencies became apparent. The easiest category of pictures to slot into our notion of a local 'school' was that conveying local imagery and specific Merseyside themes regardless of style. But even among the many paintings of exotic or foreign locations – and as at Manchester, the Liverpool Academy was often full of such 'holiday' pictures – group styles commonly suggested themselves. Coburn-Witherop's pictures, for instance, which frequently drew on Cornish sources, united natural or architectural landscape features with a steady and consistent line which encapsulated and clarified forms with great precision. His paintings owed something to the American paintings of Grant Wood. A similar fastidiousness and graphic detailing characterised the work of two contemporaries, Frank Dodman and Allan Tankard. This pair went on a sketching holiday to Yugoslavia with Huggill and Sharp in 1937. "During that holiday," Dodman later recalled, "we were continually amused at the way Tankard insisted on wearing a three-piece blue serge suit all the time – you can imagine the heat in August; on one occasion, as a great event, he did remove his waistcoat."[2] The story conveys the formal and proper countenance of a man who imposed great exactitude upon topographical studies of architectural or landscape subjects. Dodman's work also relished the struggle to master the full detail of topographical views.

The gradual re-emergence of the Liverpool Academy during the inter-war years was accompanied by a decline in the number of private galleries. Liverpool possessed 20 galleries in the early 1920's. Agnews had a Liverpool branch between 1873 and 1909. By 1967 only two established picture dealers – Boydell's and Davey's – operated in the city, while ten years later Jonathan Blond's Allerton gallery was alone in representing both serious Victorian and modern paintings. The decline in the number of galleries helps explain why the Liverpool and indeed Manchester Academy exhibitions became such important events. Blond later repeated the assessment made in John Willett's book that "though old Liverpool pictures, especially of a topographical nature, are in considerable demand, both Boydell and Davey feel there is practically no market for the present generation of artists."[3] Blond's experience was similar to Boydell's, for Liverpool collectors usually travelled to London. Boydell also remarked that he had never sold a work in Liverpool by any major French painter. Andreas Kalman, in marked contrast, had been much more successful, with Vlamincks, Soutines and other leading Continentals at his Crane gallery in the early 1950's.

Despite the difficulties traditionally encountered by private galleries in Liverpool, there is an abundance of public works throughout the city. Although public commitment to art on Merseyside has at best been sporadic, allowing for no coherent, chronological or representative collection to accrue, public monuments date back a long way in the city's history. Charles Bell Birch's large, bulky bronze of Disraeli is one distinctive example from the nineteenth century. In more modern times, Herbert Tyson Smith's two war memorial sculptures, and Jacob Epstein's *Spirit of Liverpool Resurgent* speak for the experience of the twentieth century. George Breeze, director of the John Lewis department store, was responsible for commissioning the large standing bronze figure sited above an entrance to what Willett described as the store's "exceedingly undistinguished building." The same writer explained that "not only was it one of Epstein's less successful works but the immediate focusing of spectators' attention on the figure's genitals has remained distracting to the citizens . . . all the same the commissioning of the Epstein was a bold effort, a decade later the example still seems to nag at the corporation."[4]

The corporation may here have been called into question regarding its poor commitment to public art, but there were other isolated examples of enlightened patronage on Merseyside. A Catholic school at Kirkby commissioned a long horizontal abstract relief by Robin Riley. The work is a typical 1950's post-cubist relief that uses geometrical shapes, linear arabesques and hollows to create a forceful rhythmic interplay of successive elements. A similar vein was repeated in the pronounced linear style of John McCarthy's metal gate for the Mathematics Building of the University. Basil Spence, architect of the new Coventry Cathedral,

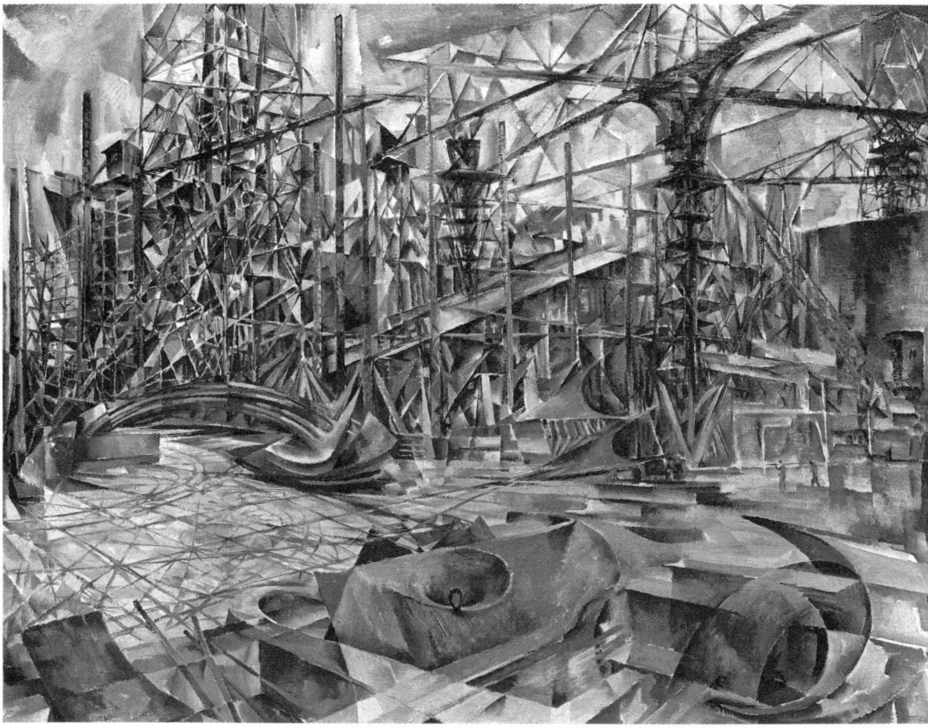

George Mayer-Marton: Shipyard, Liverpool, *oil 1953.*

designed the Physics Building on the same campus, and three tall upright forms by Hubert Dalwood were sited outside. More patronage from the Catholic church led to John Piper's windows for the Roman Catholic Cathedral, which was consecrated in 1967. Liverpool sculptor Arthur Dooley produced thin lanky figures for the Stations of the Cross at St Mary's, Leyland. An abrasive, physically strong man from a local family, Dooley was described as working "in bronze, and his figures of men and animals, at once religious and revolutionary in conception, have considerable strength and feeling for their material and in their clumsier way belong to the same tradition as those of Henry Moore."[5] Nevertheless, the Leyland figures, wrapped in taut, linear clothing, remind one more of Giacometti or Richier than of the voluminous Moore. Leonard Rosoman executed a large mural of Liverpool waterfront for Barclays Bank. The job would have been given to the well known local artist Mayer Marton, but for his sudden death. William Mitchell produced a large cast relief sculpture, in a style superficially reminiscent of Paolozzi, for a building facade on Hope Street.

A collection of works from this modern generation can also be seen in the public collections on Merseyside. One objective of the John Moores exhibitions from 1957 onwards was to allow Merseyside a glimpse of the most vital currents of contemporary British art. Of the Liverpool artists who won through from 2,000 submitted works to the last 150 selected entries of the competition, none secured the final prize, though John Edkins and George Moore won minor prizes in 1965, and Sam Walsh had a picture bought for the Walker at the 1963 show. The handful of Liverpool artists who did enter the final selection – like Arthur Ballard, Coburn-Witherop, Nicholas Horsfield, Robin Riley and Stu Sutcliffe – often had at least one of their works acquired for the Walker collection. John Willett's contemporaneous book about the distinctive features of the art of this city dealt in a frank way with the respective merits and weaknesses of this group. The book has something of the community-minded approach of Denys Val Baker's *Britain's Art Colony by the Sea* (1959), though Willett's approach was far more rigorous and expertly judged than Val Baker's less intellectual St Ives book.

The Merseyside artists covered by Willett in *Art in a City* were generally sophisticated provincials, working in various modernist modes away from the real cosmopolitan centres that were the breeding grounds for genuinely new art. Yet, as St Ives showed, artists could work in a radical, progressive manner at a remove from the cosmopolitan centres. Willett continually sought to evaluate the quality of work produced in Liverpool by putting it in a wider context, just as the John Moores competition pitted Liverpool artists against the highest category of contemporary British art.

Like St Ives, the north has had its self-taught naïves. Fred Yates was one from Manchester, while on the Wirrall Gordon has painted both Liverpool and Manchester street subjects in a Lowry-esque manner, though with greater naivety. Like Alan Lowndes, Brian Gordon homes in on the soul of northern street life – childhood memories, characters, fairgrounds, markets, are all depicted against the classic red brick and grey slate backdrops. Gordon used old roof slates, which after cleaning were engraved with small chisels, and then painted in a precise, mechanical and painstaking way. A modest though growing reputation has led to shows at London's RONA Gallery that represents the Register of Naïve Artists. Nothing could be further from the work of Warrington-born Clifford Fishwick, who studied under Will Penn in Liverpool, before branching out as a 'neo-romantic' landscape painter. Fishwick, who in later years ran the painting department at Exeter, approached landscape using sharp visual memory, a far cry from the literal approach of the naive artist. Fishwick, as an intrepid hiker and hill climber, constantly sought unusual, inaccessible and dramatic landscape views, and by necessity had to rely on memory to work up highly detailed, though often composite landscape paintings back in his Devon studio. Although a native of the north west, Fishwick's career was spent in the south. Nicholas Horsfield, in contrast, was a southerner whose career was spent almost entirely in the north, particularly in Liverpool, and it is to his important Liverpool career that we will next turn our attention.

Horsfield is usually associated with Liverpool, the city in which he settled. Yet a southern background, highlighted by an education at Charterhouse and the Royal College of Art followed by years of painting visits to Normandy, have moulded him into a sophisticated, individual, and in the best sense, provincial painter. Horsfield's style, language and subject cannot easily be tied to any one place or time – certainly not to the 'kitchen sink' realism or to the industrial expressionism of any so-called 'northern school.' There are, though, indirect links with the grey, postwar realism of northern painting. In any case, we continually find occurrences of French-inspired sensibility at play in much northern painting. It is immediately apparent in Valette's suffused impressionism, in the private school that Sickert set up in Manchester and which created a wave of followers within Manchester painting, and again in the wartime work of Claude Rogers at Southport or that which Julian Trevelyan, Graham Bell and Will Rothenstein produced at Bolton as Mass Observation artists. The sophistication of Slade or Royal College artists allowed a coherent and competent handling of mundane northern motifs that, applying the conventional criteria of beauty, seemed perverse or ugly.

Nicholas Horsfield, born in 1917, trained under Rothenstein at the Royal College, though the mark making language he later evolved derived as much from Sickert or the Euston Road. He chose motifs that perhaps owe more to the great outdoors so cherished by the impressionists (broad landscapes, large looming skies, and so on) than to the grubby interior or dark architectural recesses that proved so crucial to his Camden Town and Euston Road predecessors. Indeed, Horsfield's landscape painting has never looked towards the blighted marks of industry and urban gloom: his local subjects commonly feature the coastal, dune-filled landscape, crowned with dramatic clouds, that stretches from his Crosby home towards Southport After nearly ten years as Regional Visual Arts Officer for the Arts Council based in Manchester, Horsfield became a lecturer at Liverpool School of Art, where he worked until full retirement in the early 1980's. Being based in the college life room for so many years led to much studio-based work; one associates him with a prolific output of life drawings, classically constructed figure sketches modelled with, and lost in, an intricate linear web and maze of soft marks that often unify two or even three figures. Horsfield studied at the Royal College in the three years leading up to the Second World War. The first year, beginning in the autumn of 1935, coincided with the last year of William Rothenstein, from whom Horsfield received no direct teaching. Nevertheless Rothenstein encouraged the

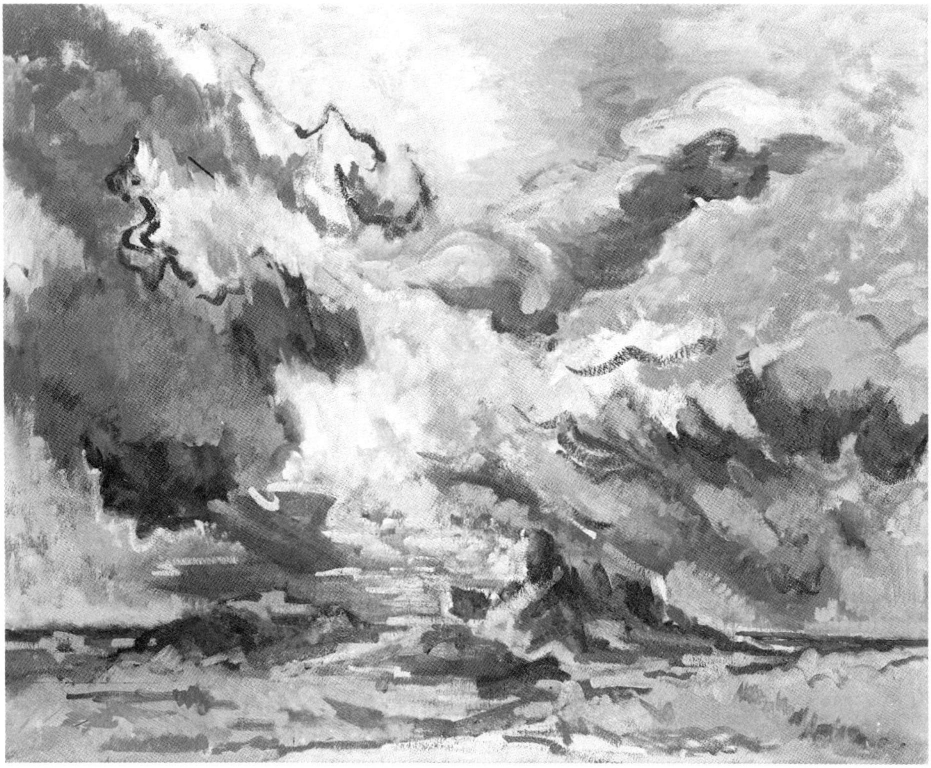

Nicholas Horsfield: The Large Sky, *oil 1982.*

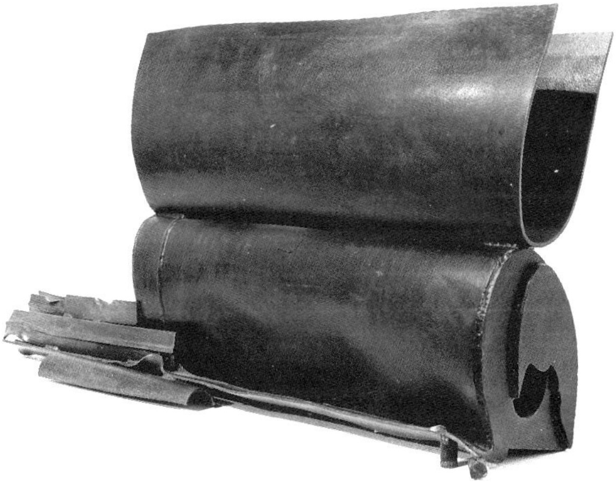

Barbara Lander: Abstract sculpture in welded steel.

young 18-year old student who found the going tough in the first few terms. Horsfield's father, retiring as a naval officer, moved via Plymouth and Kent to Guildford. A distant relative of the Horsfield family, Keith Baynes, recommended that Nicholas apply for the Royal College which, he maintained, was better than the Slade. Horsfield may not have received any direct teaching from Rothenstein, but he did benefit from other lecturers who included Vivian Pitchforth, Percy Horton (who taught Horsfield something of the skilful manipulation of pencil in drawing), Gilbert Spencer and Percy Jowett, who took over Rothenstein's position as college head. Jowett had none of the historical perspectives that the experienced Rothenstein possessed, but he was nevertheless encouraging and expressed approval of Horsfield's use of colour.

With the threat of war, the art market had collapsed, partly explaining a generally dull period in a college that produced very few noteworthy individuals. However, one postgraduate, Ruskin Spear, wedded Sickert's taste for the colloquial with a new contemporary imagery taken on board in a brash way that signalled the eventual rise of a new and popular visual culture. Horsfield had brief, insignificant contact with Spear, with whom he was to share a certain common stylistic approach under the Sickert banner. Gilbert Spencer, a valuable instructor, confirmed Horsfield's belief in the importance of tone and contrast. Spencer advised Horsfield on two major ways to paint: the first using a predominant middle tone against which dark or light patches could be later emphasised and worked in. The other method required that contrasting areas of light and dark be put down early on, and used as preliminary markers, guiding the employment of a whole range of intermediate tones across the rest of the surface. Horsfield opted for the direct, spontaneous, *alla prima* treatment of the former. Allowing for a painterly and gestural vitality, this method integrated drawing and painting in a single, unified pictorial activity. In veering away from the mechanical jigsaw puzzle approach practised by Stanley Spencer, this method led Horsfield towards a manner of British painting that evolved from Sickert to the Euston Road, from Bomberg to Auerbach and Kossoff. While continuing to embrace a coherent motif or subject, such traditions by passed rigid verisimilitude and mechanical reproduction of detail in order to keep pictorial art fresh, spontaneous, and true to the painterly medium and the visual language.

Horsfield's drawing has always formed an important, complementary side to the painting; it could not be any other way for a painter who so skilfully integrates drawing with modelling and painting. Drawing was an activity given due importance in his student days at Exhibition Road. He learned much from a fellow student, Brian Elliff, who developed a dot and line method of measured composition at the same time as Coldstream. During the winter of 1938 and 1939, Horsfield shared a Soho studio with Elliff. Alan Sorrel, then teaching life drawing at the college, insisted both on precision of angle and direction of line. But of all the teachers Horsfield felt most indebted to Elliff, who went on to design costume jewellery. In May 1939, recently graduated from the R.C.A., Horsfield answered a *New Statesman* advert for a Berlitz school of English teaching position in Leipzig. Few students came to his classes in Leipzig and he was advised to leave quickly. A week before the declaration of war he left for England on a troop train. During the war years, he was absent from England, spending time in India, Burma and Ireland. India he was fascinated with, an interest which helped compensate for the lack of available artistic pursuits.

Horsfield's return was saddened by the death of his father and the young artist struggled to regain the momentum provided by his art school training during the 1930's. He managed to obtain a post teaching art two days a week to reluctant pupils at a public school, Dover College. It was a difficult job but useful experience. After this, he obtained a job at the Arts Council, which launched him on his professional life in art. Keith Baynes recommended the job, and pointed the way forward. He served 8 years in Manchester as the arts officer, enabling him to see and assess the whole northern art scene. He worked under Gabriel White. Horsfield lived in Didsbury, and became acquainted with the Manchester Academy (with whom he occasionally exhibited) and the Midday Studios group (which he found too provincial). But he was drawn more to Liverpool, which had a thriving artistic community (Geoffrey Wedgewood, Martin Bell and Arthur Ballard included) and where he subsequently made many friends. In 1956, he moved over to Liverpool after obtaining the post at the Liverpool School of Art. Yet it was Manchester that gave him the chance to acquire knowledge of the northern arts scene, and he formed friendships as well as acquaintanceships with its artists. He knew Emmanuel Levy, who lived near Horsfield in Didsbury. Levy painted a portrait of Horsfield in the early 1950's, *A Man in a Ginger Coat*. Friendships grew with Margo Ingham, Alan Lowndes and Harry Rutherford. With Lowry it had to be more of an acquaintanceship. Once, in 1954, Horsfield took tea with the older Manchester artist at the City Art Gallery. Conversation turned to the subject of Lowry's latest picture. Lowry said that *The Funeral Party* was a depiction of what he termed his crazy family. Horsfield asked about the whereabouts of Lowry's mother in a picture that did not seem to include her. As if to cover the sadness of his revered mother's death 15 years before, Lowry answered that she had gone to the shops, a reply that did not fool the younger man. Horsfield visited Lowry's home in Mottram: experiences he found enjoyable. Horsfield had the unassuming temperament to get the best out of Lowry, and found him kind, amusing and encouraging.

Shortly before moving over to Liverpool, Horsfield managed to obtain a year's unpaid leave from Arts Council duties. He went to Dieppe for six months, spending time with his close friend, the critic John Willett. He also went to Venice, where in spite of poor weather he produced a Venetian painting. The period of leave was beneficial. His painting of Le Pollet Cliffs, near Dieppe, is now in the Walker Art Gallery. A useful experience was the visit, made in 1953, to the Varengeville studio of Georges Braque. Accompanied by Hans Herse, then director of York Art Gallery and a friend of John Willett's, Horsfield saw Braque's agricultural paintings. It was a notable experience that could only have confirmed him in the seriousness of the artistic life, and in the value and meaning of professionalism. He married in 1955, and continued to live in Manchester, at Didsbury, until his move to Liverpool in 1956.

Teaching was certainly a profession that suited him, allowing for an ideal blending of practical studio-based art activities with the more intellectual pursuit of art historical studies. Horsfield began teaching in the painting school at Liverpool School of Art, but soon went on to conduct life drawing classes before shifting over to full time art history, between 1963 and 1977. The trouble with teaching was its arduous and demanding routines. Although the ambiance of an art school was an idea one for a practising painter, the reality was that Horsfield was able to paint in a serious full time capacity only during the summer vacation or during much valued sabbaticals. In the autumn of 1961 he was awarded six months' leave, which allowed him to paint a series of pictures in France, notably at Guernes-sur-Seine. An exhibition at Liverpool's Bluecoat Chamber soon after included the spate of small French pictures. Horsfield's longstanding close friend, John Willett, recommended a sharp rise in Horsfield's prices, a policy that did not prevent the exhibition from being a sell-out. Again in 1967, he obtained an Arts Council award which gave him six months to travel and paint. He chose Poland, and the drawings and small paintings made there furnished a number of larger paintings on Polish themes produced back home in the following few years. These culminated in *The Polish Grove* (1970), with its numerous attendant studies. Finally, in the 1973-4 academic session, he obtained a year's sabbatical, allowing him to paint at La Roche Guyon near Giverny, following in the footsteps of Renoir, Cézanne and Braque. The on-the-spot sketching and note-taking gave him enough material for studio paintings back home to last for the second half of the 1970's.

It will be apparent that Horsfield studiously avoided painting the industrial north. A use of colour that draws heavily on naturalistic and toning sources discouraged industrial landscape painting which would require a schematic, expressionist, or emotive palette. Horsfield's importance to the north is as an intelligent and articulate perennial – first as an arts administrator, then as a teacher and finally as an urbane and sophisticated painter. His artistic pedigree is strongly orientated towards the French, absorbing at first hand both the lessons of French Impressionist landscape practices – the plein air oil sketch leading to larger studio canvasses – and the anglicised Post-Impressionist vernacular of Sickert, the Euston Road and the Bomberg 'school.' A peculiarly sensual handling of paint taking as one of its main characteristics a successful integration and subsuming of drawing into painting, together with a Cézanne-inspired range of italicised brushwork used spontaneously in an *alla prima* capacity, these are all characteristics of Horsfield's work. So too is a stock of unassuming subjects that tend to celebrate not so much the mundane aspects of human geography and architectural environments, but rather the glorious spectacles of nature. Such subjects include cliffs at Le Pollet, the Varengeville coast, views on to Dieppe, the dune-lined coast near his Crosby and Blundellsands home, cloud studies or simply self-portraits.

If the search for the exotic, the distant, or at least the foreign has been germinal to modernism in painting – beginning with Gauguin – then the traditional remove of the Cornish or northern French coastline has proved to be the more moderate outlets for the worthy, if unadventurous, artists of the Manchester Academy and of the northern school in general. Alex Kidson, in referring to Horsfield's "typical preference for places abroad" has expressed an imperative at the heart of Horsfield's work – the avoidance of familiar or mundane home terrain. Kidson has speculated that "his choice of a landscape to paint is intimately bound up with its separateness from home ground . . . even a site close to home such as the Hightown dunes being attractive for a particular quality of transience."[6] In the search for the new and exotic, many northern artists looked to Cornwall, chosen for a foreigness even within our own shores. Contemporaries like Horsfield's friend Alan Lowndes, and later Bob Crossley, settled in St Ives. Horsfield lost touch with Lowndes until 1972, and never visited Cornwall. Instead, Horsfield's escape route was to Poland, but particularly to the Normandy coast that provided constant source material for landscape painting. The soft, translucent Normandy light, that around Dieppe appears to rise up from the reflective sea and slate roofs, has helped mould a multivariant, but always naturalistic orchestration of colour. John Willett has referred to the "Normandy light, which was the same . . . for Bonington, for Monet, for Sickert," and which resulted in "that lovely but unfashionable thing – 'la belle peinture.'" In the same article, Willett went on to declare that Horsfield's work is "proof of how much tension lies beneath the surface of an apparently 'belle peinture', Beauty of this kind is the opposite of slick."[7] The tension that Willett referred to as lying behind the beautiful artifice of a Horsfield painting has, I believe, something to do with what Alex Kidson, in an equally perceptive catalogue introduction on Horsfield's work, has spoken of as a "task of advance sensory clarification, rather than to rehearsing the transcription itself. Transcription is always fraught, a tension builds up between accumulated knowledge, the long evolution of a language of painting which has served in the past and cannot simply be jettisoned; and, on the other hand, the need to forswear formula and to answer spontaneously the demands of a fresh motif, which makes almost any rehearsal undesirable."[8] Clear in Kidson's remark is a sense of looming dilemma for an artist like Horsfield, who has the problem of making graphic or pictorial marks "obey a clear perception of the motif that is residing within him" while at the same time honouring a perception honed to "living in a landscape and feeling a landscape, clarifying its essential structure, before definitively painting it."

On a broader, more philosophic level there is another important element of struggle inherent in Horsfield's project as a Liverpool-based, and French inspired, painter. It is a problem of provincialism – and the 'combativeness' inherent in the provincial stance has been explained in Sir Kenneth Clark's (unpublished) essay on the subject as the catchword of provincial art in its struggle to free itself from the dominating style." Great virtue is therefore attributed to a quality of quietism residing in an artist who is (correctly) deemed to favour pictorial beauty in the traditional (French) sense, a struggle against modernist or internationalist orthodoxy and a dominating style, and finally a rejection of media promoted art fashions. Instead, use is made of traditional, undemanding subject matter and a middling path is taken between abstract vitality and disciplined figurative credence.

Vivian Pitchforth was not only a prolific watercolour painter of the English landscape, but was also one of the most well travelled artists. The extent of Pitchforth's travels across the length and breadth of the British Isles recalls the endless journeying in pursuit of landscape subjects common among peripatetic painters of the eighteenth and nineteenth centuries, Turner providing us with the most shining example of an itinerant life dedicated to great artistic output. Pitchforth, arguably this century's greatest watercolour reporter of the English landscape, with its moist atmosphere and constantly changing skies, made a number of painting visits to Lancashire, and Southport in particular. That he came is inevitable, yet is also the responsibility of one man, Harry Ratcliffe, who ironically became one of the most influential and valuable personalities in the South Lancashire art scene after the second war. I say ironically because Ratcliffe was never a painter; instead he studied design and textile design at the Royal College between 1935 and 1937. Ratcliffe did, though, attend the life classes on Exhibition Road run by Pitchforth. He found Pitchforth an excellent teacher who would demonstrate, in front of the struggling student, methods of attacking formal construction on the paper. It was an essentially sculptural approach to drawing that analysed the figure in terms of segments and volumes, surprising considering Pitchforth's later use of fluid, flat, and atmospheric washes of colour in his landscape work. The drawing that Ratcliffe undertook at the Royal College began a long association between the two men which would eventually lead to Pitchforth's later missions to Lancashire in search of landscape motifs.

Ratcliffe also shared with Pitchforth a Yorkshire background. Born in Keighley in 1913, Ratcliffe studied painting and decorating for a number of years at the local art school, before winning a scholarship to the Royal College. These studies enabled him to gain employment, during the first half of the 1940's, at Salford School of Art, where he taught textile design. From 1946 until the end of 1949, he was head of the art department at Huddersfield, going on, in January 1950, to Southport Art School. There he became Principal. The 'Eagle' magazine was largely a product of Southport Art School at this time, and its characters like Dan Dare based on the School's staff. In 1952, Ratcliffe also became part time curator at the Atkinson Art Gallery, which houses an important collection of early twentieth century British painting, and which put on, each Spring, a significant exhibition of contemporary art by often well known national, as well as local, figures. In 1973, Ratcliffe retired from teaching, and became the District Keeper of Fine Art for the newly formed District of Sefton, a part time position whose main duty was to co-ordinate the activities of the small but long established art galleries at Bootle, Crosby and Southport.

For over twenty years, Ratcliffe held reign over both the local art school in Southport and the Atkinson Art Gallery. The Atkinson held the annual Spring show, the local Palette Club exhibition, and several travelling exhibitions usually circulated by the Arts Council. He also had the freedom to build on the Atkinson's already impressive collection, and in spite of having to operate on tight funds was able to make some progress in his desire to improve a sculpture collection that lagged far behind the works on the walls or stored in the picture racks. He was largely instrumental in forming the Friends of Southport Art Gallery, a society that helped raise funds and promote acquisition policy. Through the Friends, Ratcliffe was able to purchase Epstein's *Head of Maria Donska,* a telling portrait of Epstein's pianist friend. In 1965, after this important Epstein acquisition, Ratcliffe was taken by Vivian Pitchforth to see Henry Moore in Much Hadham. Pitchforth and Moore were old Yorkshire colleagues who went back to very early student days. The meeting, over tea and cake, was a talkative and jovial affair, in which much nostalgic reminiscing over the old Yorkshire days led to an important outcome. Ratcliffe's mission was to purchase a recent Moore sculpture for Southport, and he decided on the middle-sized abstracted bronze *Three Way Piece, Points,* after seeing it in plastic form at Moore's studio that day. Ratcliffe contacted the Victoria and Albert Museum, which contributed half of the reduced price for the work; the rest of the money was provided by the Friends of the Atkinson and by the Southport Corporation. Moore was very helpful, clearly indicating that he wanted it to go to Southport. The sculpture acquisitions included work by the Liverpool sculptor, Arthur Dooley, and an abstract screen sculpture in buckled aluminium by Ralph Brown, whom Ratcliffe met while visiting the Royal College. Southport's acquisition policy included the purchase of works by local artists, regardless of style or creed, who had made a recognisable name for themselves, either locally or on a more significant national level.

As a discerning scout for the Atkinson, Ratcliffe was advised to join the Chelsea Arts Club, where he was able to meet many practising painters. Although the club was full of fashionable portrait painters like Henry Carr, or of Royal Academy members, there was also scope to meet more *avant garde* or simply less spotlighted artists of interest. Through the club, Ratcliffe re-established contact with Vivian Pitchforth for the first time since their pre-war days. Pitchforth had never before worked on the north- west coast, but in 1953 was invited north by Ratcliffe to do a series of paintings. Ratcliffe picked him up from the railway station, and drove him the following day up to the estuary of the river Kent, where Pitchforth was left to paint. The artist took lodgings at Grange-over-Sands, and for a week made colour sketches and notes that led, back in his Chelsea studio, to a series of elaborate watercolours on north Lancashire themes. Pitchforth was collected at the end of a busy week, and taken on to Glasson Dock for a couple of days. Ratcliffe finally took him back to Southport and the following day saw him off on the train back to London. Pitchforth returned with a folio containing many watercolours, conclusively proving the value of the week. Indeed, the artist was struck by Lancashire's spectacular cloud formations, light, and abundant sea, sand and sky combinations, all of which were of such primary concern to Pitchforth's kind of work. He was not a painter of trees, finding them too solid and opaque as objects. One story relates the occasion when Ratcliffe showed his artist guest a spectacular Lake District landscape only to find that the motif contained too many heavy greens and trees to be of any interest to Pitchforth.

Another trip north was made the following year. This time Pitchforth was taken by Ratcliffe to Sandside, where the artist stayed at an inn overlooking the estuary. A number of watercolours resulted from these estuary views. On another occasion, Pitchforth stayed at the Knowsley Hotel at the far end of Southport promenade. On this same front, though in a more central position, Claude Rogers had painted a number of war time panels depicting the fairground and sea front from the upstairs windows of a hospital where he was convalescing.[9] Pitchforth produced several views looking down from the hotel onto the front. He also delighted in the long beach, and the marine lake, and one large watercolour, *Boating Pool, Southport*, (Atkinson Art Gallery), typified the artist's ability to place boats, as individual zones of bright primary colour, across grey or blue washes. Unusual or difficult subjects were attempted including a view of the sunset over Southport beach, and a detailed view of Southport Town Hall at night which is also in the Atkinson collection. He also executed a number of watercolours looking from the sand dunes, and was commissioned to do a series of views from Crosby looking out towards the coastline of Wallasey and Birkenhead. Pitchforth clearly enjoyed Southport, with its coastal position, its Edwardian flavour and its wide central shopping area of Lord Street. On another occasion, Ratcliffe took Pitchforth further afield to an estuary in Galloway.

The Southport Spring exhibition aimed for a balance between artists of national standing who were invited, and others who were subject to the usual selection procedures. There was also a blending of local artists' work with contributions from many parts of the country. Work was sent in by agents in Glasgow, Manchester, Liverpool and London. The art agents and shippers, Borlase, collected works from artists' studios in London. The Chairman and Vice-Chairman of the Southport Corporation Library and Arts Committee, and the curator, were on the selection panel. An effort was made to introduce new blood into the shows, and some committee members made visits to London in preparation for the exhibitions. Meanwhile Ratcliffe's contacts through the Chelsea Arts Club won over several London artists to the Southport cause. A lecture was given by Harry Ratcliffe on the history of the gallery in early March 1976. In it, Ratcliffe traced the origins of the gallery which had been founded by Knaresborough-born William Atkinson in 1878. In 1862 he had moved to Southport on account of his wife's ill health. Atkinson's wealth had been accumulated as a Preston cotton manufacturer. He provided £8,000 towards the gallery, and was also a benefactor to the Southport Infirmary, and to several Anglican churches. Public opinion had pressed for an art gallery and library, and Atkinson's funds helped provide the building for the Southport community. A letter appeared in the local paper as a result of Ratcliffe's lecture. The letter strove to dismiss Atkinson as a financier rather than art patron. Others were given credit for being the real patrons and founding members of the library and art gallery. They were Richard Nicholson, a Liverpool shipowner and Liberal Councillor during the 1870's, Benjamin Clark, Thomas Holland, the church minister, and Samuel Boothroyd, the local draper.

Shortly after Ratcliffe's history lecture, a small memorial exhibition of Lowry's work was staged in the gallery, to celebrate the life of a great local artist who died in the early months of 1976. Ratcliffe had first encountered Lowry at the Midday Studios, and had subsequently advised Monty Bloom – the Southport collector who was to become one of the leading holders of Lowry's work in the world – to begin collecting Lowry. Margo Ingham, then living in Southport with her third husband, Bert Drake, came to Ratcliffe and suggested that Southport put on a small memorial show that would include both her own collection of drawings and paintings, and the Pendlebury Street scene which had been acquired by the Atkinson for £20 from a pre-war Spring exhibition. Two oils belonging to Ingham, *Going for a Walk* and the memorable *Midday Studios,* were prize features among the works on display. Ingham wrote that when "the gallery lease ran out in 1951, Lowry painted a large oil *The Midday Studios, Manchester* for the closing celebrations." The *Telegraph's* Trevor Bates considered "the paintings to have great historic value because it was the Midday Studios that staged Lowry's first one man show in 1948. He had received a raw deal from Manchester up to that time. They felt he was just a man who painted funny little figures with big boots."[10] Among the seven Lowrys belonging to Ingham were two non-Lancashire drawings, *Yorkshire Fishing Village* and *Gentleman at South Shields.* It was an ironic outcome to the four-year seclusion of these particular works inside a National Westminster safe deposit that once on the 'safe' walls of the Atkinson, they should have been stolen. An audacious gang had carefully scaled the Atkinson building and successfully entered the gallery through a skylight. It was estimated at the time that £30,000 of work had been stolen – the insurance value of the Midday Studios oil alone was put at £12,000. Ingham, clearly upset, called it "a pointless and wicked theft," but anxieties as to the eventual outcome of the missing Lowrys was partly eased in a Peter Hetherington article for *The Manchester Guardian* which quoted Ingham as claiming that the works were "so well known that I can't imagine anyone being able to sell them or display them . . . they may go into a collection for a so called art lover who will simply sit and gloat over them."[12] The paintings were eventually recovered by Scotland Yard from a Victoria Station luggage locker. The discovery coincided with Ingham's birthday in August, and prompted her to declare that the discovery was "the best birthday present I've ever had." The recovery of the works came in time for their inclusion as ex-catalogue items in the great Lowry exhibition – planned as a retrospective during Lowry's lifetime, but subsequent to his death early that year, changed into a memorial exhibition – at the Royal Academy.

The painter and printmaker Max Blond was born at St Annes, near Blackpool, in 1943. He moved to Liverpool with his family in 1947, and went to Corsham School of Art in the early 1960's. There he was impressed by both Birkenhead-born Henry Mundy and Howard Hodgkin among the teaching staff. He was happy at Corsham, but went on to the Slade where he was taught, though not influenced, by Patrick George. Blond found the rigid drawing of the Euston Road and Slade traditions antipathetic to his more expressionist, figurative and symbolist intentions. By the time he left the Slade in the mid-1960's he had evolved out of a melting pot of influences a figurative and expressionist style and was intent on relaying a political or realist message. Blond married while at the Slade, and family responsibilities meant his moving back to Liverpool, where he worked for his father, Leslie Blond. Described by John Willett as "cinema proprietor, property owner and patron-cum-landlord of the arts,"[13] Leslie Blond once worked as an area salesman for Universal Films, and saved enough to purchase a cinema. This business grew and enabled the purchase of several others. Hope Hall, which was later to become better known as the Everyman Theatre, was Blond's first cinema.

By the mid-1970's Max opted for the more precarious career of full time painter. Having left his father's business he moved to the Wirral, where his work went from strength to strength. Clearly indebted to the German Expressionists and Gauguin, Blond's humanitarian pictures sometimes hover on the edge of a surrealistic symbolism. Nevertheless, a tangible, empathetic vision gives his work a social and realist relevance. Like the German

'Brücke' artist, Blond has developed the woodcut, usually gouged out in order to portray faces, though one landscape, *Across the Mersey* (1983) uses the peculiar directness of the black and white woodcut print to express in cogent graphic terms, and with sharp interplay between positive and negative space, the unmistakable architectural profile of Liverpool skyline seen as if from a ferry midway across the Mersey. Max Blond has been a prominent and active member of the contemporary art scene in Liverpool, and had a couple of exhibitions at his brother Jonathan Blond's Liverpool gallery during the middle years of the 1970's. But he shied away from involvement with the Liverpool Academy, and when approached by a past president, Nicholas Horsfield, with the suggestion that he might provide the fresh impetus needed to relaunch the defunct Academy, declined the offer. It was too big a responsibility on top of his painting and his having to support a large family. But other contemporary Liverpool artists, like Stephen Dowsing and the arena group, are at the time of writing hoping to revive the Academy.

Jonathan Blond's Allerton Gallery opened in Liverpool in August 1974, and continued for three years. In 1978 Blond moved south and opened Blond Fine Art in Sackville Street, off Piccadilly. But whereas the London enterprise, since relocated, has continued to show modern British and contemporary art (including for a time that of his brother Max), the earlier Allerton gallery specialised in nineteenth century pictures. Nevertheless Blond put on three contemporary shows a year in Liverpool, and also dabbled in the twentieth century British wood engraving, drawing and painting areas on which he was to concentrate in London. He felt that most significant collectors in Liverpool then were interested only in the local Liverpool branch of the Pre-Raphaelite movement (for instance, William Huggins), in topographical watercolourists or in Japanese prints. The few twentieth century collectors tended to travel to London in order to purchase, while those interested in contemporary art often purchased directly off the artists themselves. Blond at the time had the only commercial gallery in a city then in the depths of post-industrial depression. The enterprise was a useful experience for a new dealer, undertaken on safe home territory before the decisive move to London's West End.

Jonathan Blond undoubtedly inherited some of the business acumen and cultural missionary fervour from his father, who played a not insignificant role in the artistic life of Liverpool. As well as owning the cinemas, Leslie Blond, the son of Lithuanian immigrants who originally came to Liverpool via Ireland, supported local artists, many of whom he befriended. Austin Davies, Arthur Ballard and Robin Riley were some who were befriended.

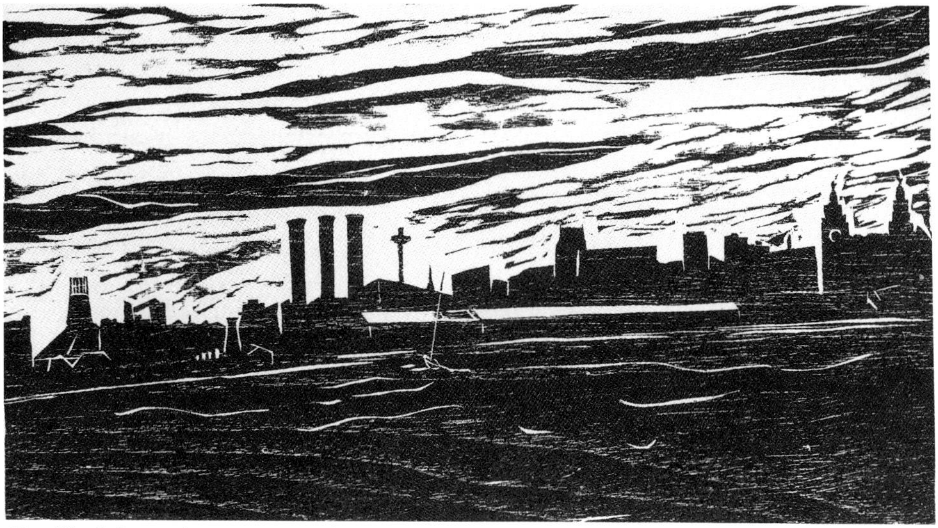

Max Blond: Across the Mersey, *woodcut 1983.*

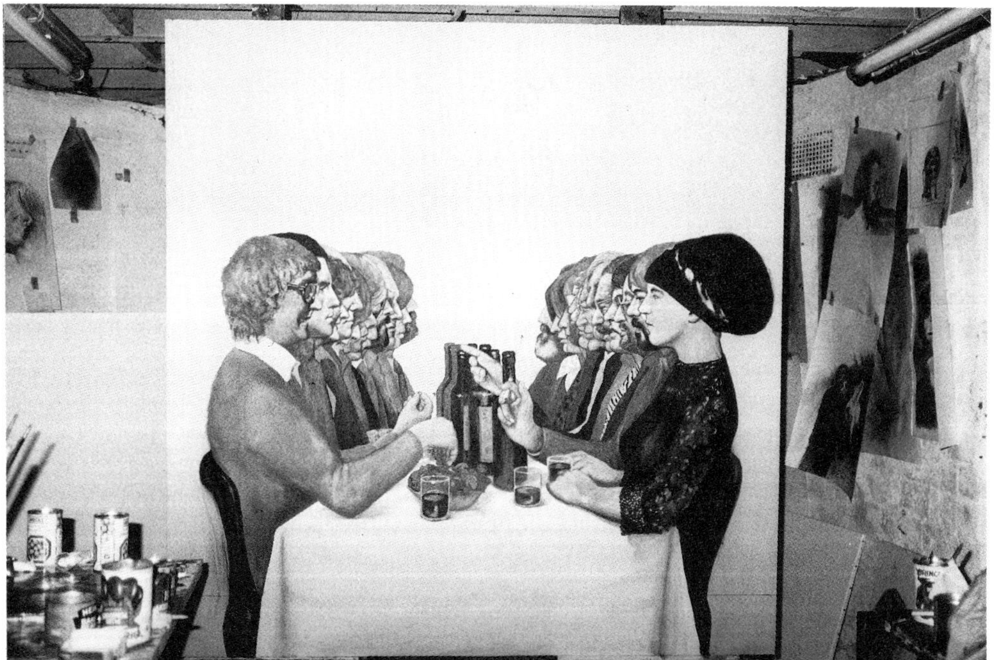

Sam Walsh: Dinner Party (22 people and me) *photographed in the artist's studio.*

A nude sculpture *Standing Figure* by Liverpool sculptor Robin Riley was ordered to be taken down by an advertising firm, Arthur Maiden, from its prominent setting on Bold Street; Leslie Blond came to the rescue of a ridiculous incident and placed it in his own garden. Sam Walsh and Donald McKinlay also became friends. He also supported two of the Merseyside Arts Festivals, held in the summers of 1962 and 1963, which were organised by a later member of the *Scaffold* pop group, John Gorman. Use was made of Blond's Hope Hall premises near the Catholic Cathedral. Those premises also provided facilities for poetry readings, and John Willett wrote that in the hall "Blond has shown, besides local painters, an exhibition of paintings by Bomberg and mixed shows from the Waddington and St George's galleries in London."

Wallasey and Birkenhead also feature in the general history of art in the region. Liverpool-born George Jardine was a product of Wallasey School of Art. Completing his studies at the Royal College, Jardine went on to teach for many years at Liverpool School of Art. Surrealist influences persisted in the work of an artist closely associated with Roderick Bisson and the Sandon Studios Society. Using the technique of conjuring up an air of fantasy through juxtaposition of disparate imagery, Jardine later painted richly personal fantasies symptomatic of an inner universe. A different kind of surrealist tenor - a more humorous satirical one - ran through the early student work of John Lennon, who studied under Jardine, Horsfield and Ballard at Liverpool School of Art.

The Williamson Art Gallery, built in the mid-1920's, often provided exhibition space to honour some of Birkenhead's or the Wirral's more distinguished artists, who included Will Penn. Wilson Steer was born locally in 1860 and the Williamson has many of his works. The town also possessed a respected local art school, where the local artist Henry Mundy (born 1919) studied between 1937 and 1939. Harry Mundy's education, interrupted by the war, resumed at the renowned Camberwell art school between the years 1946 and 1950. Although the college was in the stranglehold of a Euston Road style that habitually chose pub room, street genre, or rooftop subjects, Mundy later pressed his claim as an abstract painter. His work developed a strong feeling for architectural order which translated itself in rigorous pictorial structuring and surface composing. For nearly a decade he taught at one of the liveliest and most radical art schools, Corsham, and married the painter Gillian Ayres. Ayres moved out of London in the early 1980's to rural seclusion in north Wales. In 1961 Mundy won first prize at the third John Moores competition in Liverpool, and spent the later 1960's teaching at St Martins. In addition to exhibiting regularly at the Hanover gallery – in the sixties firmly on the gallery map of London – Mundy was honoured internationally when, in the space of a few years in the early sixties, he showed at the Carnegie Institute in Pittsburgh.

The period that saw Mundy rising to prominence was definitely a time when young artists could assert themselves and break new ground. In 1960, Mundy exhibited in the important and heraldic exhibition 'Situation' at the R.B.A. gallery. That exhibition contained paintings by 20 abstract painters who worked on a large scale, and by excluding the St Ives artists whose abstract paintings contained closer assocation with nature and landscape, the exhibition ushered in a newly-felt allegiance to American 'post painterly abstraction.' Alan Bowness detected not long afterwards that the "common ground is a rejection of expressionist brushstroke: the touch becomes anonymous, the composition formal: flat fields of colour the dominant element."[14] All the same, Henry Mundy retained painterly nuance, a degree of unpredictability with thin and dribbled paint application, and some organic drawing within a generally geometricised compositional layout.

The taking on of American influences, first seen in the 'pure', autonomous, or more plastic pictorial conventions of the 'Situation' artists, has grown and developed in the hands of a still younger generation of painters. American influences infiltrated the St Martin's sculpture department during the 1960's when the British sculptor Anthony Caro (born 1924) revolutionised the department by promulgating both his own directly welded industrial steel sculpture and the all-important example of the American steel sculpture of David Smith (1906-1965). A vigorous painting taking its inspiration from the early waves of American 'abstract expressionism' developed alongside the St Martin's sculpture boom, and has continued to take hold in this country ever since. Many of the younger practitioners of a free-wheeling, gesturally lively, and colourful abstract painting have, in recent years, been shown at Manchester's Castlefield Gallery. The story of post-war abstract painting in this country perhaps falls into two broad categories. If the so-called 'middle generation' belonged more to a European modernist tradition (indebted especially to French influences such as Braque, Soulages, de Stael, Manessier and so on), then the other tendency has manifestly been more American. This contrasts markedly with the slightly earlier 'middle generation' by virtue of its having no direct landscape references. Even in the hands of one of the more American-influenced St Ives painters like Peter Lanyon (1918-64), landscape references were always of prime significance. The more purely abstract shape, form and colour that is a hallmark of the plastic pictorialism of Hans Hofmann and his New York colleagues , have been more relevant to artists like Sheffield-born John Hoyland, Frank Bowling, Albert Irvin, and the younger painters who came to work at centres like the Stockwell Depot, Greenwich or Wapping during the 1970's. One painter very much a part of this 'group,' Peter Hoida, was born in Birkenhead in 1944. Ever sensitive to the effects of light exuded from, or externally reflected across, his colourful and gesturally assertive canvases, Hoida never allows the work the 'soft option' of a hedonistic or distracting naturalism.

Hoida's mother had spent a year at Birkenhead art school, and the artistic encouragement fostered at home led to Peter's visits, from a very young age, to the Williamson Art Gallery. There was plenty to fire the imagination of a young boy – models of every kind of Mersey ferryboat were complemented by vivid and romantic marine paintings depicting ships on stormy high seas. A white marble copy of Michaelangelo's *David* was a highlight of visits to the public library in Birkenhead. Hoida later became familiar with the Lady Lever Art Gallery at Port Sunlight, with its collection of Pre-Raphaelite pictures and Art Nouveau items. The classical building was built during the Great War by Lord Leverhulme, in memory of his wife. The gallery also possessed a pair of Stubbs' hay scenes, a Gainsborough, Raeburn and Richard Wilson. Yet the Chinese and Persian ceramics also on view were to become equally important sources for a developing aesthetic sensibility as was the will to sexual liberation of a few Victorian paintings. The ceramics appealed for their purity and integrity of form, promoting a sense of perfect craftsmanship. The mother's artistic flair was complemented by his father's occupation as a draughtsman for a local firm that worked on Cunard liners. Good examples of Art Deco design were thus brought home for young Peter to enjoy. This led to an appreciation of the wealth of design apparent inside Liverpool's Kardomah coffee house which he visited once a year as a youth. But all of these early, perhaps formative, influences were upstaged by the discovery of the larger Walker Art Gallery in Liverpool. There he saw Van Gogh as the first impression of modern art, and the effect was naturally an inspirational one, which helped alleviate familiarity with the drab terraced Birkenhead housing where he and his extended family lived. Examples of 1920's architecture and design in the area appealed – the entrance to the Mersey tunnel being one – while Art Deco was favoured for plush, flashy elements within broad design.

In 1958, when aged 14, Hoida moved away from Birkenhead as a decline in the shipping industry compelled his father to seek work elsewhere. He found alternative employment in the furniture business. The family moved to Malvern, and Hoida entered Worcester Grammar School. It was a relief to be in a more educationally-minded environment, and a natural artistic inclination led to an afternoon a week at Worcester Art School. Upon finishing school he studied in nearby Cheltenham as a landscape architect and went on to work in that field for London County Council. He spent lunch breaks in the National Gallery, but visits to the Tate meant most, with its ample displays of modern painting. Although he was interested in poetry and jazz, the example of Jackson Pollock spoke loudest to him and in 1969 he entered Hammersmith School of Art. There a good, though traditional approach to art was instilled by classically orientated draughtsmen and social realist painters like Joe McGill and Ruskin Spear. But this had only limited appeal to a painter intent on non-figurative 'pure' painting. He was at best only tolerated at Hammersmith, though a year at Goldsmiths put him in the company of more like-minded staff, who included Bert Irvin and Basil Beattie. In the early 1970's, Hoida moved with his young family to Stroud where cheaper living conditions and plentiful studio space enabled him to pursue large scale abstract pictures in an unpressured environment. A friendship with the painter Alan Gouk, who then lived in the Stroud area, led to Hoida's peripheral association with a large network of semi 'underground' abstract painters centred on group studios like those at Stockwell and Greenwich. His interest in poetry led to a meeting with W.S. Graham in Cornwall, through whom he met Roger Hilton, and in 1980 he translated into English the poetry of Blaise Cendrars for Penguin Books.

The area to the north of Liverpool contains a low lying belt of rural land. Ormskirk is a small market town mid-way between Wigan and Southport, only a few miles north of Kirkby and the outskirts of the northern edge of Liverpool. Two important contemporary sculptors, both of whom are enjoying a rapidly growing reputation in the field of steel sculpture, were born in Ormskirk. Barbara Lander, born in 1956, and Stephen Lewis, born three years later, began their art studies in the locality. Lander joined St Helens school of art, where she studied textiles and ceramics. From 1975 to 1978 she studied sculpture at Stoke. Under Les Thornton she 'played around' with carving, modelling and casting, as well as with the construction of steel and wood that was eventually to be her chosen course. But Stoke provided little opportunity for working seriously in steel, and the course seemed more geared to crafting materials than to artistic ideas, aesthetics, or matters of style. In 1979 she obtained a position as technician at Hertfordshire College of Art, where her husband, the painter Richard Lander was also working. Making use of an ample steel stock at the college and enjoying the properties of steel which she began to manipulate with a rapidly expanding range of welding skills, Lander developed a sculptural feeling through this most difficult and unyielding of materials. Yet the uniquely flexible quality of steel resides in its ready use in an additive (or subtractive) collaging process. Her degree of sensitivity to the steel medium, no doubt aided by earlier ceramic and modelling studies, was quite exceptional. The abstract painter Graham Boyd, who in 1967 had a work accepted for the John Moores exhibition (and purchased by the Walker) introduced her work to Anthony Caro. Caro recommended her to visit the Triangle summer workshop in New York State, which she did in 1987. Both Michael Fried and Clement Greenberg saw her work there, Greenberg encouraging her to cram and densely pack the sculpture. Finding her work seriously rated by Greenberg was a great boost for an unsure northern art student of ten years earlier.

The constructive criticisms of the leading post-war American critic naturally spurred her on to a period of intense output, enabling her to consolidate her growing reputation. The degree of formal innovation as well as the individuality of look consistently reached in Lander's work is astonishing in the case of a young artist who was walking a well-trodden path. Her youth gave her the luxury of choice as she looked at the options offered by a daunting historical legacy and a well developed tradition of modern steel sculpture. Not interested in putting her sculpture at the service of any pretentious or 'high brow' art historical dialogue with that modern tradition, she has been able to develop as an artist with the typically hard headed, direct and pragmatic approach of the northerner. Her employment of form has a peculiarly northern 'no-nonsense' cutting edge to it, and she has been adept enough to benefit from the criticisms and influences of Caro and Greenberg without becoming infiltrated by their dominating minds.

Being outside the orthodox St Martin's and Stockwell orbit has therefore been to the advantage of an unmistakably individual and self-determining steel welder. The secret of her success resides firmly in working slowly, ever true to her own feelings, along an organic path of discovery. The training at Stoke, where materials were held to be of such prime importance for conception, process and final outcome, was perhaps the chief factor in her down-to-earth, material-based approach to the difficult art of sculpture. Lander has used both gas welding and arc welding for specific effects; the former enabling the malleable red hot steel to be moulded into organic, softly rhythmic shapes; the latter allowing for collaging and piecing together (at decisive points of concentrated heat) of eccentric or harmonious varieties of offcuts, geometric tubing and other 'found' elements, onto the sculpture's basic structural spine or armature.

Stephen Lewis' career has followed a similar course, though he has been more orientated towards artist groups. A year at Southport art school led, in

1977, to his entry to a three-year degree course at Manchester. Keith Godwin was head of sculpture at Manchester, and together with Trevor Crabtree, Mike Lyons and Mike Mason, exerted a helpful influence on both Lewis and the other students. Mason, best known for his wood constructions, was born at Ashton-under-Lyne in 1935, and began studying art in the local art school. He went on to Manchester School of Art in 1954, and later began teaching at each of the two colleges in which he had trained. Lewis' entry into sculpture followed naturally from a youth spent constructing things from plasticine, cardboard, mechanical toys and model ships. His eventual move to the art studios in Greenwich was not however on account of a love for ships, but was rather his need to be involved in an active artistic milieu. Such a need saw him participate in John Foster's Hardingham sculpture workshop in 1986, as well as take a role in the Castlefield venture in Manchester; in 1985 he had an exhibition there of dark stained wood sculpture. Since then Lewis has chosen steel as his material, able to draw on a technical knowledge of welding learnt as much from his father's occupation as a welder and fitter in Liverpool as from art school in Manchester. He has endeavoured to use thin sheets, rods or small offcuts in an effort to emphasise the flexible, linear aspect of modern sculpture first suggested by the lyrical and playful 'doodling' of Gonzalez and Miró.

Another Lancashire-born artist who moved into one of the Greenwich studios in the 1980's was Kay Saunders, born in Blackpool shortly after the war. She started painting in Australia, where she lived for several years in the late 1960's. Evening classes in Sydney were followed, upon her return to England in the early 1970's by a four-year course of study, first at Wimbledon and then at Kingston schools of art. From that point on there was no looking back for this painter with a natural gift for colour. She studied colour theory, though such theory never indulged in the mystic but fostered a practical spirit of experimentation, using colour in search for pictorial dynamism. The example of Hofmann's 'push and pull' theories of colour dynamics within pictorial space, as well as the absolute images of Noland's shaped canvases, naturally exerted an influence. But her very personal range of colour – lilacs, turquoises, crimsons and violets – had a sparkling freshness that suggested joyful celebration 'à la Matisse' of the sensations of the natural world. This association with naturalism was confirmed by her frequent watercolour work of floral, plant or tree forms within a landscape.

Saunders' greatest eye-opener came with her move to a studio at the Stockwell Depot in south London, then a powerhouse for young artists practising broadly abstract expressionist styles, respectful of American precedent, but also proud of a national painterly tradition of which St Ives and the 'Situation' abstract artists were a part. Jennifer Durrant, then painting her large canvases full of swirling biomorphic shapes suggestive of the organic world, had a big impact, as did the sculptors Peter Hide and John Foster. But above all, contact with a like-minded painter, Geoff Hollow, led to a close personal and artistic collaboration. In common with Lander and Lewis, Saunders went on a Triangle workshop summer session, where she worked in company with, and under the critical eye of, Helen Frankenthaler, Ken Noland, Tony Caro, Larry Poons and Clement Greenberg. The workshop experience loosened up her composition, which began to shake out any residual references to the outside world. She has worked fluid and atmospheric pools of water-based acrylic colour onto canvases lying unstretched on the floor in the classic post-Pollock manner. In a quest for spontaneity and directness, cropping – a kind of visual 'editing' – has assumed an important role in the shaping of the final picture.

Since 1985 a gradual re-complication has occurred in her work, heralding a more confident use of what was an evolving abstract style. She began creating textural variation within often singular colour 'grounds,' dragging one carpet of luminous colour over another. The distinction between 'ground' and surface became blurred. Intersecting bands of contrasting colour created spatial tensions, vitality or sensation. Added to the 'push and pull' dynamic, a 'dynamic equilibrium' between opposing colours of intersecting bands, owed something to Mondrian. Resisting an adhesion to a set formula, however, has impelled her to break up the edge-to-edge bands, replacing them with short stump-like residues of radiant colour that hover above optically shifting and light exuding grounds of speckled colour. Saunders is a dedicated, talented and slowly rising painter of whom Lancashire, and Blackpool in particular, should be proud.

If the recent trend has been for talented artists to leave their native north west to pursue their difficult profession in the London melting pot – what one may term the artistic 'big apple' – then instances of a reverse trend have also occurred during the 1980's. In the case of Liverpool, this has led to initiatives, first set up by Patrick Jenkin and Michael Heseltine, to make Liverpool a cultural and tourist attraction. The Liverpool Garden Festival exhibited many sculptors in good outdoor settings. The two big cities, Manchester and Liverpool, have now both 'opened up' with expanding possibilities for contemporary artists, not least the opportunities for cheaper studios and living conditions. One noteworthy event during the 1980's, though one with a greater social than artistic significance, has been the gradual growth of the so-called 'Ideal Village' in Skelmersdale, a new town situated between Wigan and Liverpool. An unprecedented influx of people, practising the Indian technique of Transcendental Meditation, has occurred in a town with the special advantage of unusually inexpensive housing. A 'golden dome' was erected and opened in 1988 allowing for large group meditation practices. Among the community, the commercial artist Stephen Whittle has a successful etching business that produces prints of tranquil rural scenes bathed in a rich, golden light. Appropriately meditation was originally popularised by Liverpool's supreme group 'The Beatles,' whose studies under Maharishi at Bangor, north Wales in 1967 sadly coincided with the death of their legendary mentor Brian Epstein.

NOTES

1 *Art In A City* John Willett (Methuen 1967), p66 'Views of the Past '
2 Letter to the author Frank Dodman 16.3.89
3 *Art in a City* John Willett p120
4 *Art in a City* John Willett p92
5 *Art in a City* John Willett p173
6 Alex Kidson Catalogue introduction Ayling/Porteous Gallery, Chester, 1988
7 John Willett Catalogue introduction Nicholas Horsfield exhibition at Camden Arts Centre, London, October 1984
8 Alex Kidson Chester 1988
9 The Hospital is now the Byng Convalescent home on Southport promenade
10 *Daily Telegraph* 16.8.76 Trevor Bates
11 *Liverpool Echo* 3.5.76 Margo Ingham
12 *Manchester Guardian* 4.5.76 Peter Hetherington
13 *Art in a City* John Willett p129 'Questions of Taste'
14 *Recent British Painting* Alan Bowness p13 Lund Humphries 1968

Two

Liverpool Academy

The Liverpool Academy was founded in 1810. It is thus considerably older than its Manchester counterpart, though the Manchester Academy, unlike Liverpool, has managed to survive as a worthwhile and coherent group by preserving its annual spring show.

A full history of the Liverpool Academy begins early in the nineteenth century and is beyond the scope of this book. However, Nicholas Horsfield's foreword to the Academy's 150th anniversary exhibition in 1960 will suffice to summarise what the Academy had meant during the first century of its existence. "Its career has not always been smooth nor its work unblemished. The foundation of the Academy occurred as part of that great nineteenth century drive for voluntary education within the industrial towns in which Liverpool was peculiarly prominent. The primary aim of the society was to teach and its exhibitions were held as a means of publicising, and in part financing, this function. But the too frequent award of the prize to a Pre-Raphaelite painter - in the 1850's, very advanced in this country - led to a schism in the Academy and ultimately to its virtual eclipse. The members, however, maintained their association without exhibiting and classes continued until the new century. Although efforts were made from time to time to revive interest and a good exhibition was held in 1906, for the most part the Academy became a reactionary force and a butt for the new and independent Sandon Studios Society."[1]

For the purposes of the present survey, a history of the Liverpool Academy between the relevant years of the mid-1930's and the 1960's has been undertaken.

By 1960 the Academy was enjoying a resurgence of vitality, prompting Horsfield to write that "we believe that today we offer an exhibition that is alive and contemporary in feeling and professional in its outlook and standards." Back in 1936 nearly 2,000 works were submitted, indicating the popularity and esteem of the annual exhibition. A photograph of the time shows an all-male selection panel, containing white-haired, bespectacled gentlemen sitting studiously in their formal attire of sober dark suits. The President, Terrick Williams, the well known impressionist painter of Cornish and Breton harbours, was then aged 76. Williams had been born in

Liverpool. After a full art education in Antwerp and under Bougereau and Constant at Julien's Atelier in Paris he became a president of the active St Ives Society of Artists. In 1933 he was elected a Royal Academician. In spite of his high regard for Plymouth as a painting subject, he never attempted to tackle the similar theme of his native Liverpool. The Liverpool Academy's annual general meeting was held at the Royal Institution and, in 1937, the new President, R. Hinchcliffe, presided over the election of Ian Grant and Marjorie Brooks as associate members and Martin Bell as a full member.

In the same year, the Walker Art Gallery held a memorial exhibition for two prominent local Liverpool artists, Joseph Andrews and Alison Martin, who had recently died. Andrews was an amateur painter who worked for the Royal Insurance Company and had exhibited at the Royal Academy, the Walker and other Lancashire museums. He was also an active member of the Liverpool Artists' Club, the Liverpool Academy, and the Merseyside Art Circle. A local newspaper reported that Andrews "used a gay palette and his paint was applied with a full brush. He loved painting farm yards, and the little whitewashed cottages of Anglesey." In spite of his status as a part-time painter (Lowry was a 'part-timer', while two presidents of the Manchester Academy, James Chettle and Maxwell Reekie, were also amateurs), Andrews clearly reached high achievement in his career. This prompted the Walker director, Frank Lambert, as well as many Liverpool Academy members, to attend the opening of his posthumous exhibition.

During these community-minded years the Liverpool newspapers often reported the number of local artists who had succeeded in getting work into the Royal Academy summer exhibition. In 1937 no fewer than two dozen Liverpool artists appeared on the walls of Burlington House and fully justified the local pride expressed in the local press. Among the successful in 1937 were William Penn and Stanley Reed (both showing portraits), John Gauld, Coburn-Witherop (showing a Thames etching and a watercolour of Billingsgate, but nothing of the Mersey) and M. Adshead.

The autumn show of the Liverpool Academy, which represented these artists, was opened in the Bluecoat Chambers by W. Chrimes. His reactionary speech warning against the advances of modernism and abstraction was reported in the *Liverpool Echo*.[2] An appeal was also made by the President, Hinchcliffe, for the public to support their artists by purchasing examples of their work. In spite of hard times Hinchcliffe felt the Liverpool Academy offered the finest provincial exhibition of its kind. He commented that "a depression may hit business men badly but it almost annihilates the artists. We are emerging from the depression so now we ask for a wider circle of people to come forward and buy pictures. I am satisfied that they will find a new interest in life, out of all proportion to the effort or cost. We must help to bring together, therefore, artists and the buying public."

Chrimes' warning against modernist intervention was lost on the local sculptor Edward Carter Preston. His half machine, half man sculpture *Arms and the Man* prompted George Whitfield to write in the Echo,[3] that "never before has the Academy - which always has an eye for tradition - been so revolutionary or 'modern'." Whitfield continued by calling the sculpture with its Bernard Shaw title "a dreadful figure of the modern machine, not only of production, but of thought and policy which is crushing the humanities to the following of a mechanical idea, or 'ideal' as the dictators call it." Despite the disturbing futuro-modernist connotations in *Arms and the Man*, Carter Preston was capable of executing some contrasting, sentimental and, some would argue, equally grotesque carvings. An example is the larger-than-life Figurehead of Nelson, hewn from a 3½ ton block of teak, for HMS Conway moored at Liverpool. Whitfield found further traces of the modern in the work of Martin Bell who "is going more and more modern without being able to forget Van Gogh and Gauguin." A tame, though appropriate, description of Ian Grant's contribution said he "states the mystery attaching to simple houses and the community of lives lived amid the hills and dales." Similarly pleasing notes were provided for equally conventional themes such as a "lovely episode of the sea and coast as seen from Anglesey", that was attributed to R. Fraser's *Menai Straits*, and good floral still lifes by Frank Copnall and Wallasey artist Will Penn.

At the opening of the next Liverpool Academy exhibition, comprising nearly 40 artists, the Lord Mayor, Cory Dixon, made proud reference to the longest established annual exhibition in England after the Royal Academy itself. But local urban themes were not in great evidence, as if to emphasise Liverpool's decline. Nevertheless, the city had a spirited population, which flowered in the 1960's. Liverpool became famous, not for high classical culture, but for the Mersey Sound, with its numerous pop-groups headed by the Beatles, as well as for its two football clubs.

The sculptor Carter Preston complemented his cherrywood and yew figures in this academy exhibition with some wash landscape drawings. Irvine Hertford's *Sound of Iona* was described by George Whitfield as a "masterpiece of its kind", which seemed to follow in the footsteps of Peploe and the Scottish Colourists. Watercolour landscapes, "competent as ever", by Percy Lancaster were matched by equally conventional family *genre* subjects by Will Penn. Penn's Edwardian interiors, highlighted by sparkling cutlery or furniture items, were particularly fine academic set pieces in the tradition of William Orpen's *Homage to Manet* in the City Art Gallery, Manchester. Grainger Smith's landscapes of North Wales were applauded along with contributions in a similar manner by Charles Sharp. Frank Copnall's portraits, and his wife Teresa's customary floral studies, continued this conventional vein. But Whitfield was forced to doubt whether Coburn - Witherop "intends you to recognise *Chester* as such, but he always has his own method of taking places to pieces and putting them together again in his own composition, and here . . . he shows a work of much attraction."

It is doubtful whether Coburn-Witherop's mechanical and obsessive approach to detail represented any truly inventive pictorial or formal statement. It is clear though that he managed a fresh approach by choosing to depict a local subject, as well as one with many attractive and historical features. Witherop lived in Liverpool on Mount Street, but was associated with St Ives. He was a quiet man, tolerant but conservative in taste. Like John Bold he adopted the precise, delineated style of the artist who perceived and translated nature literally. For many years he served as a picture restorer at the Walker Gallery.

On the theme of the beautiful, James Mann and Fred Allen sent in the kind of Cornish pictures that were a ubiquitous feature of almost all provincial art exhibitions of this kind. Fred Allen was coming to the end of his life. This Birkenhead artist, whose nomadic life in a caravan took him to many parts of the country, had studied under Will Penn at Liverpool School of Art. Allen served in the 1914-18 conflict, and later specialised in landscapes of the Wirral, North Wales and the Lake District.

Oswald Garside's *Stockton Heath, Warrington* reflected the studies that the Southport-born painter had undertaken at Warrington School of Art. The son of a chemist, Garside's early talent had shone sufficiently for him to win from Lancashire County Council a scholarship to the renowned Julien's Atelier in Paris. He repaid the debt by becoming a member of both the Liverpool Academy and the Liverpool Artists' Club - and also by honouring local subject matter, as was indicated by his contribution to this 1938 Liverpool exhibition.

The 1938 autumn exhibition of the Liverpool Academy was opened by Sir Kenneth Clark, director of the National Gallery. The selection panel for this exhibition at the Walker included Director Frank Lambert, Grainger Smith, Academy President R. Hinchliffe and a group of councillors. They proved to be a competent team. Liverpool's Lord Mayor, Cory Dixon, who had opened an exhibition earlier that year, made a speech at the annual dinner of the Liverpool Artists' Club, referring to the artist as a corrective force in the modern world. "We looked to machines to do our work," he said, "and we are in danger of thinking in terms of machines. The artist stood for self-expression." Poignant words, spoken less than a year before the outbreak of the century's greatest global conflict. The growing Nazi menace certainly gave a tangible context for Carter Preston's *Arms and the Man*, the sculpture that had made such a vexed impact earlier in the year. One picture that stood out at the Walker that autumn was Will Penn's *Portrait of Joseph Greene*, a superb *contre jour* view of the sitter playing the piano in a grandly ornate and well furnished room set against a large window.

During the early months of 1939, the grim signs of international trouble were felt everywhere, and at the opening of the Liverpool Academy spring exhibition the new mayor, Sydney Jones, laid great emphasis on the need to cultivate greater levels of appreciation for beauty and art. These would help neutralise the growing speed, danger and carelessness of the age. The trend in Liverpool was for artists to seek a better deal and eke out a living from their work by moving to London. This was thought a regrettable trend that undermined the vitality of the Merseyside art scene. Thus the Academy exhibition presented subjects that did little to advance appreciation of the local scene. Suffolk landscapes by Grainger Smith, Philip Connard's *Ferry Farm*, Coburn-Witherop's painting of St Ives, Cornwall and "an epic of virginal pastoral" by Percy Lancaster. The rural theme was also pursued by John Bowes, whose *Formby Asparagus Fields* did represent an altogether more authentic local landscape. Two of Martin Bell's contributions came nearer to realism in their depiction of the local scene. One, *Seven Chimneys*, prompted a local critic to describe it as "an industrial study which is sufficiently striking to withstand the competition of a fairly large portrait above it." The other work, *Mild and Bitter* was described as "a novel viewing of a smoke room scene."[4] These interesting pictures by Bell had to compete with a large number of portrait paintings in the Academy from Will Penn, Ian Grant and Charles Oliver. The exhibition also contained paintings by Julius Olsson, whose renowned Cornish seascapes suffused with sublime light would have touched the maritime sensibility of the Liverpool public. Local sculptor Tyson Smith, who that year had a 30-foot Irish giant figure erected at New York's World Fair, exhibited small bronze plaques. A series of miniature pictures by women artists was another feature of the exhibition. During the war the Walker Art Gallery was taken over for food and fuel control, and the prize possessions of the Walker collection were sent to safer havens. An exhibition of Polish art initiated a season of theme exhibitions put on to satisfy the local need for art during the war. The war

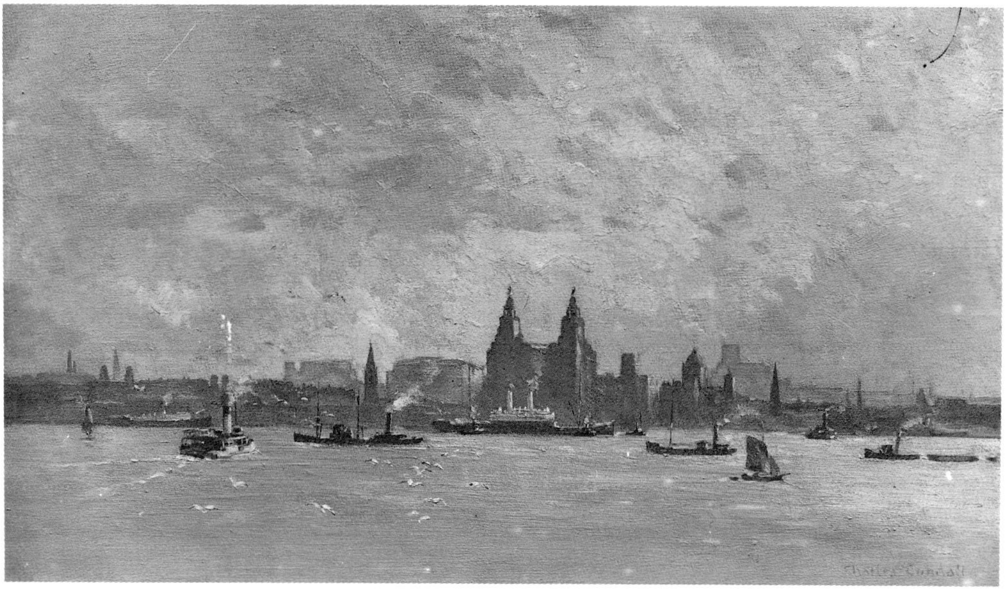

Charles Cundall: Liverpool from the Mersey, *oil 1944 (courtesy: Manchester City Art Gallery).*

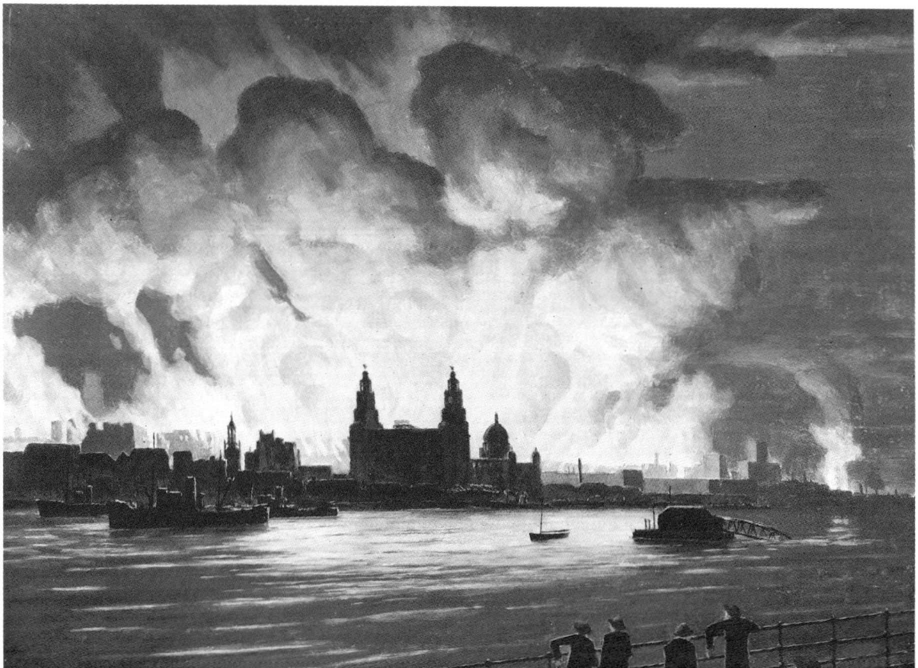

Grainger Smith: The Enemy Raid, *tempera, 1941.*

itself did little to shake Liverpool artists out of their complacency, until heavy bombing in May and June 1941 shook the city and prompted memorable paintings such as Grainger Smith's *Enemy Action* (Walker Art Gallery).

An exhibition entitled 'Art in Wartime' at the Bluecoat seemed to sum up the attitude of Liverpool artists. One local newspaper stated that "artists are curiously aloof sort of people. They hardly seem to notice the war. If one may judge by this exhibition, they were far more excited by the deep snowfall last February than in anything that has happened since. Snowdrifts and still life, white sails and washing on a line, flower pieces and farms!" In this exhibition only a handful of paintings actually expressed war conditions. Among those that did were Winifred Humphrey's *Neighbours*, depicting a group entering an air raid shelter, Grainger Smith's *Home Guard*, and Bertha Tippin-Moreton's small statue *Refugees*. Regular exhibitors like Frank Copnall, Will Penn, Stanley Reed and Charles Sharpe, however, studiously avoided war themes. In February 1941 Will Penn was honoured with a one-man exhibition at the Williamson Art Gallery, Birkenhead. Among the many official portraits from his hand was one of Liverpool's Mayor, Sidney Jones (Walker Art Gallery).

In June 1941, the Bluecoat was damaged during a night of heavy bombing. The west wing, housing the Sandon Studios, remained but the concert hall was gutted. Although the main walls and fabric of the fine Georgian building were unimpaired, the roof and interior of one side were substantially damaged. An account in Roderick Bisson's valuable *The Sandon Studios Society*[5] confirms that the Bluecoat was not directly hit though "flames from an adjoining building set the east wing and the Concert Hall alight." Bisson went on to tell how Herbert Tyson, Chairman of the Society, instructed the Rochdale fire fighters to leave the unimportant building they were tackling and go instead to save the historic Bluecoat buildings. "The fire was arrested, the walls stood and, though the Concert Hall and much of the east wing were gutted, the west wing remained intact." Dedicated Sandon members like Will Penn, Tyson Smith and Donald Lynch made maximum use of the existing facilities, however. Various musical and social events were put on and small annual exhibitions were mounted in the Music Room. One social event soon after the bombing was the 'To Hell with Hitler' party, organised by the Sandon in true fighting spirit. In this same spirit an exhibition containing 30 artists was put on in the Sandon's Music Room. The idea was for each artist to donate paintings for public purchase, to raise funds for the Bluecoat's restoration. It was in this context that Grainger Smith's *Enemy Action*, painted in tempera at his Wallasey home during the night blitz on Liverpool in May 1941, was first shown. The dramatic picture is notable for the reflections of an eerie, fiery light across the waters of the Mersey. The unmistakable silhouette of the Liver Building and its neighbouring towers stands as a dark architectural feature against the burning city in the background. In 1943, a period of little exhibition activity, the Sandon's Music Room held a small four-man exhibition by local artists Charles Sharpe, Geoffrey Wedgewood, Martin Bell and Edgar Grosvenor.

During the middle years of the war, two prominent North West artists, both active members of the Liverpool Academy, died. The first, Richard Hinchliffe, was born in Manchester, trained at Liverpool School of Art and the Slade before finishing his studies at Julien's Atelier in Paris. Hinchliffe exhibited at the Royal Academy as well as Liverpool. His successor as President, Henry Huggill, was a Royal College of Art man. Huggill took on the presidency after first serving in the Artists Rifles during the Great War, then as head of Southport Art School, and finally for ten years as Principal of Liverpool School of Art. The second artist to die (also in 1943) was Oswald Garside. It was written that Garside "will be much missed by the Liverpool Academy of Arts and other artistic coteries here whose social gatherings were greatly enlivened by his droll reminiscences and droller manner of relating them." The following year, Sir Edwin Lutyens, architect of the Liverpool Roman Catholic Cathedral, and Liverpool Academy member also died.

After a short period of inactivity during the depths of war, a Liverpool Academy exhibition was held at the Bluecoat in 1944. Once again few works came to terms with the war. Instead visitors were offered harmless, though competent, portrait paintings by Will Penn and Frank Copnall, which were complemented by an Ian Grant landscape, a characteristic Teresa Copnall flower study, and works by other regulars such as Coburn-Witherop and Grainger Smith. Another Academy exhibition, in the Music Room, presented similar themes, though two noteworthy portraits by Frank Copnall and Will Penn celebrated sitters who were ultimately of national significance. Copnall's portrait of W. Cuff, President of the Football League, Vice-President of the Football Association, and Director of Everton Football Club, was given to the Liverpool solicitor by the shareholders and supporters of Everton, in recognition of half a century of service to football. A portrait of W. McIvor, Vice-President of the Birkenhead Chamber of Commerce, painted by Will Penn, was presented at Birkenhead Town Hall in September 1946.

Between 1945 and 1947 three exhibitions were held at the Bluecoat

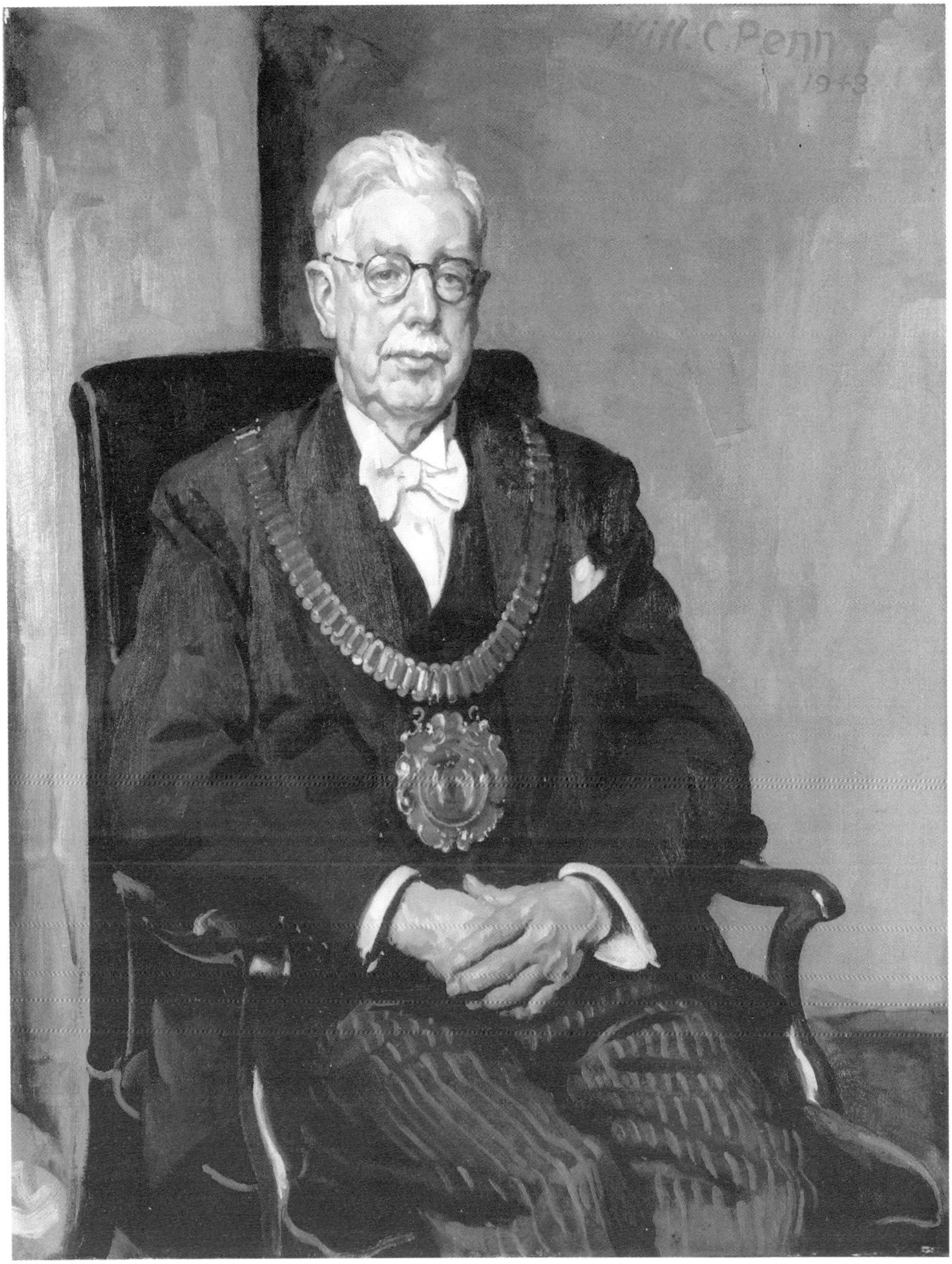

W.C. Penn: Sir Sidney Jones, *oil 1943.*

Chambers. The artist Roderick Bisson explained that with "the relics of war all about and the probability that in post-war years other buildings would disappear, the 'Recording Merseyside' exhibitions were organised."[6] It was appropriate that Bisson should cite Herbert Thearle - an "architect of fine buildings in later years," as the initiating intelligence behind this scheme. It was the war damage that inspired the architect to want to see painters record parts of the city that were gone or changing. As well as contributing his own painting, Charles Sharpe also helped organise this exhibition series. "These were an outstanding success," according to Bisson. "Not only did many artists and architects rise to the occasion with fine, imaginative work but enthusiastic patrons supported the scheme financially. The corporations of Liverpool and Birkenhead and private purchasers acquired more than half the pictures." Many of the works were subsequently illustrated in the *Liverpool Daily Post.* Geoffrey Wedgwood had reproduced the portrait he had painted of the Bluecoat when it was a school. Percy Lancaster's *Blitzed area, Pitt Street, Liverpool* was featured, so too was Coburn-Witherop's *Gate House, Canning Half-Tide Dock.* Charles Sharpe's *Toad Hall Farm* managed to link architectural detail with a broad, impressionistic play of light and shadow across the late 17th century Birkenhead cottage. James Mann's superb *Liverpool Pierhead, from the River* successfully integrated the Mersey seafront's tall buildings with tugs and ocean liners. In the same manner as Mann and Sharpe, Grainger Smith's *Williamson Square* and *Old Theatre Royal, Liverpool* managed to convey the complexity of architectural detail, though in a way that did not stop an impressionistic handling of light, expressive of sharply contrasted sunlight and shadow across both buildings and a busy street. Manchester-born Allan Tankard pursued a rigidly topographical style, in his *Rodney Street, Liverpool.*

Appearing at the Bluecoat shortly after the war was an exhibition comprising 20 Liverpool artists who had survived their service in the Forces. Among these were watercolours that recorded bomb damage by William Warden, and Stanley Reed's depiction of signal operators at work. The 1946 Royal Academy exhibition in London was again mentioned in Liverpool newspapers because of contributions from Liverpool artists. Although well down on the pre-war number of two dozen, the eight individuals who did get in showed strong work, particularly Will Penn, Teresa Copnall and Molly Garland. Will Penn also featured strongly in the 1946 Liverpool Academy exhibition held at the Sandon Music Room. Frank Copnall's portraits were of local dignitaries, themes matched by Stanley Reed, whose portrait of the Lord Mayor, Luke Hogan, in full regalia, was reproduced in the *Daily Post.* Reed, a consistent performer in

Academy exhibitions with his competent portraits, was an art master at Manchester Grammar School. He was born in Ullock, and later his blacksmith father moved his family down to Liverpool, where young Stanley studied at the School of Art under Will Penn and George Marples. He later won scholarships and his portrait *Danae* - of sculptor Tyson Smith's daughter - was purchased by the City of Liverpool. Coburn-Witherop, Percy Lancaster and Charles Sharpe each exhibited customary rural subjects, while Martin Bell answered calls for a nearer-to-home realism with *The Canal, Chester.*

The years immediately after the war were therefore quiet, reconstructive ones but new enterprising attitudes emerged as early as 1947. Lord Leverhulme, President of the Sandon Society, led a campaign to retrieve the Walker Art Gallery from the Ministry of Food. He remarked that "the good name of Liverpool is not helped by the present misuse of the gallery." There was some good news, however, in the *Liverpool Daily Post.*[7] Plans were being laid for the restoration of the historic Bluecoat Chamber. Secondly a gift of 138 paintings by Italian and Flemish Primitives, all from the Roscoe collection, had been made to the City of Liverpool. William Roscoe, eminent Liverpool lawyer, banker and man of letters, collected these treasures in the late 18th century. The pictures were handed over to the Royal Institution following Roscoe's bankruptcy. The Institution was subsequently administered by Liverpool University, becoming the centre for extra-mural studies.

Liverpool Academy exhibitions continued to be shown in the Sandon Society Music Room. By 1950 the Academy exhibition, though very much smaller than that offered by the Manchester Academy, proved pleasing to local *Echo* critic George Whitfield, who expressed his pleasure in a complimentary review.[8] Stanley Reed's characteristic portraits were complemented that year by his display at Burlington House of a memorable portrait of the Archbishop of Liverpool. Teresa Copnall's flower paintings - "crisply painted in a high key and beautifully designed" - were liked by Whitfield. Martin Bell and Will Penn once again featured prominently. Towards the end of November 1950 Percy Lancaster died in Birkdale. His death led the *Southport Visiter* to run a long front cover tribute, including a reproduction of his portrait painted by Henry Vitofski. In the picture Lancaster gazed intently outwards with decisively folded arms.

1951 was marked by the Festival of Britain. The Liverpool Festival of that year, directed by Alfred Francis, contributed to these national celebrations, and Coburn-Witherop and J. Keates organised an exhibition entitled 'Fifty Years of Liverpool Art.' Drawing from public and private collections, the exhibition recorded the changing patterns of art during the first half of the century. In November, the *Liverpool Daily Post* reported on three local societies whose annual exhibitions coincided.[9] Regulars like Stanley Reed, Will Penn and Martin Bell highlighted the Academy exhibition, while Geoffrey Wedgewood's remarkable *Overhead Railway, Liverpool* won justified attention. The Wirral Society of Arts exhibition, which "aims to discover and encourage new talent", even if many of the exhibits were unexciting floral subjects, was held at the Williamson Art Gallery in Birkenhead. Finally the Liver Sketching Club's exhibition was distinguished by a series of topographical drawings of Liverpool by Gordon Hemm.

Two men were considered by *Guardian* critic Charles Sewter to dominate the 1952 Liverpool Academy exhibition. They did so on the basis of work that expressed the unique mood of the 1950's, with a gritty style combining neo-romantic tautness of design, poignancy of feeling, a palette of ochres, purples and greys, and an over all feeling of 'angst'. The two, Austin Davies and Mayer-Marton, had nearly 50 works shown between them - far too many for the health of a thriving Academy. Davies' alienated figures, bathed in a Kafkaesque mood, were described by Sewter as "moving and pathetic documents". The critic went on to describe how his use of paint "with its dry earthy quality and the dull ochre and slate colours, evokes a sense of elemental anxiety."[10] Sewter was less enthusiastic about Mayer-Marton's brand of modernism, finding in the work too literal a depiction of movement, that betrayed a superficially adopted influence of Severini and the Futurists. Nevertheless Sewter concluded that "apart from these two painters, there is little enough of note in the exhibition." There were, however, some "painstakingly conscientious portraits by Stanley Reed and Will Penn." In complete contrast the *Liverpool Daily Post* decided that the exhibits on display in Liverpool that autumn "make an excellent show".[11]

An Academy ruling in 1954 restricted the number of works from individual artists to six. Sewter wrote that the "result is a more balanced but less interesting show, and the new restriction does not prevent the personalities of a few artists from securing predominant attention."[12] Nevertheless, the hanging of 50 works by only two members the year before was a situation that had to be quickly remedied. Austin Davies' dock scenes, "low in tone, elaborately linear in execution", were complemented with very different portraits "of great refinement and sensibility", as Sewter called them. The "elaborately linear" approach of Davies towards dock subjects used emotive, romantic and taut imagery that owed much to cubist design.

Arthur Ballard also impressed Sewter and seemed to be going from strength to strength. Sewter said Ballard was "simplifying, broadening and softening his style, without losing the sombre mood of realism which previously emerged from his subject matter rather than from his treatment". The artist was undoubtedly feeling his way towards a kind of late 1950's painterly abstraction - inspired by de Stael and other post-war Parisian abstractionists - that somehow never quite lost the reference point of natural form or allusion to the outside world. The block-like slabs of knifed pigment were often composed to resemble a de-focussed segment of landscape, a still life or a group of figures. Ballard's subjects were taken from motifs suggested to him in North Wales, and his contribution to the 1954 exhibition was the axiomatic *Derelict Cottage, North Wales.*

The 1954 exhibition succeeded in tempering the usually sceptical, and sometimes caustic, criticism of Charles Sewter. "As Academies go, this is a lively exhibition," he was able to say.

In the years leading up to the 150th anniversary exhibition in 1960, the general quality of the Liverpool Academy was judged to have risen considerably. "Martin Bell's gentle townscapes," wrote Sewter in his *Guardian* article, "rather in the manner of Utrillo, are pleasing and sensitive in colour, but a little tame." Tameness certainly did not apply to Mayer-Marton's "ingenious essays in a revived futurism", but this was "the application of a complicated intellectual and theoretical approach to a vision without inherent originality." Mayer-Marton's *Merseyside Patterns*, "a picture of cranes, criss-crossing rails and rigging", impressed Sewter most, though even this interesting composition "loses expressiveness by its excessively jazzy effect of colour." Of the older members Sewter wrote, "the cold and meticulous landscapes by Coburn-Witherop look rather colourless; and the official portrait of the Mayor of Birkenhead by Stanley Reed appears to have strayed from Madame Tussaud's." The need to bring a hint of inspiration to Academy exhibits seemed nowhere more evident than in the work of Allan Tankard, whose topographical watercolours of Liverpool streets showed a "dramatic and romantic mood which he would do well to cultivate, even at the cost of sacrificing some of his neat architectural detail." The 1955 annual exhibition of the Academy, held at the Walker, was the 144th of its long history. The show had unexpected range with Austin Davies exhibiting a portrait of Mrs E. Braddock M.P. "She is a very good sitter," Davies remarked, "mainly because she is used to sitting still for long periods at political meetings." There was nothing inert, however, in the final image which conveyed a strong, decisive character.

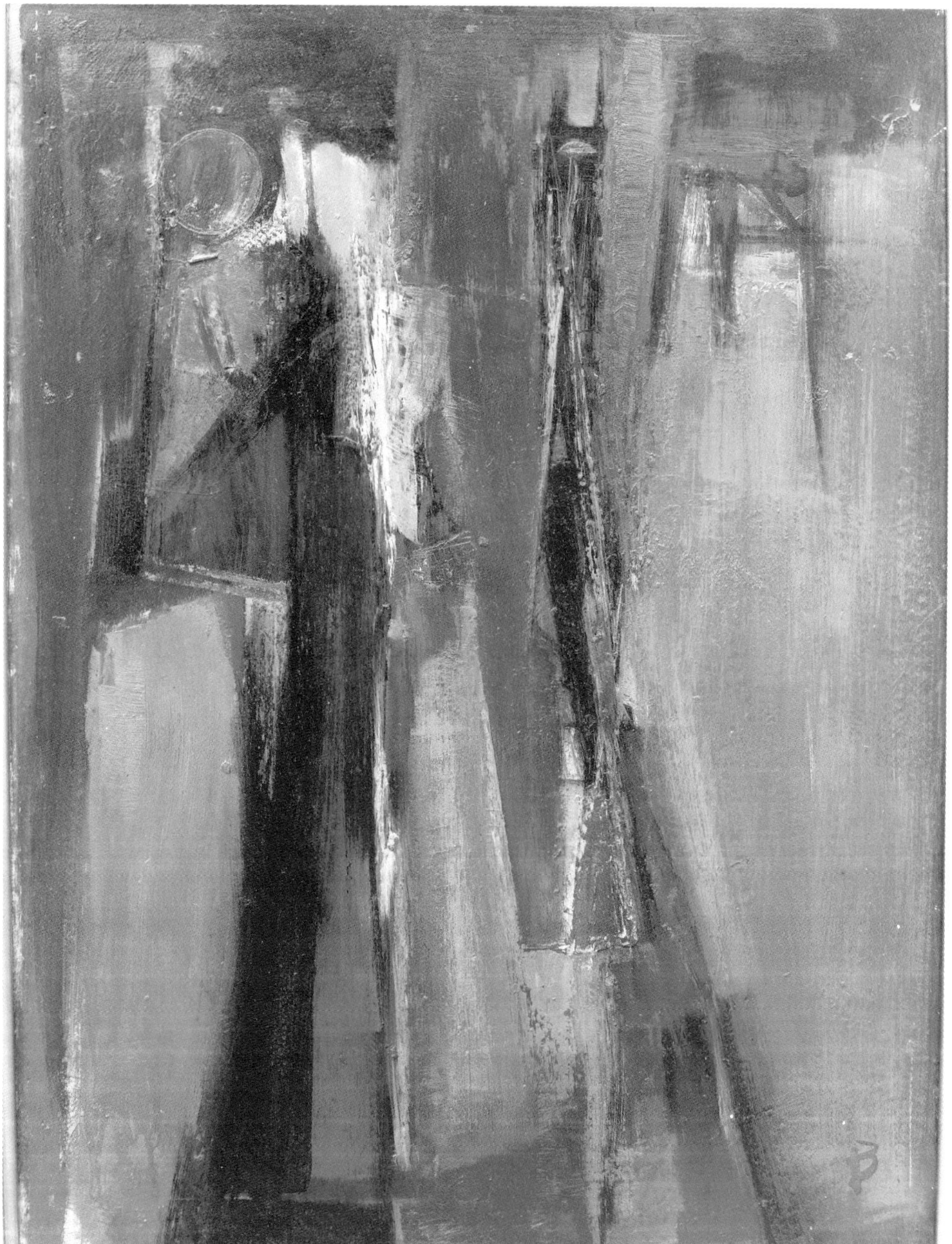

Arthur Ballard: Non Figurative Painting *(courtesy: Walker Art Gallery)*.

The painting aimed at realism by placing the subject against what the artist described as "the squalor and darkness of Liverpool." Davies dressed the sitter in a casual jacket, realised in the picture by a criss-cross of light and sinewy lines to emphasise the folds of alternatively taut and loose drapery.

An exhibition of work rejected from the 1955 Academy exhibition was held in the basement of the State Building in Dale Street. There were 150 works by 80 artists on display but the reporter for the *Daily Post* found "the rejected works are generally of a mediocre standard."

One outcome of that year's Academy exhibition was the decision to purchase five paintings for the Walker collection. Hugh Scrutton, as gallery director, together with two City Councillors, selected *Forest Fungus* by Austin Davies, *Farm* by Arthur Ballard, *Le Pollet Cliffs* by Nicholas Horsfield, and an example each by Robert Percival and Margaret Hughes.

The 1956 exhibition proved to be a dispiriting experience for Charles Sewter. His *Guardian* piece even doubted the need for any further Academy shows.[13] Sewter claimed that Academy exhibitions were once indispensable as the only way a worthwhile artist might exhibit his wares. The local pride and community feeling generated by such regional exhibitions made them a central event in the cultural calendar of any large provincial town. But in the modern age of private galleries, Sewter wondered if the Academy with its inward-looking and sometimes nepotistic juries had outlived its usefulness. "The municipal galleries themselves could serve the public, and the cause of art, better," he speculated, "by inviting only the artists who, in the opinion of their directors, were worthy of public notice." Sewter therefore suggested that much of the work, particularly that by open exhibitors, should have been excluded. Stanley Reed, Mayer-Marton, whose two Austrian scenes were judged to be "in a class by themselves," Millicent Ayrton and Martin Bell whose work was "rich in colour and pleasing in design," particularly impressed Sewter. However, another front rank performer, Austin Davies, was not exhibited to best advantage, his excellent paintings being dispersed throughout the exhibition.

Sewter was much more generous with the 1957 show. "A respectable and moribund body shot through with disruptive pangs of modernism, has suddenly become young and vigorous."[14] Sewter was also able to applaud the new look catalogue and a more spacious hanging in which all the major exhibitors had their work hung together. Indeed, in his own review, Nicholas Horsfield referred to "a decently hung exhibition of able professional work that with only a little further sifting could be shown anywhere."[15] Arthur Ballard, whose abstracted landscapes seemed to hang in a nocturnal mood, was regarded as being at the forefront of this renaissance. Sewter credited Martin Bell with continuing "to deal with the theme of picturesque, architectural squalor on the outskirts of old cities, but his treatment has become more constructive." Austin Davies, who on this occasion attempted still life subjects, continued to sparkle with a period palette of blacks, browns, greys and purples which together conveyed a dramatic mood. Davies' taut, linear strokes, his use of evocative colour and scratched or physical paint surfaces, were to some extent mirrored in the work of Brian Bradshaw, who "shows three powerful pictures, all of which have a dramatic tension in every brush stroke." Donald McKinlay's powerful surfaces, the product of a flirtation with the then current tachist painting technique, were mentioned for their sheer visual impact across the rooms of the Walker. The tachisme attempted by Donald McKinlay was at that time being practised in France by the likes of Manessier, Hartung or Mathieu. On the other hand the warm, intimate and painterly study, *Studio Table*, by Richard Young and George Mayer-Marton's series on the theme of the artist and model in the studio, employed motifs that owed more to the older French tradition of Braque and Bonnard. All such influences were absent, however, from Allan Tankard's neat and very English topographical watercolours of Chester, which according to Nicholas Horsfield "must be as accomplished as any now being done in this genre." Horsfield explained that Sewter had "recently made harsh criticism of provincial academies," and speculated that those criticisms of six months before "would seem to have gone home, for the present exhibition is not the usual hotchpotch of ill assorted works that passes for a provincial academy."

As a run-up to the next Liverpool Academy exhibition, in May 1958, the *Liverpool Post*[16] included a photograph of six artists - Mayer-Marton, John Hart, Nicholas Horsfield, Martin Bell, Arthur Ballard and W.L. Stevenson - whose works had recently been purchased for the City by John Moores. Two days later Charles Sewter reported on the continuing vitality of the Liverpool Academy exhibition which he described as "a livelier show than any of our other provincial academies have produced for decades."[17] Arthur Ballard was again leading the field with six abstract paintings which "have a conviction, a sonority of colour, a weight and solidity of pigment, and a controlled power of rhythm." An encouraging aspect of the show was the number of works that revealed awareness of contemporary art movements. Even Austin Davies seemed to shed the taut, neo-romantic garb, with what Sewter considered was "a much bolder and freer abstract expressionist manner in which his natural feeling for linear rhythm, for telling and subtle opposition of colour, and for the expressive textures of paint surface, is allowed new scope." And Martin Bell, although continuing with architectural subjects, used more expressive brushwork, "released from the task of description."

A year later, the Liverpool exhibition of May 1959 displayed many abstract pictures, prompting F.W. Fenton to write that "it is no slave to academic tradition."[18] Fenton's *Daily Telegraph* report spoke of a genuinely avant-garde exhibition, where even figurative works, such as Yankel Feather's clown, Millicent Ayrton's *Amphitheatre, Verona*, and works by John Bowes and Brian Bradshaw were considered modernist. Philip Hartas' *Crying Child*, reminiscent of Epstein, was a feature of the small sculpture section. Charles Sewter went further, saying Liverpool's art was now of "metropolitan standard."[19] Sewter himself was in no doubt that Ballard and Davies stood out as the best. Davies' "manner, as always, is more linear and more involved than Ballard's, but is also rich in textures and in suggestions of movement and recession." John Hart, Nicholas Horsfield, Robert Percival and Martin Bell impressed, while Brian Bradshaw's drawing *Lamplight* "attains a power which he somehow misses in his paintings." Sewter cast his critical eye on Richard Young and wrote that "in spite of a heavy debt to Bratby he clearly possesses an individual gift for colour." John Bowes showed "quiet and unpretentious but evocative watercolours." Sewter finished his commentary by suggesting that the "situation of the Liverpool Academy, too, is healthier than that of its London counterpart, for it represents virtually the whole local artistic activity, and this is predominantly of what may be termed a progressive character."

In June 1960, the Academy celebrated its 150th anniversary exhibition. The historical section presented works shown at the Academy from its foundation in 1810 to 1867, supplemented with paintings shown at Liverpool art societies from 1774 until the birth of the Academy. David Cox, William Etty, Turner and Holman Hunt were included. The contemporary section was made up of 180 works from regular contributors. Millicent Ayrton's *Delphi* and Brian Bradshaw's waterfall subject were on the figurative side of the contemporary avant-garde, which contrasted with Arthur Ballard's *Drifting Shapes*. The influence of de Stael could be seen in John Hart's vividly textured abstract which, like Ballard's, was illustrated in Mary Bennett's fine 150th anniversary catalogue. Neville Bertram's *Pierced Form*, also illustrated, was an upright, carved piece, abstracted into sensual curves. It was a distillation from the figure, which looked too close to Barbara Hepworth's style.

President Nicholas Horsfield wrote that if "we feel today that we are on an upsurge, we cannot accept this complacently: the Academy's future depends entirely on the character of its members. But we may hope that as

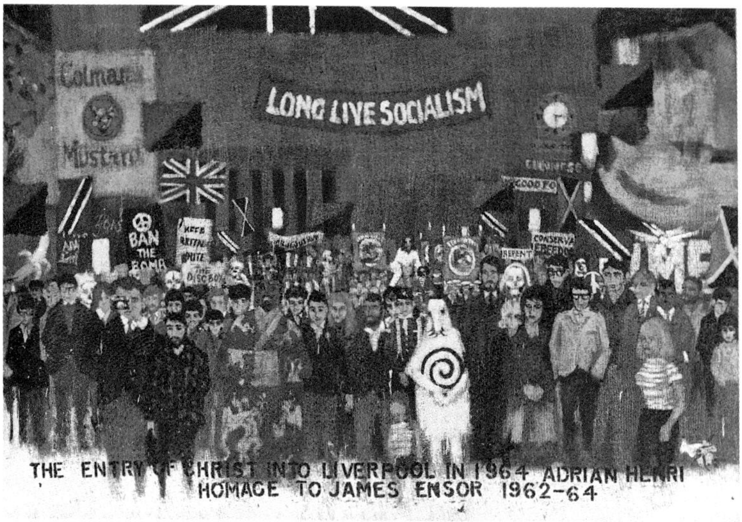

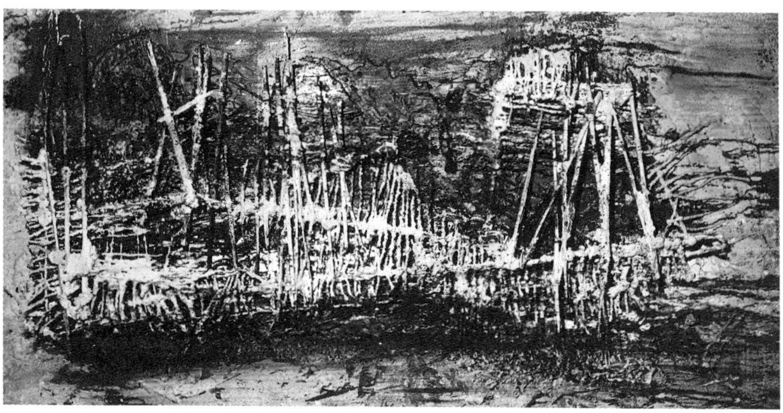

Adrian Henri: The Entry of Christ into Liverpool, *oil on hessian and Donald McKinlay:* Composition D, *wood, wax and oil, 1959.*

Liverpool has maintained a body of professional artists through a hundred and fifty years, so the Academy in the future may still continue the tradition." The fact that this situation continued for only another 20 years was due firstly to difficult economic circumstances that set in after the optimistic 1960's, then to the continuing centralising influence of London on regional art, and finally, in Liverpool's case, to a degree of financial mismanagement. Ian Grant said much later that the Liverpool Academy had "an inefficient council at that time and lost paintings until I became fed up and resigned."[20]

In the exhibition of May 1961, Anthony Tucker was able to confirm the encouraging level of invention and vitality detected in Academy shows in the late 1950's. Tucker wrote "Perhaps, quite simply, Liverpool has a better nucleus of home-grown artists than most provincial cities, for the annual exhibition manages to be broader, brighter, and less dotted with triviality than its brethren elsewhere."[21] Referring to the 'New York School,' Tucker said that "there is plenty here to demonstrate that neither intention nor scale determines success. Violence, brilliance, vigour, and even invention remain secondary to control, and the paintings here which strike deepest are seldom those which first claim attention." As an example, Tucker referred to the "quiet grey sensitivity of Richard Young's interiors" and the "very fine colour sense of Nicholas Horsfield." As always, the Francophile sophistication, sensuality and *belle peinture* ethos practised by Young, Horsfield, Ballard and others, won commendation.

The emergence of Pop Art influences on Merseyside should not surprise us, given the global impact of the Beatles and Merseybeat. Liverpool had been put on the map in the popular imagination. Adrian Henri, well known Liverpool poet and Pop painter, was closely involved with this popular movement, and he became the last President of the Liverpool Academy. Indeed, the 1964 Academy exhibition, reviewed by M.G. McNay for the *Guardian*, commentated on Henri's challenging gesture: "the dada is not the painting by Adrian Henri with the plastic flowers glued to the surface, but the act of the hanging committee in hanging a meticulous traditional flower painting beside it.[22]

Adrian Henri and Dublin-born Sam Walsh became the Merseyside Pop painters par excellence. Henri's large *Entry of Christ into Liverpool* (1962) anticipates the collaged crowd scenes, full with famous faces, of Klaus Voorman's and Peter Blake's record cover for the Beatles' 'Revolver' (1966) and 'Sgt Pepper' (1967). The fascination for larger-than-life fame found its perfect image in cinemascopic scale. Sam Walsh's large close-up portraits, notable for their thin and dribbled painterly surfaces (giving the effect of seeing a face through rain) celebrated the amplified aspects of 'popstar' culture. Cinema also romanticised heroes of the past and Peter MacKarell's Napoleonic history scenes owe something to Larry Rivers. Mackarell's, Walsh's, and Henri's retention of painterly values and personal mark-making reflects Rivers' position in modern America art as a transitional figure between abstract Expressionism and Pop Art.

The visual diet of Liverpool was enhanced, not only by the Academy exhibitions during the late 1950's and early 1960's, but also by the annual John Moores painting competition, which saw many of the best contemporary British painters submit their work in competition for a lucrative prize. Many humorous and affectionate stories have come out of those years, but not least the tragi-comic episode in 1963 when a drunken Roger Hilton, anticipating his prize, impatiently interfered with the official civic ceremony and demanded the prize cheque without further formality. The chaos was exacerbated when the Mayor collapsed, and later died. Jack Smith won the first John Moores prize in 1957, followed by Patrick Heron in 1959, Henry Mundy in 1961, and Roger Hilton in 1963. Later prizewinners were to include David Hockney, John Hoyland, John Walker, Euan Uglow and Richard Hamilton.

Nicholas Horsfield retired as President in 1965, and the Presidency was taken over first by Arthur Ballard and then by Adrian Henri. The Academy continued until 1981, when it went into liquidation, though not due to Henri's Presidency, which was both lively and open. The small premises on Renshaw Street used as the Academy's own gallery were run by Glenys Davies, an ex-student of the Liverpool School of Art. The gallery ran small group and one-man members shows, and was financed through sales and Academy subscriptions. Adrian Henri was more ambitious and succeeded in acquiring larger premises on Pilgrim Street. Arts Council subsidies were raised, and a paid outside administrator, Murdock Lothian (the *Guardian* writer) was appointed. The Academy was forced to close in 1981, thus bringing to a sad end a long and eventful story.

NOTES

1 Introduction to the Liverpool Academy's 150th Anniversary Exhibition catalogue 1960 Nicholas Horsfield
2 *Liverpool Echo* 31.5.37
3 *Liverpool Echo* 2.6.37
4 *Hoylake and West Kirby Advertiser*
5 *The Sandon Studios Society* Roderick Bisson Parry Books, Liverpool 1965 pp198-199 'Surviving the War'
6 *The Sandon Studios Society* Roderick Bisson pp200
7 *Liverpool Daily Post* 17.9.47
8 *Liverpool Echo* May 1950 George Whitfield
9 *Liverpool Daily Post* November 1951 E.S.
10 *Manchester Guardian* A.C. Sewter 'Two Men Dominate the Show.'
11 *Liverpool Daily Post* October 1952 E.S.
12 *Guardian* 1.11.54 A.C. Sewter
13 *Guardian* 1.11.56 A.C. Sewter 'Art Academies - Are they Needed?'
14 *Guardian* 4.5.57 A.C. Sewter 'An Academy Grows Young'
15 *Art News and Review* 11.5.57 Nicholas Horsfield
16 *Liverpool Daily Post* 10.5.58
17 *Guardian* 12.5.58 A.C. Sewter
18 *Daily Telegraph* 15.5.59 F.W. Fenton
19 *Guardian* 18.5.59 A.C. Sewter
20 Ian Grant Letter to the author 6.2.89
21 *Guardian* 18.5.61 Anthony Tucker
22 *Guardian* May 1964 M.G. McNay

Three

Strands of Manchester Art: Past and Present

The purpose of the present chapter is to look at a pot pourri of talents who have differing degrees of association and involvement with Manchester. A broadly chronological approach is taken, through which it is hoped a wide historical view will emerge, suggesting a distinct Manchester tradition. Art has undergone such changes since the 1930's that any regional history will inevitably echo the macro-developments of British art as a whole. But any close identification of a 'northern school' with a kind of Lancashire urban and industrial landscape painting needs to be qualified with a look at the two main urban centres that contained important artistic institutions - these institutions were associated with the Royal Academy in London. As a result they were committed to showing art that did not necessarily represent the northern locality where it was shown. Many of the conservative strands indicated in a history of art in Lancashire are attributed to academic institutions that supported and contributed to a national school: a school in which landscape painting was a prime genre, and which was epitomised by safe impressionist styles loyally employed in the production of traditional or commercial imagery.

The starting point is difficult to define but the intention of dealing specifically with the period from 1930 to 1960 is based on the assumption that this period saw the battle lines of modernity and tradition drawn up for combat. The main stylistic ingredients of 'modernism' filtered through not only to the insular London art scene, but also to the British provinces. These styles competed with one another, triggering off lively debate by a legion of critics representing all levels of taste. The dull Manchester cultural scene early this century is partly highlighted by a French impressionist, Adolphe Valette, who produced the most memorable images of the city during this time. Henry Lamb, a fine British painter, though hardly a modernist, found Manchester wholly depressing and culturally uninspiring. Born in Australia, Lamb grew up in Manchester, where his father Horace Lamb was professor of mathematics at the University. Despite the lifelong aversion felt by Lamb towards the city of his childhood, it is possible that Manchester helped shape his personal and artistic identity. Even if, as Lamb's biographer Keith Clements suggested "it is only accountable as a negative force against which he reacted so vehemently,"[1] then at least Manchester succeeded in eliciting an emotional response. For many less bohemian artists the response triggered by Manchester would be a much more positive and fruitful one. The Hallé Orchestra and the well laden annual Manchester Academy exhibitions certainly provided the highly talented Lamb with plenty of cultural stimulation.

Horace Lamb, the son of a Stockport cotton mill foreman, went first to Stockport Grammar then on to Cambridge to study mathematics. He taught the subject at Manchester's Owens College, before spending a decade teaching in Australia. Henry Lamb was born there. Horace Lamb obtained the Chair of Mathematics at Owens upon his return, and his administrative abilities contributed to the transformation of the college into the new University. The Lamb family lived at Fallowfield, and at school the young Henry Lamb was taught drawing by the local painter, Joseph Knight, whom Lamb described as "a most excellent, discerning fellow." Knight, who had been a Vice-President of the Manchester Academy, encouraged Lamb in his pursuit of art. Another early influence was Francis Dodd, whom Lamb met through Knight. Dodd arrived on the scene in Manchester in 1895, and went on to paint a particularly evocative 'bohemian' portrait of the young Henry Lamb. Lamb also met Muirhead Bone, Dodd's brother-in-law. Although Dodd had met Whistler in Paris, his own style was pedantically topographic, and he was not then highly regarded in circles such as Chelsea and Bloomsbury, which were later to adopt him as one of their exciting protégés. But early on Dodd helped open many doors for Lamb, and both artists maintained their Manchester connections by sending in work almost every year to the Manchester Academy exhibitions.

Lamb entered the medical faculty of Owens College in 1901. He was an active member of the university, but although academically talented never had his heart in the medical studies he had undertaken to appease his family. Activities pursued at University included music, drawing and debating. His political views were liberal rather than radical, and this middle-of-the-road attitude reflected an artistic career that never veered far from the acceptable post-impressionist style. Yet his bohemian dress and manners and his precocious talent with a pencil, endeared him to Augustus John.

In the spring of 1905 Henry Lamb became the first student to have three works shown at the City Art Gallery in the annual Academy exhibition. At the same time the university magazine reproduced several of his pencil sketches. In his final term as a medical student he left early without a degree. Then he met Nina Forrest at a university summer ball. Forrest, whom he was to rename 'Euphemia', became his first wife, and in July of

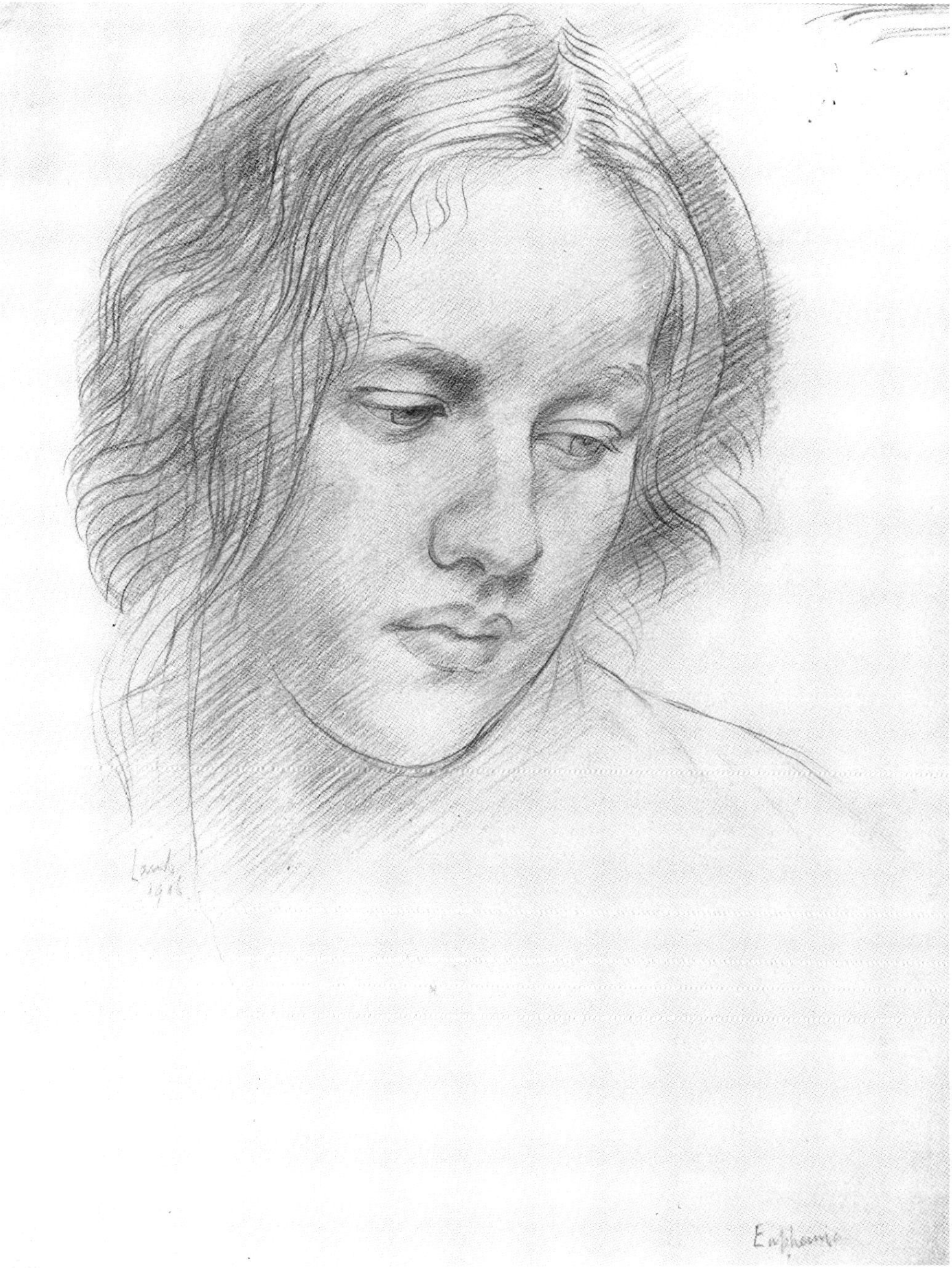

Henry Lamb: Euphemia, *pencil drawing 1906*.

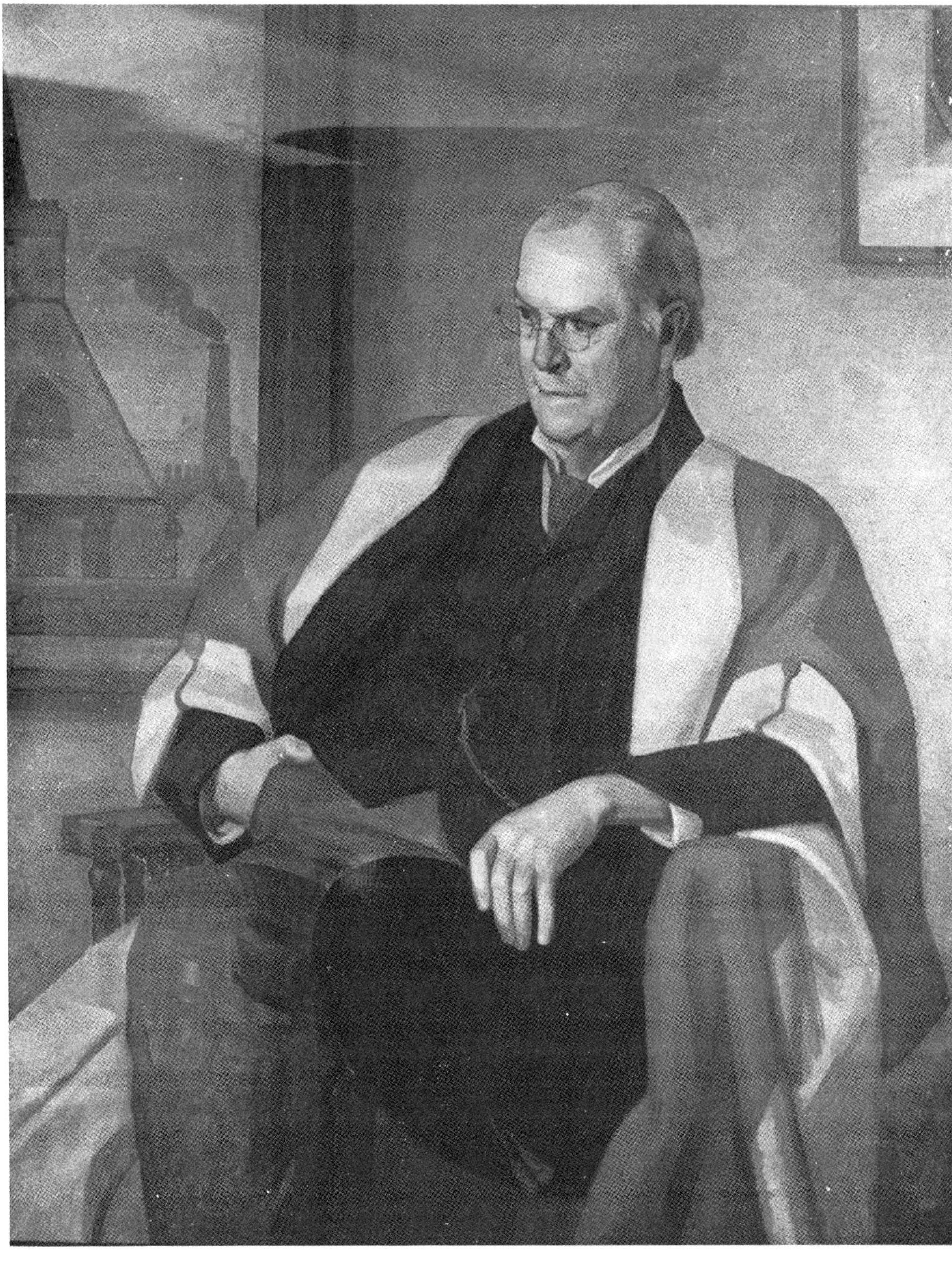

Henry Lamb: Professor Horace Lamb, *oil 1914 (courtesy: University of Manchester).*

that year they moved to London to seek their fortunes in the art world. Lamb was aided by a stipend from the Alexanders, a wealthy family from Didsbury whose son had been a schoolfriend of Lamb's. The first year struggling in London was also financed by money from the *Manchester Guardian* for Lamb's drawings. James Bone, the brother of Muirhead, was London editor of the famous Manchester paper and became another early supporter. In 1913 Lamb undertook a commission from the University of Manchester to paint a portrait of his father, in recognition of nearly three decades of service. The painting was executed in "a large light room" at the University. The sittings went reasonably well, though an unwelcome view of Manchester through the window and an increasingly restless and garrulous Horace Lamb gradually irked his son. In November that year the picture was presented to the University.

Another artist raised in the Manchester area who left early for London was Oldham-born James Fitton. Born in 1899, Fitton was 16 years younger than Lamb, and the gap shows in their work. Fitton's art seemed closer to the kind of sophisticated naïve painting exemplified by the 7+5 Society between the wars. Fitton's work is anecdotal and affectionate in its portrayal of the small incidents of everyday life. It is not until later in Lamb's career that such subjects, tinged with humour, make an appearance - for example, street scenes with their shoppers and cyclists, or domestic records of family life. Fitton loved to incorporate into his pictures window signs, billboard lettering, advertising slogans and so on, giving to his scenes a convincing contemporary feeling. Born into a working class family Fitton was, like Ruskin Spear, always drawn to the unpretentious, although he was quite capable of painting in a highly accomplished and 'classy' manner. Fitton started work at 14 years of age. During the years of the Great War he worked as an apprentice to a fabric designer in Whitworth Street, an experience that no doubt gave him a keen eye for the possibilities of pure design that would allow into pictorial composition an assortment of unconventional elements such as lettering. He attended evening drawing classes at Manchester School of Art, where he met Lowry. "In some ways the two were kindred spirits, particularly in their keen observation of contemporary life, but whereas Lowry always was rather a recluse, Jim was an extrovert,"[2] wrote Sidney Hutchison. This ignored the very apparent differences in their work. Fitton was always a jollier, livelier painter, using more brightly coloured palettes and a more cogent narrative style. Fitton moved to London in the early 1920's, and became a regular Royal Academy exhibitor during the remaining 60 years of his life. He died in 1982.

The life and career of William Maxwell Reekie are those of a socially

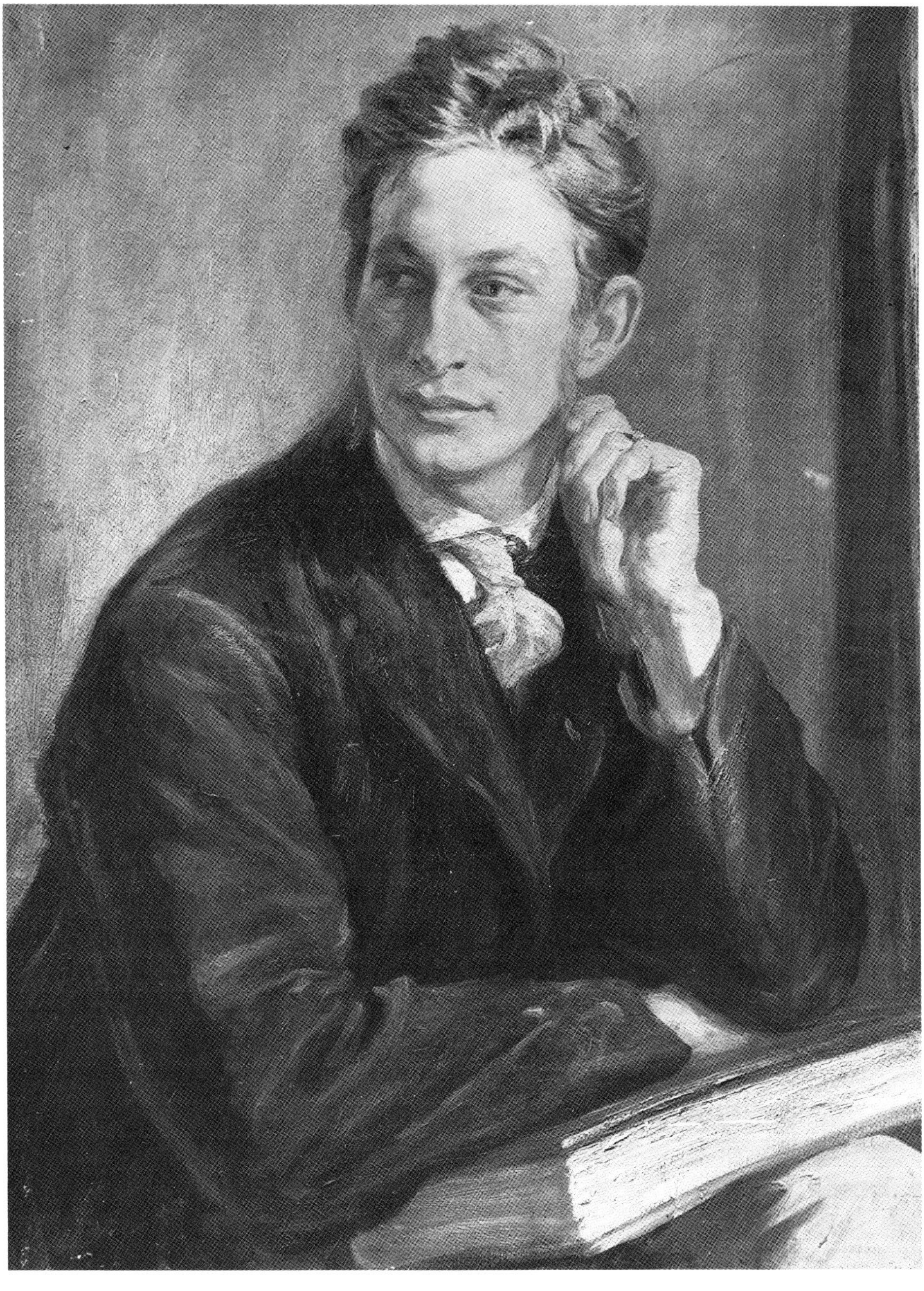

Francis Dodd: Henry Lamb, *oil 1905 (City Art Gallery, Manchester)*

responsible artist-gentleman. He successfully integrated a significant artistic career with influential activities in the business life of Manchester. In common with other Scottish painters Maxwell Reekie remained a loyal and active member of the Manchester Academy. His father, John Reekie, was a cotton merchant whose family came from Fife. William was born in Manchester in April 1869, and attended Manchester Grammar School, before joining the firm of Robert Barbeur, cotton exporters. Between the wars Maxwell Reekie made three trips to India on behalf of the firm. India then supplied the raw cotton which was subsequently processed in Britain before its re-exportation back East. Once the Indians learnt to process raw cotton themselves, the Lancashire cotton industry suffered immediate damage. His first trip, taken through the Suez Canal in 1917-18, resulted in a series of small paintings recording the journey. He returned with 22 panels, depicting such subjects as Burma, the Indian cities of Delhi and Benares, and the magnificent architecture of the Taj Mahal. One of these pictures, *Off Suez*, dated November 1917, and painted on the ship to India, is composed with light blues and ochres, and conveys in simple terms the heat and clarity of daylight. The slightly earlier *Evening Glow, Red Sea*, showed the artist's sensitivity to specific light effects. *Pagodas on the Irrawaddy* of February 1918 was notable for the cleverness of reflected detail across water disturbed by wave ripples. This ability to record reflections on water was also evident in his landscapes of Scotland. He painted on Skye, and in 1924 produced a particularly fine view of St Andrews from the golf links. The artist's final journey east, during the winter of 1935-6, was taken when he was a company director, a position held until his death in 1948 at the age of 79.

Such an active and distinguished business career should not overshadow our assessment of Reekie as a painter. He had always been interested in art, and made many friends in the Manchester art world. These included Tom Mostyn, Charles Oppenheimer, James Chettle, Egbert Steinthal and Hugh Paton, the etcher, who was a particularly close friend. He liked the young Ian Grant, and also the older Lowry, whom he considered a very substantial painter.

Each year he spent several weeks away painting out of doors before completing the pictures in his attic studio. Favourite locations included Lincolnshire, North Wales and Scotland. A family holiday taken every Easter usually meant a motoring trip to one of the principal cathedral towns. Bath, Wells, Salisbury, Lincoln and York were some of the cities visited. In a style consistent with his English impressionist pedigree Reekie avoided pedantic graphic detail in his renderings of cathedral subjects. Instead he delighted in small, delicate pochades that used a wide array of small colour inflections to elaborate an overall study of light and shade. Rather than succumb to an expression of Gothic grandeur, solemn topography and dramatic colouring typical of Constable's Salisbury Cathedral series, Reekie took his cue from Monet at Rouen. He drew from his buildings a sense of the exotic or unexpected, particularly with regard to the behaviour of light and the modulation of colour across architectural surfaces. It was as if Reekie's trips to the Orient had permanently enriched his vision and given him a heightened palette.

After 1912 summer holidays were always taken on Anglesey, where he never failed to take the opportunity to paint. Many seascapes were produced here demonstrating Reekie's particular skill with clouds and the silvery glow of daylight across water. Annotated crayon sketches and photographs were used as memory aids back in the studio. Often large canvases were painted at home in this way, one late example being *Calaverock Castle*, completed just before he died. This picturesque ruin on Solway Firth had been knocked about by Cromwell, and illustrates the enduring attraction of historic sites for the artist. Despite his age, the treatment of this subject (and of one very like it - *McLellan's Castle)* showed the artist in full control of the medium.

Maxwell Reekie's regard for the purple, orange and rusty ochre of autumn, his love of the fresh greens of spring, and of bluebells and daffodils, was entirely consistent with an impressionist manner of painting distinguished by its relish for free associations of positive colour. He was often drawn back to Scotland, and stayed in Kirkcudbrightshire near the home of fellow Manchester Academy member, Charles Oppenheimer. They had a great respect for one another's work, and Maxwell Reekie would always look in at Oppenheimer's large and orderly studio. This concern for order was a lesson not lost on Reekie. He was aware that the strength of a picture was built on solid, compositional foundations - a product of solid structure and harmonious spacing of principal forms undertaken early in the picture's development. Often Reekie would turn away from a motif in order to look back at it through a mirror. Later, with artistic licence, he would rearrange in his mind's eye objects seen in the mirror in an attempt to make them cohere as aesthetically satisfying pictorial units. The colouring could then be taken from direct contact with the subject.

Interested in art since childhood, Maxwell Reekie studied part-time both at Academy classes and at Manchester School of Art. In common with his contemporary, Forrest Hewit, Reekie studied under Sickert when the famous Camden Town painter came to teach in Manchester during the 1920's. Another of his early teachers was one-time Manchester Academy President Tom Mostyn.

For Reekie, painting was best pursued as an innocent, if demanding, activity, free from the need to make a living from it. Certainly he used every spare moment, particularly during holidays, to paint, and many of his letters were ornamented with pen and ink sketches. The autumn was always a busy time for Reekie. When he returned from the family holiday, he worked solidly in his studio to create five pictures for the Manchester Academy exhibition to be held early the following year.

Reekie never painted industrial scenes. This perhaps weakens his credentials as an authentic Manchester painter, though it should be remembered that his business commitments undoubtedly restricted the time available for painting local subjects. An oil of the town and bridge at Ironbridge was undertaken, not for the subject's industrial character, but because of the same historical aura that so regularly drew him to cathedral subjects. He never painted portraits, an activity he found too demanding. An unsuccessful attempt to paint his daughter alerted him to his limitations in this genre. Maxwell Reekie certainly got to know many artists in the city, particularly through his role on Academy selection and hanging committees. Near his West Didsbury house, home from 1910 until his death, lived Laurence Haward, director of the City Art Gallery. The two became good friends. Another neighbour was Hal Yates, whose four sons were friendly with Reekie's own children.

Reekie exhibited regularly with the Manchester Academy from the 1920's. Twice he had works accepted, but not hung, at the Royal Academy, a source of great disappointment. But he was delighted when the Walker, Salford and Manchester Art Galleries purchased his works for their permanent collections. His paintings were popular at the Manchester Academy exhibitions, and he would usually sell three or four of the five paintings submitted. He arranged his colours in the order of the spectrum on a large palette board. Black was rarely used. To obtain darks, the artist mixed primary colours. He often worked in the evenings after dinner, particularly if working to an exhibition deadline. He enjoyed music, hosted musical evenings, and Sybil Thorndike once visited the Reekie household. Maxwell Reekie's greatest friend, Philip Gilchrist, was also a businessman and part-time painter specialising in seascapes. After retiring Gilchrist went to live above Morecambe Bay. Reekie went there in 1946, and a canvas resulted in which the sands are embellished with the wrecked carcass of a ship.

One of Maxwell Reekie's closest colleagues at the Manchester Academy was an exact contemporary, Forrest Hewit. The lives of these two painters follow a remarkably similar course. Hewit, who died in 1956, could not match Maxwell Reekie in the field of landscape painting. Yet it was Reekie's own weakness in painting figures that proved to be Hewit's main strength. The studies undertaken in Manchester under Dugdale, but particularly under Sickert, helped Hewit realise his genuine talent when introducing figures into his usually outdoor settings. He could also paint interiors. The picture of an ornate northern ballroom with distinct echoes of Malcolm Drummond's *Palais de Danse* phase provides a good example, though in the series of café subjects, Hewit opts for the outdoor that spills onto Continental streets.

Hewit was also clever with buildings, enjoying in particular the play of strong daylight across façades then reflected in still sea front, lake or harbour waters. The task of depicting demanding architectural mass or of a complicated section of natural scenery frequently let him down. He was happiest when recording a scene as an impressionistic network of highlights, shadows and colour rhythms. Emmanuel Levy wrote in 1927 that Forrest Hewit "is an artist's man, and he will have to wait fully fifty years before that mysterious but ultimately reliable judge, 'the man in the street' will accept his work."[3] We should remember that at this time his work slotted into a safe, conservative English impressionist holiday style with few modernist innovations. The one great influence that Hewit did take on board - and this is why perhaps his work appeals to us today - was that of his mentor and teacher Sickert. Hewit clearly learned enough about drawing from Sickert for him to deal with ambitious figure-within-architecture settings as unified elements of pictorial composition.

At its best, Hewit's work has the look of Sickert or Thérèse Lessore. Figures within the pictures are animated, or if sitting, are still convincing enough to bring the whole picture to life. The ballroom scene seems to have the artist himself as the main subject with his wife at a table on the edge of the dance floor. There is something photographic in Hewit's composition, imagery and format, almost as if the artist were painting, in the late Sickert manner, from snapshots. Hewit did in fact use *in situ* drawings and photographs as memory aids while working up an oil in his studio.

Unfortunately Hewit never chose to depict his native city in his work, preferring instead to paint what were essentially holiday pictures: trips to the Swiss lakes, the Mediterranean coast, China, or closer to home the New Forest and Jersey. Such pictures, hung in the annual Manchester Academy exhibitions between the wars, helped precipitate the many criticisms that

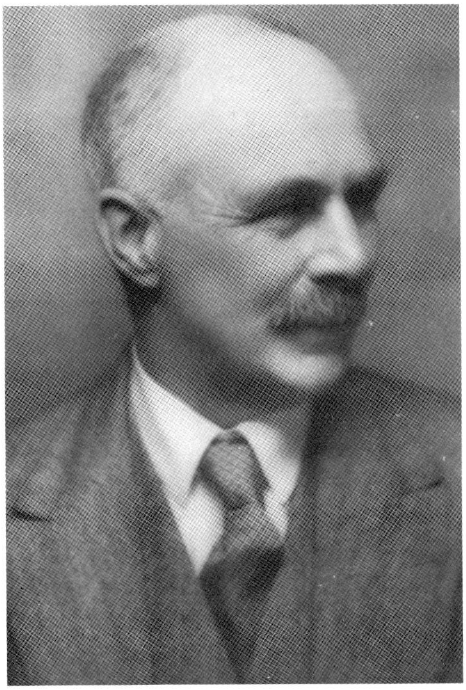

Forrest Hewit, and below, his painting
Northern Ballroom

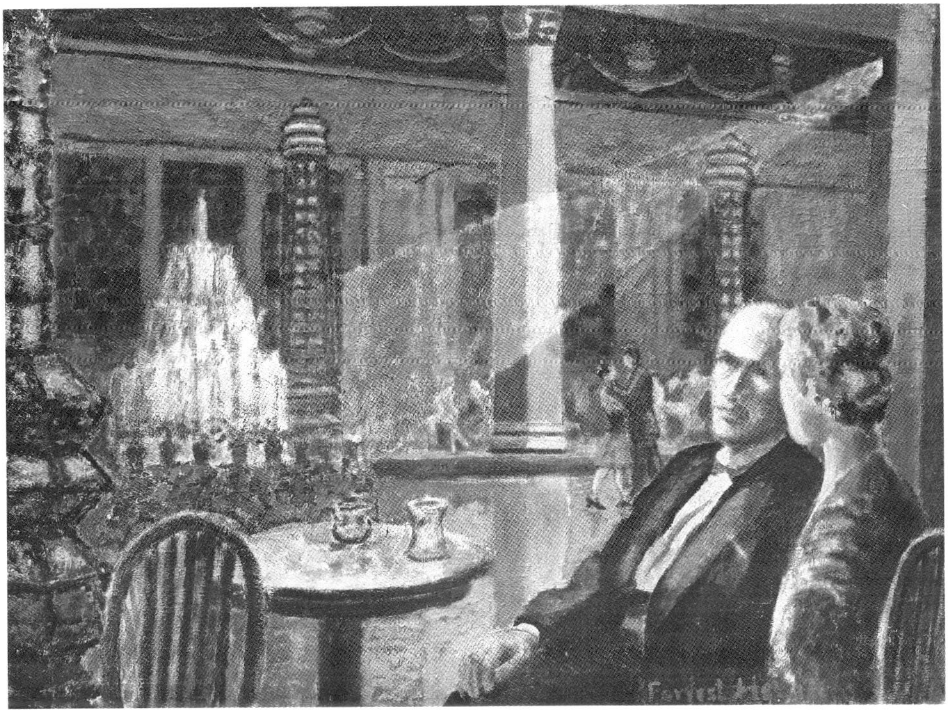

few local painters chose to depict their own area. Sickert would certainly not have approved. One of his specific tenets on the use of subject matter was a frank embrace of mundane, sordid, realist motifs. One of the few local subjects that Hewit did use, however, was the area around 'Overhill', his home at Wilmslow. Hewit was a jovial, formally dressed man, known for his generosity and support towards less well-heeled painters. He often bought their work. The only television in the Hewit household was in the studio; more evidence perhaps of photographic or 'movie' culture influences in his painting. Although he seldom used local subjects, one of his largest canvases, and probably the finest picture he painted, was *Calico Printers Ball*, an ambitious figure composition celebrating his own position as Vice-Chairman of the well known Manchester textile printing firm.

Hewit was not the only Manchester artist to adopt the mannerisms and painting modes of Sickert from his teaching days in Manchester during 1925 and 1926. Harry Rutherford was also much influenced by Sickert. Rutherford and Hewit were accompanied at Sickert's one-day-a-week class by Hartley Mooney, Maxwell Reekie, H. Fairhurst, Hannah Ritchie and Mrs Steinthal. Rutherford and Hewit were certainly the most receptive students. Sickert was particularly respectful of Rutherford's work. Rutherford had written earlier that year to Hewit about the need to find new premises for drawing classes following the demise of Sickert's highly popular weekly class.[4] Not long afterwards Hewit received a letter from Sickert: "It has been a grief to me to have failed my promised visit to the Rutherford Studio." Sickert then continued "I will make it up and if I don't I may say that I attach more importance to having proved my theories by the *accouchement* of Rutherford than to any of my own canvases, the permanent interest of which is problematical."[5]

Sickert was clearly flattered by this willing group of enthusiastic young painters. He wrote another letter to Hewit, describing Rutherford's promise: "Rutherford has this additional advantage of his artistic gifts. He has, as the French say, *la langue bien perdue*. He invariably capped all I said with a remark which showed that he not only had understood, but was able to carry every idea a step further. By explicitly making him my intellectual heir and executor I have of course strengthened his hands for his debut as a painter. I would like you to read him this letter and the more you quote my opinion in Manchester the more good you will do."[6] In regarding Rutherford as his "intellectual heir and executor" Sickert was paying tribute to what he regarded as a most outstanding young talent, not only in the north, but in England generally. Sickert must have known that Hewit would never have the natural gifts, still less the time, to become a really top class painter. But Sickert did see Hewit as a worthy, if average, painter who practised in the accepted style of the master and shared a remarkably similar approach to the idiosyncracies of modern life. Forrest Hewit wrote a number of letters and notes that outlined in considerable detail the techniques and approaches that Sickert instilled in his students. Hewit noted that Sickert attracted as many as 20 artists to his classes. He went on, "for nearly two years he came down every week in the afternoon one day, held the class in the evening, and returned by the earliest train the following morning. This ultimately told on his health and he had a breakdown which ended the class in Manchester."[7] An exhibition was held at the Salon Club to commemorate the two years of Sickert's lessons. Sickert's poor health prevented his attending the exhibition of pupils' work, but Hewit noted that "he has sent a telegram expressing his interest."

The exhibition prompted Hewit to write to the *Manchester Guardian* elaborating Sickert's methods. Hewit felt that Sickert regarded drawing and painting as separate disciplines, drawing being from the particular to the general, painting taking the general to the particular. Sickert wanted an artist to draw 'centrifugally', relating parts back to a central starting point, and he warned his students against copying the style of an established master. The key to success was simply to remain free to one's own perception and modes of vision. Lack of attention to the element of scale in a composition was felt to be the one great flaw in conventional art school training. Plastic shading, in the form of hatching that traversed the rigid boundaries of pedantically drawn outline, helped unite foreground detail with the background in a way that unified the overall picture. Hewit completed his letter by reminding readers that "Sickert, of course, never allowed anyone to rub out. He claimed that the first impression, depicted by the first outline, was of great value and had a personal quality."[8]

Hewit went on to describe Sickert's method of 'squaring up' small drawings for transfer onto larger canvases. Many of Sickert's drawings and paintings have deliberately retained the 'draughtboard' grid pattern. The colouring of a pre-drawn composition involved working from darks to lights. The colouring process was the final stage and was preceded several weeks before by an all-over monochromatic painting, involving the laying down of a tone set within a narrow compass. Colouring was the crux of painting; the final hurdle that would claim most casualties. "Sickert would look at a very decently worked out canvas and say doubtfully, 'now, take it away and spoil it.' In the matter of texture paint," Hewit continued, "he recommended the paint to be the consistency of soft butter." Despite the tentative, even laboured nature of Hewit's paint surfaces he had learned enough of drawing to give adequate surface structure, and his use of colour was both refreshing and credible.

If Hewit owed a debt to Sickert, then the best known artist he in turn helped was Frances Hodgkins. The New Zealand artist, adopting England as her home, visited two friends, Hannah Ritchie and Jane Saunders, who taught art at a leading Manchester girls' school. It was noted that "long a musical centre, Manchester was then enjoying a small boom in the visual and dramatic arts. Frances accompanied her friends to the theatre, painted with them in the wild country beyond the city and used them as models."[9] Hodgkins spent a year in France after her first trips to Manchester, but the ever-restless artist returned in early 1925. Planning a return visit to her native Australasia that summer, she once again visited her women friends in Manchester. Ritchie and Saunders went to a drawing class held by Sickert one of the nights and Forrest Hewit, as another pupil, was invited back by the two women to meet their important guest. When Hewit eventually met Hodgkins she greatly impressed him, and only a couple of days later he offered her a job as designer at his Calico Printers Association with a salary of £500 a year.

This provided her with considerable relief after the hardships of the previous few years, but unfortunately her contract was not renewed after the first six months. The specialised skills required for fabric design proved too much for her freewheeling spirit. Her friends offered help and accommodation but the death of her mother in April 1926 resulted in one of her frequent bouts of depression. Nevertheless, by November that year she had a successful one person show at Manchester, which proved rejuvenating. The *Manchester Guardian* voiced a cautious note, suggesting that her "experimental" work seemed too responsive to modernism at the expense of a firmer control of basic craftsmanship. It was a verdict that proved her to be ahead of her time, especially for certain sections of the Manchester public. But money from the exhibition made further travel to the Continent possible, and she left what she described as the "soot and depression" of Manchester for the French port of Tréboul. Here, Hodgkins found herself in the congenial company of many painters, including Cedric Morris and Christopher Wood. Dorothy Selby, a wealthy Londoner, gave her money to help keep her in France, and in return received some tuition. Correspondence with Lucy Wertheim in Manchester confirmed the connection between the influential gallery owner and these artists working in France. A Frances Hodgkins show at the Claridge Gallery in 1928 - her first London exhibition for five years - included *Lancashire Family*, a typically sensitive and poetic portrayal of two boys with their mother. The artist's

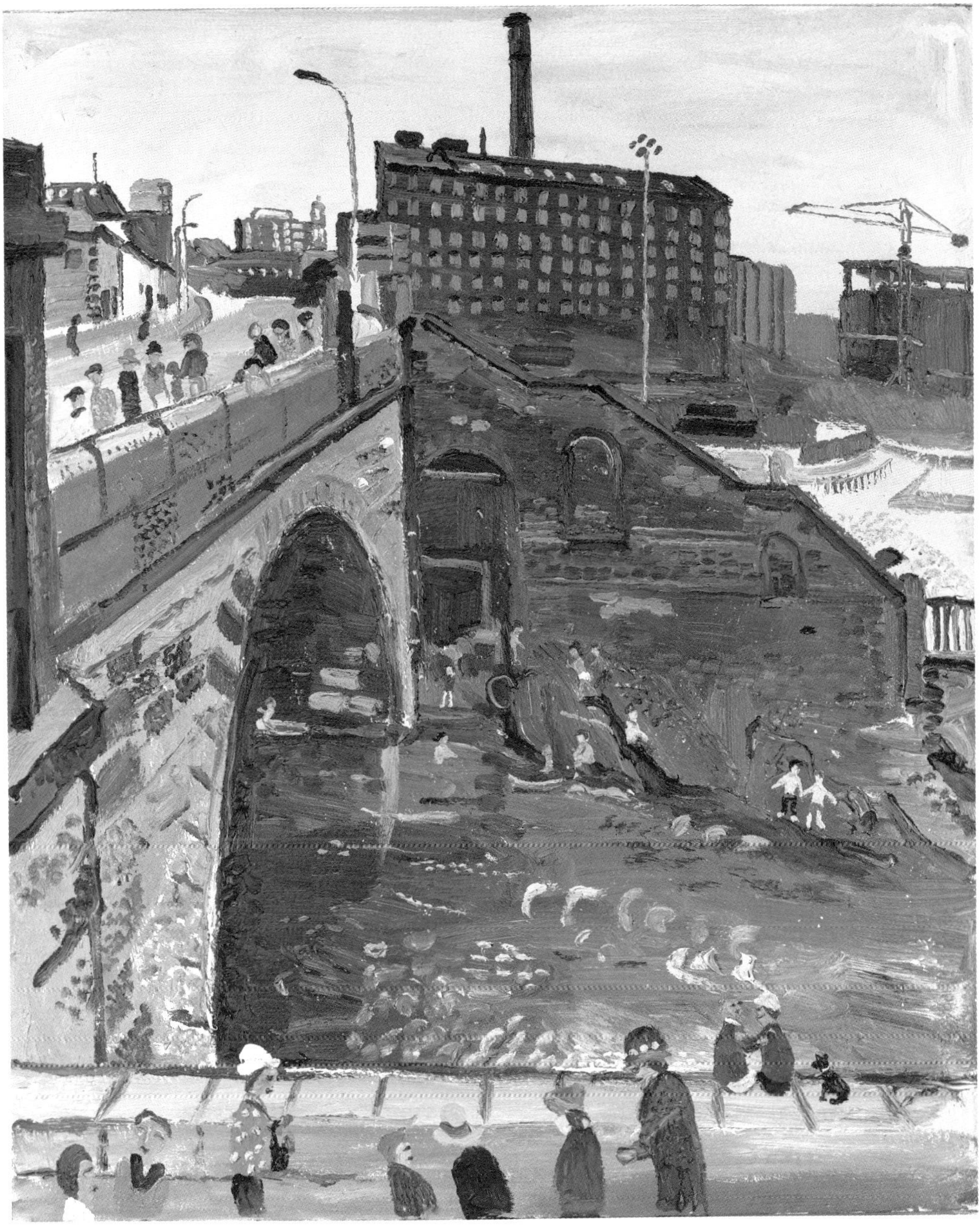

Fred Yates: Stockport Viaduct, *oil*.

love of the sea shows through even in this, as the boy is holding a model yacht. The Claridge Gallery show helped her obtain her first professional contract, which came soon after in 1930 through the St George's Gallery.

Fred Yates is a colourful and popular artist who comes into our story for several reasons. He is a more recent example of a Lancashire painter who migrated to Cornwall, and to St Ives in particular. Early in the century Preston's John Park and Southport's Arthur Hayward started the trend which was followed by painters like Harry Rutherford from Manchester and Coburn-Witherop from Liverpool. Rutherford's ambitious study of Penzance, a resolved maze of architectural facets alternately in light and shade, is now in Southport's Atkinson Museum. In later years the Oldham potter Trevor Corser went to St Ives to work with Bernard Leach. Colin Johnson and Preston born Bryan Ingham both had spells in the fertile artists' crescent of west Penwith.

The northern naïve artist par excellence must be Manchester's Fred Yates, who also left the North to live in south-west Cornwall. Yates and his twin brother Arthur were born in 1922 into a family from Ardwick. Yates later recalled how the brothers "would visit Stockport market with mother. Winter's magical clock in Undergate, the flares of the open market with free lumps of cheese to taste and the river Mersey, then flowing freely at the back of the Co-op, all served to provide a theatrical backdrop to an otherwise uninteresting town."[10] One would not discern an "uninteresting town" in Yates' colourful and densely textured oil paintings of Stockport. They celebrate in affectionate, nostalgic terms, the wonder of a child's delight in Stockport's rich architecture. The old red brick terraces, the rough slopes near the viaduct, or the arches of that famous railway crossing, all found their way into his paintings. The people and events of the town bring the whole pictorial performance well and truly to life. Visits when young to local pantomimes and ballrooms alerted him to the scintillating splendour of scenery and costume. It may have been low culture and populist entertainment, but the impact was powerful. During the war Yates served in the Grenadier Guards, then "for five years I lived like a foreigner in sophisticated Bournemouth." After a teaching career that lasted nearly two decades Yates finally made his move to Cornwall, where like Lowndes, he continued to mix the grey skies and red brick of northern themes with bright and sunny Cornish subjects.

Another very different kind of artist who ended up in St Ives was Tom Cross, born in Manchester in 1931. Educated first at Manchester's St Bede's College, Cross entered the Manchester Regional College of Art in 1949, where he studied until 1953. He then spent three years at the Slade where he won a Robert Stanbury postgraduate scholarship. Other scholarships led to travel in northern Italy, attendance at the British School in Rome and spells working in Paris and Provence.

Cross had entered art school to study architecture, and in his first year at Manchester was introduced to the broad principles of basic design - as useful to painting as to the applied arts. A tutor, John Holmes, had devised this broad course at Manchester. Cross described Holmes as "an extremely interesting and sympathetic man who was a painter, but who had also taught at the Architectural Association and had visited the Bauhaus in the mid-1920's." He later wrote that he felt "this course was the first basic design course in an English art school and it continued in the post-war years with an enthusiastic and young staff."[11] Another young member of staff, Ruth Hopwell, encouraged Cross to make the decisive move to painting, which he pursued at the College's All Saints premises. Cross described the painting studios as "very cramped and crowded but rather nice purpose-built studios overlooking the square." Direct instruction was given in drawing, composition, life painting or still life painting. There were limited library facilities, but "a brief and cursory survey of art history was taught by one of the painting staff, Ian Grant, mostly remembered for his abilities as a car driver in scramble events."[12] Contemporary art was introduced through magazines and visits to exhibitions in London. Nevertheless exhibitions of recent European art could be seen occasionally at the City Art Gallery. Cross helped organise the first exhibition of the Northern Society of Young Artists, which later became the important annual Northern Young Contemporaries exhibition, and was a valuable launching pad for artists recently out of art school.

The first exhibition, held at Oldham Art Gallery in September 1953, had Lowry as President and Peter Carey as Chairman. The second exhibition, in August of the following year at the Whitworth Art Gallery, had Tom Cross as Chairman. A third show followed in April 1955 at the Walker Art Gallery. The 1954 exhibition at the Whitworth drew favourable remarks from Charles Sewter in the *Manchester Guardian*. He referred to the emergence of "several painters of distinct promise." One of these was Tom Cross who, Sewter felt, possessed "a natural flair for the medium of oil paint, while the directness and forthrightness of his execution matches the conviction of his response to his subject."[13] Sewter considered that Ian Fothergill was a more romantic kind of artist. Others like Alan Windsor, Shirley Ford, William Whittam and Sheffield's John Corbridge led Sewter to observe that "the quality of the exhibits and their modest prices have already attracted a number of purchasers." Also included in the show were:

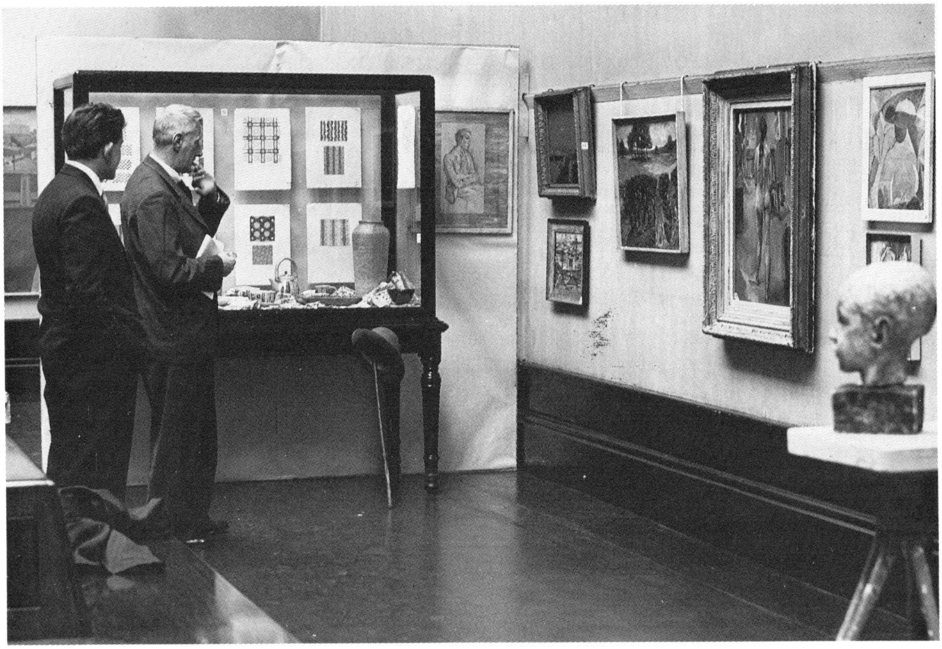

L.S. Lowry and Tom Cross study pictures at the Northern Young Artists Exhibition, Oldham Art Gallery, September 1953.

R. Baskerville, Brian Bradshaw and Margaret Gumuchian. An introductory note for the second show said, "It is our contention that in the North there is much talent and industry being devoted to the arts. For a variety of reasons it is often difficult for young artists, as yet unestablished, to show and sell their work, and by these exhibitions we hope to bring to the notice of the public paintings, drawings, sculpture and works of applied art that they may find of interest and beauty." The three selectors for the 1955 show, held in Liverpool, were Lowry, Hugh Scrutton and Nicholas Horsfield. Each exhibitor had to be under 30 and "normally resident in the North." Each of the 30-odd participants was limited to four works. Each year the Gimpel Fils Gallery exhibited eight young painters from the Young Contemporaries stock. Unfortunately this initiative did not lead to any long-term connections between Manchester and the well known London gallery. Among those shown at Gimpels in the autumn of 1955 was Alan Windsor, who one commentator discerned "has a natural exuberance without the intellectual affection."[14] Elizabeth Blackadder, Pamela Lloyd, Hazel Underwood and Tom Cross were also exhibited there.

Soon after Cross began his studies - and coinciding with the peak period of activity at Margo Ingham's Midday Studios - the Crane Gallery opened at

35 South King Street. The gallery was launched at the end of 1949 by the Hungarian émigré Andreas Kalman, who paid £2 a week rent for a basement that had once been used as an air raid shelter. The humble beginnings led to an unrivalled success story, as the private gallery awakened Manchester with some challenging mainstream European and British exhibitions. Kalman came up the hard way. Entering Britain in 1939, he studied leather chemistry at Leeds University in 1940, then worked for the leather trade in Leeds and later Manchester. Kalman returned to Hungary for a year in 1947, where he cleared up the affairs of his family which had been eliminated by the Nazis. After this Kalman never looked back. An interest in the film world and a flair for playing professional tennis did not sidetrack him from running a modern art gallery. By 1950 Kalman was already in touch with Ben Nicholson who had seen the young Hungarian play tennis at Wimbledon. From then on Nicholson often sent Kalman pictures from St Ives, and a permanent link was made between the leading British abstract painter and Manchester's leading private gallery.

The prestigious galleries then operating in London, for example the Redfern, Gimpels, the Leicester and Lefevre, often helped Kalman by lending him work by important artists for sale on a commission basis. Matthew Smith, Ivon Hitchens, Ben Nicholson and Henry Moore were soon seen on South King Street. So, too, were even more spectacular names: Vlaminck, Bonnard and Soutine. Marlborough lent some of the major Parisian masters. Kalman also acquired more modestly priced works from a host of *petits maîtres*. One such artist was Boitel, whose attractive painting of a girl on a lawn was purchased by Lowry. Lowry had strolled in to meet Kalman within the first month of the opening. Lowry himself, but often the Lefevre Gallery, provided Kalman with his stock of Lowry pictures.

The Bibby family, whose wealth had been created in Liverpool from the cattle cake industry, were early Crane backers and clients. Christopher Bibby went into partnership with Kalman, though the artistic side of the gallery remained firmly in the hands of Kalman. Kalman always had a clear idea of the art he wanted to represent. He favoured the figurative, with a particular fondness for *la belle peinture*, with its broad, positive colouring and generous handling of paint. His mid-European taste for expressionist colouring and confident handling helps explain why he supported local painters like Alan Lowndes. Their first meeting led to a lifelong association. Lowndes asked Kalman to his humble Stockport studio. The slow, circuitous bus ride to Stockport rewarded the dealer. His first impressions of Lowndes' work was of its rawness, honest originality, interesting colour, texture and personal vision. Kalman also discovered in Lowndes a surprisingly erudite and intelligent working class man, whose sometimes abrasive views betrayed the difficult circumstances of Lowndes' background. Nicholson, Bacon and Sutherland, whom Kalman exhibited regularly, also betrayed an element of unwavering intolerance towards other artists. Lowry was more tolerant, often giving moral support to indifferent artists. Lowry's criterion for encouragement was based on the detection of a touching dose of artistic sincerity. Kalman felt this was due to Lowry's reluctance to hurt - a sure sign of his own vulnerability and humble artistic origins.

The courting of clients from the world of popular entertainment was an essential ingredient in the story of Kalman's rise as a dealer. It helped too in the establishment of Alan Lowndes. One Lowndes picture of 1949, *The Power and the Glory*, made much of the juxtaposition of St Peter's Church and a nearby power station. With its mocking, ironic title, this picture caught the eye of Ralph Brinton, art director for the film based on Shelagh Delaney's *A Taste of Honey*. It inspired him to visit Stockport and use the same view for an opening sequence in the film. In a similar way, Tony Warren, creator of Granada's *Coronation Street*, based the idea on an Alan Lowndes painting of uniform, purple brick terraces that was also titled *Coronation Street*. The Crane Gallery, being near the opera, encouraged visits from theatre people such as John Boulting, Charles Laughton, Sydney Bernstein, Richard Attenborough, Robert Morley and Mai Zetterling, many of whom purchased paintings. An Alan Lowndes picture of the time, in his customary rich colouring and palette-knifed impasto, records the rich scene of ornate frames and vividly coloured pictures on the gallery walls. The early days of the Crane were not easy, however, and Kalman relied on help from other galleries. He eventually put on a show of Soutine and Modigliani, then a Kisling show, at the Redfern. The Crane Gallery's success, particularly after the move to London's Brompton Road in 1957, was due to the good business sense and sound aesthetic judgement of a dealer who looked after the interests of his clients.

A gallery that Kalman himself was able to help was Dorothy Almond's Great House Gallery, opened in 1962, which came to show many of the artists who once exhibited at the Midday Studios. Richard Weisbrod, José Christopherson and Margo Ingham were among those who exhibited with Almond. Weisbrod, who came to England from Switzerland in 1933, eventually married Christopherson in 1970. He became one of Almond's artists and she continued showing his work even after her gallery outside Bolton closed in 1984. Other exhibitors here included Reg Gardiner, Charles Tunnicliffe, Scottie Wilson, Wilson's friend Audrey Johnson, Claude Harrison, the naïve painter from

Preston, Jeremy Merek, Gladys Cooper, Michael Goddard, the sculptor Graham Bentham, and the peripatetic painter Colin Johnson. Goddard's travels to the Middle East led to an exhibition of desert paintings. Colin Johnson, who for many years made annual painting trips to St Ives, finally settling there in the mid-1980's, had a thematic show of market scenes. A local Wigan-born sculptor Alex Simpson was taken up after his exhibition of carved stone heads in a neo-primitive style at Salmesbury Hall, Blackburn, had impressed Almond. Simpson's wife June also began showing work there on a regular basis. Lowry was a friend and visitor to the gallery, while F.W. Fenton, the Manchester-based critic for the *Telegraph*, came to most openings. One particularly ambitious group exhibition, held in the autumn of 1967, was reviewed by Fenton.[15] He remarked on the refreshing mixture of lesser known local talents with nationally known artists. The work of artists such as Vanessa Bell, Carel Weight, Winifred Nicholson, Mary Newcomb and Alan Lowndes was borrowed from Andreas Kalman.

Not all promising artists found their way into the annual Manchester Academy exhibitions. A recent survey of the art of Lancashire from the nineteenth century up to today entitled *Lancashire South of the Sands* came in three parts, and toured the museums of Lancashire between 1986 and 1988. The first two exhibitions of the series, entitled *The Rural Landscape* and *Industrial Landscape,* traced artistic responses to the development of Lancashire from a rural county to an industrial centre. The Industrial Revolution brought the growth of railway and canal networks linking the mill towns and provided evocative source material for many contemporary artists. The 'rape' of nature, seen in the form of the gradual encroachment of the urban sprawl, was often recorded by artists. The third and final phase of the exhibition, *The Contemporary Landscape*, offered a different post-industrial reality reflected by the work of younger artists. Frank pessimism in the face of gradual de-industrialisation and economic decline, although imperceptible at first, characterised much post-war art that demonstrated the rapid changes that had set in. Yet the contemporary landscape, cleared of the industrial smog seen in Theodore Major's work, benefited from the Clean Air Act. New and quite different threats to the environment were hinted at by Salford-based mural artist Walter Kershaw. His painting *Cooling Tower Fantasy*, expressed in the large scale, technicolour, photographic style of Pop-Art, conveyed a forbidding, close-up industrial reality where no man dare go.

Walter Kershaw's huge plywood panel, painted in acrylics, apes the style of the outdoor muralist. He is perhaps best known for mural painting, and a large work of his at Trafford Park in Manchester is the world's largest industrial mural. Nevertheless he is capable of equally pertinent imagery on a smaller scale. His *Canal : Littleborough* and *Ogden Reservoirs* provided memorable images from the Lancashire exhibition. The former, in particular, reveals how an all-powerful nature is re-encroaching on the mill and canal in an area where the urban and the rural meet. In contrast, Kershaw's large *Cooling Tower* picture is less compromising. Huge cooling towers are seen from base up or looking down from all-revealing aerial perspectives. The meeting of hot and cool air streams is indicated by colourful air balloons, one of which has been dangerously sucked into the cooling town funnel itself. This extraordinary juxtaposition of composition elements is a typical feature of mural art. The message is not commercial as in billboard art, but more in the nature of social comment.

Kershaw was born in 1940 at Rochdale, but was educated at Salford and Durham University. He has a large studio at his Littleborough home and has turned mural painting in the North West into a personal career, and has also worked for the British Council in Brazil on large scale decorative projects. Kershaw's interest in the grandeur of industrial buildings and their often dramatic lighting at night – and "the way they contrast with the subtle curvature of the hills" – ties in with Trevor Grimshaw's pencil sketches of northern towns, in which the skyline of industrial architecture is silhouetted against the undulating hills. What fires Kershaw is his interest in the morphology of industrial architecture. In contrast to many mural artists, Kershaw is not therefore conveying before all else a pointed ideological message.

One local artist who distinguished herself in the final phase of *Lancashire South of the Sands* was Lesley Young. Her impressive painting *Waiting on the Tenth Floor, Ancoats* was shown at the 1988 Manchester Academy exhibition and purchased by the City Art Gallery Gallery. Lesley Young was born in Carlisle in 1942. After a year at Carlisle Art School she went on to study painting at Newcastle University, graduating in 1966. One of the teachers at Newcastle was Richard Hamilton, whose work struck a chord in the powerful use of corrupt or debased advertising imagery in the world of fine art. Young's own work was then largely abstract. Large freely painted biomorphic shapes, derived from plant forms, had affinities with work that later made Jennifer Durrant famous. Shortly afterwards, she relinquished lyrical abstracts for the exact topographical and figurative painting for which she is recognised today. Her student days were followed by a spell teaching at Hornsey College of Art until 1966 when she married. She moved back to Manchester in 1967 and began painting again in the early 1970's. An accomplished portrait of an old Salford jazz musician was shown and sold at the Royal Academy summer exhibition in 1975. During the second half of the 1970's Young exhibited her slow output of painstakingly detailed painting either at the Manchester Academy, or at mixed exhibitions at the Portico Library Gallery and the Portland Gallery. She taught art history at

Bolton art school, did some foundation teaching at Salford and had a spell as an art therapy teacher at Salford's Hope Hospital.

Occasionally Lesley Young undertook straightforward landscape painting, and a solo exhibition at Carlisle Art Gallery contained pictures of her native Cumberland. Her increasing interest in portraiture is partly autobiographical and her work features husband, mother, and friend, all within a landscape setting, often seen through a window. Her *Waiting on the Tenth Floor, Ancoats* is perhaps her grandest achievement using this device. There is also a psychological level to her work, one that exposes the history, background and present circumstances of the sitters. There is an implied social or political solidarity with the weak or vulnerable. Many of the pictures are melancholy in mood. The portraits of her elderly mother, or of the two women at the Ancoats tenth floor window, are good examples of this spirit. The Ancoats flat belonged to an Iranian student whom Young had taught in Manchester. The student sits with her companion, displaying a sombre, introspective air and grave resignation, against the Ancoats skyline.

Blackpool, November 1987 is a quite different painting of the blustery Blackpool seafront on a dimly lit winter's day. Her husband and two colleagues provide the focus of human interest. Blackpool, dedicated to pleasure, but portrayed in its unfamiliar, out-of-season aspect typifies Young's pursuit of a darkly romantic or melancholic mood. A more recent canvas uses another black girl as the foreground figure against the stark background of the St Helens power station.

Oblique social references to decline, change and renewal emanated from the work of artists like Bolton-born Ray Haslam. His *Crushed Cortina, Lancaster* (1983) portrayed in an admirable photo-realist style, a crunched-up motor vehicle parked on a garage forecourt. Obsolescence, epitomised in the condemned hulk of useless scrap, is the theme in this memorable and unpretentious picture. The stillness and lack of human presence in the crashed Cortina picture are repeated in Charles Hickson's close-up views of anonymous motorway boundaries, pathways and roadsides. Hickson's work hints at the gradual Americanisation of local culture which is seen as increasingly impersonal. Michael Exall has also taken a small section of landscape and magnified it by enhancing the formal qualities of the seemingly mundane. By painting tiny segments of a garden path, Exall elevates mundane local detail to decorative pictorial significance.

Similar concerns characterise Paul Hatton's work. His collaging of gravel, found debris or sand onto the picture plane clearly owes something to Mark Boyle and to Kurt Schwitters. Hatton is a founder member of the Luneside Studios, an artists' space overlooking the River Lune in Lancaster. Any art that surveys the changing face of an area's landscape inevitably uses the documentary power of photography. Paul Haywood used the technique of multi-exposure to express something of the history of an industrial area, while Andy Goldsworthy has used Morecambe Bay to make intentionally ephemeral sculpture from flimsy natural materials encountered on walks across the landscape. These are then photographed as permanent records of the way nature has been used in the artistic process. Perhaps in his eccentric, whimsical way Goldsworthy is creating a metaphor for the transmutation of natural landscape into a man-made environment.

In Manchester, the formation of a self-help artists' studio complex has been extended to include an auxiliary art gallery, the Castlefield. The Castlefield grew out of the Manchester Artists Studio Association, which started in 1983, and made use of a Victorian building off Whitworth Street close to the University. Although grants were obtained from the Arts Council, a need was soon felt to raise funds from associate members. Two members paid by the City Council Education Committee taught life drawing classes. An all day drawing session was held on Saturdays. The main problem was that there was only enough space for a dozen artists.

Ten founder members of MASA went on to found the Castlefield Gallery, which was adminstered by members of the studio group. The voluntary exhibition organiser was later paid through financial help from various councils and the Gulbenkian Foundation. A committee met every fortnight to discuss the many exhibition applications. The committee had an egalitarian policy. It ignored names and considered applications solely on the basis of the work itself. Even so, the Castlefield successfully sought out Anthony Caro, who became the patron, and a long series of exhibitions followed John Hoyland's opening show in March 1984. The Castlefield came to represent a vital, though somewhat marginalised, 'school' of contemporary abstract painting in Britain. Sculptors like Anthony Caro, Stephen Lewis, Mary Shemilt and Jeff Lowe were complemented by painters like Geoff Rigden, Frank Bowling, Tony O'Malley and Garry Wragg. Tricia Gilman, David Sweet and Tom Watt also had exhibitions that provided variety within this strain of contemporary art.

An exhibition late in 1985 of work by Geoff Hollow, Marilyn Hallam and Paul Tonkin revealed how well figurative and abstract painting could go together, when a common approach was inspired by the Matisse-Hofmann-de Kooning axis within colour painting. A more recent exhibition of alternatively crepuscular or diaphanous abstracts by Clyde Hopkins continued this, though Hopkins' nervous graffiti-like marks owe rather more to Miro.

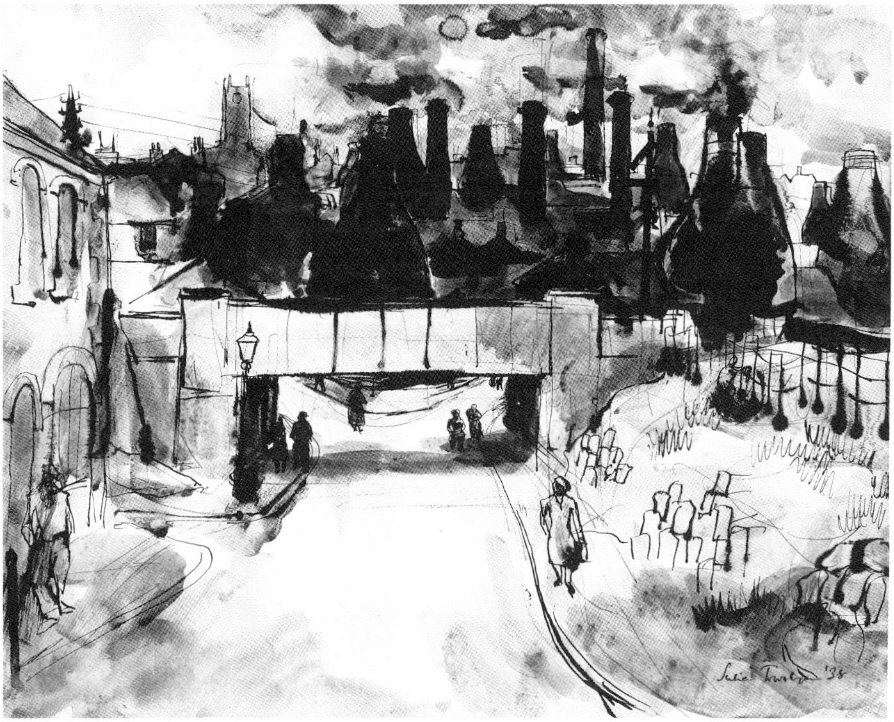

Julian Trevelyan: The Potteries, Bolton, *pen and wash 1938*.

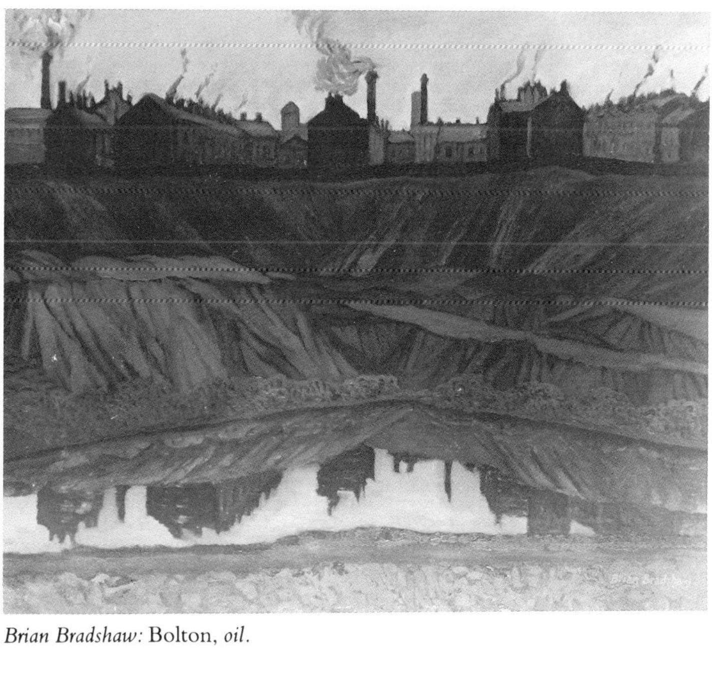

Brian Bradshaw: Bolton, *oil*.

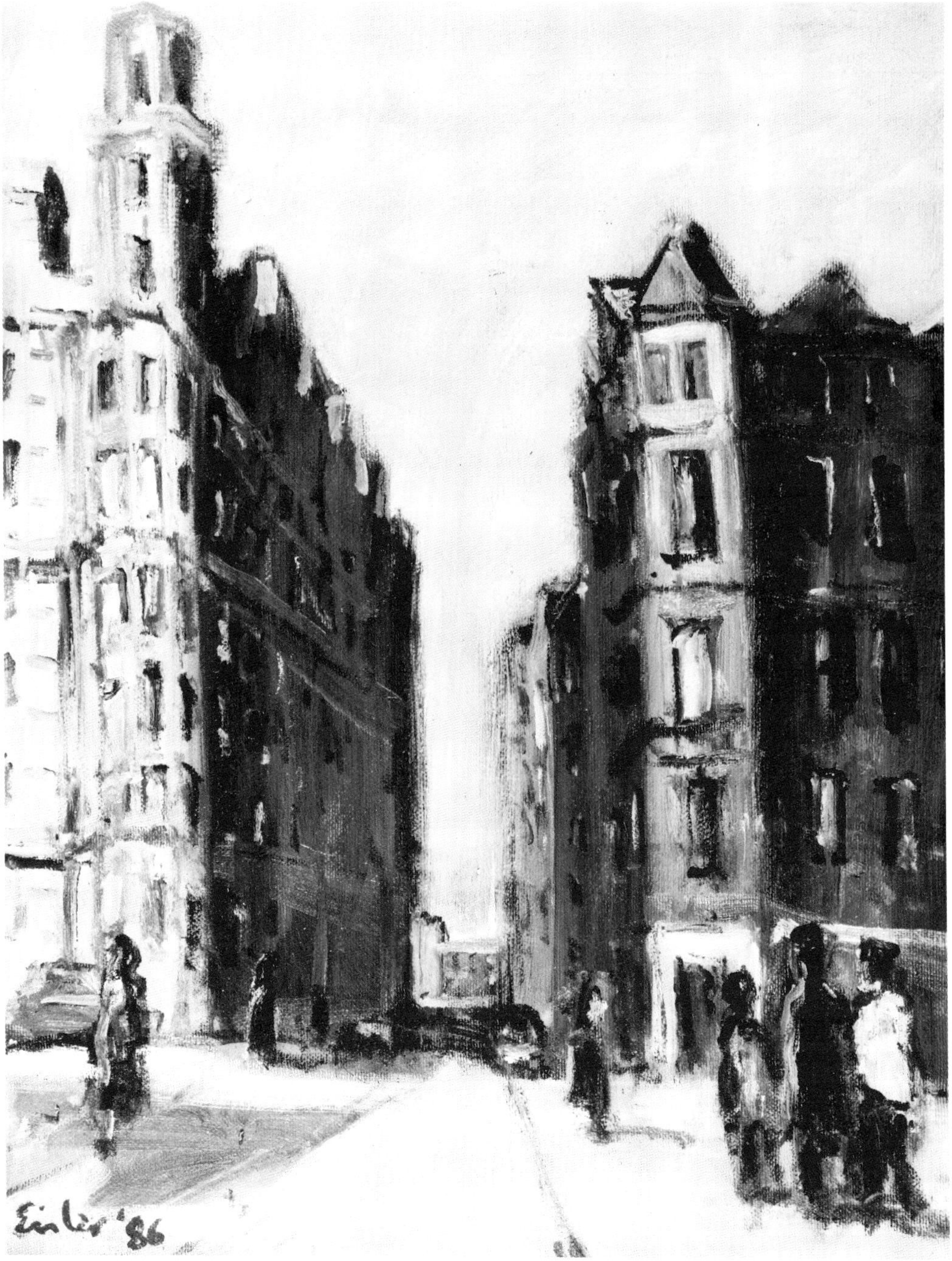

Georg Eisler: Whitworth Street, Manchester, *oil 1986.*

MASA member Kevin Lewis studied art at Salford and at Manchester Polytechnic. Taught by David Sweet, Lewis began painting larger, coolly composed abstract pictures which employed large discs of colour flatly and uniformly painted. The use of large scale formats represented a romantic post-Pollock desire to be 'in' the painting, both psychologically and physically. All this of course represented a very different outlook from that of the tradition-minded Manchester Academy. While welcoming painters of whatever style the Academy would have been unable to accommodate a large group of experimental artists. The Manchester Academy exhibitions during the 1980's have continued to benefit from contributions by members such as Ian Grant, Margaret Gumuchian, William Turner, Roger Hampson and so on, but many new faces have come to the fore. Among those who have established themselves in recent years are Ted Roocroft (sculptor of carved wooden pigs) and Academy Secretary Vera Lowe.

The Academy President during the second half of the 1980's, Norman Jaques, has risen to the top after being a member for over 40 years. Jaques was born in Manchester in 1922 and educated locally at a junior art school during the 1930's. Thus at an early age he studied still life and plant drawing, pattern designing, and the independent laws of colour. After winning a scholarship, he attended All Saints art school for two years. With drawing as the core subject, this course extended to many specialist areas. Another two years were spent studying pictorial design. A broad-based approach to illustration and graphic design broke down into the kind of studies now sadly lacking in art education: history of illustration, lettering and typography, book design, history of costume, mechanical methods of reproduction were only some of the skills taught. "Looking back," Jaques declared, "I think I was fortunate to enter art training as attitudes to art were beginning to change and the modern movement take hold." He also remembered that the All Saints staff "were a wonderful mixture of the 'old school' with strong academic backgrounds but aware of the changes taking place and in sympathy with shifting emphasis towards expressionism and abstraction." Paul Keene (illustration), Doris Taylor (history of costume) and Jack Willock (history of style) were considered outstanding tutors, though Ian Grant also had a hand in Jaques' education. In 1948, when aged 26, Jaques was awarded the Proctor Travelling Scholarship, allowing him to travel to Paris and Italy. In 1961 he was awarded a Yates Bequest grant to study art education in Paris. The result of these studies was specialisation in print making. Jaques in turn became a senior lecturer in the design faculty at Manchester. He was commissioned by many important commercial bodies and has exhibited his paintings and prints, notable for a strong sense of abstract or decorative design, at the Peterloo Gallery in Manchester and at the Royal Academy.

Jaques remembers with affection how the Manchester Academy opening was once a conversazione, attended by civic dignitaries and decorated with carpets and flowers. The occasion was also augmented a few days later with a lavish dinner at which a quartet played. Two outstanding presidents who always gave an inspiring speech at the dinner were Harry Rutherford and Roger Hampson. The centenary anniversary exhibition in 1959 was celebrated by a grand banquet in the Manchester Hall, with Lord Derby as guest of honour. A modified version of the old annual dinner is still held, though without the civic formality of the old days.

NOTES

1 *Henry Lamb* Redcliffe Press, Bristol 1985 Keith Clements p.4
2 Oldham Art Gallery catalogue 1982 James Fitton memorial exhibition
3 *Manchester City News* 26.3.27 Emmanuel Levy
4 Letter dated 11.4.26 Harry Rutherford to Forrest Hewit
5 Letter dated 20.10.26 Walter Sickert to Forrest Hewit, written from 7 Old Steine, Brighton
6 Sickert to Forrest Hewit Letter from Globe Hotel, Exeter
7 Forrest Hewit notes courtesy of the artist's grandson, Donald Hewit, Bath
8 Letter dated 23.10.30 Forrest Hewit to W.P. Crozier at the *Manchester Guardian*
9 *Portrait of Frances Hodgkins* Oxford University Press 1981 E.H. McCormick p.99
10 Fred Yates Letter to the author March 1989
11 Tom Cross Letter to the author 6.2.89
12 Tom Cross 6.2.89
13 *Manchester Guardian* 2.9.54 A.C. Sewter
14 Art 15.9.55 G. Makonvag 'New Names and Old Faces'
15 *Daily Telegraph* 20.9.67 F.W. Fenton
16 Norman Jaques Letter to the author

Four

Manchester Academy: 1929-38

The origins of the Manchester Academy of Fine Arts go back to the early nineteenth century. The Royal Manchester Institution, as it was first known, was founded during the 1820's out of a pressing need for the thriving and growing business centre of Manchester to nurture a full artistic identity. The building in Mosley Street, which is now part of the Manchester City Art Gallery, was designed by Sir Charles Barry in the late 1820's. It was handed over to the City of Manchester in the early 1880's. In 1859, the Manchester Academy of Fine Arts was born out of the Royal Manchester Institution, and the first Academy exhibition took place soon after, with a formal civic opening. The annual Academy exhibition (which survives to this day) had, by the 1880's, become established as the central feature of a range of activities that included drawing classes for both the full time and amateur artist. Unfortunately the first Academy President, J. Hammersley, was unable to win royal patronage, in spite of Prince Albert's commitment to the arts. The Academy only gradually evolved egalitarian policies. The first women were not admitted as Academy members until the 1870's and amateurs were excluded until after the Great War. James Chettle was the first amateur to become President, holding the position from 1935 to 1944. Although the Academy continued to enjoy full use of the City Art Gallery for its annual exhibition, difficulties arose over alternative premises for Academy life drawing classes. Locations like Brazenose Street and John Dalton Street were unsatisfactory. They were later superseded by the Acomb Street premises. By the early 1920's there were vastly increased attendances at the annual show, partly because admission was now free. Soon afterwards the Academy invited well known national figures to become members, a move designed to add prestige to the flagging exhibitions. During the 1920's prestigious names such as William Orpen, Charles Holmes, Henry Lamb, Terrick Williams, and Walter Bayes were recruited. Francis Dodd, President in the early 1920's, was responsible for this development, while his successor, Bertram Nicholls, concentrated on improving the educational side of the Academy. At the beginning of the period under focus in this chapter, an all important rule was introduced specifying that non-members be allowed to submit work in return for a small hanging fee.[1]

By the end of the 1920's, therefore, the characteristic blend of established big-name painters with lesser known local artists was becoming a feature of the annual exhibition. Many who became full members because of their reputation in London or Paris, also had significant local connections with Manchester. The 1929 exhibition contained many works by such artists, who often used French subject matter, which suggested that holiday visits were put to good use. Even the North West's very own Percy Lancaster, a watercolourist renowned for his Lancashire and Lakeland rural scenes, chose to step outside the North when he included a work of Steerian flavour, *Chepstow Castle*. Similar, though even more distant imagery was present in the pictures of James Chettle and Charles Cundall, both of whom painted the harbour at La Rochelle. Perhaps they travelled together to the west coast French port? John Park contributed two typical Cornish pictures, while the President Bertram Nicholls emulated Chettle and Cundall with a French coastal subject, *The Brittany Coast*, depicting castle, beach and sea with dark, dramatic lighting. The pronounced dark blue sea, in particular, and the composition and subject in general, resembled the lochside Scottish landscapes of D.Y. Cameron. Drama of a different kind was presented in Francis Dodd's excellent *A Willow Tree in Winter*, in which the unfolding central image of a large tree, silhouetted against the vivid but cold sun of a winter's afternoon, looks down on figures skating below. The commentator in the *Manchester City News*[2] suggested that this likely Hampstead outdoor scene represented Dodd's finest contribution to any Academy exhibition. That year Holyhead-born and Manchester-raised Francis Dodd became a trustee of the National Gallery. The *Daily Dispatch,* commenting on the year's Academy exhibition, said that no artist had ever "seized and rendered so beautifully and so sympathetically the suburbs of a modern town and the curious outer edge of humanity."

The La Rochelle painting by Charles Cundall was accompanied by *Wolverhampton*, a picture that was closer, both geographically and spiritually, to the Academy's Manchester base. Cundall was at his best when portraying the length and breadth of an industrial or urban skyline, seeming to relish the array of architectural detail that would certainly have defeated less able painters. Even closer to home were Charles Holmes' *Pendle from Whalley*, Herbert Royle's *Bolton Abbey*, and Ronald Allan's *Snow in Cheshire*. The latter was praised by a *Guardian* reporter who found that this small work "represents a breakaway from tradition." Allan at 29 was one of the youngest exhibitors that year. His exquisite small paintings experimented boldly with the harmonising of rich colour. At the opening, President Bertram Nicholls implicitly justified the policy implemented by his predecessor, Francis Dodd, whereby Academy doors were opened to prestigious artists no longer directly involved with Manchester. He referred positively in that speech to the self-willed nature of Manchester people. He also suggested that it was no longer possible for serious painters to stay in Manchester and make a living. Yet it was important for the northern city to kindle an interest in, and to support, many of the artists who had their roots in the North West.

The frequent use of Continental subject matter may have been a feature of Academy exhibitions at this time, but an open-armed embrace of advanced Continental modernism certainly was not. The *Manchester Guardian's* reporter noted how a "staunchly conservative" show resisted any such Continental stylistic influences. He commented on "the thoroughgoing, conscientious, co-ordination of facts and places closely observed," that led to the demure realism of pictorial travelogues holding fort. Tom Dugdale was credited with providing the greatest contribution: "His range would seem to be somewhere between Sir John Lavery and Sir William Orpen, though actually he is a greater realist than either. Essentially objective in temperament, instead of imposing his own vision upon reality as they can do with such entrancing verve, he finds reality an ample field for his fluent, perfected technique." This was fair comment. The allusion to the "entrancing verve" of the work of Lavery and Orpen was based on the perception of an academic slickness and formula-bound precociousness abounding in the easy, virtuoso manner of these two highly fashionable and acclaimed artists. Dugdale was a more earnest and honest labourer; his portraiture, if less spectacular than theirs, stands up better to a more sober scrutiny.

Another portrait painter, E. Hartley Mooney, met with the comment that "his acuteness of vision is such that he has rendered his sitters with almost photographic realism, even to the faintly strained expression induced by posing." This quality, though variant with Dugdale's more robust and rugged kind of painting, failed to achieve any greater degree of verisimilitude. Instead, the sheen and cosmetic perfection of the resulting photographic likeness became the dubious end-product of a stiff technique of contrived painterliness. Yet Hartley Mooney's manner was one that found friends in high places. One has only to think of contemporaneous portraits by Gerald Brockhurst or Meredith Frampton to see that a demand for this particular kind of easily assimilated painting existed. Charles Oppenheimer's landscapes, portraying his native Kircudbrightshire in a late afternoon light, though set in this exhibition of Italian scenes, were praised for their "diaphanous luminosity in a high key." No mere cosmetic trick this, but an expert rendering of the fall of light across different landscape surfaces.

In October of 1929, there was an exhibition of the five Manchester Arts Clubs: the Attic Club, the Athenaeum Graphic Club, Modern Painters, the Sketch Club and the Society of Miniature Painters. Professor C. Reilly, opening the exhibition, remarked that the position of the contemporary artist was a very precarious one. He pointed to the need for northern towns to have a healthy artistic community; the public at large needed to support and appreciate their artists. Emmanuel Levy, who in those days was supplementing his activities as a portrait painter with regular art criticism for the *Manchester City News*, wrote of the "heroic attempt at self-expression,"[3] undertaken by modern artists. "It matters little," he speculated, "whether the subject be a vase of flowers, a figure, a landscape, or a Michaelangelesque conception, provided these resolve themselves into such significant arrangement of form, line and colour." Levy went on to advocate the need for the artist to have a strong and independent personality. Slight but differing complexions were noted in the five clubs - Levy correctly applauded Janet Kirk's black chalk drawings of old Manchester alleyways, full of architectural detail, but found the intellectual level of her work low. Nevertheless, her drawings have a documentary interest today as many of her subjects have since been demolished. The same can be said of Lowry's drawings of the urban landscape, which Levy, interestingly, praised for their transcendence, not only of illustrational or documentary roles, but also of conventional codes of aesthetic beauty. There was an "individuality expressed in his smoke stacked landscapes," that enabled Emmanuel Levy to see "a philosophic rather than an aesthetic beauty."

The 1930 Academy exhibition echoed many themes of the year before. John Park once again sent in what were referred to as "bright and breezy" St Ives paintings, while James Chettle contributed another La Rochelle painting, and Oppenheimer another Italian scene. Isobel Dacre sent in a classic piece of English picturesquerie with her painting of Ludlow Castle, while flowers expertly transformed into paint by Malcolm Milne, and hayfield subjects similarly treated by Percy Lancaster again featured in the show. Charles Cundall also repeated habits of the previous year and displayed French subjects. Francis Dodd contributed a noteworthy portrait of Isobel Dacre, an unflagging energy within the Manchester art scene. Dodd's painting was a form of recognition and piece of flattery, if not of the ageing face of a woman in her 80's, then certainly of a senior Academy member, elected as early as 1884. Such long-serving loyalty was one valuable commodity: another was the introduction of new blood, as advocated by the *Guardian* reporter, along with the need to invite former

Manchester painters (like Matthew Smith) who had forged national reputations. Among the relatively few new exhibitors, Charles Tunnicliffe was mentioned as the most promising. Tunnicliffe's *Macclesfield Cattle Market*, depicting activity in his native town below the distinctive church, was a wonderful piece of townscape.

Bertram Nicholls was deemed by the *Guardian* reporter "to reduce boats, buildings . . . and all the elements to the cunning jigsaw of his design, finished and polished to the grain of linoleum." Nicholls, born locally in 1883, had studied at the Slade and served in the Great War before settling in Sussex. He exhibited at the Royal Academy and won the useful support and critical approval of such leading critics as P.G. Konody and Frank Rutter.

Nicholls answered the criticisms that had been made in the *Guardian* concerning the contents of the Academy exhibition. In the same newspaper he explained that low public consciousness had not made a new art gallery possible. Local artists tended to move away, or show their work in London where sales were more promising. To help remedy this regrettable situation he promised that artists of quality would always be very welcome at the Manchester Academy.

Nicholls' explanations for the inertia and unadventurousness of the Academy exhibition did not stem the flow of criticisms that were not only voiced in the *Guardian.* W. Weatherby, for instance, wrote in the *Manchester City News* about a show that had "little or no spirit; no joie de vivre."[4] Weatherby could see many competently painted and worthwhile works of art on offer but he was forced to conclude that, "throughout the exhibition there is scarcely a comment on contemporary life. Does all the rearrangement, the rebuilding, the demolishing and reconstructing, material, mental and spiritual, mean nothing?" Weatherby's lamentations on the failure of most Academy pictures to express contemporary life, were echoed ten, even twenty years later by local critics like Sewter, Senior and Willett, who also witnessed an unwillingness on the part of Manchester Academy painters to celebrate local urban themes. Weatherby prophesied the need that was eventually fulfilled by Margo Ingham. "Is the younger element," he asked, "given any place in the organisation? Is there sufficient interest in new blood?" Nicholls wrote to the *City News*, and rebuked Weatherby for failing to quote one single work in an article that dwelt unfairly on the stodginess of the Academy. Nicholls was also quick to point out that many regular Academy contributors, like himself, also made telling contributions at the equivalent annual exhibition in Burlington House. Writing in the same newspaper as

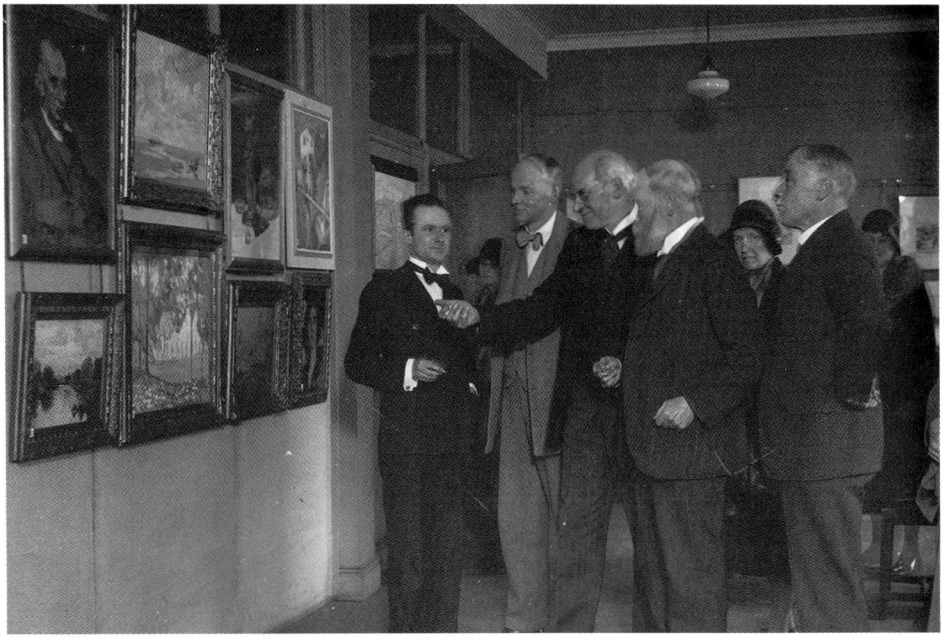

Manchester Academy in early 1930s. James Chettle, W. Maxwell Reekie and E. Steinthal examine pictures at the Academy.

Weatherby, Emmanuel Levy confirmed that the exceptionally good work in the spring exhibition was not in bountiful enough supply to break down an overall feeling of mediocrity. In words that paralleled Weatherby's, Levy advocated "a lowering of the pedestal, a little widening of the gates, and a still further embracing of the more varied and vital forms of art."[5] Senior members, and mature painters like Dodd, Dugdale, Nicholls and Oppenheimer, were the high points of excellence within an exhibition of only average quality.

A painter who quietly made his presence felt in Manchester exhibitions was Byron Cooper, a local painter whose first exhibition in his native city was at the Salon Club. This was followed by a distinguished exhibiting career not only with the Manchester Academy but also with the Royal Academy. As early as 1905 Cooper had one of his Cornish seascapes *Godrevy Light, Cornwall* (1903) acquired by the Manchester City Art Gallery. Alderman Todd, opening the artist's first exhibition in Manchester, voiced customary Council conservatism when he expressed pleasure in seeing works that "have not been influenced by the freak movements in the art world." Cooper was quoted in the *Daily Express*, and explained that the absence of people in his paintings was due to his growing "tired of depicting old aldermen and stout mayors with gold chains. Women are more interesting to paint but there are not many beautiful enough for an artist."[6] Instead, Cooper followed the example of Cornwall-based painters Moffatt Lindner, Julius Olsson and Borlase Smart and concentrated on romantic seascape and evocative moonlit scenes. In this he was typical of many artists of the 1920's who, like the Scottish colourists, reacted against the follies and traumas of the Great War by searching for spectacular natural scenery on the geographic periphery of Britain. This painter who found people a "blot on the landscape," and called Manchester "an awful hole" seemed to know exactly what he wanted, but was prone to bombast when describing his likes and dislikes. His occasional outspokenness was backed up by such excellent achievements as *The Incoming Tide*, a marine painting exhibited at the Academy in early 1931. The painting grasps the full force of the incoming mountains of water, crested with sparkling foam. Basing it on a view of the Atlantic invading a Cornish beach, Cooper here emulates the work of Cornish painters Smart and Olsson. "Manchester itself is ugly," he declared, as if justifying his painting of Cornish marines, "not because the architects are bad but simply because they are not given a chance. The town planning is all wrong." Cooper found Italian town planning more to his taste, and discovered that country to be an altogether more art-loving place. Yet in England nature compensated for a phlegmatic, philistine society: "there is more variety and more beauty in the English countryside and seashore than in any country." These sentiments echoed those of the much travelled contemporary painter Frances Hodgkins, a New Zealand-born artist who had lived in both Manchester and St Ives, after finally making England her home.

In August 1930 Tom Mostyn, who was known in London art circles as 'the Manchester Painter,' died. This distinguished landscape and portrait painter had once been a Manchester Academy President. Mostyn was born in Liverpool, but was educated at Manchester Grammar School and later studied under the renowned Herkomer in Bushey. Training at Herkomer's enabled him to paint figures and portraits with classical strength. Later he turned to the romantic depiction of imaginative, quasi-Arcadian landscapes, highlighted by golden light, pronounced shadow, and rusty autumnal textures. An interest in overgrown gardens and trees was also a feature of his landscapes. His abounding energy led him to open his own school at Charlton-cum-Hardy. This enterprise was later emulated by his daughter Marjorie, when in 1938 she opened the still-existing St Ives School of Painting with her fellow portraitist and husband, Leonard Fuller. The rosy romanticism of Arcadian gardens and mythological beauties mixed the detailed Pre-Raphaelitism of English painting with the florid colours of Monet's late garden and waterlily pictures. Tall, silent woods and untrodden vistas - in spite of the English or Italianate settings - touched the Nordic mood of Munch and the Symbolists. In complete contrast, Mostyn's commissioned portraits, such as those of Manchester businessmen James Thomas Blair (1863-1917) and J.K. Bythell (1840-1916), conveyed the sober, dark, realist style of Victorian and Edwardian portrait painting. Blair was a collector and benefactor of the City Art Gallery. Bythell was chairman of the Manchester Ship Canal.

The kind of painting that integrated portrait and still life subjects into one compounded interior setting was practised by Leonard Fuller and Marjorie Mostyn, and was equally successful in the hands of William Wildman. His painting *The Smiths at Breakfast*, was exhibited in the 1931 Manchester Academy exhibition. This picture of a mother breakfasting with her two daughters was suffused in sunny morning light and rendered with bright, positive post-impressionist colour. The picture was illustrated by the *Manchester Guardian* whose reviewer referred to its "clever and lively handling of the foreground." The reporter also admired Charles Tunnicliffe's drawings, while John Park's use of paint was cited as being the most sophisticated on offer; even if "his gusto, instead of making his skies go back into the distance, plasters his clouds about among his houses and harbours, to the utter confusion of the latter." Emmanuel Levy, again writing for the *Manchester City News*, acknowledged an improvement in the 1931 show, though continuing to advocate the need both for the greater freedom of expression and use of colour that was a distinguishing feature of contemporary mid-European painting. Levy maintained the exhibits were often painted in too straightforward a manner, leading to the exhibition's overall "soulless" character.

As if to echo his own talents for colour, Levy referred to "two spirited flower studies by Malcolm Milne, both sparkling with colour and playful light."[8] Charles Holmes presented a powerful Edward Hopper-type Manhattan street scene *Forty Second Street*. Charles Cundall's painting of Hamburg Docks slotted into an *oeuvre* that includes similar subjects, such as the Liverpool sea-front seen from the Mersey, or panoramic views of Manchester and Preston. Francis Dodd's *Spring in the Suburbs*, " with lovely pearly colour and skilful design," seemed to Levy to catch "the essence of a suburb street in its dismal quietness." Sensitive as ever to the effects of colour, Levy admired "a mastery of tone values" in Charles Oppenheimer's landscapes, although the portrait painting of Dugdale seemed too pictorially flat. Yet Dugdale was far more than a stiff, formal portrait painter: *Lunch at*

Chelsea Arts Club or *Night* were complex figure scenes, full of animated social interaction, rapture and frenetic activity. One exhibition that Levy could not review was his own one-man show at the Salon Club; his first in Manchester for five years. W. Weatherby, writing on the exhibition for the *Manchester City News*, applauded the individuality of Levy's style, based on a solid structure and positive colour.

The relative luxury of debate, commentary and critical evaluation was temporarily eclipsed in late February by the City Council's drastic decision to withdraw an annual grant of £2,000 for buying paintings. Bertram Nicholls wrote to the *Guardian* lamenting the decision. He noted that Manchester artists were "prized in public and private collections all over the world; but not in Manchester must they look for recognition or support."[9] Further gloom came with the death of Gertrude Wright, who had been born and educated locally. Her statuettes, in a style of refined, classical naturalism, were notable contributions to the normally scant sculpture section of the Academy shows. In spite of the Council squeeze, a gift of 55 lithographs by John Copley was made to the City Art Gallery. This included *Alassio, Starry Night*, a print with a Van Gogh title which in fact recalls Matisse. An element of psychological intensity is provided by the proximity of the face of an elegant woman behind which lies the romantic vista of a Riviera resort.

The deprecatory remarks made about Manchester by Byron Cooper and many others who sought to justify their continued production of holiday scene pictures, was countered by a nostalgic Francis Dodd who reminisced to the *Guardian* by giving his impressions of Manchester at the turn of the century. Dodd wrote: "There are times when the mist of Manchester is as soft and caressing to the eye as the colour of a dove's wing, and the lights in the street gleam like an opal."[10] Such descriptions had already been translated into eloquent visual statements in Adolphe Valette's blue and grey monochromatic pictures of Manchester's canals, buildings and streets veiled in a suffused mist. In the Spring Academy show of 1932, the usual St Ives harbour scenes by John Park were accompanied by similar subjects from Hartley Mooney. Emmanuel Levy again found a "persistence of mediocrity" at the heart of the Academy show, attributable in his mind to a reluctance to experiment. A rare landscape, *South Downs*, by the flower painter Malcolm Milne which "pulsated with light, colour and movement" once again impressed Levy. A small-scale portrait of David Garnett by Henry Lamb was mentioned, while William Wildman's excellent *Oyster Dredger* found its way into the Manchester City Art Collection.

Soon after the Academy exhibition, an exciting display of French painting was seen at the City Art Gallery. Gauguin and Pissarro were well featured in an exhibition that stretched back to the seventeenth century, to include legendary and classical landscapes by Claude and Poussin. Such riches did not end there. In October, Charles Holmes opened a Van Gogh exhibition on Mosley Street. Emmanuel Levy, reporting for the *City News*, dispelled the myth of Van Gogh's madness, finding in his pictures lucidity, control and coherence. The skilful opposition of warm and cool colours, so important to Van Gogh, was acknowledged by Levy when he wrote of the "hot golden sunlight and the cool blue skies . . . which moved him deeply."

The next Academy show, in early 1933, was destined to be a disappointment after the displays of Gauguin and Van Gogh. Malcolm Milne's floral still lifes and Terrick Williams' Concarneau harbour scenes did, however, provide undisputed points of beauty on the Academy walls. Weatherby noted in the *City News* that the "keynote is always sound, serious workmanship," but echoed the views of many commentators both before and after when he complained of "those holiday productions which belong to 'Diary of a Happy Holiday,' or 'Recollections of Whit-week.'" But Lowry's *Dwellings in Jersey Street* presented a realistic perception of local industrial habitation.

Significant events that followed the spring show included an exhibition at the City Art Gallery of three English painters: Charles Ricketts, William Orpen and Ambrose McEvoy. At the end of the year, an exhibition of work by Rowley Smart took place in the same gallery. Smart, born in Cheetham Hill in 1887, aped the Bohemian lifestyle and flamboyant artistic manner of Augustus John, with whom he lived briefly in Dorset. Sporting a beard and long hair, Smart had renegaded after only a term at the Manchester School of Art. Later he moved to Liverpool, and eventually went to live in Sweden suffering from ill-health. Yet in many respects, Smart's work exuded the sobriety of an artist interested in the structure of hills or streets - subjects he habitually chose for his watercolour work. Less than a year after his Manchester exhibition, in August 1934, Smart died. The *Guardian* wrote that a "nervous, restless energy began to creep into his work, accompanied by a greater understanding of the plasticity of form."[11]

Three other notable Manchester artists died during 1933. Isobel Dacre, the Salford-educated feminist, who became a President of the Manchester Society of Women Artists, died at the age of 90. Annie Swynnerton, who had studied art at Manchester and then in Rome with Isobel Dacre, died aged 88. She had married the sculptor Joseph Swynnerton, with whom she lived in Rome. Encouraged in her early years by Burne-Jones and Sargent, she made history in 1922 by becoming the first woman associate member of the Royal Academy for a century and a half. Manchester appreciated its distinguished woman painter, and gave a civic reception to her exhibition held in 1923. Her carefully executed portraits included a study of Henry James. The *Guardian* noted that her "portraits of children were especially adroit."[12] Her landscape style was however imaginative and colourful. The other major loss of that year was Byron Cooper, who, like the two women painters, was from the generation of the long distant 1840's. Cooper's art studies at Manchester were augmented by a spell under one of the finest French artists, Carolus-Duran. He had a studio in the Royal Exchange at Manchester. His obituary noted that he was a sincere rather than an original artist, though it conceded that his "strongest claim to originality was in his paintings of moonlight, which is not a matter of piling on blues and black. Moonlight has its own complex colour harmonies, and Byron Cooper made it his special study."

An exciting Lowry subject, *A Football Match*, was a feature of the 1934 Academy list. Later that year the *Guardian* illustrated Charles Cundall's superb football scene that depicted with stunning virtuosity a thronging Wembley crowd witnessing Manchester City winning the F.A. Cup. Harry Rutherford silenced those 'Diary of a Happy Holiday' critics by submitting a superb holiday picture *Great Yarmouth, August*. Formally, this Sickert-inspired artist has succeeded in blending, with a high level of figurative drawing, relaxed but animated human activity within a complex architectural composition. The colour and light of this happy holiday scene proved a good deal brighter and more varied than the habitually rich or dark renderings of Sickert's Normandy seaside scenes.

The *Guardian* and *The Times* both found Henry Lamb's *Girl in Black* to be the best portrait in the Academy show. The *Observer* critic, Eric Newton, described the Lamb painting as "a typical example of the artist's favourite set of colour harmonies - rose and russet and pale olive green."[13] Yet Newton also found Tom Dugdale's *Portrait of Captain Adrian Jones* a brilliant piece of portraiture that "has far more of the texture and the 'feel' of flesh surfaces than Mr Lamb's." The year saw James Chettle take over the Presidency from Bertram Nicholls. Chettle, the first amateur painter to become President, speeded up the policy of opening the doors of the Academy to new, younger exhibitors from a wider artistic background. Newton speculated that such new blood "may not be, on the whole, better painters, but they certainly tend to have a fresher and less traditional outlook." Among the younger artists, Malcolm Milne, whose colourful floral painting Newton found "thoroughly individual," was praised for paying "least homage to academic tradition." The successful introduction of such gifted

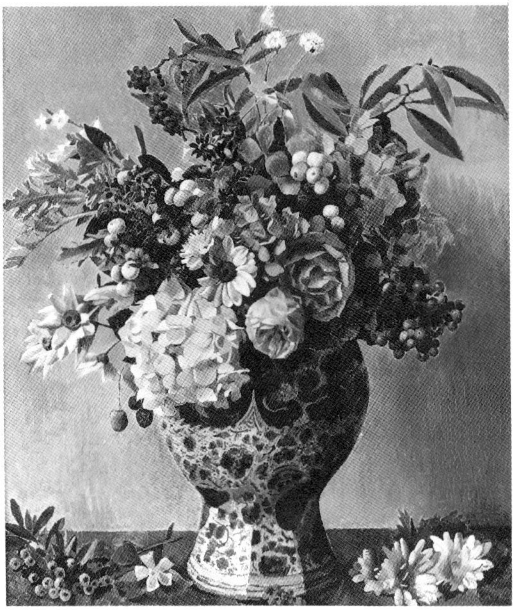

Malcolm Milne: Bowl of Flowers, *oil*.

Harry Rutherford: Penzance *(courtesy: Atkinson Museum, Southport)*.

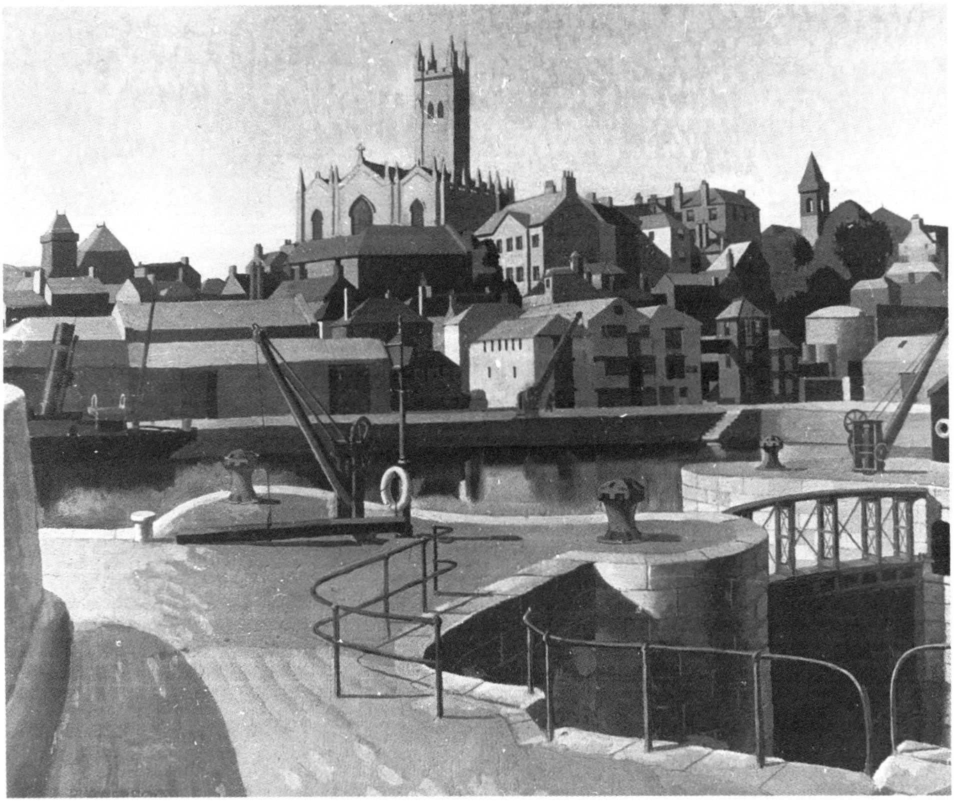

young artists led to an improved level of attendance at the 1934 exhibition.

Thomas Dugdale's impressive interior, *Lunch at the Chelsea Arts Club* was a notable exhibit in the 1935 Academy spring exhibition. The painting successfully integrated a crowd of artists sitting at lunch in the Club's dining room. It showed Dugdale stretching his figurative talents, and revealed the artist in lighthearted mood celebrating jolly, social occasions. It certainly represented a side of Dugdale's art quite different from his formal and darkly lit commissioned portraits. William Grimmond's *Sunday Afternoon on Hampstead Heath* was another excellent London subject, though one of many that bore little relevance to the industrial North. In similar vein, Harold Workman (1897-1978) - who later contributed a marvellous composition of Manchester workers and factory machinery, *Printing Camouflage Cloth* for the Haward war commissions - often used London subject matter. A painting of Hyde Park Corner was a lively, busy study of buildings and traffic, while his *Manette Street, Soho* (1935), portrayed tall, imposing buildings cast into alternate planes of light and shadow. The empty street below reminds one of Hopper, though the contemporary style and mood of the Camden Town artist Malcolm Drummond is most readily called to mind.

Another North London scene, though of an altogether different kind, was the one by Charles Cundall entitled *Cup Final, 1934*, celebrating Manchester City's victory at Wembley. The whole carnival-like atmosphere of Cup Final day was conjured up in this, as well as in other football subjects, such as the one celebrating Arsenal's 1936 victory over Sheffield United. Arsenal also appeared in a painting of a match against Chelsea. Cundall used the Stamford Bridge ground as a vantage point to look beyond to the Lots Road Power Station. Another painting of a Manchester day out in London was set in the less salubrious location of the Corinthian Casuals' grounds below Crystal Palace. *Corinthians versus Manchester City* (1927), and *A Chelsea Cup Tie* are further evidence of Cundall's interest, through the game of football, in the 'big day' occasion with its large figure groupings.

Returning north, a superb piece of architectural topography, *Manchester Renaissance* came from Levenshulme artist Vincent Reade. This recorded, not a football stadium, but the equally spectacular Manchester skyline with its assortment of office buildings, smoking chimneys and factory hinterlands in the distance. Harold Hemingway made an early contribution to the same Academy show, while more seasoned exhibitors like Maxwell Reekie showed a colourful study, in complementary blues and pinks, with the Whistlerian title *The Opal Sea*. James Chettle's opening speech expressed pleasure that the City had restored a grant for the purchase of art. The 1936 Academy exhibition was hung by a very competent trio: Tom Dugdale, Harry Rutherford and Hugh Wallis. The President, James Chettle, spoke at the opening of the need for the City to help living artists by purchasing their work. He applauded Charles Rutherston's foresight in acquiring works before they became too expensive. Harry Rutherford also made an address, welcoming the demise of futurism in art. The *City News* reported that "Rutherford refused to be convinced that the human figure could ever look like a set of organ pipes nor the human eye a poached egg."[14] Clearly, Rutherford was anchored to a Degas-Sickert orbit and wished to dismiss modernistic modes that strove to break up or disorientate the world of classical form. His Gilman-like *The Green Dress* was a feature of the 1936 exhibition. Colloquial, social-realist subject matter, allied to sound academic drawing, would remain Rutherford's banner, although he also displayed a sensuous feeling for paint. In 1930, Rutherford's canvas *Penzance* was purchased by Manchester. Depicting each building of the elaborate Penzance skyline as seen from the harbour pier, Rutherford uses a sharp, delineated style in order to do justice to the bright, Cornish light and the cutting granite architecture. In contrast, Rutherford (seen in his dull, tonal and Sickert-like *Folkestone*, 1964) later sacrificed the pedantic detail and finish of *Penzance* for a summary tonal treatment and a looser handling. Rutherford had no more to worry about concerning the infiltration of modernist decadence into Manchester Academy shows than did Alfred Munnings at the Royal Academy in the late 1940's.

Indeed, the constitution of the 1936 show continued along familiar lines, with some excellent examples by artists who practised only a conservative form of modernism: Terrick Williams, John Park, Maxwell Reekie, Francis Dodd were among the familiar names. From Scotland Charles Oppenheimer sent down his *Engineering in Concrete*, a celebration of a large scale dam-building feat that resembled Cornish painter Borlase Smart's contemporaneous study of the building of the Burrator Dam. Not for the first time Henry Lamb won praise for *Girl with a Wine Glass*. The *Guardian* claimed it "has the power to come to closer grips with the shapes and solidities of things than any other artist exhibiting this year."[15] Tom Dugdale's less broken brushwork and smoother modelling did not lead to a better portrait. The same newspaper referred to his "unevenness of vision." James Chettle's 'affectionate eyes' resulted in typical examples of 1930's rural calm, rustic tranquillity and poster-like boldness of composition. Significantly, Lowry won critical attention for appearing to rise above the rest of the exhibitors in the field of landscape painting. The newspaper declared that "by far the most creative of the landscapists is Mr Lowry . . . who sees his Lancashire with the intensity of an Italian Primitive. He paints

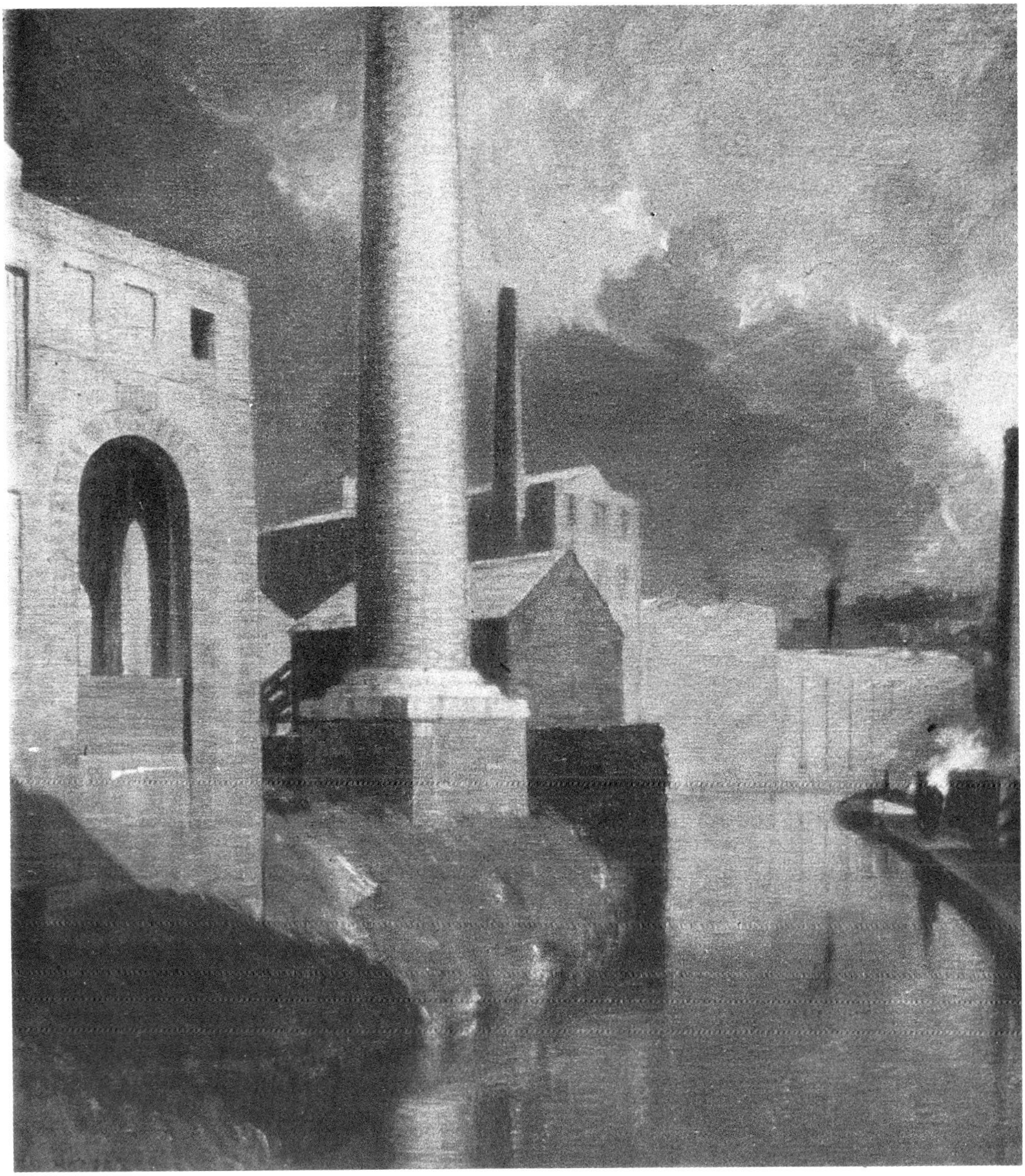

Charles Holmes: Near Greenwood Mill, Blackburn, Lancashire, *1928 (courtesy: Salmesbury Hall, Blackburn).*

chimneys as Lorenzo Monaco painted saints. These are real works of art, and the strength of their wild unreality makes their photographically conscientious neighbours seem dim and unconvincing by contrast."[16] This spring show was followed by an exhibition of Chinese art, and the third annual dinner of the Manchester Academy was held at Kettners in Soho, underlining the fact that so many Academy artists were resident in London.

In June a long-standing Academy exhibitor, and one of the first women members, Emma Magnus, died in Fallowfield. She had studied at the Slade after attending Manchester School of Art. In December 1936 an even more significant member, Charles Holmes, died in London. This distinguished painter and critic, who became a Director of the National Gallery, was born in Preston in 1868. His father was a hard-working clergyman. In 1880 Charles had entered Eton. An uncle, Sir Richard Holmes, was Librarian at nearby Windsor Castle. The schoolboy was thus introduced to the print collection at Windsor, stimulating an interest in art, though he also developed a passion for fishing and football. After Oxford, Holmes went into publishing, and became a proof-reader for Ballantyne and Hanson. He met the artist Charles Ricketts, who encouraged him to take up etching. Holmes learnt painting largely on his own. He went on to work as manager for the Vale Press, founded by Ricketts. He also shared art criticism with Roger Fry for the magazine *Athenaeum*. In 1903 Holmes was invited by Fry to come to the rescue of the recently founded *Burlington Magazine*, which was in financial trouble. Holmes became both the magazine's editor and manager soon after, and eventually succeeded in making the *Burlington Magazine* one of the foremost cultural periodicals. In 1904 his remarkably distinguished career saw him become Slade Professor of Fine Art at Oxford. He later graduated from the Directorship of the National Portrait Gallery to become Director of the National Gallery itself in 1916; a position he held until resigning in 1928. After that he dedicated most of his time to painting, and published an autobiography, *Self and Partners*, in 1936. He wrote several books, including studies on Constable and Rembrandt. He was knighted in 1921. Frank Rutter paid just tribute to his enormously active and responsible life by writing that he "proved the truth of his later contention that the taste and habit of mind of an artist is in no way incompatible with business aptitude."[17] Holmes was part of a generation of artists - Forrest Hewit, James Chettle and Margaret Pilkington among them - who were part-time and self-taught, but who greatly expanded the social standing of local art through their active business and social lives. Yet, they also epitomised a respectable suburban status quo that was inevitably at odds with bohemianism and the vanguard ramifications of radical and progressive art.

In spite of the privileges and eminent positions that Holmes enjoyed and held throughout his life, he was an artist who seldom shied away from an honest depiction of his native industrial North West. He was genuinely interested in industrial architecture and was drawn, in particular, to canals near factories, stagnant ponds and furnaces. He also painted industrial scenes in Yorkshire. Several Sheffield scenes, executed as early as 1914, anticipated the much later kitchen sink realism of Greaves and Middleditch. In the late 1920's he was commissioned by Salmesbury Hall, Blackburn, to produce a series of paintings along the Liverpool to Leeds canal at Blackburn. *Near Greenwood's Mill* is a dark picture that records the sombre grandeur of mills and chimneys reflected in the stagnant waters of the canal. He looked for a kind of classical power, a fullness of form in industrial buildings. As if adapting the Cézannian principle of the cube, cylinder and circle to both nature and the man-made environment, Holmes emphasised the roundness of the chimneys and towers that were an ubiquitous feature of the industrial scene before his eyes. Frank Rutter wrote that "Holmes went on to invent a new genre for himself when, struck by the effect of industrial buildings in juxtaposition to rural surrounding he proceeded to paint his first industrial landscapes." He was also drawn to more conventional examples of beauty, and painted in the Lake District to the north of the Lancashire industrial belt. The *Guardian* spoke of his "quick summarising eye and a good memory."

At the opening of the Manchester Academy spring exhibition in 1937, the President, James Chettle, absent because of illness, had his address read out by Hartley Mooney. That address once again implored the public to support their local artists "who are having a thin time." The exhibition included: Essex landscapes by John Park (who served on the hanging committee), a portrait of Cecil Beaton by Henry Lamb, and a magnificent roof-top view of Canterbury by Francis Dodd, that emulated the finest example of topographical townscape provided the year before by Vincent Reade. Once again the exhibition threw up a high incidence of non-northern subjects, and even Rochdale's young Harold Hemingway showed an untypical southern subject, *Vauxhall Bridge*. But Lowry did not fail, sending in *A Footbridge* and *Industrial Landscape*. Nor did Charles Holmes' final contribution *Long Preston* deviate from local subject matter. The Holmes picture - shown posthumously at the Academy - was noted in the *Liverpool Daily Post*: "Holmes discovered paintable qualities in the industrial townscapes of his native city. Sombre skies and mill chimneys were his specialities, and even his landscapes looked grim. *Long Preston* is far from grim. It is a majestic painting of heavy lowering clouds blowing up upon a desolate moorland, where the evening light lingers."[18]

In more rural vein, Maxwell Reekie presented a picturesque view of a Scottish castle. Janet Kirk's *Cranes* was purchased from the exhibition for the City Art Gallery. Henry Lamb was again steeped in critical praise, and for the third year running the *Guardian* indicated Lamb's contribution to be the best in the entire exhibition. His portrait of Cecil Beaton was deemed "quite the most distinguished work in this year's exhibition," even though the *Guardian* reviewer wished Lamb would, "add a few new colours to that familiar, bland palette of his." The 1930's were the decade of Lamb's portrait painting, culminating in the 1938 portrait of the then Prime Minister, Neville Chamberlain. He relied on portraits such as these to support a young family which he was rearing in the quiet village of Coombe Bissett near Salisbury. His faithful support of the Manchester Academy belied his disagreeable feelings towards the city in which he grew up. But in spite of a formidable network of important artists and friends, Lamb always believed in the local life of provincial art societies and groups. The reporter admired Lamb's recent work for its eschewal of the "literary or romantic" elements that had once motivated him to try his own 'blue' period containing mythic nudes in a landscape.

The *Guardian* remarked that even if Lowry were never to paint again he would be remembered, indicating - quite correctly - that he had already reached a considerable level of achievement. John Park and James Chettle contributed paintings - of Essex and Suffolk landscapes - that "serve to remind us that the Constable tradition is still alive." Similarly, Charles Cundall and Francis Dodd created "meticulous documentary records, recalling the high days of Canaletto." An exhibition that "owes much to the excellence of its presentation," seemed to benefit greatly from the service of the experienced John Park on the hanging committee.

The temporary restriction imposed in the 1930's on the acquisition of art by the City had lifted sufficiently by 1937, enabling the Art Galleries Committee to state that a number of interesting works had been purchased during that year. In addition to the acquisition of works by local artists such as Lowry and Rutherford, the committee reported that "acquisitions included a characteristic painting by Christopher Wood, a striking canvas by Adrian Allinson, a fine portrait by Jacque Emile Blanche depicting Thomas Hardy in old age, an intimate full length portrait of Mr Francis Dodd by Stephen Bone and a typical example of Stanley Spencer."

A heap of alternating praise and criticism characterised responses to the 1938 Academy exhibition. Henry Lamb's *Lord David Cecil* used the artist's characteristic range of muted purples, greens, pinks and ochres, and was deemed the best portrait on offer. Tom Dugdale's *Polly*, a portrait of a maid with a tray of drinks, integrated portrait and still life *genres*, and recalled the late work of Harold Harvey. Lowry's work continued to convey the morbid mood that was a pronounced feature of his life and work while his mother lay on her deathbed. His contribution included *Empty House*. The *Liverpool Daily Post* wrote that "Lowry's mordant townscapes, and his painful portrait of a half-witted child attract attention, while Harold Workman's *Salford* is another industrial landscape which records - though less critically than Mr Lowry's - the more sordid works of man."[19] Emmanuel Levy contributed a portrait, while Vice-President Hartley Mooney's *Listening In* managed, in similar vein to Dugdale's complex figure-within-interior groupings, to dress a difficult and complicated group pose in gay, contemporary garb. It was to be the last of the Vice-President's contributions to the Academy. The floral and portrait painter died in April, shortly after the spring show. He painted several mayors of Manchester and also pursued musical interests. Another successful figure grouping, though one set outdoors, was Harold Workman's *Derby Day Incidents* (1937). Both Forrest Hewit and Maxwell Reekie showed loch subjects, while John Park sent in a typical *Morning Light, St Ives*. One of the largest pictures that year was Francis Dodd's *The Roundabout*.

George Pollard was another contemporary critic who, reporting for the *News Chronicle*, exposed the failure of exhibitors to embrace authentic industrial themes. Pollard expressed, in crystal clear terms, the inability of Academy artists to grasp the powerful, implicit aesthetic of the 'ugliness' and squalor of the bleak northern scene. In the right hands the stagnant, polluted wastegrounds of urban blight could be transformed into a powerful metaphor depicting the folly of human interference with nature. The highly emotive First World War battleground imagery, used to such devastating effect by Nevinson and Nash, had achieved this. So too had any number of contemporary expressionist artists in Germany. An old war artist like Francis Dodd chose, in the quiet years of the 1930's, to turn his considerable documentary skills towards a tame and sober recording of pleasant southern suburbs and townscapes. Not for him the dark satanic mills of the North. Francis Dodd's *The Roundabout* is a far cry from the macabre and robotic depiction of the same subject by Mark Gertler. Created shortly after the Great War, this was a cynical comment on the vicious cycle of war, technology and rampant nationalism. It was all very well for Harry Rutherford to applaud the demise of futurist art as a major threat to his more cautious modernist programme. But the perennial reluctance of the pre-war Manchester Academy exhibitors to come to grips with the ugly power and compelling energy emitting from the industrial landscape was considered a serious flaw, both by George Pollard and by a whole succession of intelligent critics from then on.

Indeed, Pollard wrote that the 1938 exhibition "confirms my impression that the artist believes Manchester is a very good place to leave behind."[20] It needs to be remembered, however, that the weather and drab industrial character may not have been the major factors behind an exodus of artists from Manchester. A significant number of opening speeches referred to the need for the people of Manchester to support their artists with greater fervour and commitment.

Pollard alluded to the "charming bits of Cornwall and France, of the Lakes, of Derbyshire and Yorkshire" that frequently cropped up on the Academy walls. Pollard confessed to have visited the exhibition "in search of the work of an artist who had pictured some aspect of the vast industrial life of the area - and left disappointed. In its great machine power, its factory strength, its teeming industry, the north has beauty to be revealed and interpreted, and what might be lost in colourful pleasantry would surely be gained in vitality and truth."[21] Even in the picturesque 1930's, a nucleus of northern realists - notably Lowry, Hemingway and Holmes - stuck out in the large annual group exhibitions. Academy Secretary Louise Bancroft reported in the *City News* that nobody wanted to purchase pictures "due to the present times."[22] It was a regrettable situation for which Manchester could not be blamed - the ominous signs of a looming European cataclysm were on the horizon. In the war that was to follow it was the great industrial heritage of Manchester that enabled the city to function on a level of national importance. Furthermore, as we shall soon see, industrial activity when suddenly put to urgent task attracted war artists to the area, and helped to trigger off industrial subject matter as a utilitarian as well as aesthetic ingredient in contemporary art.

NOTES

1 For further early history of the Manchester Academy see *A Short History of the Manchester Academy of Fine Arts*, published in 1973 by the Manchester Academy as part of the 1973 Manchester Festival. Previous short histories were published in 1959, as part of the Academy centenary celebration, and in 1969. Research and text was the work of Hal Yates, who in 1959 was the honorary literary secretary.

2 *Manchester City News* 6.2.29

3 *Manchester City News* 19.10.29 Emmanuel Levy

4 *Manchester City News* 8.2.30 W. Weatherby

5 *Manchester City News* 15.2.30 Emmanuel Levy

6 *Daily Express* 13.5.30
7 *Guardian* 10.2.31
8 *Manchester City News* 14.2.31 Emmanuel Levy
9 *Guardian* 25.2.31 Bertram Nicholls
10 *Guardian* 6.1.32 Francis Dodd
11 *Guardian* 10.8.34
12 *Guardian* 25.10.33
13 *Observer* 4.2.34 Eric Newton
14 *Manchester City News* 7.2.36
15 *Guardian* 1.2.36
16 *Guardian* 1.2.36
17 *Sunday Times* 13.12.36 Obituary by Frank Rutter
18 *Liverpool Daily Post* 3.2.37
19 *Liverpool Daily Post* 29.1.38
20 *News Chronicle* 29.1.38 George Pollard
21 Ibid.
22 *Manchester City News* 5.2.38 Louise Bancroft

Five

Manchester Academy: The War

Between 1938 and 1960 the Manchester Academy showed great vigour and durability. The period saw L.S. Lowry transformed into a national figure. In this, Manchester played a more substantial role than the artist was in the habit of acknowledging. The period also witnessed the rise of a younger generation of local talents, who, after the war, gradually replaced the more traditional impressionist and post-impressionist painters who had filled the Academy of the inter-war years with attractive, but often irrelevant (as far as Manchester was concerned) subject paintings. Irrelevant because their pretty Cornish and Mediterranean harbour subjects, floral still lifes and genteel portraits seemed to ignore the grey realism of the industrial society that existed in Manchester and the north west.

Local newspaper reviews of the Academy Spring Exhibitions commented on the lamentable absence of pictures - Lowry and a few others apart - with discernible local themes. Whether or not the new generation after the war outstripped the conservative impressionistic painters of the 1920's and 1930's in craftsmanship is open to argument, but certainly their new and direct realist painting marked a change in the meaning of subject matter. The emphasis became one of direct expression, often with a social or socialist sensibility underpinning the realism.

It is somewhat ironic that several of the affluent older artists submitted pretty, non-industrial pictures to the Manchester exhibitions, painted during holidays or periods of leave taken from their activities as dignitaries, merchants or industrialists. Richard Weisbrod, for instance, was the prosperous owner of a silk mill near Preston. Hal Yates was a wealthy seed merchant, while an older painter, Forrest Hewit, represented the kind of socially eminent painter typical of the Manchester art scene in pre-war years. Hewit was a highly respected local industrialist and the *Manchester Guardian*[1] reviewed in June 1938 his one-man exhibition at the Manchester Academy. The newspaper report was tellingly headlined 'Industrialist as Artist.' Hewit's contributions to local industry were formidable, while his artistic pedigree, if never quite as spectacular as his secular positions, was none the less sound enough. Manchester-born, he studied under Sickert at the great Edwardian artist's Manchester school, and there also received instruction from the portrait painter Thomas Dugdale. To some extent echoing the example of Lowry, success to Hewit came first in London, where he enjoyed exhibitions at the Burlington Galleries and at the Royal Academy itself before Manchester rewarded him with his first one-man exhibition in his native city. During the late 1920's Hewit exhibited, alongside other Sickert pupils, with the Salon Club in Manchester. The influence of Sickert is evident at once in street genre pictures like *Cafe Nero* (Manchester City Art Gallery). Other continental or Far Eastern pictures also in the collection of the Manchester City Art Galleries, *Boats at Meneggio* (1930) or *Shanghai Landscape* (1937) are good examples. They indicate the dependency on traditional views and the use of popular, attractive or exotic subjects, to the exclusion of northern industrial themes.

In a picture like *Beech Trees in the New Forest*, Hewit comes closer to home, though in a style nearer to Spencer Gore's Richmond Park series than to Sickertian modes. But it is clear that Hewit represents a common tendency of his generation to draw on an English Post-Impressionist style and a happy sunlit rusticity. England's green and pleasant land seemed to inspire him more than the local mills that would later become emotive source material for the younger expressionistic painters.

In addition to featuring Hewit, the 'Industrialist as Artist,' the *Manchester Guardian* reported in June 1938 on the purchase by the Manchester Academy of the home of Mrs Elias Bancroft at No. 10 Acomb Street, Whitworth Park. Mrs Bancroft had been an Academy secretary for 16 years, but was now stepping down for reasons of health. The new Acomb Street premises were the first permanent home where Manchester Academy could stage its own exhibitions, since the Salon Club closed in 1933. "Apart from a short and unsuccessful period as a shirt factory, the house has a long and unbroken association with Manchester artists . . . Muirhead Bone and Henry Lamb were amongst the artists who exhibited their work there. The Academy's new tenancy continues an association that has lasted since 1922, when the studio was rented from Mrs Bancroft for the Academy classes. The original use of the house as a drawing class for the Academy owed much to Francis Dodd who affectionately nicknamed it 'The Red Elephant's Castle'."

A second exhibition at Acomb Street, in October 1938, featured over 50 paintings in oil and watercolour by James Chettle, the Academy President. Life drawing classes started at Acomb Street in October and continued until March in adjacent studios. In November an exhibition of work by northern artists met with the criticism in the local *Evening Chronicle* that the display was "featureless and disappointing." The reporter explained that the exhibition "is not likely to create much controversy, the subjects are largely commonplace and the treatment orthodox. Nothing here reflects these troubled times. Many northern artists appear to have become escapologists and sought some quiet backwater." The criticism no doubt refers to the tendency to choose cosy or picturesque subject matter at the expense of a grittier realism. The escapology rebuke also seems to mirror an unpreparedness for the possibility of European cataclysm. The complacency of the Chamberlain government towards German expansionism is further evidence of English provinciality at this time; a factor so evident in the insular nature of much 1930's British painting. Reflecting a native artistic tendency towards the sublime or tranquil, Harold Williamson's *Picnic* and Sickert's *Ballet at Her Majesty's* were given an admiring notice by the reporter. 1938 ended with the prominent Academy painter Maxwell Reekie winning the Heywood Medal. This prize was set up in 1821 by Benjamin Heywood, who gave the governors of the Royal Manchester Institution £500, from which an annual prize would be given for the most meritorious production of science or art.

The big event early in 1939 was Lowry's all-important first exhibition in London, at the prestigious Lefevre gallery. The exhibition was shared with Martin Block and J.D. Fergusson. Although Block and Fergusson were better known painters, the acclaimed critic Eric Newton chose to spend most of his *Sunday Times* review on Lowry whom he maintained was "the kind of artist who is apt to be ignored just because he is entirely original . . . it is a limited vision, but it owes nothing to any other artist." Newton went on to speculate that despite his then belonging to no school, Lowry was likely to become the founder of one. Newton found Lowry's work pervaded with a compassionate, affectionate response to the sordid and dilapidated areas he portrayed. Newton even found "implicit religious quality" in Lowry's art, though he did not indicate a puritan parsimony residing in the Manchester painter's predominantly black and white palette. Instead he compared Lowry to the Italian Primitives, finding in his work "the same delicacy and richness of surface, the same cleanness of colour (even his smokey greys are somehow clean) the same tendency to draw his figures only in front view, back view or profile. Yet despite these superficial naivities his composition is often subtle and sometimes masterly." Two months later, in March 1939 Manchester's *Evening Chronicle* proudly noted that Lowry's *Dwellings in Oldfield Road*, purchased by the Tate Gallery from the Lefevre exhibition, was the first Salford landscape in a major national collection.

Spring, 1939 saw the 80th annual exhibition of the Manchester Academy.

John Gauld together with the popular Lancashire and Lakeland watercolourist Percy Lancaster, served on the hanging committee. At the opening the President, James Chettle, lamented the drift towards London of many Manchester artists. "Manchester was the art centre of the north of England, but the support given here to those who practised the visual arts was not sufficient to prevent them from gravitating to the better opportunities afforded by London." These words by an unbiased traditional painter were later echoed by the émigré dealer Andreas Kalman, who in the late 1940's argued in the local press that Manchester did not have a major art scene because of inadequate public appreciation for, and awareness of, significant contemporary art. Be this as it may, no one can deny the flourishing nature of the Manchester Academy Spring exhibition, which in 1939 boasted 350 works by over 80 artists. Of these only 15 were sculpture, underlining the fact that the Salon - like the Academy Spring show - was a fundamentally pictorial affair.

Key works in the 1939 show included Charles Cundall's *Liverpool from the Mersey* (Manchester City Art Gallery). The panoramic view of Liverpool's waterfront, with its fine Victorian architecture, showed Cundall at his best in the detailed portrayal of urban skylines. Other works in this vein included his magnificent *Preston* (Harris Museum, Preston) which portrayed the entire breadth of the Lancashire railway town with a breathtaking mastery and control of topographical detail. Cundall's Liverpool skyline was accompanied by the altogether different subject of a Venetian scene. Tom Dugdale's grand portraits continued to outshine all other examples of portraiture, while Ronald Allan, John Bowes and Arthur Hilton were three artists who later became leading spirits in the post-war Manchester Group at the Midday Studios. Percy Lancaster exhibited virtuoso watercolours such as *Harvesting in North Lancashire* that mastered the fleeting impression. But even further from Manchester urban themes, came contributions by Charles Tunnicliffe, Malcolm Milne, Agnes Drey and James Chettle, which presented wildlife, floral, St Ives and Dorset subjects respectively. Indeed, Chettle's *Early Morning, Poole Harbour* (1937) revealed the early rising *plein air* painter, working in warmer British climes, to produce a picture that would have graced Bournemouth Arts Club exhibitions, but which was acquired by Manchester City Art Gallery. Forrest Hewit's typical *Jura Mountains* - yet another Continental picture from him - was cited as being "excellent simplification by an artist who knows how to seize on essentials."

The newspapers which seriously covered Academy exhibitions were the *Guardian*, the *Evening Chronicle* and further afield, the *Yorkshire Post* and the *Liverpool Daily Post*. Dugdale's portrait *A.P. Herbert* won a favourable response in the *Guardian*, whose reporter hinted at a dilemma common to artists. While criticising an apparent uniformity of treatment in the Academy exhibits he warned against artists indiscriminately trying out new styles simply for the sake of novelty. There was nothing wrong with using a well-trodden impressionist style so long as the artist "feels that impressionism is his creed, and provided he uses his creed not as a mere dead formula but as a living stem onto which he can graft his own personal contributions and convictions." The reporter saw little evidence of any originality, but did refer to the temperamental drama of Chettle, based on a pronounced use of shadow and on a predilection for pure picturesque themes.

A child portrait study *Miss Beryl Samuels* by the Liverpool artist Stanley Reed was a much publicised item from the show, and resembled, if not emulated, the quality of Dod Proctor's neo-classical figure pictures of the period.

Preston-born John Park's work was referred to as "traditional painting in the best sense. He does not say 'This is how I saw it' but 'This is how it was,' and he seems to add 'if you think you can paint the reflections on troubled water better than I can, just you try! and frankly there are not many contemporary painters who could." After periods of study at the Colarossi School in Paris, Park went to live in St Ives, Cornwall. In this famous artists' haunt he became a foremost practitioner of outdoor landscape painting, specialising in deftly coloured impressionist views of St Ives harbour mirroring in its waters a dazzle of coloured reflections from moored fishing vessels. This was a theme repeated at Brixham, where he went to live late in life, in 1957. Soon after, Park returned, via Folkestone, to his native Preston, where he died early in 1962. Some of John Park's early paintings reveal his Lancashire, and specifically Preston, origins. His portrait of *Trader Horn*, a well-known local Preston character who had sailed to many countries, is in the Harris Museum at Preston. Park is best remembered, though, for the Cornish harbour impressions, a subject used by another Lancashire painter, Southport-born and Warrington-trained Arthur Hayward (born 1889).

Reporting on the 1939 Academy Exhibition the *Daily Mail* (28.1.39) noted that 'Artists Won't Paint Their Own City'. In over 300 pictures, the newspaper's reporter could find only two depicting Manchester. Instead, examples of Welsh, Scottish, Irish, Cornish, Italian and French scenes abounded. The newspaper asked "Are they ashamed of Manchester?" The inclement local weather seemed to be the principal excuse. The months following the Spring Exhibition - an ominous period leading to the outbreak of war in September 1939 - saw an exhibition of 42 drawings by the Manchester portrait painter Emmanuel Levy, held at the Contemporary Bookshop in Oxford Road. "Wizened old ladies, Jewish patriarchs, and dilapidated buildings are Mr Levy's favourite subjects," the press reported. Many of the works were produced from life in the Cheetham Hill Home for aged Jews. In July 1939 came the death of the local sculptor John Cassidy. Cassidy was born in County Meath in 1860, and came to Manchester School of Art to study modelling. Among his best known achievements were the statue of *King Edward VIID* in Whitworth Park, and the *Adrift* group in Piccadilly Gardens. A bust of the Victorian painter William Frith is in Manchester City Art Gallery. He produced 200 busts, and acted both as an adjudicator of students' work at the art school and as Treasurer to the Manchester Academy. After the declaration of war, it was agreed to permit the Manchester City Art Gallery to continue as much as conditions would allow.

Despite war time restrictions, the 1940 Spring Exhibition was able to present a number of entries equal to any of those in the 1930's. Lowry submitted three works, compared to one the previous year. Yet, unusually for him, only one of the three was of a Manchester subject. The *Guardian* illustrated John Garsides' superb *The Breakfast Table*, a woman-at-table interior subject that emulated Leonard Fuller or Marjorie Mostyn at their very best. An Ian Grant self-portrait was described as "the most serious of the smaller portraits." The newspaper also noted that "there are not many signs of war in this year's exhibition. The quality of the paintings has not suffered. No sitter wears a steel helmet." This was evidently less a reflection of the 'escapology' criticised in reports of previous Academy exhibitions than the fact that the north west had not, by the spring of 1940, been directly scarred by the war. But Chettle's bitterly ironic *War Memorial Manchester* of 1941 recorded the castle-like ruins of a bombed building that was a smouldering monument to intense enemy bombing during 1941. Early in 1940 Lawrence Haward, Director of the City Art Gallery, wrote in the *Manchester Guardian* on the plight of museums in war time. He drew comparisons with the experience of the Great War, and spoke of the need for museums near factories to remove their treasures to safer places. Manchester pursued this sensible policy, and a few years later in 1945 Emmanuel Levy celebrated the end of the war by producing two commissioned pen and ink drawings, *Loading the Pictures, Aberystwyth*, and *Manchester Pictures in the National Library of Wales* which recorded the reloading of pictures for their return from temporary storage havens in Wales.

Haward brought a glimmer of hope for artists by citing the example of the Pilgrim Trust in making large grants for the encouragement of the arts in war time. Haward hoped that out of the conflict of World War 2 a group of paintings might result that would emulate those by Spencer, Nash, Lamb, Nevinson and Dodd from the 1914-18 conflict. Following the example of the year before, Charles Cundall contributed another Liverpool picture *Building the Catholic Cathedral at Liverpool* that again revealed his masterly blending of architectural detail with pictorial harmony.

By 1941, however, war damage inflicted itself on the Academy Spring Exhibition which had only about 200 pictures on display. A marked decrease of submitted works reflected the interference of war. Yet Derek Senior, writing in the *Guardian* (1.2.41), found a positive effect in reduced numbers. He praised the Academy for putting on an exhibition at all. "The reduction in total numbers," he wrote, "is, on balance, an advantage." To maintain a Spring Show throughout the war years was a notable achievement, and showed that the north west was not as vulnerable to enemy attack as the south. The lively Bournemouth Arts Club and its neighbouring Poole and East Dorset Art Society both had to severely curtail their operations during the war. Senior was quick to air his disappointment over the contents of the Spring Show, though regretting that the war "has hardly ruffled their placid temper." The critic was clearly looking for the kind of gutsy picture that expressed the suffering of war. He deplored paintings that oozed an insular sentimentality and consoling cosiness. The exhibition displayed "the same mixture of good, bad and indifferent as before, with perhaps a little more emphasis on indifferent." The reduction in numbers did not prevent regulars like Norman Janes, Charles Tunnicliffe, William Grimmond, Malcolm Milne, John Gauld, Tom Dugdale, L.S. Lowry, Ian Grant, Forrest Hewit, Percy Lancaster or Maxwell Reekie from exhibiting. Lowry's contribution, *The Footbridge*, "ignores the strange new aspects of the drab town life he knows so well," according to Senior. Forrest Hewit contributed one of the *tours-de-force* of the 1941 show. *The Calico Printer's Ball, 1882* was made up of detailed figures in period costume set in the imposing Gothic architecture of the Manchester Town Hall interior. Hewit was a director of the Calico Printers' Association.

Derek Senior did, however, get an opportunity to see current war paintings in an exhibition brought to Manchester by the Ministry of Information. The exhibition, in January 1941, was of paintings by official war artists. In the middle of January Senior noted that a predominantly documentary tenor ran through the work, but congratulated the authorities for having the vision to engage some "of our livelier artists" to record the condition of wartime England. Yet he felt those conditions inhibited even some of our best artists for "even on the home front inspiration sometimes flags. Francis Dodd's factory studies are dull and static." In the same way he found that air-raid damage was recorded "dispassionately" by the fine English topographic and atmospheric watercolourist, Vivian Pitchforth. Senior was difficult to please; for him the more emotive and romantic renderings of Graham Sutherland's vision was lurid. He most enjoyed the pen and watercolour sketches by Anthony Gross, which were preferred to what he termed Edward Ardizzone's "stylized semi-comic sketches."

Events of the latter part of 1941 included the acquisition by Manchester City Art Gallery of James Chettle's *War Memorial.* The traditional image in English painting of the picturesque castle, left in partial ruin by the gentle passage of time, is here duplicated but with the very different suggestion of more immediate and violent damage. James Chettle, in his capacity as Academy President, opened a one-man exhibition of Lowry's work at Salford in October. The 54 picture retrospective covered a 20 year period. Derek Senior, who was in the early 1940's singlehandedly the chief spokesman for the Manchester art scene, found the recent Lowry paintings on display less optimistic, though this would presumably have pleased a critic who wanted Academy exhibits to veer away from the tranquil towards a frank and realist statement of the effects of war. "There is still a vein of humour, but the smile is withered by a fiercer undertone of bitterness," Senior wrote in the *Guardian* in October 1941. This darker mood may have had less to do with the war than with the loss of his mother, who had died in 1938, at the very moment when Lowry's labours over 20 years had reaped the reward of an impending exhibition in London. The event that marked his crucial breakthrough was, tragically, not one he was able to share with his revered mother. The pictures from this forlorn period that epitomised "the undertone of bitterness" were the disparate *Head of a Man* (1938), the lonely *Bedroom, Pendlebury* (1940) and the sombrely coloured *Blitzed Site* (1942). The latter is a rare example of Lowry's recording in direct, tangible terms the effects of war. *Blitzed Site* to some extent fulfilled Derek Senior's wish that Lowry paint Manchester's war. The critic explained that Lowry's preoccupation with the seamier aspects of life "is enforced by his honesty of vision and stimulated by freedom from the distraction of 'beauty.' The conditions of war would not have radically shaken the foundations of an already pessimistic integral vision that, come rain or shine in external ever changing circumstances, found its apotheosis in Lowry's frequent reference to the 'battle of life'." Yet by 1943, in a notable picture like *Britain at Play*, based on Angel Fields, Manchester, Lowry

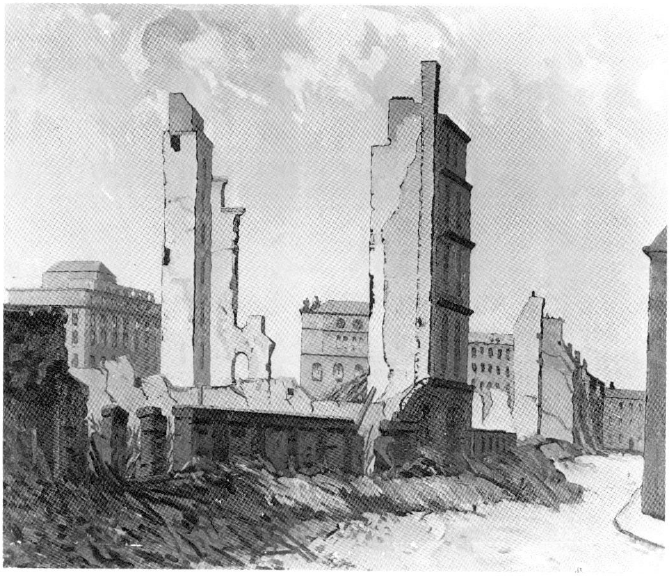

James Chettle: War Memorial, Manchester, *oil 1941 Harold Workman:* Printing camouflage cloth, *oil (both illustrations courtesy: Manchester City Art Gallery).*

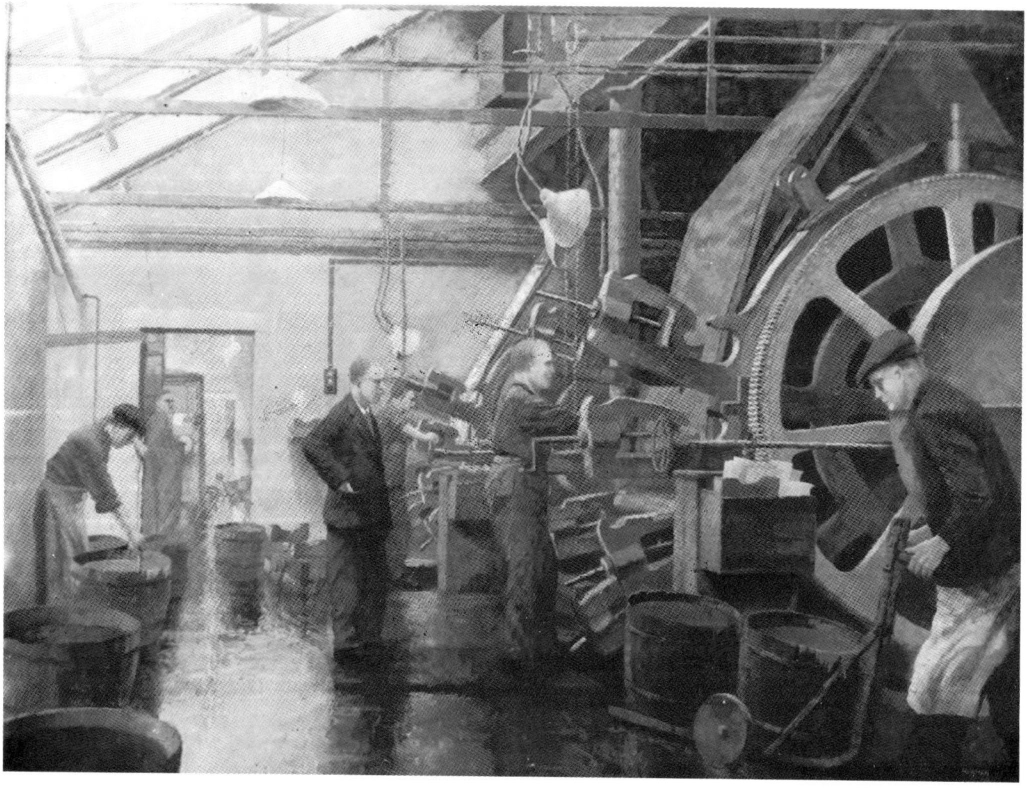

showed himself in much brighter, optimistic mood.

The Spring exhibition of 1942 was an altogether bigger affair, attracting a third more exhibits than the previous year's total, and featuring 150 artists. Continuing the theme of a greater overall consistency of middling quality, Senior remarked that there seemed "fewer first rate pictures than there used to be - but there are fewer bad ones." Portraits appeared to be particularly common with Pamela Fisher and Emmanuel Levy exhibiting 'outstanding' examples of this *genre*. But the most significant feature of the exhibition, Senior wrote, "is the interest which some of the artists are beginning at last to take in the aesthetic aspects of a world at war . . . some are content to record the picturesqueness with which bombs, no less than time, can clothe a ruin. But Lowry's *Street Scene* hurts like a broken tooth, and John Copley's *Destruction* - the finest picture in the show - makes grey faced figures beside wreckage expressive not only of poignant emotions but also of a bitter sense of unreason."

The beginning of 1943 saw a second Lowry exhibition at the Lefevre Gallery in London, a show that included the picture *Britain at Play* which Eric Newton described in the *Sunday Times*: "the Satanic mills of South Lancashire, the cobbled streets crowded with a strange beetle-like race of men and women and dogs, the smoke-laden skies." At the same time the Manchester Academy Spring Show was a source of new enthusiasm for Manchester's senior critic who could write that "the general improvement is the more striking because several distinguished members are not represented this year; Dugdale, Cundall, and Lowry are conspicuously absent. But by way of compensation other regular exhibitors have excelled themselves." As in the previous year, Senior found John Copley author of the best contribution, though "Emmanuel Levy emerges as a serious picture maker in full control of his exceptional abilities with *Europe* 1942." Levy's empathy with the plight of his fellow Jewish people was a regular theme in his work, and the depths of the war gave the Mancunian Jew from Cheetham Hill prime motive to express that empathy. Chettle and Hewit were praised for use of colour and brushwork, while John Bowes - a later exhibitor in the Midday Studios group - and Janet Kirk were also favourably mentioned.

The Spring exhibition of 1944 was the 85th of the Manchester Academy's history. The exhibition saw contributions from artists who would become prominent in the post-war Manchester art scene. These included Theodore Major (who contributed an impastoed, Vlaminck-like still life *Rhododendrons)*, Arthur Hilton, Harold Hemingway, John Bold, Leila Haffar, Brian Bradshaw and Richard Weisbrod. In July, Lawrence

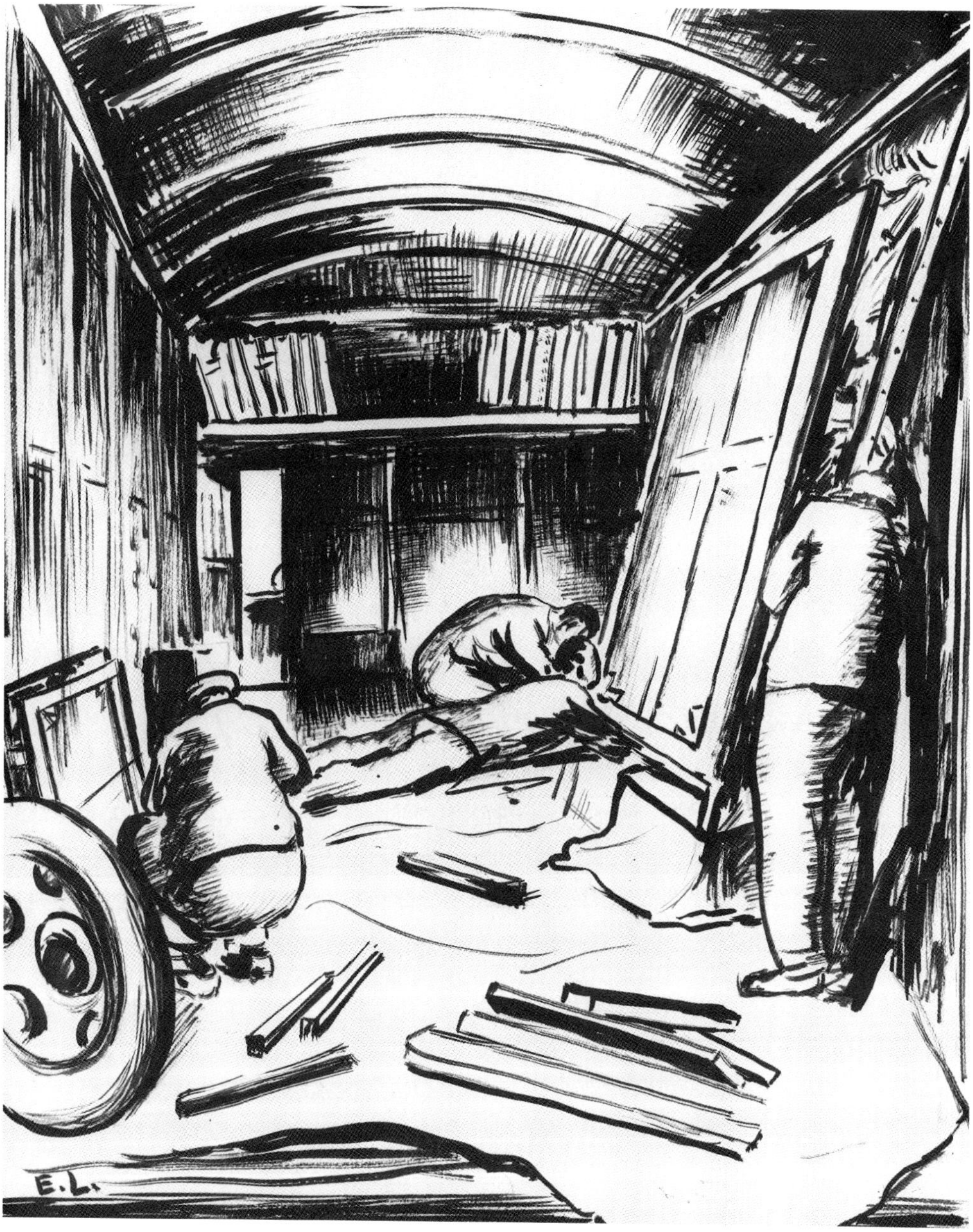

Emmanuel Levy: Loading the Pictures, Aberystwyth, *pen and ink 1945 (courtesy: Manchester City Art Gallery).*

Haward retired from the Manchester Art Gallery, where he had curated since 1914. Haward's successor was David Baxandall, who had served with the Royal Air Force and been a Keeper of Art at the National Museum of Wales. To mark the end of Haward's extraordinary service on Mosley Street, the Manchester Art Gallery Committee commissioned Henry Lamb to paint his portrait. They had been friends for many years, drawn together not only through art, but also through a shared love of music and literature. Answering some controversy concerning the likeness of Lamb's portrait, Haward wrote in the *Guardian* that "in fifty years time it won't matter who it looks like, what will matter is that Manchester will possess an exceptionally fine painting."

Several notable Academy people died during the war. Elizabeth Chapman, a former honorary treasurer, and Oswald Garside were two, while James Chettle, the President, died at the end of 1944. Born in Sale, Chettle came from a merchant family, and himself ran a textile firm. He was elected President of the Academy in 1934 (he had joined in 1927) and was the first non-professional painter to become President. His colleague Maxwell Reekie affectionately wrote that his "subjects were mainly landscape and his favourite haunts were the uplands of Derbyshire and the low-lying marshes of Suffolk. No fewer than 15 public galleries have bought examples. He was a man of kindly and sympathetic nature. All that he asked for was sincerity." The loss of Chettle was noted by Senior in his review of the Academy's 1945 exhibition, which he found inferior to the previous year's: "it is as though the whole Society had been subdued by the loss of its president." Although Senior felt that "John Bold and Emmanuel Levy show signs of fresh development, the one in design and the other in colour," he regretted that an exhibition again without the stalwarts contained "little that stimulates." He did however, cite newcomers like Terry McGlynn, Richard Weisbrod, and Harold Hemingway as containing sparks of promise for the future.

An interesting outcome of the war, and indeed of Lawrence Haward's long and distinguished career at the City Art Gallery, was a scheme initiated by Haward for paintings to record war-time Manchester Industry. Haward wrote in the *Guardian* that he wanted to see art express the behind-the-scenes industrial war effort, an aspect that was as crucial to victory as the fighting on the front. What made this theme so important to Manchester was that all the war industries were represented in Manchester. By recording the chief industries a precise identification could be made of Manchester's huge contribution to the war effort. Haward approached the big firms and asked them "to commission certain artists . . . to make records of what was considered each firm's main contribution to the war, which the directors would then present to the art gallery. In this way the citizens of Manchester would be able to see pictures of the industries on which the prosperity of their own city largely depended . . ." Seven engineering firms participated, including the research laboratories of I.C.I. and the Shirley Institute. Haward declared that he "only had to put the case clearly to have it received in a most friendly and co-operative spirit and with a northern determination to see the job properly through." There were three main criteria for choosing what aspect of the firm's work in the war effort to depict. Firstly, the pictorial suitability of a particular activity then the intelligibility and communicative power of the final image that would be offered to the public, and finally the degree to which a chosen theme was typical of the firm's overall output.

The works that resulted were nine drawings produced by Henry Lamb in the Rosser Factories, Trafford Park; a William Grimmond painting of Avro Lancaster bombers in their factory at Roe; a Francis Dodd picture *Delivering the Goods* depicting the Renold and Coventry Chain Company in Manchester. Charles Cundall worked in the 'D' Aisle of the Metropolitan-Vickers factory, while Henry Rushbury used his documentary skills to illustrate the Manchester Docks from Trafford Wharf. Lithographs like *Cathode Ray Tubes* by Ethel Gabain were produced at Ferranti's, while Harold Workman's *Printing Camouflage Cloth* was presented by Simpson and Godlee to the Manchester City Art Gallery. In addition to having the specific reference point of wartime industrial production, their works fall more generally in the wider category of industrial painting that not only typifies the 'northern school' in purest terms, but also reflects a *genre* within British art as a whole. Laura Knight's vividly detailed factory paintings of turban-headed women at work on the production line comes immediately to mind. The inherent and marked zest of these works was, according to Haward, attributable "partly to the strange and exciting nature of the industrial scenes portrayed and partly to the fact that the artists knew that these records were planned to form a homogeneous group and to find a permanent home in the City Art Gallery." The Haward project marked the end of his remarkable professional contribution to Manchester art and also resulted in an enduring artistic record of the war.

Six

Manchester Academy: 1946-59

Manchester could scarcely have chosen a better way to celebrate the end of the war than by having an exhibition of recent work by Picasso at the City Art Gallery. Ironically, some of this work had been created by an artist who was dreaming and lying low in Nazi-occupied Paris. The Picassos generated much controversy in the Manchester newspapers. John Gauld, a head of Bolton School of Art and a future Academy President, wrote about a hedonistic or, at best, an aesthetic pleasure at work behind what he termed Picasso's "self-expression through a kind of hieroglyphic art." Unlike *Guernica*, the Manchester Picassos did not seem to Gauld to express the true horrors of war. Derek Senior, on the other hand, waded into the arguments over the Picassos and remarked in the *Guardian* that recent modern art escaped from academic decadence, in a quest for essential content and true plasticity. This he claimed led to an integrity and coherence in the visual arts that would appeal to and promote aesthetic experience. Although impressed with Picasso, Senior criticised the newly founded Arts Council for putting on a misleading selection of recent Picassos that by virtue of their newness were unrepresentative of the formative phases that led up to his 1940's work. Nevertheless, Senior responded to the "joyous brilliance" of *Royan* and the "splendid vitality" of *Still Life - Skull with Leeks*, descriptions that adequately sum up our common assessments of Picasso's value today. The inevitable denigratory advance publicity for the show was swept aside by Senior, who, being the sharp critic that he was, could not fail to appreciate the importance to Manchester of an airing of the recent paintings from the greatest living artist. Picasso had an enormous post-war influence on many contemporary British (not to mention Continental) painters - the neo-romantic painters were only one group under his spell - some of whom were themselves soon to show work in Manchester.

The imaginative wartime scheme initiated by Lawrence Haward had the desired effect of employing Manchester Academy artists to document the city's industrial contributions to the war effort. This project went some way towards introducing a greater degree of honesty and realism into Manchester art. At the same time Haward's project recalled the civic commissioning of the celebrated Ford Madox Brown murals in Manchester

Town Hall. Both projects pinpointed Manchester's civic pride in the unique blend of heroic labour and industrial enterprise - though the artists chosen to illustrate the city's industrial war effort came far closer than the Victorian murals to an authentic celebration of its industrial importance. The phenomenon was an antidote to valid criticisms made by several newspapers concerning the "escapology" or "placid temper" of early wartime Academy exhibitions. It has been noted how Derek Senior found Francis Dodd's factory scenes "dull and static" and Vivian Pitchforth's scenes of bomb damage dispassionately recorded. Even before the war started the *Daily Mail* had run the telling headline 'Artists Won't Paint their Own City,' in response to a Manchester Academy exhibition that included no more than a couple of pictures about Manchester. Even Lowry's wartime painting avoided any direct comment on the emotional and human costs of the war. Although Lowry's work, with its psychological distance, touched upon philosophical truths about the human condition, it is doubtful whether his work ever penetrated the hard realism expressive of the social or political conditions that moulded the life and times of the world he dispassionately looked at. In the capacity of a wartime fire warden, Lowry experienced many a morning after the blitz. One painting that resulted from these walk-abouts was *Blitzed Site*. The central image is of a man, bewildered and shell-shocked, rising from the wreckage of a bombed house. The expressed theme of the picture is not so much of the pity of war, as of the unusual empathy that the artist felt towards dereliction, loneliness and abandonment. Such themes, filled with autobiographical intensity, had long served Lowry's vision, whether in war or peace.

The sunny disposition of the Manchester Academy exhibitions did, however, slowly begin to change during the 1940's - a number of prominent, older generation, traditional artists died during that decade - bringing a more realist pictorial tenor that would be in keeping with the general move in the post-war period towards a more socially committed art. The Academy, while continuing to represent a hybrid collection of styles, started to accommodate a new generation - Harold Hemingway, Alan Lowndes, Roger Hampson, Theodore Major, Brian Bradshaw among them - who seemed to represent an authentic Lancashire voice contributing towards post-war realism. The so-called 'kitchen sink' realists, artists like Bratby, Middleditch, Greaves and Fullard, represented England's most coherent version of a wider European realist movement that used the khakis, ochres and greys of the ration book economy. The contemporaneous rise of American Abstract Expressionism, drawing on Surrealist, Primitivist, and Post-Cubist sources, was an opposite, very un-English alternative that began to emerge during the second half of the 1950's. This proved to be a style irresistible to progressive British artists who wanted to identify with the modernist mainstream. In the context of these international historical currents, Lancashire and in particular Manchester art would inevitably make only a partial, provincial contribution. As the contents of post-war Manchester Academy exhibitions swung gradually away from the pretty postcard imagery or rustic idealism of the 1930's, so it was replaced by examples of a sometimes parochial realism. In the meantime reactionary forces like Maxwell Reekie, James Chettle, or most vociferously Hal Yates, made sure that the new abstract painting - what Yates called 'monkey painting' - was resisted head on.

The first post-war Academy exhibition, held in the spring of 1946, therefore witnessed a blending of older stalwarts - William Grimmond, Maxwell Reekie, Tom Dugdale and Charles Cundall among them - with the new generation. One of the younger painters, Harold Hemingway, contributed a relevant piece of contemporary documentation, *V.E. Day, Lancashire*, an admirable painting that portrayed the roof tops and chimneys of a Lancashire town with a remarkable degree of mastery over the close-in topographical detail of townscape painting at its best. The picture recalled both the Poole townscapes of the 1920's by Henry Lamb, and the urban views of Charles Cundall. Another Hemingway, *Cabbages in Cumberland*, was praised for its decorative, down-to-earth quality that anticipated, in rural terms, the mundane scenario favoured by the 'kitchen sink' realists. In a rather more conventional vein, John Gauld showed *The New Necklace*, which portrayed a mother sitting at a bedroom mirror with her daughter looking on. In spite of its admirable craftsmanship, the picture looked back rather than forward, recalling the smart Edwardian interiors of Orpen, the later work of the Newlyn painter Harold Harvey, or of Gerald Brockhurst and Meredith Frampton. The new mix of pre- and post-war artists was alluded to by *Guardian* reviewer Derek Senior. He suggested that a "mixture of dignity, accomplishment, and well bred dilettantism with a modest leaven of good painting bring back old times." An English talent for watercolour was noted, allowing Norman Janes, William Grimmond, John Gauld and Charles Tunnicliffe a newsworthiness for being exemplary exponents of this medium. At about this time Lord Crawford reopened the Whitworth Gallery, following repair work to damage sustained from a direct enemy hit on the Royal Infirmary nearby.

The next two Academy exhibitions were thriving events. The 1947 show displayed nearly 300 works (from over 700 submitted).

Controversially, nearly three-quarters of the selected works were by members, and the exhibition led to a much publicised debate between Ned Owens, then representing the rival Midday Studios, and Academy President Maxwell Reekie. Owens offered the Midday Studios as a kind of 'Salon des Refusés' for those outsiders he felt unfairly rejected by Academy nepotism and élitism. Reekie, meanwhile, defended the Academy by vouching that selection panellists would judge both members and artists off the street with impartiality. Derek Senior did not see the issue of selection procedures as being significant, but wrote that "academicism is not necessarily inconsistent with spiritual enterprise and intensity of feeling or even with technical experiment. The trouble with this show is that the bulk of it is laboured, pretentious, and dull." He speculated that much of the work was the result of uninspired force of habit. He undoubtedly also felt that the Academy could only be as good as the overall quality of art that Manchester could produce. Theodore Major's powerful *Kippers*, glowing with Vlaminck-like colour and rich impasto, was deemed "out of place" in the Academy context, whilst older stalwarts like Lamb, Cundall and Dugdale - who were of proven stature and undeniable appeal - seemed to Senior to be represented "only in the ceremonial sense." Whatever imperfections may have been perceived, nearly 60 works sold from an exhibition that drew almost 22,000 visitors.

The following exhibition, in early 1948, had Senior commenting positively on "heartening signs of . . . emergence from a rut." Despite, or perhaps because of, the absence of Cundall and Lamb, Senior's optimism was based on the fact that "a liberal welcome has been given to unorthodox talents and promising beginners." These "promising beginners" would include Terry McGlynn, Harold Hemingway and Fred Yates. Margo Ingham made a rare contribution to this exhibition while Ian Grant showed four pictures, including a typical semi-rural scene near his Stockport home, *The Canal, Marple*. Frank Dodman showed a series of Arran landscapes (a subject also used by John Bold), while Kenneth Craddock exhibited Herefordshire wood engravings. Kenneth Craddock (who later attracted Bolton painter Roger Hampson to teach at Hereford School of Art) became one of a number of Bolton artists who distinguished themselves in Academy exhibitions. Others were John Gauld, Stella Platts and Brian Bradshaw.

Two prominent Manchester Academy artists died in the winter of 1948/9. Maxwell Reekie died, aged 80, at his West Didsbury home. Reekie, a local man, of Scottish parents, was educated at Manchester Grammar School. He became a director of Manchester Chamber of Commerce, a president of the Royal Manchester Institution, and a member

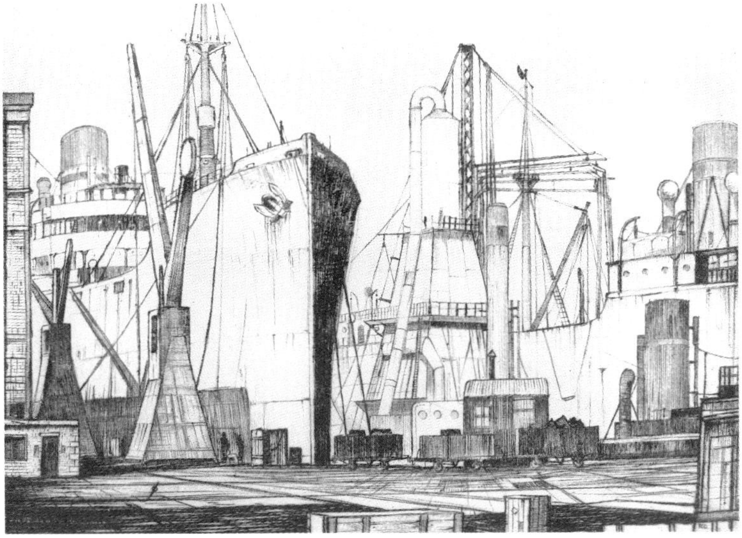

Frank Dodman: Manchester Dock, *drypoint 1940s.*

Norman Jaques: Three Trees, *oil.*

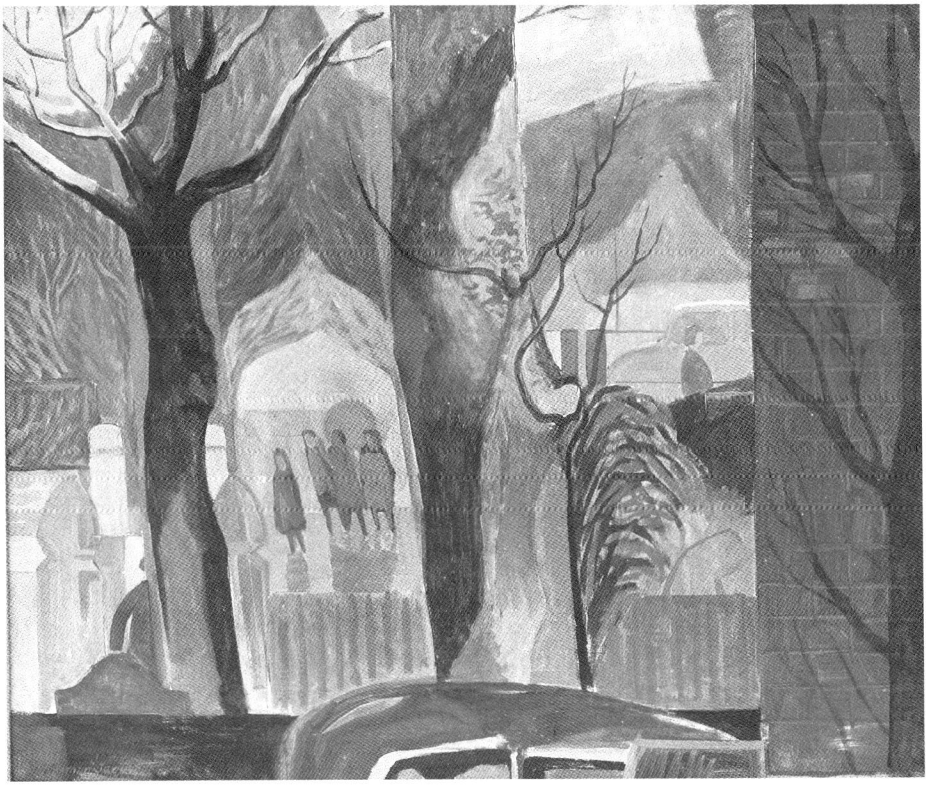

of both the Manchester Reform Club and the Graphic Club. Such a high level of active involvement with the civic and business affairs of the city was common for many Academicians during the first half of this century. The post-war experience was a different one - young, art school-trained painters emerged with avant garde leanings in aesthetics, and left-wing sympathies in politics. Reekie was a Liberal of the old school, and in 1938 was awarded the Heywood Medal for an outstanding contribution to Manchester life. The other loss that winter was of Francis Dodd, who died during the spring show of 1949, the Academy's 90th annual exhibition. Dodd was quintessentially one of the grand old men of Manchester art. He was born in 1874 in Glasgow, the son of a Wesleyan minister. Dodd studied under Newbery at Glasgow, where his outstanding promise won him a scholarship to Paris and Italy. In Paris, Dodd visited Whistler who warmed to him and advised a trip to see the Tintorettos in Italy. This he did, and after returning from the Continent settled in Manchester, embarking on a series of pastel drawings depicting Manchester suburbs. Having received invaluable advice from Whistler, Dodd went on to become an important source of encouragement for many of his contemporaries. Henry Lamb, for instance, was persuaded by Dodd to give up medical studies for the life of an artist. In 1897 Dodd met Joseph Knight, the head of Bury School of Art, who introduced him to Isobel Dacre. Dacre, a leading Manchester artist, exerted a great influence and Dodd used his considerable gifts to produce many portraits of her, one of which, *Signora Lotto*, is in the Manchester City Art Gallery. Among the many other artists whom Dodd painted were: Henry Lamb, Muirhead Bone, Jacob Epstein, Randolph Schwabe, George Clausen, Charles Cundall and Henry Rushbury. No doubt inheriting some of his minister father's eloquent, persuasive powers, Dodd encouraged many young artists to pursue the artist's life. He was thus a generous source of support to many young painters and his death removed from Manchester art life an irreplaceable and authentic source of inspiration.

The 1949 exhibition continued the practice of the previous couple of exhibitions and blooded fresh talent. The hanging committee was John Davies, Harold Riding and Percy Lancaster. A *News Chronicle* article by Margaret Roberts spotlighted Lowry and was headlined, in suitably Blakean terms, 'The man who paints the Dark Satanic Mills.'[2] Lowry's habit of roaming the Oldham Road area with his sketchbook at the ready was highlighted in the feature. The artist confessed that "it has a fascination for me which I can't explain. There is something particularly squalid about it which no other district, Pendleton, Hulme, or Ancoats, possesses." While Lowry's growing reputation was assured by the increasing effectiveness of the media after the war, Manchester saw out the final months of the 1940's with a succession of exhibitions featuring the work of protégés. The City Art Gallery showed Henry Moore's work. Robert Colquhoun, Robert McBryde and John Minton were shown at the Midday Studios. The St George's Gallery exhibited new German paintings (Nolde included) while the Whitworth Art Gallery exhibited modern German art (prints and drawings) at the end of the year. John Willett, later to become an acclaimed writer on art of the Weimar period, wrote sympathetically on German art, which he described as possessing "a coherence which no other country could boast today . . . a willingness to attempt the big scale treatment, its relative freedom from the wish to be 'provocative' and its search for originality in themes rather than manner."[3] An Arts Council exhibition of Polish Folk Art, shown at the City Art Gallery, rounded off a lively series of thought-provoking exhibitions.

John Willett's enthusiasm for the German art shown in Manchester during 1949 was not, however, matched by his response to the 1950 Manchester Academy exhibition. Writing in the *Guardian* at the end of January he found "a dull show, full of insipid, ugly colours, humdrum subjects, and a general atmosphere of lifelessness. What Manchester thinks today (or rather, Monday) London thought 30 years ago: Paris and Rome perhaps never thought it at all. This is a sad contrast with the exhibition of art students' work which has just ended at the Manchester School of Art."[4] Willett continued to rub in salt by lamenting that the show "recalls the jigsaw puzzles and tradesmen's calendars of its childhood." Norman Janes, Percy Lancaster and Ethel Gabain were none the less described as "notable" talents, while the true "element of promise" lay with Theodore Major who conveyed a "very personal style of Wigan-cum-Vlaminck." John Bowes' Academy picture that year was striking for its unusual image of a trio of nude bathers on an industrial canal bank facing a colliery on the opposite bank. In late February Willett again exercised his critical pen, finding further fault with the exhibition of Manchester Academy rejects at the Midday Studios. The experience convinced him that "the Academy's fault is not of rejecting too many masterpieces but of letting in too much trash."[5]

Derek Senior had for many years voiced qualified criticism of cosy or unadventurous art at the Manchester Academy; now, with a new and less charitable critic in John Willett, the *Guardian* had an outspoken and strict commentator who would take to task any feeble amateur tendencies at the Academy and elsewhere. Despite Willett's criticisms, the 1950 exhibition contained some new faces and marked several new points of departure. Alan Lowndes showed a portrait, *Audrey*, the first of his contributions to any exhibition in Manchester. The inclusion of a portrait from the hand of a painter more accustomed to, and specialising in, the urban scene of his native Stockport, is further evidence of the Manchester Academy's bias against pictures depicting the industrial locality. Lowndes' evening class tutor at Stockport, Emmanuel Levy, also showed a portrait, his *Man in a Rust Coloured Coat* presenting an image of Nicholas Horsfield. Henry Lamb's *Henrietta* was a personal depiction of his daughter, who was then aged 19.

In June, shortly after the spring exhibition of 1950, an exhibition of Manchester Academy members was seen at Rochdale Art Gallery. Arnold Taylor wrote a highly complimentary review, discerning in the work of the northern painters a "strong colour emphasis - a reaction against the common drabness of the lighting in this district." Thus in the hands of younger painters like Terry McGlynn, Fred Yates or Alan Lowndes colour could emerge as a primary expressive element while still portraying local north-western subjects. Alan Lowndes, in particular, portrayed Stockport with rich, variable and expressionistic use of colour. This prompted John Willett to praise the artist's "highly personal" April show at the Crane gallery. Arnold Taylor admired in the Rochdale show "the impulsive brush work" of Fred Yates and the liveliness of Terry McGlynn's handling of paint which "stimulates movement in his works by swiftly running dark lines." Among more traditional practitioners, Tom Dugdale, Forrest Hewit, Norman Janes and William Grimmond were also mentioned. In the autumn of 1950 an exhibition, *Modern Italian Art*, circulated by the Arts Council, was seen at the City Art Gallery in Manchester, and no doubt had an inspiring effect on the more progressive spirits in the city.

The gathering pace of change and the emergence of a group of artists who brought a new complexion to the post-war art scene in Manchester was made even more evident by the deaths of three important artists of the old, pre-war Manchester art scene. John Copley, his wife Ethel Gabain, and Percy Lancaster all died during 1950. Copley was born in Manchester, and as a young man received inspiration and encouragement from Ford Madox Brown, when the Pre-Raphaelite was working on the murals in Manchester Town Hall. From Brown Copley learnt about the structure and movement of the human body, though his formal education was gained from the Royal Academy Schools. Here he began making lithographs, a medium for which he showed real aptitude. In the late 1930's Copley turned his talents to etching as well as to tempera and oil painting. Copley's use of lithography was matched by Ethel Gabain Copley, whose *Cathode Ray Tubes*, produced at the firm Ferranti, was part of Lawrence Haward's war artists initiative in

Manchester. In November 1950 the death of Percy Lancaster represented the loss of one of the most popular and expert exponents of the Lancashire rural landscape. Lancaster, a kind of northern Vivian Pitchforth, was born in Manchester in 1878 and studied at the Stockport School of Art before training as an architect. In spite of this architectural training, Lancaster's work concentrated on rural Welsh or Lake District subjects. An underlying order and design imposed themselves and became translated in terms of an unobtrusive, pictorial pattern that implicitly upheld and enhanced the naturalism and atmosphere of his watercolour landscapes. Lancaster's obituary said that "he had sufficient sensibility to the actual scene not to try to impose a preconceived design upon it." The adoption of Lakeland subjects owed something to his friendship with Heaton Cooper, who ran a shop and gallery in Keswick. For many years Lancaster served on both the selection and hanging committees of the Manchester Academy.

The relevance of the work that Percy Lancaster and his colleagues exhibited was called into question by the new *Guardian* critic John Willett, who wrote disparagingly of the spring 1951 exhibition. Willett noted "the prevalence in the paintings of uninteresting, muddy colour and the banality of the subjects chosen, which so frequently seem to boil down to 'How I enjoyed my holiday': the same old streams, woods, mountains and shores, seen with no very fresh eye."[6] Quintessential Percy Lancasters and Lamorna Birches represented the peak achievements of a whole array of paintings presenting this kind of pretty or picturesque subject matter, which for many years had been a dominant feature of the Academy walls. The success of a painter like Bolton's Roger Hampson, who emerged during the 1950's and was later to become an Academy President, lay with the ability to take on the naturalistic creed and academic excellence of artists like Lancaster or Lamorna Birch, then to substitute their idealised sunny landscapes, leafy trout valleys or harvest fields for a harder realism, based on the frank, unsentimental portrayal of the industrial architecture. Hampson was to represent less a stylistic break with past tradition and practice than a vigorous new approach to traditionally unsuitable subject matter. John Willett mentioned Theodore Major, Emmanuel Levy, Harry Rutherford and Kenneth Craddock as being artists who stood above the general level of mediocrity. The child portraits of Kenneth Craddock, of which a portrait of his son Julian was included in this 1951 exhibition, recalled Augustus John and Henry Lamb. Emmanuel Levy's portrait of his wife Ursula represented a well rehearsed subject with which the talented Manchester painter was to persevere into his and Ursula's old age. The sculpture section was, as usual in Academy exhibitions, very much an appendage, though the inclusion of a terracotta *Seated Figure* by the Eccles-born sculptor John Milne marked the beginning of a promising career by one of the most distinguished modern sculptors from Manchester.

John Milne was born in 1931, the youngest of a large family. His father was Scottish but his mother came from Derbyshire. After the war Milne, aged only 15, entered the Salford Royal Technical College where he began engineering studies to appease his career-minded father. But in 1946 his irresistible interest and talent for drawing saw his transfer to the college art department, where he spent the next four years studying art, particularly sculpture. His inquisitive mind led him to explore an eclectic range of sculpture, embracing that of Egypt and Assyria, classical Greece, as well as the versatile sculptural expressions of the modern movement. Manchester provided him with a good start; he was able to see the Egyptology collection at the City Art Gallery. The professor of classical history at Manchester University, Cosmo Rodewald, was befriended, enabling him to investigate Greek and other antique cultures in greater depth. But visits to the British Museum, and more importantly to Paris, proved of even greater value to the fast developing sculptor. Paris was an inspiration. At the Grande Chaumière he was instructed by Auricoste, and came into contact with Zadkine. Interest in the great modern sculptors of the Ecole de Paris helped Milne identify an early preference for bulky neo-classical figure sculpture - Dobson in England and Maillol in France were of particular interest to him. But so too was Rodin. Milne's early terracotta figures, such as *Seated Figure* seen in the Manchester Academy exhibition, were swelling, voluptuous forms, full of anatomical reference and finished with naturalistic devices such as the ripples of thin drapery across sensual, fleshy surfaces. These early figures were Milne at his most figurative.

Referring to architecture and compounded sculptural modes of the past, Milne's later work became more architectural. Making use of the Louvre and other Paris art centres was an ideal rounding off of a conscientious art education. His trip to Greece in 1951 marked the beginnings of his post-student life, and with it the launch of an independent sculpturel career. He studied Greek archaeology and his interest in ancient architecture made itself felt in many of the abstracted forms that he later churned out in his St Ives studio. Milne's student work, in wood and terracotta, was based on modelling. Not until St Ives and his apprenticeship to Barbara Hepworth, did Milne opt for carving and bronze casting as his prime sculptural modes. From Cornwall he made frequent trips to Greece and Morocco. Association with the St Ives School in general, and Hepworth in particular, led to the adoption, in his mature work, of slick linear designs and an

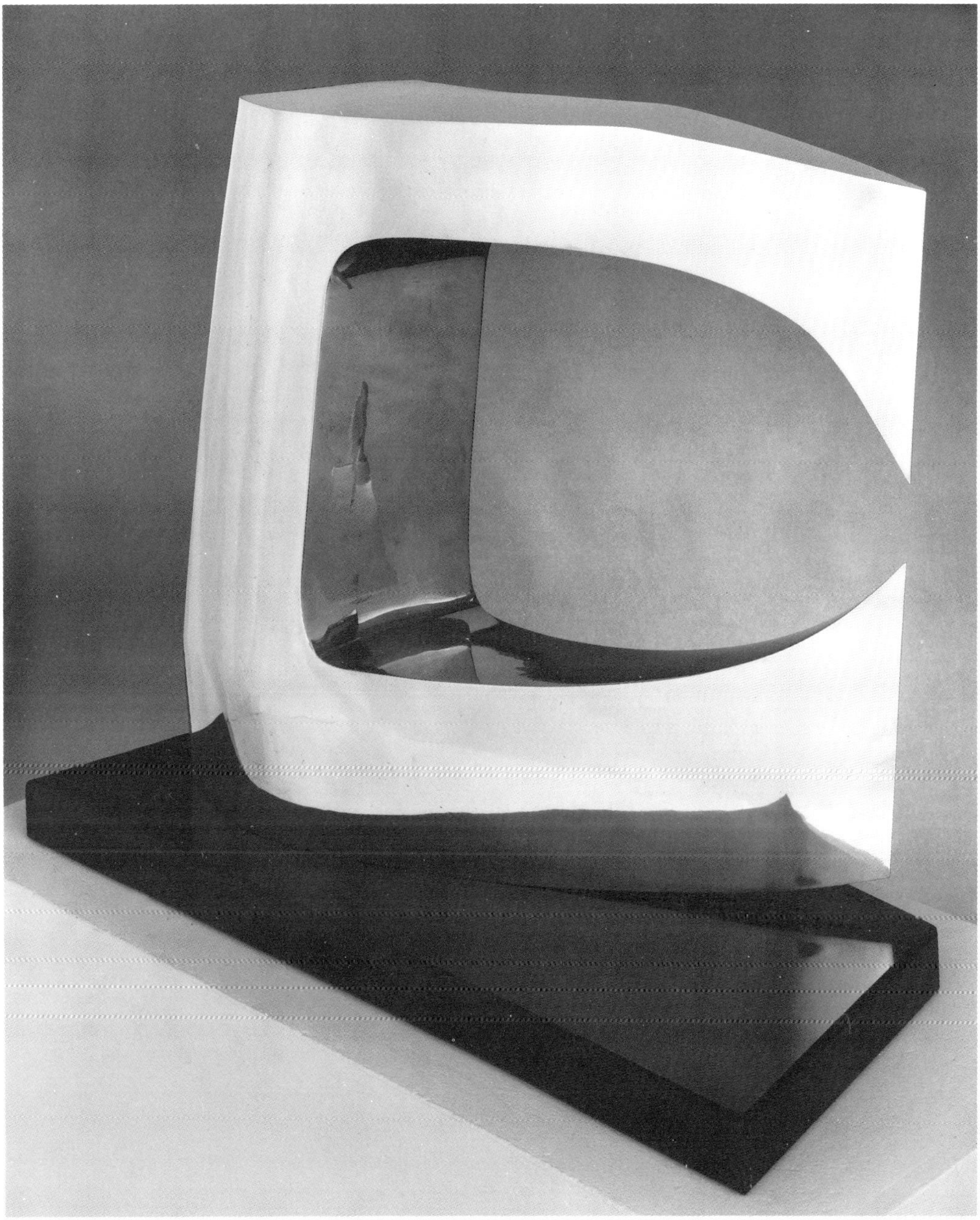

John Milne: Gnathos, *bronze 1960.*

abstract chunkiness of form.

No account of the year 1951 would be complete without consideration of the Festival of Britain and the Arts Council touring exhibition *60 Paintings for 51* which visited Manchester City Art Gallery. John Willett praised the enlightened funding that allowed contemporary British artists to work on a large scale. He equated small easel painting with a diminishing middle-class audience, and saw the large scale works suitable for public wall spaces as possessing a greater degree of accessibility to a larger number and variety of people. "It will do British painting all the good in the world if Government departments, local authorities and private firms can keep this particular ball rolling," he wrote. Citing Colquhoun, McBryde and Carel Weight as failures, Willett found Nicholson, Lanyon, Heron and Hitchens as being the custodians of excellence, and forerunners of the post-war emergence of British painting. Yet Ben Nicholson's *Still Life* 1950 proved too much for conservative members of the City Council. Councillor Westbrook suggested in a City Council meeting that the Nicholson picture "showed nothing in the way of design, or depth of colour, or perspective." The *Manchester Guardian* picked up the controversy - centred around the proposal to acquire a Ben Nicholson for the City Art Gallery - and ran a headline 'Councillors Attack Modern Art: "Product of Disordered Minds."' The proposal to buy the Nicholson was, of course, rejected. Clearly Willett was in the vanguard of radical, progressive artistic taste. His often unkind remarks about the clichéd, rustic holiday scenes that adorned Manchester Academy exhibitions bit harder than even Derek Senior's criticisms had at the conservative content of Academy exhibitions. Yet the kind of art he did support - and for Willett it would be a robust British art that successfully drew on fully understood and digested continental and modernist trends - proved anathema to the civic authorities.

The hostility aimed towards the modernist art of Nicholson came not only from the local authorities. Hal Yates, deriding what he called the 'monkey painting' of abstract or post-cubist styles, pitched into the controversy with an argumentative letter to the *Guardian*.[7] Yates' recipe for successful pictorial art was based on three time-tested pillars - verisimilitude, a balanced design to enhance an appreciable effect, and the display of an inherent sensitivity by the artist towards his chosen medium. The best works, he maintained, required all three attributes, although poetic inspiration was an unwritten quality without which a work could often appear mysteriously lifeless. Apart from what he considered were a few excellent examples from the *60 Paintings* exhibition - and they would not be the ones chosen by Willett - Yates remarked that "the only quality with which we can credit the remainder is that of size." Picking up on the William Gear painting which had been hung in the reverse way to its illustration in the catalogue, Yates dismissed the error as of no importance, since incoherence resulted in both cases. Ben Vincent replied to Yates' letter quoting Thomas Aquinas' three criteria for beauty: clarity, wholeness and consonance. "I am sure," Vincent wrote, "he looks just as handsome lying down as standing up." Hal Yates' bull-headed attitude to progressive modern art, in such marked contrast to Willett's, may be attributable in part to Yates' lack of formal artistic education. In the 1930's he had once been an unpromising amateur who had studied at the Acomb Street classes run by the Manchester Academy, yet had suddenly and surprisingly broken through to an accomplished and mature watercolour style. The flippant or easy manner of much modern art, in seeming to by-pass many sacrosanct practices, probably offended Yates' idea of art as being the outcome of honest toil and arduous struggle which he had endured in getting his own work off the ground.

The spring exhibition of 1952 was hung by Harold Riding, Harold Workman and Terry McGlynn. The "air of sobriety" that Derek Senior referred to in his review of that Academy exhibition no doubt partly reflected the social conditions of an economy still conditioned by the ration book. Senior pointed to a couple of Roger Hampson prints, less on account of any visionary power than on grounds of outstanding technical proficiency; a quality that has remained a permanent feature of the career of this sober, but none the less unusually skilled, painter and printmaker. Brian Bradshaw struck "a disturbingly fresh note," and Theodore Major "breaks new ground with a *Crucifixion* - and asserts his mastery of flower painting with a torrid canvas." Despite the *60 Paintings* exhibition that was shown on Mosley Street the previous year, few examples of progressive or abstract style seemed evident. Bob Crossley was cited as providing one of these "notable examples of unorthodox style." Crossley developed a gestural, abstract style notable for an ordered mark making using liquid paint and bright positive colour. As will become evident later in a discussion of the Rochdale artist's career, he joined the artists' colony of St Ives, Cornwall, and there found readily available sympathy for his own developing *métier*.

In August 1952 another Manchester-born artist and active Academy member, William Grimmond, died. And oil and watercolour painter, Grimmond was a product of Manchester School of Art and later worked as an architectural draughtsman, which explains his interest in and mastery of the residential buildings of North London. Among his achievements were book designs for the King Penguin series, a spell as Director of the London

Press Exchange, and regular contributions to both Manchester Academy and Royal Academy exhibitions. Another loss came in November, of an even greater member, Thomas Dugdale, who was born in Blackburn in 1880. Dugdale, educated at Manchester Grammar School, Manchester School of Art and finally the Royal College of Art, went to Paris and served in Egypt, the Balkans and the Middle East during the Great War. Manchester has several Dugdale watercolours that depict war episodes in the Middle East. In the 1920's he turned to oil portraiture and became one of the foremost practitioners of his generation. A natural empathy with human beings enabled him to render the character of his sitters. He had a strong and independent nature that made him nobody's acolyte, though the influence of John and Orpen is apparent early on with the use of broad and generous brushwork. The *Guardian* obituary observed that the best qualities of Dugdale's temperament positively moulded his painting. The obituary added that Dugdale "let his native shrewdness in the reading of character and his northern independence in the manner of expressing it dictate his style with the result that he established an easily recognisable manner of his own and produced . . . portraits which were interesting pictorially as well as faithful likenesses."[8]

A well known and quintessential Lowry painting was a high point in the Academy exhibition of 1953, which was hung by Delia Massey, Harry Rutherford and Wilfred Wood. Lowry's *Outpatients Department of Ancoats Hospital* was commissioned by the Ancoats Hospital Medical Committee as a memorial to Peter McEvedy, a surgeon who had died in 1951. The verdict that the Lowry picture "blends humour and sympathy with the stark realism of the subject" appeared in the *Evening Chronicle*,[9] and touched on the tension implicit in any hospital scene of this kind. Although hospitals - more than any other institution - symbolised sympathy and care, the outpatient hall would in addition provide a scenario full of the nervous anticipation felt by a crowd of patients. The sordid interest in cripples and in deformed humans that is characteristic of Lowry's late work, is anticipated in this picture. Formally, the composition employs the same perspectival and architectural structures that characterise Lowry's outdoor subjects. Furthermore the floor, walls and ceilings of the hospital hall - accounting for the majority of the picture plane - are painted with the same 'all-over' scheme of creamy white that had by now become a commonly practised technique of the artist to enhance pictorial unity. The many figures scattered horizontally across a middle zone of the picture are painted in their drab, early fifties uniform of grey, black or dirty ochre, highlighted at intervals by the odd red or blue overcoat. The *Evening Chronicle* justifiably

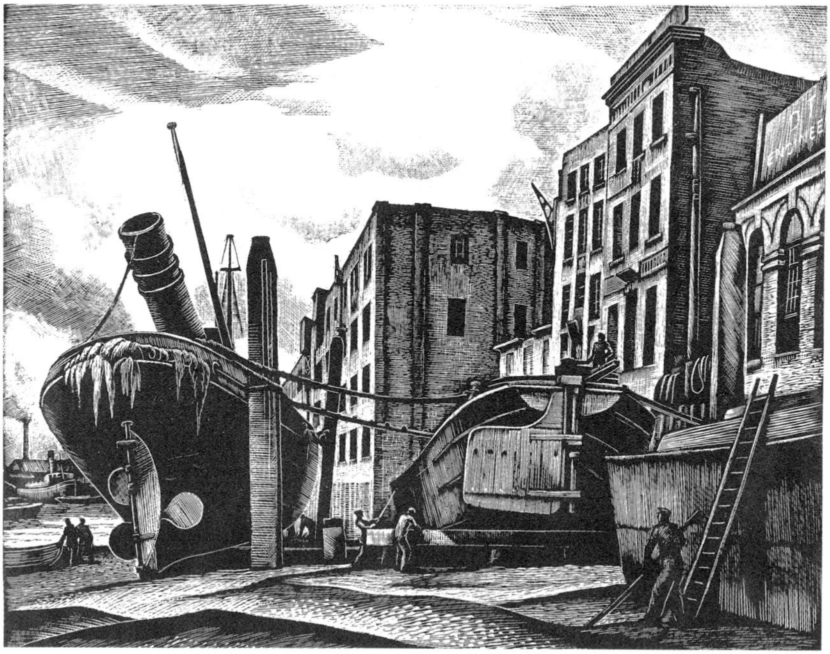

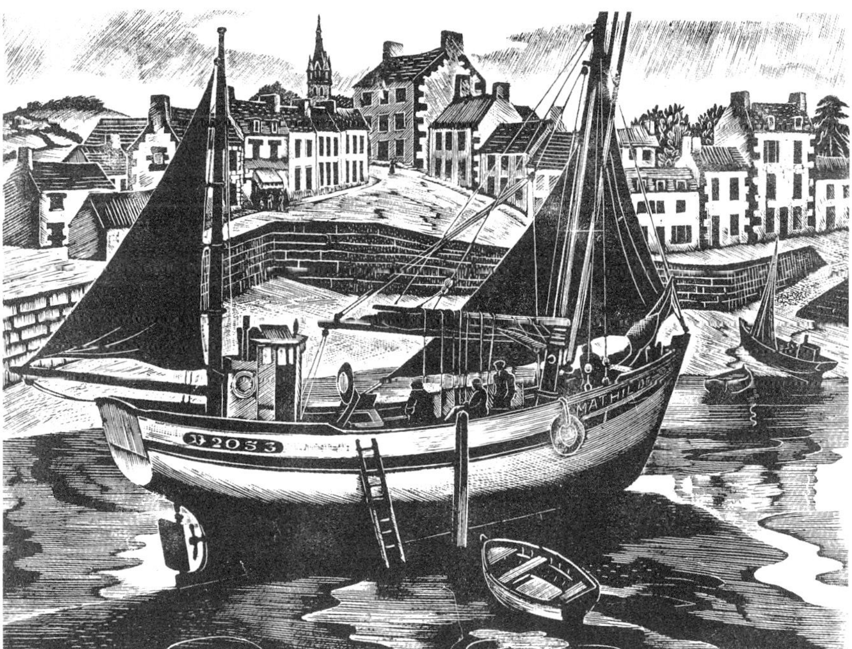

Wood engravings by Norman Janes, a regular exhibitor at the Manchester Academy.

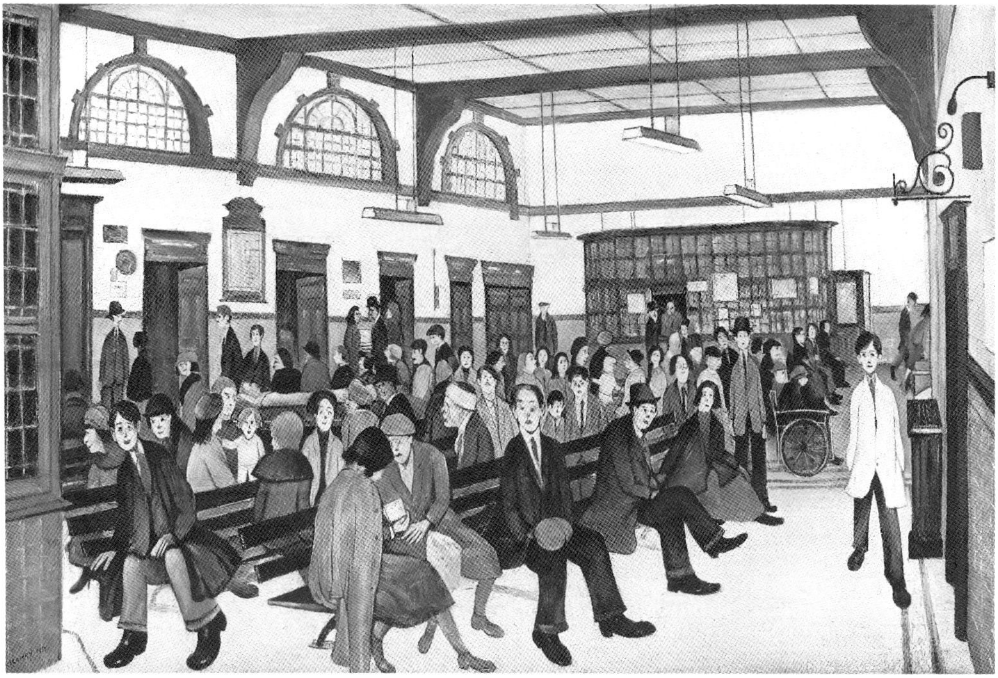

L.S. Lowry: Ancoats Hospital, Outpatients Department, *oil 1952 (courtesy: Whitworth Art Gallery).*

Below: Excavations at Manchester, *pencil on paper.*

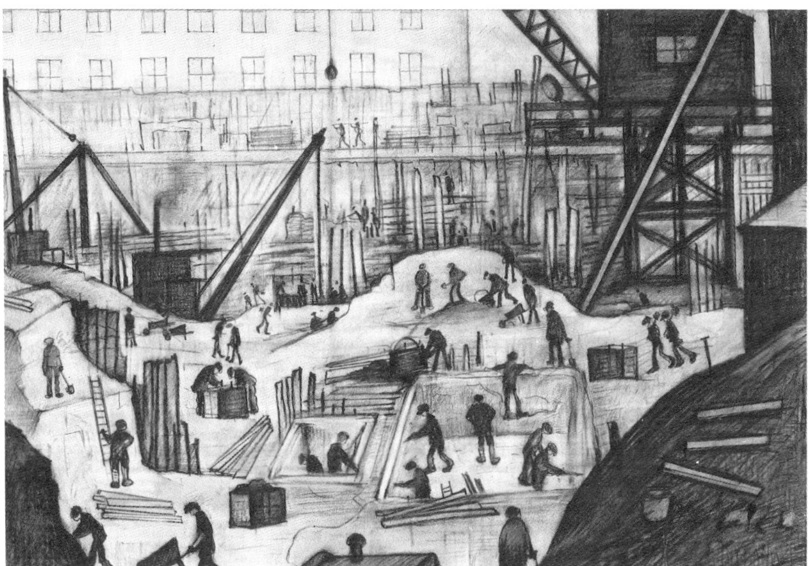

alluded to a quiet, introspective humour; not surprising in Lowry's work, though the humour is often wry and ironic. A certain kind of resignation and acceptance of the tragic side of the human condition can certainly be read into a picture of this category.

The "stark realism" the Lowry painting was considered to reveal was felt to be absent from most of the other Academy exhibits that year, although Terry McGlynn and Hal Yates, among the post-war generation, were once again credited with having "contributed several watercolours with a lively and expressive freedom of touch." The same commentator, Alan Sewter, echoed the feelings of his fellow *Guardian* critics John Willett and Derek Senior when he wrote that the show "suffers from a surfeit of technically competent but quite meaningless pictures. There are still . . . painters who delude themselves with the notion that neatly painted transcriptions of the beautiful scenery which they visit on their holidays, of the best flowers from their gardens, or the heads of their favourite uncles suffice to make works of art." This perception proved that the same tendency towards the pretty and the picturesque still dominated exhibitions.

The same commentator used a political factor - demonstrating the deepening of cold war political allegiances - with which to approach an appreciation of the next Academy exhibition in 1954. Indeed, Sewter's *Guardian* review was headlined 'Right Left and Centre in Art.'[10] Bob Crossley was cited as a left-winger in an institution dominated by the Right and Centre. The 130 artists who averaged only two exhibits each were considered "very unsatisfactory" in the sense that "too many things of no more than tolerable amateur quality have been accepted." The exhibition was criticised for chaotic hanging, inducing Sewter to advocate the setting aside of a whole room each year for two prominent Academy members. The academic right wing was associated, in Sewter's mind, with Harold Williamson's portrait of Alderman Gosling as Lord Mayor, and by Bertram Nicholl's *Conway Castle* which along with a picturesque pre-war painting like *McLellans Castle* by Academy stalwart Maxwell Reekie, continued the tradition. Sewter's claim that the impulse behind such works was the ambition to paint like a calendar reproduction of an old master should not blind us to the level of technical excellence that resided in a well worn but ultimately unimaginative range of subjects. Reekie's *McLellans Castle* (Manchester City Art Gallery) represents full control of paint and tone - the light that falls diagonally across the walls of the castle and white house in front of the ruin is reflected in a foreground river. The sensitivity to the behaviour of light and the atmospheric evocation of a time of day here reach a highly pitched level of expertise. But the idea of depicting a symbol of past feudal strength, and perhaps even imperialism, cannot avoid the rightist appellation of Sewter.

The centre ground of the politics of picture-making was held by Hal Yates, Terry McGlynn, Norman Jaques and José Christopherson, a new generation who exuded what for Sewter seemed a "vitality and individuality of style." Nevertheless Hal Yates could be as conservative as Munnings or Reekie had been before him.

A Lowry painting once again generated discussion in the 1955 Manchester Academy exhibition. The Ancoats Hospital picture only obliquely hinted at his fascination for cripples. *The Cripples* left no doubt that this was a theme that was to preoccupy Lowry frequently thereafter. The *Evening Chronicle* illustrated the picture and anticipated that it would shock the public and provoke controversy. The painting, completed in 1949 and previously exhibited in 1951 at a Lefevre exhibition, drew on the cripples and down-and-outs that Lowry collected in his mind's eye during his walks around Manchester. He wrote to David Carr, "'The Cripples' picture is progressing - I have operated on one of the gentlemen in the far distance and given him a wooden leg - I still laugh heartily at the hook on the arm of the gentleman . . . that suggestion of yours was a masterstroke."[11] The other Lowry contribution to the Academy exhibition that year was *Piccadilly Gardens, Manchester*, to my mind one of his masterpieces. Executed in 1954, the picture was first exhibited at the Whitechapel Art Gallery before its Manchester showing early in 1955. It has been noted that the painting was worked up from preliminary sketches Lowry had made as early as 1930 in Piccadilly, at the request of Lawrence Haward, then Director of the City Art Gallery. This picture, and the cripples painting, prompted the *News Chronicle* to dedicate a large two-page spread to the two contrasting aspects of city life, 'Two moods of a Northern Master'.[12]

In spite of the undeniable effect of the Lowrys there were some disagreements over the interpretation of the overall quality of the 1955 Academy exhibition. The *Daily Telegraph* found that "most exhibitors are saying much that has already been said," but admitted that "technically most of the watercolours are almost irreproachable."[13] The "quiet sparkle" of Terry McGlynn's work also struck a favourable chord, as it had many times before. In contrast to the *Telegraph's* comments, Sewter praised the liveliness of the 1955 show, applauding in particular an exhibition that seemed to him "more youthful than it has done for several years."[14] Sewter liked the "pondered and deeply felt" character of Bob Crossley's work, while Brian Bradshaw was praised for "serious and strongly designed landscapes of the Red Mountains and of Bolton." Sewter believed they

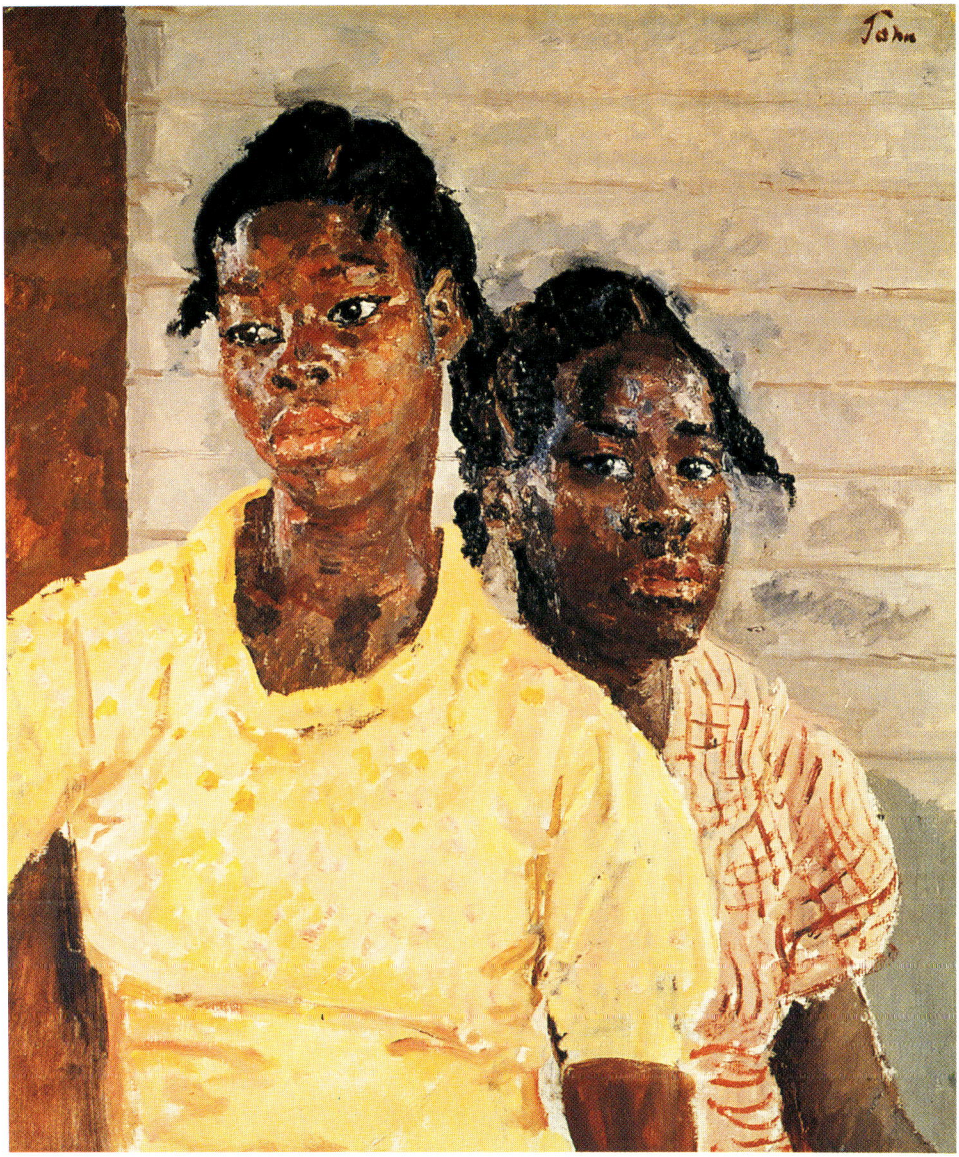

Augustus John: Two Jamaican Girls, 1937 (courtesy: Walker Art Gallery).

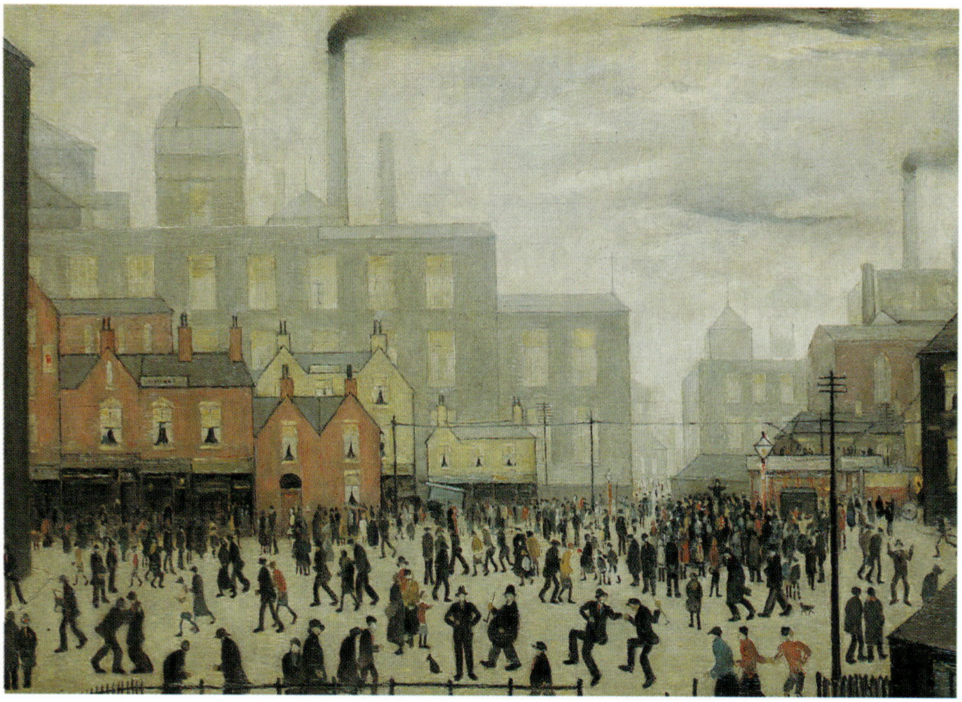

L.S. Lowry: Outside the Mill, 1928 (courtesy: Crane Kalman Gallery).

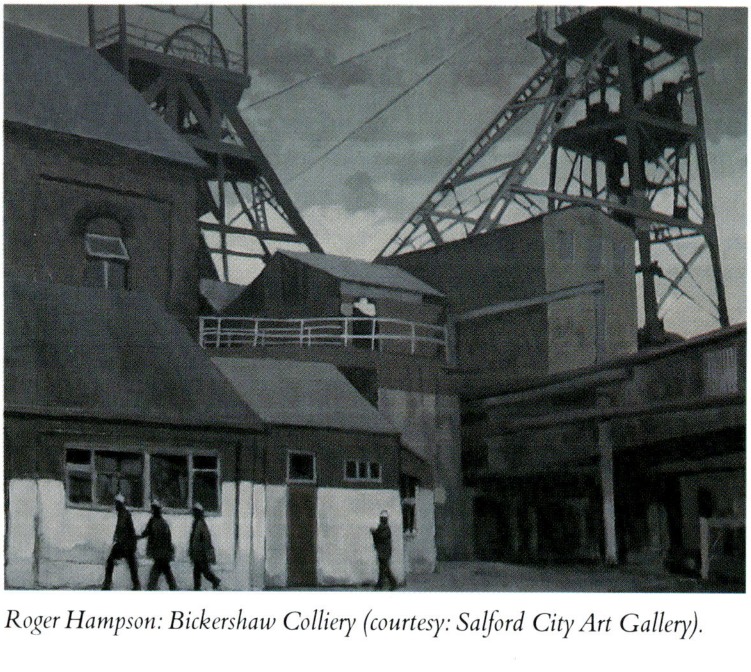

Roger Hampson: Bickershaw Colliery (courtesy: Salford City Art Gallery).

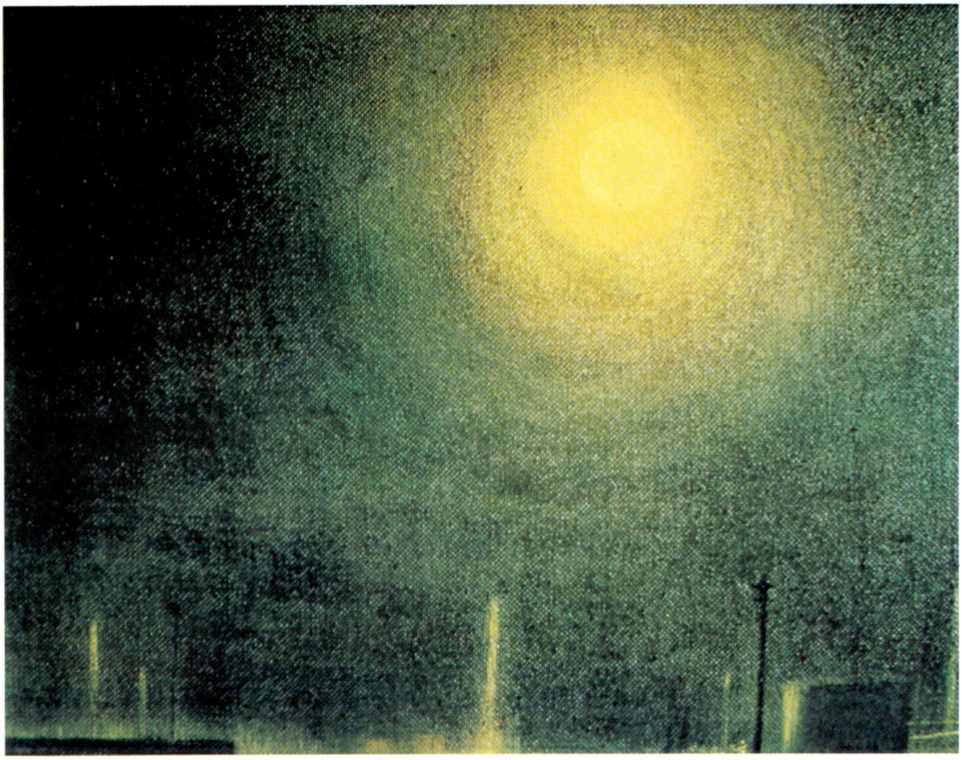

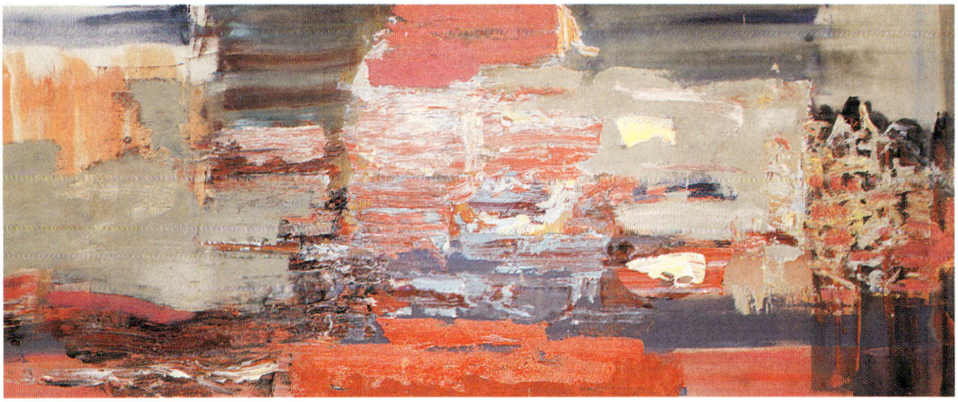

Theodore Major: Wigan Scene (courtesy: Atkinson Museum, Southport).

Peter Hoida: Weston, 1984.

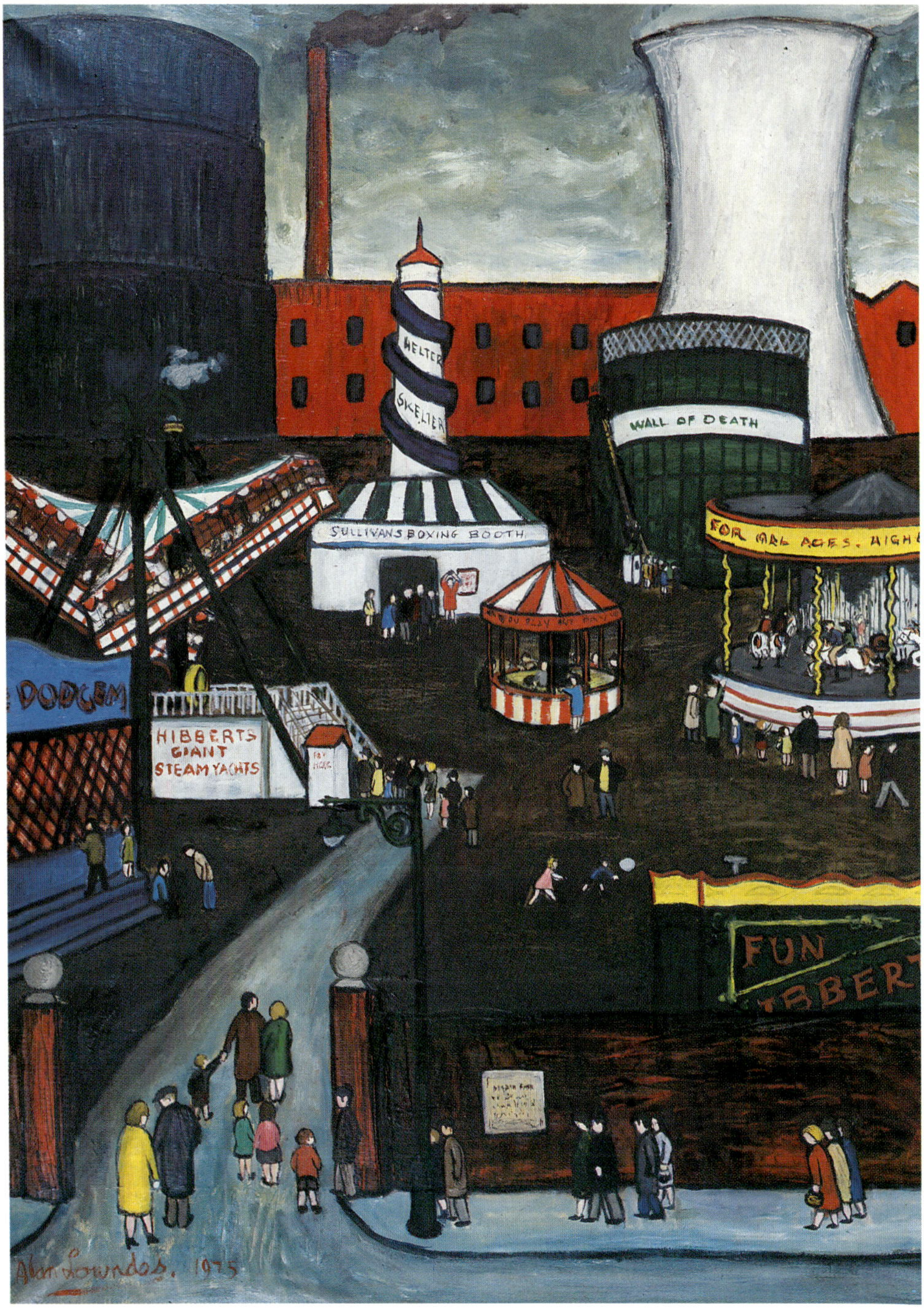

Alan Lowndes: Old Stockport Fair, 1975 (courtesy: Crane Kalman Gallery).

were "certainly among the best products of the young school of realists which has been gathering adherents in the last year." Sewter here pinpoints the mid-fifties as the period for the maturation of a group of realists. In addition to Bradshaw he would be thinking of painters like Roger Hampson, Harold Riley, Alan Lowndes and Kenneth Gribble - who all owed something to Lowry's established style, though all deviated markedly in style from that formidable example. Indeed, Bradshaw was deemed to have "developed away from Lowry by frequently following in a simplified, almost poster-like style the same kind of sober subject matter."

In a different vein the portraiture of Emmanuel Levy contributed to Sewter's detection of an improved overall quality in the Academy show, with work that appeared "cleaner and fresher in execution and in colour than before."[15] Other portrait painters, like Fred Deane and Stanley Reed, seemed to Sewter to fall between too inconsistent and variable a style in Deane's case, and "a standard photographic glossiness" in Stanley Reed's grandiloquent portraits of Lord Mayors. Sewter regretted the apparently "baneful" influence of Francis Bacon on the otherwise promising Malcolm Hughes, while Lowry, Harry Rutherford and Theodore Major all justified themselves. In September that year, members of the Manchester Academy exhibited together at Bradford's Cartwright Memorial Hall - the first time since the Academy began in 1859 that its members exhibited together outside Lancashire.

Alan Sewter detected a lapse in the 1956 Academy exhibition. Reporting again for the *Manchester Guardian*, he referred to a "bad slump" and was able to find only 40 pictures that were "tolerably good." From a total of 250 paintings, "hardly more than a dozen items show any awareness of the trends of contemporary national or international art movements. Abstraction is entirely missing; while Brian Bradshaw remains the sole representative of the younger realists."[16] Perhaps the "bad slump" can partly be explained by the absence from the 1956 show of undisputed masters like Lowry, Major, Lamb, Fitton and Cundall. Furthermore, Sewter advocated that to avoid the slump worsening into "senility" the Academy needed to recruit new blood. The outlook was not entirely bleak, however, for proficient realist painters like Kenneth Gribble and Roger Hampson were at the beginning of their Academy careers and contributing work of high quality. But one has to question why a local painter like Alan Lowndes, who by 1956 was successfully exhibiting at a rising commercial gallery and was making significant inroads into the established Cornish art colony of St Ives seemed unable, or more frequently unmotivated, to get work regularly into the Manchester exhibition.

Sewter was not alone in his admiration for Brian Bradshaw. The *News Chronicle* reported that he was "certainly the most impressive artist, his sureness of composition, clarity of detail being coupled with an enhanced sensitivity for colour."[17] The *News Chronicle* reporter referred to the "idiomatic stroke" of Richard Weisbrod's thin, Giacometti-like line work, while Bob Crossley with his "unrepentantly expressionist" style offered one of the few examples of "any awareness of the trends of contemporary art movements." The rise of Brian Bradshaw was underlined by the artist's one-man show at the now prestigious Crane Gallery in April. Despite Sewter's admiration for Bradshaw's contribution to the Academy exhibition a few weeks before, the critic found the design too much based on a linear approach that was the outcome of an artist trained in engraving techniques. While the composition seemed "well knit," Sewter found a lack of painterly richness that prompted him to prefer the charcoal drawings for being a more authentic reflection of this artist's most telling quality. He was compelled to refer to "a stolid matter of factness" in describing the mood of the Bradshaws. Further acclaim for the young Bolton painter came with a *Daily Mail* report on the year that Bradshaw had spent working and travelling in the Mediterranean. Bradshaw commented that during the year away "I saw nothing so beautiful as the road from Salford to Bolton." Bolton Art Gallery reciprocated the compliment by honouring their local artist with a one-man show. The *Guardian* touched on a raw nerve of Bradshaw's art when commenting on the blend of an "uncommonly honest" tenor with an unpromising subject matter that was "not very superficially pleasing." Sewter did, however, find pitfalls standing in the way of Bradshaw's future development. "When an artist commands a technical skill in oil paint to equal his mastery in print making," he wrote, "it is possible that his pictures may acquire a more seductive surface; but the sense of striving to encompass reality may be endangered."[18] The dilemma was not so pressing as the critic indicated. The blending of grey, thinly painted surfaces with a pronounced linear structure was a feature of much 1950's realist or kitchen sink art. The decline into indulgent impasto painting, using bright, eye-catching new pigments was no answer to a vital or honestly felt modernism, as the case of John Bratby proves.

Other events in 1956 included a Richard Weisbrod one-man show at Salford Art Gallery in August. Sewter noted the reliance in Weisbrod's art on an entangled, somewhat Gothic linear complexity and on what he termed "the contrast between the passive, open planes and the active bounding or interrupting lines" that gained immeasurably in dramatic force. Furthermore Weisbrod was credited with a period vision that "extracts from the deserted streets and squares of the Parisian suburbs in winter a certain slightly ominous and expectant atmosphere." The year was seen out with an exhibition, *Recent Abstract Painting*, at the Whitworth, an exhibition that reflected the overpowering tide of abstract painting at this time. Another exhibition, *Filling the Gaps* was at the City Art Gallery, and featured recent acquisitions. The selection included work by Vaughan, Wynter, Craxton, Freud, and also by realists such as the talented Nan Youngerman and the local man of the moment, Brian Bradshaw.

Forrest Hewit had died in the early part of 1956, a loss that represented further denuding of the old Academy bedrock which was distinguished by academic or technical excellence, if not always by innovative or challenging subjects and styles. Hewit was the amateur painter *par excellence*, who through hard work and dedication exhibited with impunity among full time professionals. Educated at Manchester Grammar School, he had to rely on brief, though valuable training, under Sickert and Dugdale at the former's private school in Manchester. Hewit made cotton his business, becoming in his time an honorary life governor of the British Cotton Industry Research Association, Vice-President of Calico Printers' Association, and Vice-President of the Federation of British Industries. He was also a member of the International Chamber of Commerce, and became a Vice-President of the Manchester Academy - an honour bestowed on account of his wide commercial experience, business acumen and immersion in the cotton industry that was so central to the economic and social life of Manchester. Hewit painted *The Delegates* as a celebration of the visit to Manchester by a group of Japanese cotton delegates. He painted full time after retiring from an extremely active business life, a luxury that led to several notable one man exhibitions. As well as exhibiting regularly with the Manchester Academy, he exhibited work at the Royal Academy and the New English Arts Club.

The Manchester Academy's 98th annual exhibition was in the spring of 1957. Over 250 exhibits by 120 artists represented "a soup in which so many ingredients have been mixed that the final flavour is utterly indeterminate."[19] The *Guardian* also illustrated what it obviously considered two prize pieces, *The Bed* by Brian Bradshaw, and James Fitton's *Self Portrait*. Sewter still seemed bogged down in the lesser issues of Bradshaw's surfaces, referring to a "hardness of surface, a rigour and tautness in his linear patterns and a deliberate avoidance of all charm in colour." Nevertheless there was a pronounced "poetic quality" in Bradshaw's striking image, couched in the terms of early Bratby, Middleditch and Bernard Buffet, of cascading sheets draped dramatically downwards from a scruffy, unmade bed in a dark, unappealing interior. The theme, of course, relates back to Sickert's or Gore's Camden Town period, though the linear treatment of the sheet folds clearly relates to the three contemporary painters mentioned above. Sewter even declared that the Bradshaw outstripped the Lowry and Fitton contributions to the show.

Sewter's answer to *A Funeral Party* was that "Lowry looked forced, laboured and uncomposed." Once again, he liked best the watercolour and drawing sections in the exhibition, which included usual contributions from McGlynn, Yates and Janes. Prints by Hampson, Jaques and a drawing by Ned Owens also made worthwhile contributions. The criticisms of the Lowry painting did not, however, limit itself to the pages of the *Guardian*. Mary Hampson in the *News Chronicle* referred to *A Funeral Party* as being "cold as a caricature, more dead than death itself . . . it looks like a Lowry who has fallen out of love with Lancashire."[20] A fair comment, but was Lowry ever in love with Lancashire? But the same reporter found a "compensating quality of vitality" in the Emmanuel Levy portrait *The Landlord* which was illustrated in the newspaper. In spite of the criticisms levelled at the Lowry, visual records of the Academy installation of that year confirm that the stark opposites of dark and light, based on the luminosity of a flake white ground, enabled Lowry's picture to stand out on the walls above many of the drab, more anonymous contributions - of river scenes in cities or dark interiors - that surrounded his painting.

The death of Lawrence Haward in November 1957 was not only a great loss to Manchester culture, but also signalled the end of an era. The artists whom he had encouraged and championed during his years of power, officiating and directing the many activities of the Manchester City Art Gallery, were now replaced by a new generation. The Academy exhibition of 1958, the last before its Centenary Exhibition the following year, featured the work of painters who had sprung to prominence in the 1950's. That 99th annual exhibition included work by Bradshaw, Bold, Gribble, Hampson, Hemingway, Lowndes, Levy and Lowry. Lawrence Haward was born in London, educated at Cambridge, and travelled widely throughout Europe. Between 1906 and 1914 this highly cultured man was a music critic for the *Times* and wrote for the *Guardian*. Between the wars Haward, in his capacity as curator of Manchester City Art Gallery, turned Platt Hall, Wythenshawe Hall and the old Parsonage at Didsbury into ancilliary branch galleries. Haward presided over the steady growth of the permanent collection of paintings on Mosley Street. He wanted to link the Athenaeum to the main art gallery building, both buildings the work of Sir Charles Barry. Haward was also responsible for the large Rutherston collection of contemporary paintings and drawings acquired through donations. In the spirit of the way this impressive collection had been assembled, Haward set up a scheme (that still exists) of lending works out to schools and other northern institutions. Using his skills as a diplomat, he obtained important donations of works through his relations with both the Contemporary Arts Society and the Northern Arts Council Fund. As already noted, he persuaded local firms to commission wartime works. The *Guardian* noted Haward's "conviction that Manchester had given him more scope for doing the things he cared about doing than he could have found in any other city."[21] After his retirement, Haward lived in Switzerland (his wife, whom he had married in 1911, was Swiss). Haward's death, followed a little over a year later by the Centenary Exhibition, drew to a close an important chapter in the story of art in this northern city.

NOTES

1 *Guardian* 27.1.48 Derek Senior
2 *News Chronicle* 16.3.49 Margaret Roberts
3 *Guardian* 16.12.49 John Willett
4 *Guardian* 28.1.50 John Willett
5 *Guardian* 28.2.50 John Willett
6 *Guardian* 29.1.51 John Willett
7 Letter to the Editor *Guardian* 5.5.51 Hal Yates
8 Obituary *Guardian* 14.11.52
9 *Evening Chronicle* 23.1.53
10 *Guardian* 25.1.54 A.C. Sewter
11 Lowry to David Carr 13.9.48
12 *News Chronicle* 22.1.55
13 *Daily Telegraph* 22.1.55 ' "Same again" at art show.'
14 *Guardian* 22.1.55 A.C. Sewter
15 *Ibid*
16 *Guardian* 24.2.56 A.C. Sewter
17 *News Chronicle* 25.2.56
18 *Guardian* 28.5.56 A.C. Sewter
19 *Guardian* 26.1.57 A.C. Sewter
20 *News Chronicle* 26.1.57 Mary Hampson
21 *Guardian* Obituary 19.11.57

Seven

Margo Ingham, The Midday Studios and The Manchester Group

The Midday Studios were situated at 96, Mosley Street, opposite the Manchester City Art Gallery. The premises were to become an important focal point in the post-war Manchester art scene, housing a continuous series of local and national exhibitions. They offered exhibition space to the Manchester Arts Club (which had previously used the walls of the Ballet Club) and the bi-annual exhibitions of Margo Ingham's own Manchester Group. The premises no longer exist, but records show that the subterranean galleries provided ample wall space for moderately-sized group exhibitions. The space was originally used by the influential collector and patron Lucy Wertheim as a gallery in which to show the kind of naïve school of painting that she liked and supported. She never especially took to Manchester, and moved away to Derbyshire soon after the war. The then head of painting at the Manchester Art School, Ian Grant, had known Wertheim from earlier contact in London, and was instrumental in the initial approaches for the taking over of the gallery by the Manchester Group. Despite some financial problems, Lucy Wertheim was writing to Ingham in September 1946, congratulating the enthusiastic young Manchester entrepreneur on obtaining the premises. The next five years were to see many exhibition openings, well attended with throngs of people enjoying a sympathetic and welcoming atmosphere.

Margo Ingham was a local elementary school teacher. She met Ian Grant in 1927, during evening studies at the school of art. Grant never found her a particularly talented student. "She drew rather like a fashion artist, she tended to draw in the way a fashion artist elongates and makes slinky." Ingham's unique contribution was not so much as a painter, but rather as the unflagging spirit and organising genius that lay behind the Manchester Group. In this capacity, she made a statement at the inaugural meeting of the Manchester Group, on November 6th 1946. She revealed that a proposal had been made by her in the summer of 1945 to acquire the Midday Studios, but it was turned down because her husband, Ned Owens, was still in the army. She went on to say that "all art lovers know Mrs.

Wertheim's Midday Studio. There she has shown many young moderns. She has given many a struggling artist his or her chance." Ingham went on to say that "Ned and my mother and I decided we would put equal money into it to launch it - Ned his gratuity, and I my savings." The gesture of risking personal savings on a venture that promised dubious financial rewards demonstrated both her eagerness to establish a gallery for contemporary Lancashire art, and the kind of overflowing enthusiasm and entrepreneurial spirit for which she is now remembered.

The talented painter, sculptor and writer Sven Berlin, then a St Ives artist, was invited by Ingham to hold a one-man exhibition at the Midday Studios in 1947. Berlin later wrote, "she was one of those women who had an almost overplus of outgoing energy and fitted into the art world with complete missionary dedication. I was almost frightened of this in a woman but went along with her invitation to show in Manchester." Because of the personal financial investment in the Midday venture, Margo Ingham adopted a businesslike attitude, with the Manchester Arts Club paying rent for mounting their exhibitions. Furthermore she wanted the stamp of officialdom. Letters were sent out to local luminaries inviting them to the Manchester Group's maiden exhibition at the premises on November 23rd. David Baxandall, director of The Manchester City Art Gallery, supported the new venture with vigour, and in his opening speech told the large crowd that he was not merely presiding over the opening of another exhibition but was witness to the beginning of something badly needed in Manchester. He applauded the courage showed by Ingham and Owens in taking on the gallery, and validated their efforts by saying that people were unable to see enough art in the provinces. Contemporary art was more important than ever, since it spoke more directly to mid-twentieth century man than did the work of past masters. Baxandall went on to declare that an artist's effect would be maximised and vindicated if the work was a genuinely rooted response to the expressive potential of the artist's indigenous region. By saying this Baxandall meant two things. Firstly he was dismissing the kind of weakly popular, indulgent and derivative romanticism lucidly identified by R.W. Wilenski in his influential book *The Modern Movement in Art*. Secondly, he was advocating the kind of unpretentious urban/industrial realism - seen in the work of Lowry and Major, then later in Lowndes, Hampson, Riley and Gribble - that represented the successful expressive response of the artist to his own environment.

The first opening ceremony at the Midday was indeed a thronging affair. Photographs of the crowded opening, taken by Tordoff, were published in

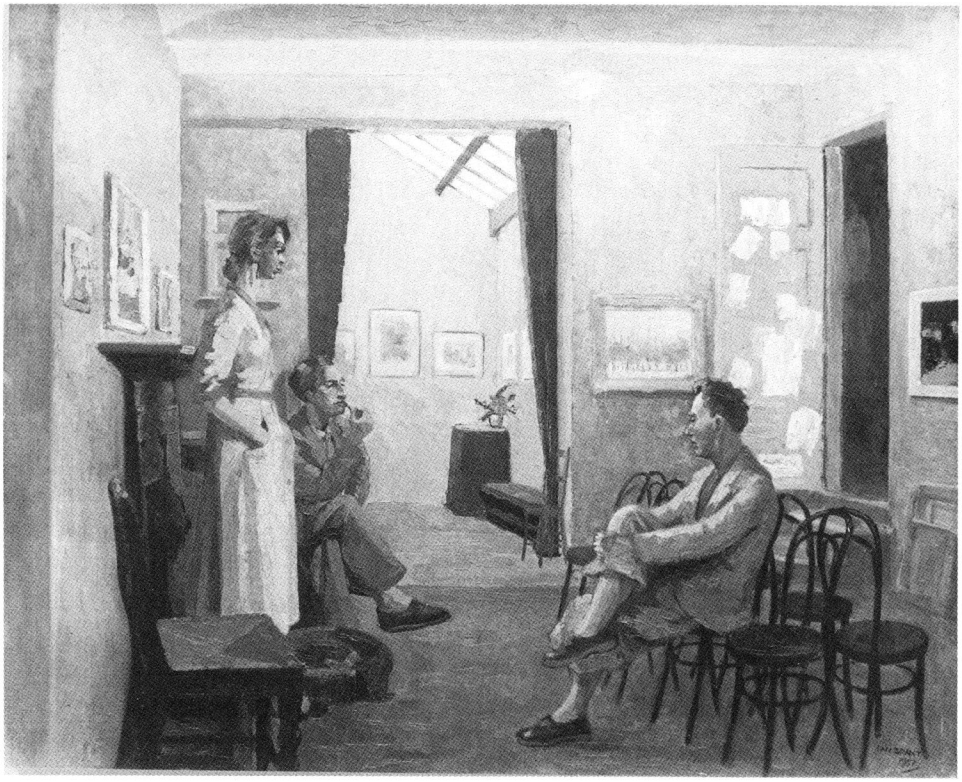

Ian Grant: Midday Studios, Manchester, *oil 1951.*

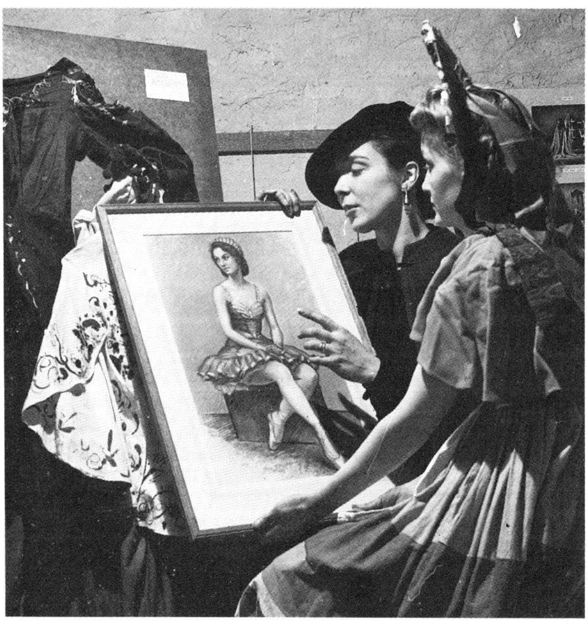

Margo Ingham discussing an Ian Grant pastel at the Manchester Ballet Club Exhibition 1946.

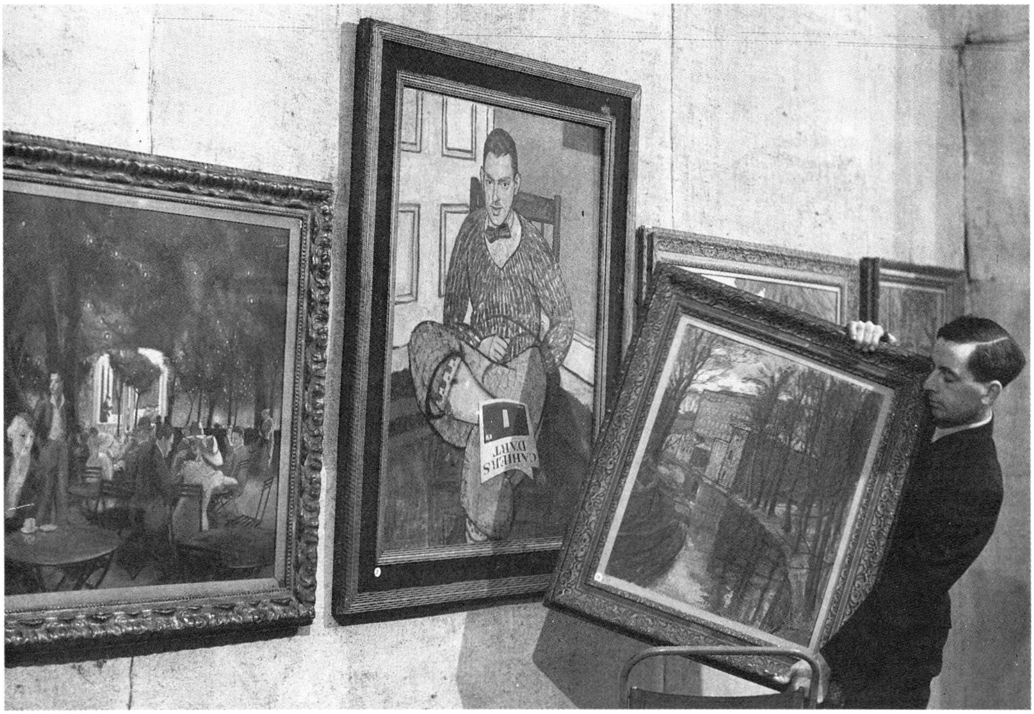

Ned Owens hanging three Ian Grant paintings at the Midday Studios in the late 1940s.

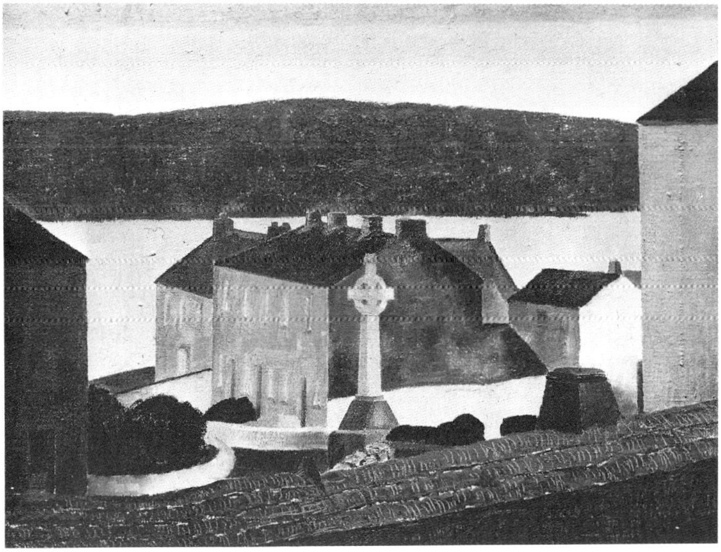

John Bold: Kilronan Arran, *oil.*

the Autumn, 1947 Journal of the Manchester Arts Club *Expression.* Seventeen artists were represented in the maiden exhibition.

Among the more thought-provoking early exhibitions was a show of artists who had been rejected from the Manchester Academy's annual exhibition held at the City Art Gallery. Ned Owens stood on the steps of the Art Gallery entrance, advising the rejected to apply to the Midday Studios. The artist was asked to pay a hanging fee of 7/6d, and to pay one third on sales in return for the privilege of exhibiting their work at Manchester's new Salon des Refusés. The relationship between the established Manchester Academy and the new Midday Studios Group was seldom as antagonistic as one might expect. There was, after all, the need for another smaller, intimate outlet in Manchester to show contemporary art. It also had something to do with the Manchester Group's oft-published declaration that it "does not represent any particular 'ism', bias or creed in painting but is an attempt to form a representative group of Lancashire artists who will exhibit their latest creations regularly to the public." Nevertheless, the role of the Midday Studios as an unofficial Salon des Refusés was a posture that seemed destined to create controversy and rivalry, and sometimes out-and-out bad feeling. A *Daily Dispatch* headline in mid-January 1947 read, "Artist starts 'Rejects' Exhibition. Call for Fair Deal." In the subsequent article Ned Owens said that "we contend that the Academy selection committee favours work of its members to whom a large percentage of wall space is allocated, artists with 'names' and influential Manchester people who may dabble in painting only occasionally." In spite of Owens' criticisms, the Manchester Group never represented any advanced abstraction or programmatic modernism such as the Penwith Society of Arts was soon to do in Cornwall. Maxwell Reekie, the Academy Vice President, refuted Owens' criticism of the Academy's alleged nepotism by saying that selection was open to all.

Despite these utterances from the two sides of Mosley Street the relationship between the Group and the Academy was generally one of concord. Some members of Ingham's group also exhibited with the Academy. One such artist was Ian Grant, who had his first one-man show at the Midday in early 1947. Grant's exhibition, comprised of work produced between 1926 and 1946, and included the well known *Cheshire Mill* (Manchester City Art Gallery). This picture, which has a fascinating story, told in the chapter on Ian Grant, was purchased for 25 guineas by the City Art Gallery. Other pictures on display included landscapes of his native Scotland, local Cheshire landscapes, views of North Wales, and a number of typical woodland and lake scenes, successful for their competent handling of a wide range of greens.

A further overlapping of Midday and Academy activities is illustrated by the fact that John Bowes, one of the Midday artists, served on the Academy's spring exhibition hanging committee along with Margaret Pilkington and Percy Lancaster. Indeed, Theodore Major showed two oils, *Kippers* and *Joan*, in that 1947 Academy show. One local newspaper reported that Major's contribution "stands out for its fresh quality. To many a visitor it will be considered the best of the show's pictures." A further statement by the Midday Studios, in the local press, said "Theodore Major's work has been exhibited by us in every exhibition since Ballet Club days, and he was scheduled to be the star of our 'Reject' show. His inclusion in the Academy show is an unexpected catholicity on their part and a blow to us. May we take a little of the credit for forcing their hand?" If tame squabbles like this indicated the lack of real aesthetic controversy in Manchester art circles (which could only be provided by an active *avant garde*) then the *Manchester Guardian*, doyen of the local papers, pitched in with alternate degrees of praise or criticism for the local artists. One article in February 1947 voiced disappointment at the exhibition of Academy rejects. "It is in fact, almost as disappointing as the Academy's own show." This was followed by a Midday exhibition of Ronald Allan's work, a founder member of the Group, who was described in the Midday catalogues as "the last of the Manchester Bohemians." Allan was born in Cheshire in 1900 and had trained at the Manchester School of Art, then at the prestigious Slade School.

The Manchester Arts Club's maiden exhibition at the Midday Studios took place after the Allan showing. The *Guardian* wrote, "It is a modest beginning. The Club seems to be rightly conceived as a hospitable fellowship rather than an exclusive coterie; it seeks to offer a congenial climate for individual expression rather than to force the growth of a distinct school. Its achievement is to be judged not so much by the quality of its early exhibitions as by the ultimate fruits of the confidence they inspire." This was a well worded description of the Group's aims. The *Guardian* comments seemed to echo the Manchester Group's magazine *Expression*, which identified a "congenial climate for individual expression", existing at the heart of the Midday's activities. They did not manifest any pointedly *avant garde* styles, but it is clear enough that the Midday artists, with their vaguely defined ethos of "individual expression", represented a break from the stiff, and self-justifying formalism of traditional academic studio practice. Sadly, because of financial pressures, *Expression* ran to only two issues. A longer running organ for the group's activities would have clarified positions, and consolidated a genuine 'movement' of young artists in the north.

Derek Senior's *Guardian* review in May 1947 reiterated recent remarks made about the posture of the Midday Studio artists. "In its second exhibition, now on view at the Midday Studios, the Manchester Group makes good its claim to catholicity and standing but does little to justify the description of its members' work as 'progressive and experimental'. In too many cases the style, though unorthodox, is static and the spirit, though individualist, is unadventurous. There is undeniable quality in the paintings shown by Ian Grant, A.C. Hilton, Lowry, Charles Messent, Terry McGlynn, Ned Owens, Richard Weisbrod, and Hal Yates."

In the summer holiday period the Midday Studio put on the first of its theme exhibitions - mixed shows by artists who shared a common subject or theme - this one on the nude. The display was accompanied by portraits of children by Frith Milward. In November the Midday presented an exhibition of paintings, drawings, and carvings by the St Ives artist Sven Berlin, whom Ingham had met in the Sloop Inn at St Ives the previous summer. Berlin showed carvings, in red alabaster, polyphant stone (which he had been given by the potter Bernard Leach) Portland stone, teak, and concrete. Among the familiar Berlin repertoire of subjects were bird and animal pieces. Berlin carved these outside his studio, dubbed the 'Tower', on the island overlooking Porthgwidden beach, St Ives. He was an active member of the St. Ives art colony, although he soon found himself at odds with the austere Penwith Society of Arts, whose artistic complexion was dictated by Hepworth and Nicholson. Berlin's final break with St. Ives came in 1953 when he moved to the softer pastures of Dorset. This was precipitated by disillusionment with the abstract straightjacket of the St Ives art scene in general, and with the demoted status accorded to traditional stalwarts of the St. Ives colony (like Leonard Fuller and the Preston-born landscape painter, John Park) in particular. Berlin's work responded to common, everyday themes - eminently accessible to the general public - with an individual expressivity courtesy of strong, flamboyant colour. The popular, romantic appeal of his work ideally suited the Midday Group. Derek Senior summed up the show, referring to Berlin as a "versatile artist with a keen eye for the significant line that epitomises a characteristic shape or posture." Certainly, Berlin's drawings of animals and insects, expressed with line work that owed something to Gaudier Breszka, display a natural empathy with nature and the animal kingdom.

Ingham's introduction of Sven Berlin reflected to some extent her own tastes. She might well have chosen from any number of painters in St. Ives but chose one who perhaps possessed the greatest gift for stimulating the popular imagination. "I did not go nor did I sell anything but the event seems to be remembered. It was then that Lowry saw my work, I expect. Alan Lowndes told me he knew of it and liked it. I have often wondered and was sorry I did not meet him. This was the year after my first London show at Lefevre. Eric Newton wrote me up in the *Sunday Times* in London but did not in Manchester. He was writing in the Midday journal *Expression* on Lowry that month." It is possible Berlin is mistaken that Lowry was introduced to his work at the Midday - the year before Berlin had his Lefevre show. Sven Berlin's brief professional encounters with Margo Ingham are recorded with resounding clarity: "I met Margo Ingham in the Sloop in St Ives . . . Margo Ingham looked like Ethel Manning, who was a novelist of the 20's and 30's. Perhaps she was influenced by her. The same black hair parted in the middle with I think plaited 'earphones' - or possibly a 'bun': both popular in those days. I believe she even wore a cloak - a black one. A pale, smiling ivory face with fine teeth. Talked a lot. A valuable person to have about. She gave an impulse to history."

The bi-annual exhibition of the Manchester Group followed the Berlin show at the end of 1947. The chairman was then Ian Grant. The fifth bi-annual Manchester Group exhibition, in November 1948 was opened by Hugh Scrutton, director of the Whitechapel Art Gallery. The show elicited favourable comments in the *Guardian* which reported, "In this show there are no bad pictures and few that would not improve with keeping. There are, it is true, no masterpieces either - apart from two perfect and quintessential Lowrys, one of which seems already to have taken on the patina of a veritable old master - but there are plenty of fresh and stimulating efforts." The reviewer also noted that the overall effect of the group exhibition displayed "a coherence of spirit that promises well for the group's future." The "coherence of spirit" was seen in the co-existence of the youngest exhibitor, the 23-year-old R. Baskerville, with the oldest, Lowry then aged 61. Joan Hargreaves' *Dutch Girl*, described as a "mature portrait" in one paper and as an "arresting piece of work" in the *Oldham Evening Chronicle*, won particular notice in the press. Mention was also given to Arthur Hilton's surrealistic life paintings, to John Bold and Ned Owens, to Terry McGlynn's Pembroke landscapes, and to a picture called *Llandudno* by Ian Grant. Theodore Major's contributions at this time were the early unsentimental portraits such as *Lancashire Girl* and *My Wife*. Both pictures were expressed with a broad, uninhibited handling of thick pigment. These early portraits depended for their instant effect on the dramatic contrast of dark colours, used to express worn faces, against a stark white background.

The *Manchester Evening News* referred to another vivid characterisation of local life, that of R. Baskerville's *The Paper Boy*, as being "a fine study of slum life in Manchester." John Gaunt called the same picture "fascinatingly grotesque" when reviewing for the *Oldham Evening Chronicle*. It was an attribution that places this apt, unsentimental portrayal of working class life in the same category as certain Lowry and Major portraits. By way of complete contrast with this dark realism, the *Guardian* noted that "José Christopherson seems to have found in Frances Hodgkins' work an influence in keeping with her own potential genius, though her colour still reflects a less wholesome discipleship." The comparison with Hodgkins was no doubt based on Christopherson's use of light fluid colour, applied with liberal abandon over expanses of partially covered white paper. Yet Christopherson's work lacked the sophisticated impressionist mark making, luminosity and strength of structure that epitomised the best of the eminent New Zealand painter's work.

Hugh Scrutton used the columns of the *Evening Chronicle* to urge the Manchester public to support their local artists by purchasing exhibits. This fifth exhibition of the Manchester Group went on an extensive tour that took in such varied locations as the Foyle Art Gallery, the British Council, the Oxford University Art Club, and Chester's Y.M.C.A. The advantage of such a tour - which is probably the envy of contemporary exhibition organisers who have to contend with the bottleneck exhibition circuits - was partly offset by the limitations of opening hours on Mosley Street. John Gaunt's comment in the *Oldham Evening Chronicle* that "it is a pity that the studio is open only during the lunch hours and the evening rush hours," highlighted the problem of inflexible opening times.

A more complete discussion of the lives and careers of the Manchester Group's principal members is contained in another chapter, but it is instructive here to glance briefly at the full membership of the exhibitors, and to quote from the short biographical notes contained in the Group exhibition catalogues. The full group, listed in the catalogues, was: Ronald Allan, R. Baskerville, John Bold, John Bowes, José Christopherson, Bernard Fairclough, Ian Grant, Leila Haffar, Jean Hargreaves, Arthur Hilton, L.S. Lowry, Terry McGlynn, Theodore Major, Charles Messent, Ned Owens, Roger Summer, Ray Taylor, Richard Weisbrod, Hal Yates and Margo Ingham.

Ronald Allan was born in nearby Cheshire in 1900, had studied first at the Manchester School of Art, and then at the Slade in the early 1920's. This was a period of particular distinction in the history of the Slade; only a few years earlier artists like Stanley Spencer, Mark Gertler, David Bomberg

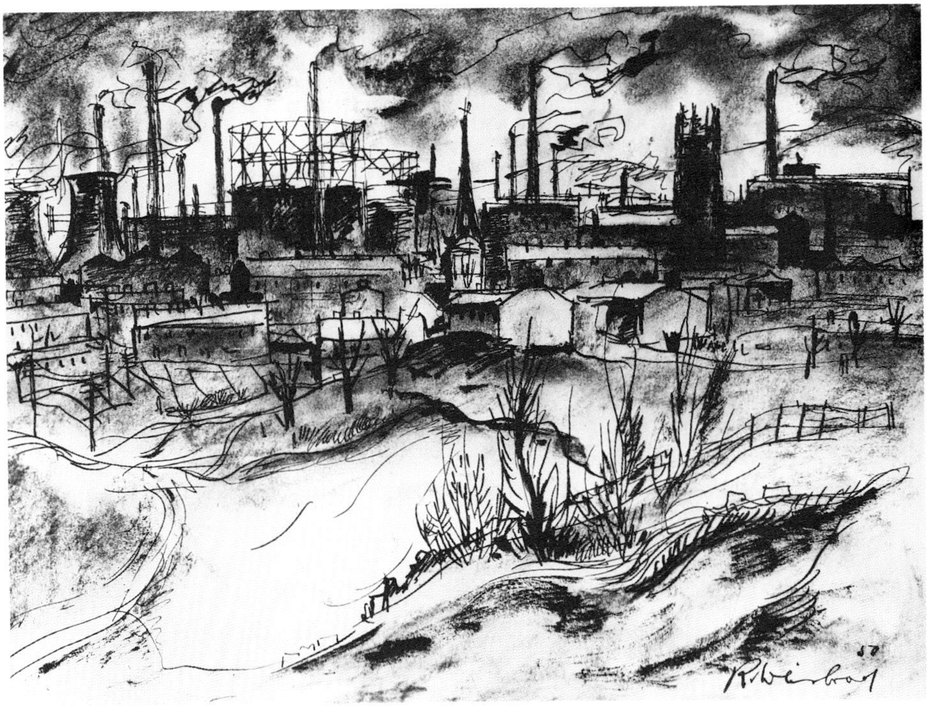

Richard Weisbrod: Lancashire Landscape, *1950.*

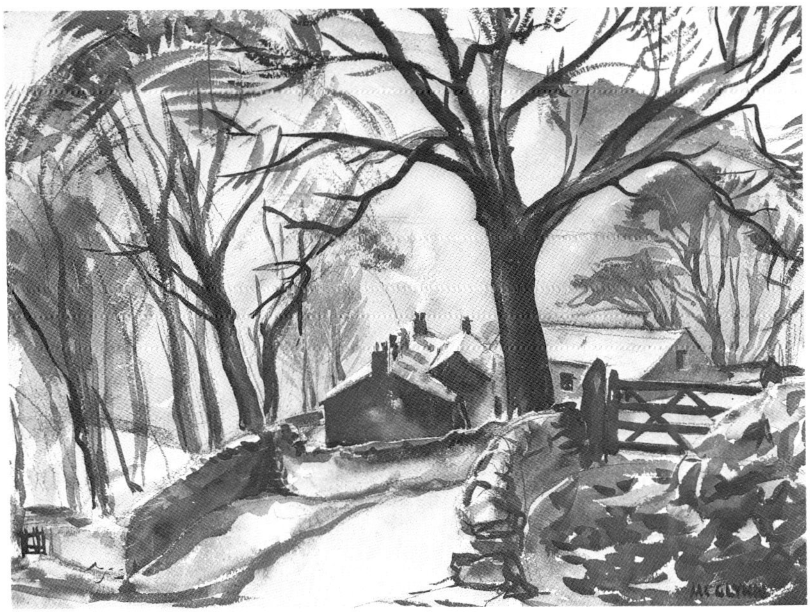

Terry McGlynn: Ashes Farm Kinder *(courtesy: Manchester City Art Gallery).*

and William Roberts had attended the school. Baskerville was born in 1926, and was trained as a photo-lithographic retoucher, though he wished to devote all his time to painting. Like John Bold, Baskerville possessed a great love of music. Bold was a quiet, introspective Manchester man, born in 1904, who used the Derbyshire hill country to the south of the city as his prime subject matter. John Bowes, born in Oldham in 1899, served in the Great War. He, too, was a keen musician - he had been a professional singer - and, during the period of the Midday Studios, was living in Southport. José Christopherson's inspiration was the ballet. Having begun painting at 16, she was something of a child prodigy. She was also interested in Chagall, particularly his stage decor work. Ian Grant, too, was interested in ballet, and like many of the artists already mentioned, pursued an interest in music, and played in an orchestra. Leila Haffar trained at the Manchester School of Art under Ian Grant. Jean Hargreaves also studied under Grant at Manchester, but unlike Haffar, this Rochdale-born painter (born in 1921) went on to emulate Grant's own training, by completing her studies at the Royal College of Art. Arthur Hilton was born in 1897 in Manchester; wounded in the Great War, he was alone in contributing abstract, biomorphic and surrealist compositions to the Group exhibitions.

Terry McGlynn was born in 1905, and produced murals for mill interiors in the Manchester area. Theodore Major and Lowry, often grouped together for their similar, uncompromising visions of northern factory towns, were both local men. Charles Messent, by contrast, was born in Felixstowe in 1911. He served in the Air Force in Egypt where he began painting on old tent canvases, and ended up as a commercial display artist in Manchester after the war. Ned Owens was born in 1911 and achieved a scholarship to art school in Durham. He was interested in stage design, which he taught part-time at the Manchester School of Art. Roger Summer was born in 1925, and like Messent, had served in the Air Force; his chief musical interest was jazz. Ray Taylor was born in 1914, and after studying at Manchester School of Art, had some harrowing but character-building war experiences, after the ship he was travelling on was torpedoed in the Channel. Taylor was picked up by enemy vessels and served the next three years as a German P.O.W. Richard Weisbrod was born in Switzerland in 1906. He was a silk manufacturer and fabric designer, for whom mountaineering provided a leisure pursuit. Hal Yates and Margo Ingham were both born locally, Yates in 1907, Ingham 1918.

It was a fairly homogeneous group of variable abilities and levels of professional training and attainment. The group's existence in post-war Manchester explains the frequent occurrence of fabric or stage design as activities which partner painting. The group also showed interest in ballet and music. Most of the artists were born locally between about 1910 and 1920.

The group's fifth exhibition at the Midday, late in 1948, prompted an invitation from Hugh Scrutton for the Group to show at his Whitechapel Art Gallery in London. The exhibition ran during February and March 1949. R. Baskerville's *Strong Man, Petticoat Lane* won much praise in the local newspapers. The same artist's *Paper Boy* also generated much interest. John Bold exhibited *Arran Village*, one of a long series of paintings he made during numerous visits to the west coast of Scotland. Bold's other contribution was the well known *Haworth Parsonage.* The buildings behind the cemetery together with the crisply defined forms of foreground gravestones under a dark, brooding winter sky divided by three upright trees, give the scene a mysterious, romantic feeling. John Bowes' contributions, *Monmouth Landscape* and *Autumn near Southport* reflected a temperament geared towards gentle landscape. José Christopherson's contributions included *Seagull Cafe, St Ives*, and *Italian Landscape*, the former showing the habit of artists from across the United Kingdom to make painting visits to the famous Cornish art colony by the sea. Jean Hargreaves again exhibited her *Dutch Girl* that won favourable response in Manchester. Ian Grant also showed a picture previously exhibited in the group's Manchester headquarters: his nocturnal view of Llandudno across the harbour. Lowry's works at the Whitechapel included *Portrait of a Young Man, Princes Dock, Glasgow*, and *Doctor's Surgery.* Theodore Major exhibited two new pictures, both still lifes. Terry McGlynn exhibited Welsh and Irish watercolour landscapes, notable for their speedy execution and strong structure. Charles Messent, perhaps drawing on wartime memories, showed an Arab scene, while Richard Weisbrod exhibited his characteristic and distinctive pen and ink urban landscape panoramas, full of detail yet bold in composition and design. His *Lancashire Landscape* is a good example of contemporary work in this style.

An interesting critical appraisal of the Whitechapel group exhibition appeared in the *Guardian* (4.2.49). The reviewer found fault in painting habits that veered too much one way or too much the other. The reviewer wrote: "Baskerville who paints rough characters with great gusto . . . is sometimes rather insensitive in his handling of oil paint. Hal Yates, on the other hand, is almost too skilfull with watercolour." In similar vein he continued "Theodore Major is perhaps too fiercely emphatic, and John Bold, though he shows taste and charm, is not quite emphatic enough." Even Lowry's much esteemed work seemed to betray polarities. "Lowry, whose queer picture of a very black ship entering Princes Dock Glasgow, is a complete success, but whose equally queer portrait of a young man falls a little short of this." Such polarities and diversities were easily explained by Margo Ingham in an article, *Art in Lancashire: The Manchester Group*. "When an exhibition is arranged, each artist is his own selector, consequently the exhibits are diverse in subject and technique and are full of interest and variety".

An uncompromising critical article 'Unregional Art' by Ray Watkinson, appeared in the magazine *Our Time*. Watkinson was forthright in his mixture of praise and denouncement. "The most pointedly local work is that of Lowry, the oldest member, and of Baskerville, the youngest. In respect of maturity of achievement, the work of Lowry and Theo Major stands out. There is little in common between them but this maturity and consistency. Major's work is loud to the point of brutality, in handling, and his colour equally verges on crudity; nevertheless it is alive and enjoyable, clearly he loves paint." Watkinson identifies and credits Major's un-English courage with thick, dramatically contrasted pigment. Yet he fails to draw undeniable connections between Lowry and Major. Many of Major's landscapes resemble Lowry's mill landscapes, rendered in definite zones of black, white and grey. Both artists tended to use their own localities - for Lowry Salford and Pendlebury, for Major Wigan - as reference points for pictures that departed from accurate topographies to a more imagined and invented place that gain a universal and un-local sense of symbolic significance. It is true however, that Lowry's work was more academic than the expressionist flavour of Major's. Lowry's composite views of remembered fragments of several places were recorded with more intricate drawing and panoramic clarity. Watkinson went on to note that "other paintings on local themes, for example by John Bowes, Ian Grant and Richard Weisbrod are utterly lacking in character, either of painter or place, and are swamped by adolescent mannerism . . . much of the work, good and bad, and even when dealing with local themes is very derivative and smacks of the art school."

By the end of 1949, art links had been fostered between London and Manchester. In November 1949 a group of the most celebrated contemporary artists from the London scene - the two 'Roberts' Colquhoun and MacBryde, John Minton and Keith Vaughan - exhibited at the Midday Studios, prompting Ned Owens' remark that "This is the first time that this distinguished quartet have ever been represented in one show together outside London." Another of their vaguely defined 'neo-romantic' group, John Craxton, exhibited with Alan Lowndes at the recently opened Crane Gallery in Manchester in 1950. In the same year the Manchester Group exhibited at the 20 Brook Street Gallery in London's fashionable New Bond Street. Back in Manchester, the *Evening Chronicle* ever loyal in covering the achievements of the local Manchester artists, related this story: "One of the two women represented in the Brook Street show, José Christopherson, contributes some Spanish landscapes; about one of them, a harbour scene, she tells a droll story. She was painting it from the sea front at Cadaques when she was embarrassed by someone roaring with laughter as he looked over her shoulder. She was not sure whether the laughter was with her or at her. Turning around, she found Salvador Dali, the famous Surrealist painter."

The rich incidence of Mediterranean colour was a feature of the Manchester Group's ninth exhibition at the Midday studios in October 1950. Both José Christopherson and Bernard Fairclough had been to Spain on painting holidays, while Richard Weisbrod, the well-to-do owner of a Preston silk mill, had painted in the South of France. The group was never exclusively devoted to a portrayal of local industrial, or even of pretty Cheshire and Derbyshire scenes. Pictures of far-away places frequently visited by Midday members brought exoticism, romanticism and colour into the Midday studio exhibitions. John Bold's Arran landscapes, Ian Grant's unpeopled pictures of his native Scottish landscape, Terry McGlynn's fluent watercolours of Wales and Scotland, Margo Ingham's St Ives pictures, and José Christopherson's Mediterranean landscapes are good examples.

Shortly before the Group's October exhibition of that year the Midday offered Theodore Major a one-man show. An article appeared in the *Manchester Guardian* to coincide with the opening of the Mosley Street show. It was titled 'A Fine Lancashire Artist' and was written by John Willett, the distinguished critic and historian who today is well known for authoritative books on Brecht, on German art, and on art in Liverpool. Willett began his appraisal by citing the unlikelihood of finding an untutored and untravelled artist painting in an unpromising environment such as a nineteenth century red brick railway town like Wigan. Willett then balanced the odds a little by quoting some unexpected advantages, "You would be free from all predigested notions of modern art; you would be able to find poetry in traditionally unpoetic scenes; you would appreciate colour all the more by contrast with the greyness outside your window; and your love of the medium would be intense enough to stand out." Willett certainly found in Major's immediately recognisable art the working of an original hand and mind, buttressed in its inherent individuality precisely by the homespun advantages the critic had noted.

But appropriate comparisons with the work of Lowry, Vlaminck and Matthew Smith were also made by Willett, emphasising the sheer impossibility of painting without some kind of (conscious or unconscious) relationship to contemporary or historic precedents. "He shows an extraordinary mixture of pictures: on the one hand his various Wigan street, pit and factory scenes, sombre and almost monotonous in subject yet immensely varied in their smokey atmosphere and dull colours: on the other hand, the quite exceptionally vivid still lifes, flower and figure paintings whose raw colours would wake up a Smith nude and put Van Gogh's sunflowers in the shade." This exalted praise of Major's paintings comparing them to those of Matthew Smith and Van Gogh should not blind us to the point Willett was making. For once English art's chronic tendency towards closely modulated, greyed-down understatement was being kicked into touch by an unlikely northern painter of unusual vigour and untutored directness. A good indication of the promise that Major was deemed to possess was revealed when a selection of Major's paintings, including *Lancashire Girl* were selected for an Arts Council Show, 'Some Lancashire Artists' which toured the North West about this time.

Theodore Major was never shy of public debate as an opportunity to vent his strong, even bombastic views. One such occasion presented itself soon after his Midday exhibition, in November 1950 and was prompted by an article in the *Evening Chronicle*, 'Does Manchester lag in art?' by Fred Isaac. The feature was based on an interview with Andreas Kalman in which the Hungarian war emigré, who had recently opened his Crane Gallery on South King Street, lamented the level of artistic appreciation in local Manchester life. A letter from Mr and Mrs A. Kilroy declared "while we sympathise with the sadness felt by Andreas Kalman of the Crane Gallery on his failure to sell modern paintings (at anything up to 1,000 guineas) we deprecate his conclusion that Manchester is not an 'art loving place.' Where else in the north can be found such a galaxy of talent and art enthusiasm as is contained in the Manchester Academy of Fine Art, the Manchester Group, the Manchester Society of Modern Painters, the Manchester Graphic Club? The City is proud too, of L.S. Lowry's international repute - a painter whose work she long nurtured and fostered." The Kilroys then went on to praise the quality of the young generation in Manchester, "and with what hope and promise Manchester looks forward to a wider acclaim of her latest star protégés - Ned Owens and Theo Major. As for apathy towards modern art in Manchester's younger generation, Mr Kalman could not have fought his way round the thronged Mosley Street Gallery during the recent exhibition of Italian Expressionism."

The hasty reply from Kalman was bluntly titled 'Manchester is not an Arts Centre.' He began by denigrating the Kilroys' statement as having "the enthusiasm and tone usually associated with bebop fans." Kalman continued with unwavering pith, "if we take embroidery-cum-knitting circles, amateur dramatics, sketching clubs, as the standards for art then Manchester is seething with art. Wax flowers, plaster plaques of sham, clay dogs, fire screens with 'nice' designs, flower paintings as different as one lampost is from another, these are all artistic. A painting by Sickert, a bronze head by Epstein, a drawing by Augustus John is ART." Kalman also replied to the Kilroys' claims that the contemporary art scene in the city was lively. "There are five or six really good artists in and around Manchester and about an equal number of talented ones. Mr Lowry is the most important of them. But did Manchester nurture him, as Miss and Mr Kilroy say? According to Mr. Lowry he had painted for 20 years before, at the age of 51, he sold a painting in Manchester, after recognition in London. As for Mr Ned Owens and Mr Theo Major, "Manchester's new star protégés," I sincerely hope they will be "nurtured" better. There are no more than two or three painters (not painters and decorators) who make a living from painting in Manchester." Kalman completed his tirade by answering the criticism that his gallery was the only one to charge an admission charge of one shilling, necessary he said, to put on expensive or rare exhibitions. Kalman never rated Manchester as a cultural centre; by the mid 1950's he was moving his gallery down to London's prestigious Brompton Road, where its reputation has continued to grow ever since. He always shared Lowry's wry and justified observations, about how the art-buying echelons of Manchester society only invested in Lowry pictures once their commercial and cultural value had been confirmed by the London art establishment.

As Theodore Major had been quoted as one of the 'star protégés,' it was apposite that the Wigan artist should pitch into the lively debate that the *Evening Chronicle* was running on its pages. Major agreed partly with both points of view. "Many people are certainly interested in art in Manchester, but from a business point of view there is little interest. But is art the buying and selling of pictures? Surely the chief interest and business in Manchester and the rest of England lies in football, cricket, racing, pools, television, cinemas, and the 'stuff' called entertainment produced by the B.B.C." Major did, though, rebuke Kalman's policy of showing established safe bets, like Nicholson, Nash, Piper and Sutherland at his new gallery, rather than the new generation in Manchester (Alan Lowndes being an exception).

A discussion of the merits of Manchester as a self-supporting centre for art came at a pertinent time, because in the following year, 1951, the brave Midday adventure ended and the studios closed. The Midday studios were given three months notice in June by Meller, Speakman & Hall, the solicitors and agents for the Trustees of Mrs E. Riddick. No reason was given for the withdrawal of their lease which had been in effect since October 1946. At the time Margo Ingham said they would search for new premises, which unfortunately were never found. In June, 1951 Ingham declared in the *News Chronicle* that "it is a blow to Lancashire art. We have spent a lot of money fitting out the cellar and we artists are not rich people these days. It will be difficult, too, finding another place so centrally situated." Just how difficult was borne out by the fact that the Group never found alternative premises. The Midday studios were also home for the 150-strong Manchester Arts Club, which during the five years of the studios' existence, met twice a week. A day after the notice was received Ingham and Owen announced the sad news at a party given to celebrate the Group's Festival Exhibition. This exhibition was organised to coincide with the epoch-making Festival of Britain, and went on to tour to the Cooling Gallery in London's New Bond Street in August, 1951. In the exhibition Lowry contributed *Burford Church*, while the same artist was affectionately portrayed by Ned Owens in *Lowry in the Lane*. Hal Yates and Ray Taylor exhibited views of Tewkesbury and Blaenau-Festiniog respectively. Charles Messent showed *Egyptian Mosque*, another example of work drawn from his wartime experiences in the Middle East, while Bernard Fairclough's romantic *Spanish Cemetery* contrasted with the closer-to-home subject of *Autumn in Southport*, a picture which together with a Monmouthshire landscape had originally been shown in an earlier Midday exhibition.

The Cooling exhibition was reviewed by Michael Chase in *Art News and Review*, which had been founded by Bernard Denvir and Richard Gainsborough in 1948. Chase's critical review declared that the show "appears to have been arranged hurriedly and insufficient attention given to the limitations of the room and scant consideration to the selection of available work." He was perhaps referring to the inherent heterogeneity of subject and style, as well as a lack of thematic arrangement. Jean Hargreaves' still lifes were criticised for their striving for abstract harmonies which missed a cohesion of design and colour. Similarly Ray Taylor's landscapes were criticised for being too elaborate. Chase showed perceptive depth when he declared preference for the more individual black and white figure studies of miners and workmen depicted in authentic, realistic north-country environments. Along these lines he wrote "John Bold's ungarnished statements of Manchesters' suburbia are strong in that they make no attempt to force the spectator's imagination in one path. Theo Major's Wigan landscape is an impressive study of light versus industrial gloom—too uncompromising for the strictly conventional *Disley Village* by Ian Grant, next to it."

The Cooling exhibition was summed up by Chase when he referred to a pair of Lowry exhibits which "confirm his established position and Burford Church strikes a note of simplicity and strength that should have given the theme for the whole show." Coinciding with this show there was a retrospective exhibition at Salford Art Gallery of six pictures - mainly in oils - by Lowry. John Rothenstein, writing in the show's catalogue, declared "I regard him as one of the best painters at work in England today." A one-man exhibition by a maturing master clearly proved a more satisfactory and coherent proposition than the speedily assembled group show by the Midday artists. Chase's observations were partly confirmed when the *Glasgow Herald* made a vain attempt to define a group style at the Cooling Gallery; the Glasgow paper's definition centred on "a steadiness, a refusal to go in for frills or attitudes, a kind of sober individuality—that is clearly north country." The *Manchester Guardian*, like *Art News and Review*, singled out Lowry's *Burford Church* for special praise declaring that "Mr Lowry heads the list, and in his *Burford Church* shows that he can bring to alien territory, in this case to the Cotswolds, the vision which serves him so well in the blacker and whiter industrial landscapes of the North. Ned Owens has done a nocturnal impression of *Lowry in the Lane* in which the artist is portrayed in his haunting garb of blue suit, cloth cap, and carrying a walking stick."

The importance to the Group of an exhibition in a prominent West End Gallery cannot be overestimated, and gave the members much publicity. A smaller Manchester Group limited to 14 members also enjoyed an exhibition in July 1951 at Liverpool's Bluecoat Chambers. The *Liverpool Daily Post* wrote "Lowry and Major both paint industrial squalor and poverty as an unsentimental commentary - a recording of a familiar pattern not intended to rouse the social conscience." It seems strange today that, except for Lowry, these very typical early 1950's northern artists should have sunk to such relative obscurity. Their neglect would have been hastened not only by the demise of the Midday studios, but also by the advent of the new American Painting after 1956 with its creed of modernist abstraction and ethos of a cosmospolitan mainstream. Such influences certainly asserted themselves in the St Ives art scene during the 1950's, in spite of Alan Lowndes' move from Manchester to the Cornish colony in the second part of the decade. If the break-up of the Manchester Group came with the loss of their premises, then the larger Manchester Arts Club found alternative premises quickly, though these were not large enough to also accommodate Ingham's group.

The Midday Studios closed in October 1951, after five years of activity. The final exhibition there was of Richard Weisbrod's work. This prosperous owner of the Darwen Silk Mill in Preston was praised in most of the reviews. Weisbrod's *Preston Station* was mentioned for its "solid, confident structure." The impressive iron and glass structure of this large nineteenth century railway station provided an ideal subject for Weisbrod's versatile linear style, that was able to pick up a wide array of detail from challenging urban panoramas or pieces of industrial architecture. Weisbrod's *Lancashire landscape* (1950) in which mill, factory, church, terraced housing, gasometer and cooling towers are all included with a confident web of pentimenti lines and ink marks, is a good example. The *Northern Daily Telegraph*, referring to an exhibition he had enjoyed at the Leger galleries in London the year before, pinpointed "the influence of de Segonzac in the virility of his pen drawing and again the clear vibrant colour of Dufy in the landscape." Yet another review of his Midday exhibition spoke in an altogether different vein by referring to "the scribbly, inconsequential gaiety that hints at Dufy." The same reviewer saved Weisbrod from condemnation by stating that "he is delivered from mere prettiness by sure taste and an extreme liveliness of line and rhythm."

In early October (9.10.51) a letter from Ted Frape, director of Salford Art Gallery, was sent to Ingham, pledging future support. David Baxandall also wrote, expressing pleasure that she had at least found alternative premises for the Arts Club. Baxandall's efforts to accommodate the Manchester Group can be seen in one of his letters: "My committee has, as a general policy, attempted to provide space for an exhibition by one local art society each year in addition to that of the Manchester Academy. I am sure, therefore, that they would receive a request for an exhibition of the Manchester Group with all sympathy, but you will realise it is unlikely that the turn of the group for an exhibition here would recur oftener than once in three years." The Manchester Group, many of whose members exhibited anyway in the Manchester Academy Spring exhibition, was to remain synonymous with the unique Midday Studios premises originally provided by the eminent collector Lucy Wertheim. The Midday Studios had been important for its time and place and undoubtedly formed an important stage in the story of Art in the North West.

Eight

Ian Grant

The Scottish-born painter Ian Grant became one of the most active members of the Manchester arts scene, exhibiting each year at the Manchester Academy and regularly at the Midday studios, which he helped to set up. He also ran the painting department at the Manchester School of Art through the difficult 1940's. He helped bridge the gaps in the Manchester artistic milieu between the local-bred artists and the academically trained, the provincial and the cosmopolitan, and the modernist and the salon painter. He was educated in the cosmopolitan art culture of both London and Paris, yet he advocated and practised a cautious, moderate pragmatism; a common sense approach to painting that was accessible to students, serious amateurs and professional painters. Each category was an important group within the flourishing art scene. In many respects, Grant also bridged the gap between two generations of painting - one a pre-war academic and conservative salon painting, the other a more exuberant and colourful, though disciplined, figurative painting that conveyed a spirit of 'joie de vivre'. Grant's work was closer to the latter, French inspired manner. With its palette knifed marks in a rich autumnal key, Grant also emulates a Scottish relish for colour, painterly impasto, pictorial texture, and gestural handling of paint.

Ian Grant first studied at Glasgow School of Art between 1922 and 1926. The distinguished Royal Academician Maurice Grieffenhagen was then professor of painting in Glasgow. "Although a small man," Grant has recalled, "he had a powerful personality and dominated Glasgow Art School. Most students were influenced by his style, but in my year a small group of us rebelled against the prevailing Grieffenhagen style." That rebellion was, of course, fuelled by what was happening in Paris, the whirlwind of change that had repercussions everywhere, particularly in Francophile Scotland. Grant visited Paris in the summer of 1925 and again in 1926, after receiving his diploma. The Paris that Grant experienced was enjoying a golden age; witnessing a remarkable convergence of talents from throughout Europe. It was a bohemia that has only been echoed since in the post-war Greenwich Village that was the setting for the rise of the New York School. Grey, cautious England had no such opportunity for exchange, innovation or experiment; but Manchester later offered a community spirit. Just as enterprises like the Diaghilev Ballet in Paris facilitated the collaboration of painters, stage designers, musicians and dancers, so Manchester's textile industry brought together painters and designers.

In spite of its invigorating atmosphere, Grant decided that "the chances of making a permanent living in Paris among the thousands of artists was slight. Starving in a garret is fine in your twenties, but looking at middle-aged painters still struggling, without much hope, I decided it was not for me." In Paris, however, Grant met some great artists. He went to the Colarossi Academy where André Lhote taught, and was influenced by him. He met Matisse in a life class at Colarossi and Picasso at a gallery, though a natural modesty and language difficulties prevented any conversation. The work of Matisse however spoke volumes, with its example of a decorative and rhythmic line that created pronounced pictorial harmonies. This interest in movement, conveyed with fluid lines and arabesques, is evident in much of Grant's work until the 1940's.

Grant returned to England and, on the suggestion of John Rivel, the recently appointed Director of Glasgow School of Art, entered the Royal College of Art. He studied there from 1927 until 1930. William Rothenstein was the Principal, and Tom Monnington, whom Grant came to like and respect, taught life drawing. In his capacity of common room secretary Grant was at the centre of college life. The students of the design school were considered then not good enough to be professional painters, but it soon became clear that the experimental creativity of the design school was more relevant to the innovations and advances of modern painting than the academic society painting taught in the painting department. The renaissance of the Royal College painting department came about under Robin Darwin in the late 1940's but in Rothenstein's day the painters tended to be conservative. "The great high priest of drawing was Ingres and you were told to study Piero della Francesca as a painter." In 1929 Grant took his diploma and the following year prepared a mural for the Prix de Rome. He also painted small cubist pictures and did freelance interior decorating. But he was attracted by the security of teaching, and by taking a first job as painting master at the art school in Southport, Grant made his move to the north of England.

Southport had a small and friendly art school, and there Grant taught painting, design and art history. He exhibited at the spring exhibition at the Atkinson Art Gallery along with Percy Lancaster who was a regular and lively contributor. Grant painted the portrait of a prominent Southport architect, Gordon Hemm, and also contributed work to arts club exhibitions as far afield as Bradford and Bournemouth. He was elected as a member of the Liverpool Academy, and showed work at the Royal Scottish Academy, the Royal Academy and the Manchester Academy. In 1937 Grant became the painting master at Manchester School of Art. During the first year of his new job, he commuted between Southport and Manchester but came to the conclusion that Southport was too flat for an artist with his southern highland background. His love of hills compelled him towards the Pennine foothills and the Derbyshire and Cheshire hill country that formed the unmistakable, undulating horizon beyond Manchester. Grant therefore moved to a leafy suburb of Stockport, beginning a long personal and artistic association with Cheshire. He had intended to return to London after five years, but the war prevented him, and he was promoted to senior lecturer. Grant therefore established himself at Manchester.

The School of Art in Manchester was very basic at this time. Paul Keene ran the illustration and commercial art courses, and Grant taught still life. Albert Dodd supervised both, and taught drawing. Hanna Martin taught composition, and Peter O'Brien, a talented water-colour landscape painter, taught in the design school. At the beginning of the war Grant was asked to run a camouflage school, teaching the principles and techniques of camouflage design to army and aircraft personnel. The tops of factories needed to be disguised as roads and houses. He also recoloured the interiors of munition and aircraft factories in what contemporary psychologists believed were uplifting colours for the workers. Grant spent the final part of the war, less strenuously and urgently, talking to troops about the theory and practice of art.

Soon after moving from Southport to the Manchester School of Art, Grant met Margo Ingham, who was then an evening student. Margo had tremendous energy and drive. After the war, she used that enthusiasm for starting a gallery that would exhibit work by local Manchester artists. Grant advised Ingham, and her husband Ned Owens, in this venture, and put them in contact with his old acquaintance, Lucy Wertheim, who ran the Mosley Street Gallery. Shortly afterwards this became the Midday Studios. Grant enjoyed a one-man exhibition at these galleries in 1947, and an article he wrote about his work appeared in the short-lived Midday magazine, *Expression*.

Throughout his long career, Ian Grant performed at a consistently high level of attainment, using portrait, figure, still life and landscape subjects with flourishing confidence. He inclined towards landscape later on, replacing his earlier inclination towards portrait painting. He felt unable to paint a satisfactory portrait unless the sitter first interested him. Consequently Grant avoided professional portrait painting. The commissioned portrait would have been a stultifying, barren area for this moderate, but individual modern painter. The ability to paint a good portrait led to some animated figure compositions set in Parisian cafés and showgrounds. There is one particularly fine, personal painting, depicting himself in animated conversation with Ned Owens and Margo Ingham at the Midday Studios. The personally significant details include the unmistakable, though muted image of a Lowry hanging on the wall beyond the figures. It is an affectionate chronicle of the post-war Manchester art scene.

Photographs of the hanging, by Ned Owens, of Grant's one man show at the Midday in 1947 show a series of head and shoulder portrait drawings of women. These are constructed with firm, steady lines, in pencil or conté, embellished with confident hatching that overlays, traverses, or simply fills in the boldly constructed outlines. Subtler shading, with smudged thumb or nuanced pencil marks, add volume to the faces. In the full figure, semi-nude drawings, the form blends in with drapery or with domestic architecture and furniture, achieving a robust moving silhouette and pronounced linear arabesque. This suggests the artist's interest in Severini (whom he met in Paris), the Futurists, and the decorative domesticity of Matisse. The head and shoulder drawings, with their interest in physiognomy and the pattern of hair, recall, in more controlled terms, the freely drawn and hatched pencil portraits of John and Lamb.

Ian Grant has acknowledged the dilemma of the artist with a talent for portrait painting. He said, "I am naturally a portrait painter, but I'm not temperamentally suited to be a professional portrait painter. I can't paint people unless I'm interested in them. If I am then I can produce a rattling good portrait." One particular "rattling good portrait" was of a subject that has interested him the most down the years. His large oil self-portrait of 1949 (Collection: the artist) depicts the artist at his easel. Grant stands in his painter's coat with a large palette board in his hands. The sideways glance of the artist indicates that the image presented itself to the artist by way of a large mirror. The painting achieves a satisfying balance between tone and temperature contrast; the pink, red and ochre of the flesh is complemented in the cooler green, blue, and grey areas of the clothing and the surrounding dark interior. The self-portrait has formed a major strand in his work. A series of portraits of his wife and daughter in their Cheshire home has been a natural development out of the self-portrait series.

Drawings in pastel or pencil of ballet dancers have also been produced,

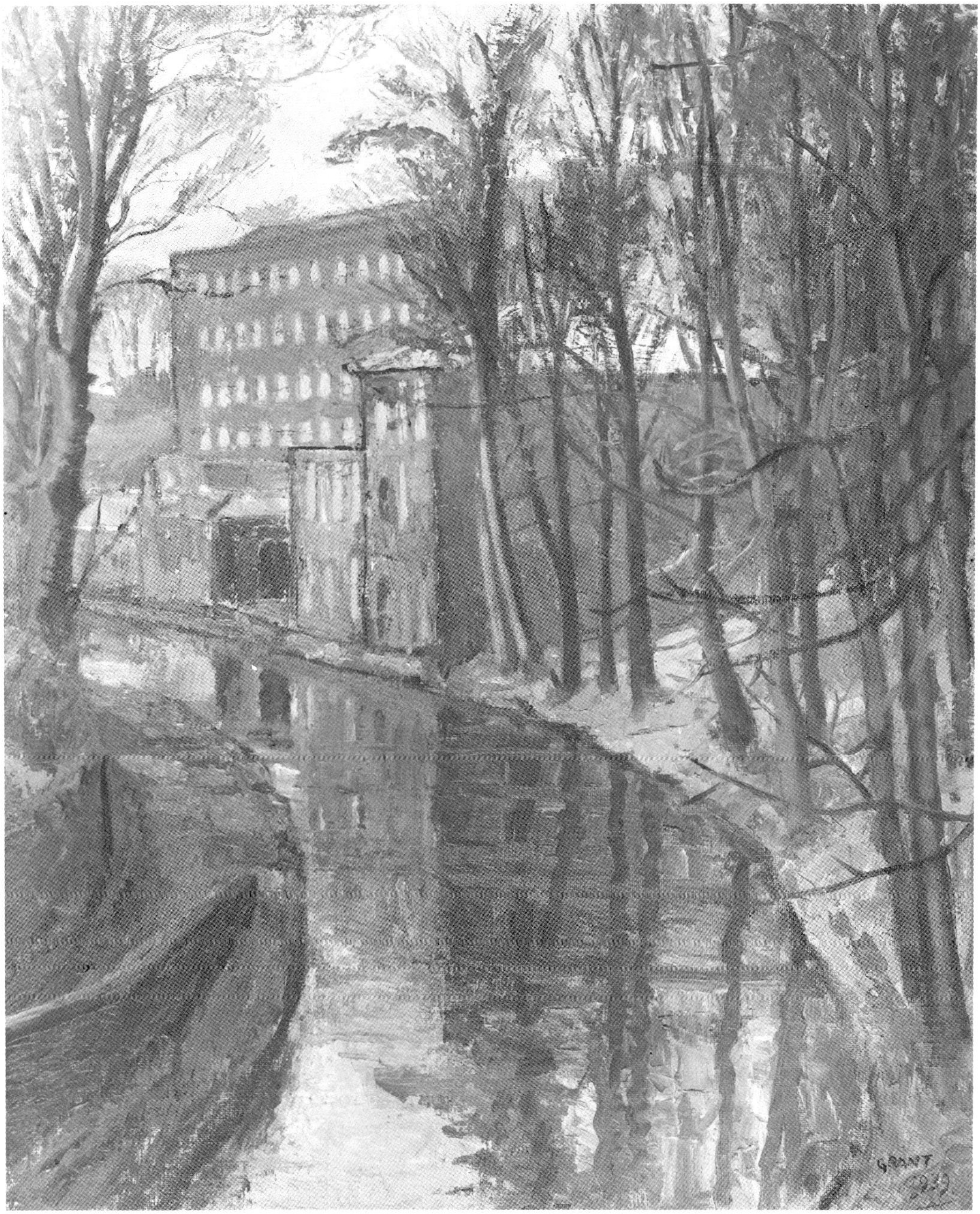

Ian Grant: Cheshire Mill, *oil 1939 (courtesy: Manchester City Art Gallery).*

particularly after the war, through connections with the Ballet Club and Margo Ingham. Grant portrayed Margo Ingham in striking red costume sitting against a blue background. Nudes reclining in relaxed or languid postures across modern sofas have been the theme of many paintings and drawings.

The interest in landscape painting, that became prominent later on, found its first expression in the trips he made with groups of Manchester art students to prime sketching locations outside the city, in particular the rural parts of northern Derbyshire and Cheshire. *Cheshire Mill* (1939: Manchester City Art Gallery) depicts a mill on the High Peak canal near his Cheshire home. The picture was painted entirely out of doors which is unusual, for the artist tended to paint in the studio from 'plein air' drawings. Grant set up his easel at a spot on a canal bridge near the canal tunnel. The mill and an avenue of trees cast shadows and reflections across the water, soon to be disturbed by a coal barge, which, for a mile-long stretch of tunnel could not be pulled by horses and had to be paddled by bargees. The day was breezy and Grant was painting with a palette knife loaded with paint. A sudden gust of wind blew the painting off the easel, and the wet canvas picked up dust from the ground. Most of the dust was scraped off but the picture retained a certain textural roughness. Grant sent it barely dry to the Royal Academy, where it hung in the last exhibition of peacetime. Afterwards *Cheshire Mill* was lent to the Art Exhibition Bureau, and went on a touring exhibition around provincial galleries. On the tour, which took in Brighton, Southampton, Leeds and Liverpool, the painting survived a number of near misses and mishaps. At Leeds the picture, waiting to be unloaded, was among a mass of cargo that was bombed. It was one of only a few paintings that survived. In Liverpool an enemy bomb exploded outside Johnson's warehouse. The building was reduced to rubble, but the paintings were thrown outside by the force of the blast. Remarkably, Grant's *Cheshire Mill* sat unimpaired above a pile of damaged paintings. The picture was exhibited after the war at the artist's one man exhibition at the Midday Studios, where it was purchased by the Manchester City Art Gallery.

Grant had another exhibition, in February 1953 at the Salford Art Gallery, which offered a series of one-man shows to local artists. Charles Sewter described Grant's work as being "the gentle art of recording his perception of a landscape, a figure, or an interior." Sewter's assessment that Grant was an artist "not driven to find expression for an intensely felt emotion," seemed the result of being "too conscious of the demands of design composition, and consistency of surface, so that intuition, on which

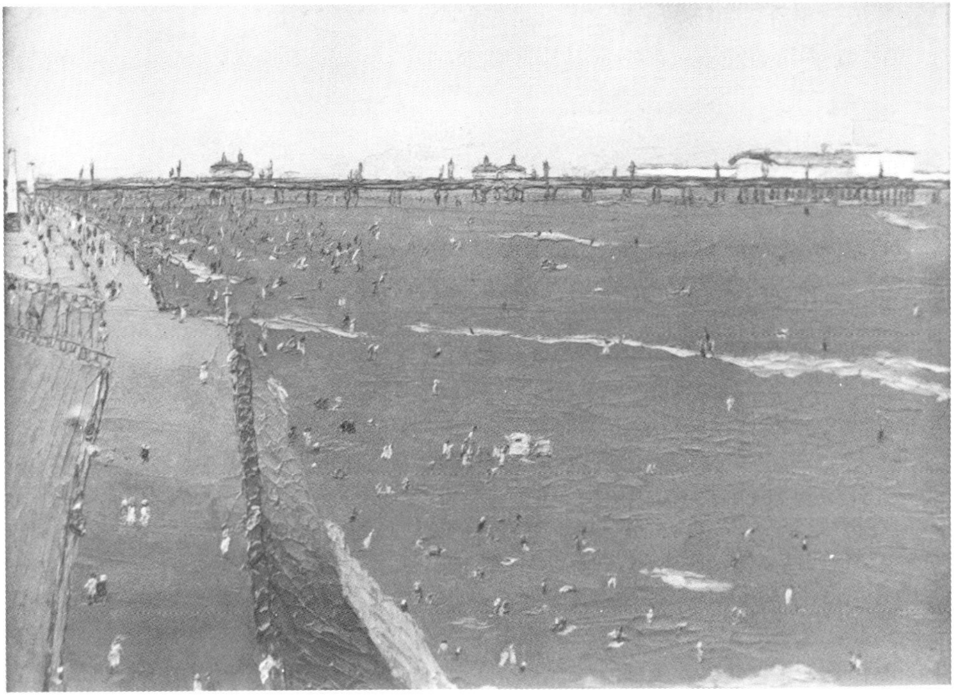

Margaret Gumuchian: Beach Scene: Blackpool, *oil 1951*.

everything ultimately depends, is liable to be swamped." In other words, Grant seemed to him a conventional artist; executing his craft to a high level of refinement, at the expense of spontaneity of execution, and of expressivity of mood. His work, if not expressive of a pronounced or distinctive response to the world, nonetheless gives us a pleasurable sample of nature conveyed through an extremely fine attunement and balance of drawing, composition and colour. His fine mind and even temperament made him a good art historian and lecturer, as well as an important force and diplomat in the art scene of Manchester during the post-war years. He helped maintain contacts between the Manchester Academy and Margo Ingham's Midday Studios group that included artists who had been rejected by the Academy. His period of experimentation was over by this time, although for a while in the late 1950's he adopted abstract painting - still using the autumnal, rich earth colours of his naturalistic landscape painting - but in general, the artist painted landscapes that were informed by his use of on-the-spot watercolour reportage. The artist declared: "I was going for the spirit in the landscape rather than absolute details. Some are more detailed than others." Grant made regular visits to his native Scotland, and to Cornwall. A spate of paintings were produced of Cornish subjects, such as the harbours at Mousehole (where he and his wife stayed), Newlyn, and St Ives. The trips to Cornwall continue to the 1980's. On one Mousehole visit, Grant sold most of his small works before he returned north. As early as the 1920's a trip Grant made to Newlyn enabled him to meet, and witness working with their renowned 'plein air' methods, several of the later members of the Newlyn School.

In 1953, Ian Grant married one of his former Manchester students, Margaret Gumuchian. Born in 1927 at Birch-in-Rusholme, of Armenian parents, Gumuchian taught for two years and then studied painting and textile design for her National Diploma. At the Manchester School of Art there was an emphasis on industrial landscape but Gumuchian sidestepped this and studied the bright harmonies and light colour key of Impressionist painting. George Allsop taught her to use gouache, while Edwin La Dell and Vuillard exerted a more general influence. Conscious from an early age of the indefinable relationship between nature and art, her imagery was often derived from spectacular shafts of sunlight flooding onto a landscape, or from snow reflecting light upwards. These compelling natural images act as metaphors for the meeting of the enlightening rays of artistic consciousness with the expansive landscape forms of nature. She has used winter's bare branches to effect a marked pattern across her pictures. Her first contribution to the Manchester Academy was a studio painting made from a sketch standing outside the Metropole Hotel in Blackpool: *Beach Scene: North Pier, Blackpool (*1951:Manchester City Art Gallery*)*. It was a homage to her shipper and cotton merchant father and the vivid memories of the holidays he had taken the family on each year. Lithography was a liberating medium, while the inevitable influence of Ian Grant led her to produce many landscapes distinguished by a pronounced seasonal lighting. Snow scenes and scenes of early spring were often painted outdoors, with a hot water bottle keeping the artist warm. Poetry pervades the soulful landscapes of an artist sensitive, like Grant himself, to the specific, atmospheric and climatic conditions of the seasonal cycle. What better subject for a painter than this changing cycle, that demands such versatility in the colour register. She went on, during the 1950's and thereafter, to exhibit at most annual Academy exhibitions, and was elected a member in the 1960's. She has also shown several times at the Royal Academy. One contribution, a gouache of a sheep-crowded Welsh landscape (which was exhibited at the 1968 exhibition at Burlington House), won her an annual invitation to the Woman of the Year lunch at the Savoy Hotel. During the late 1950's she taught painting at evening classes in Cheetham Hill, and

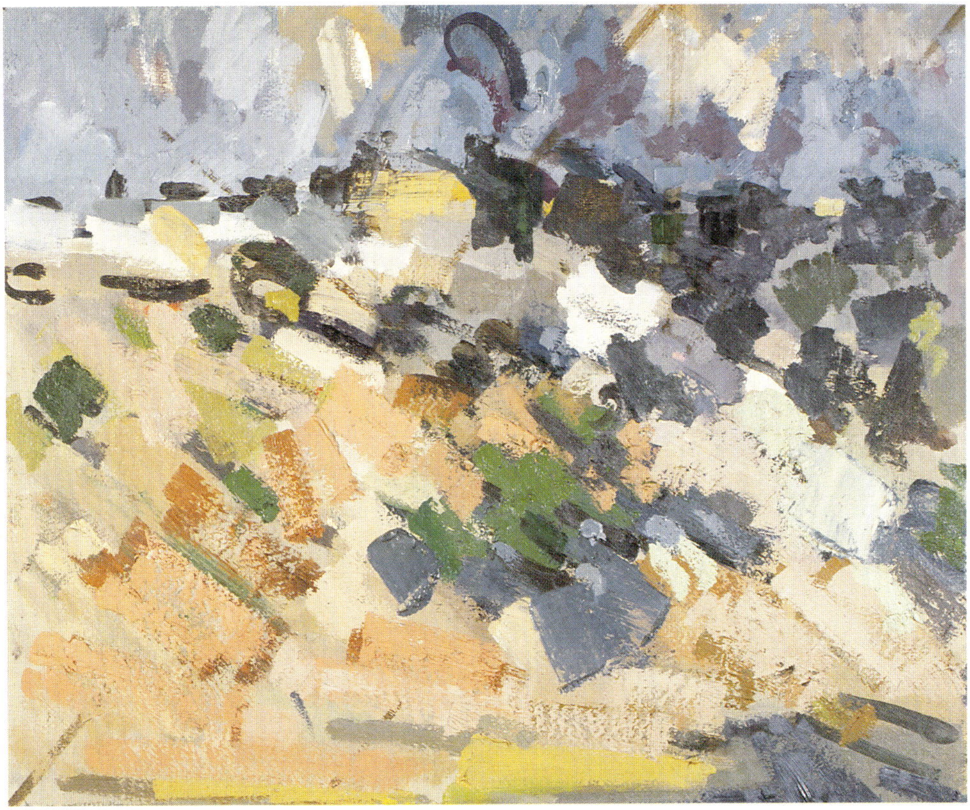

Nicholas Horsfield: Landscape.

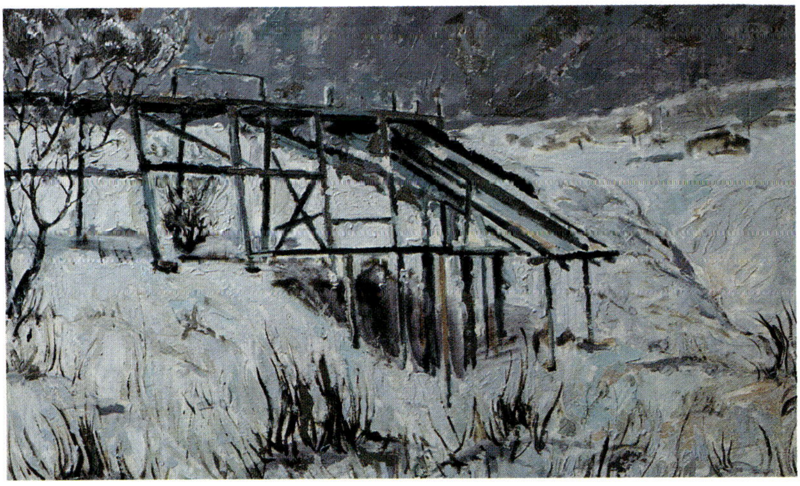

Bob Crossley: Disused Pit, Denshaw, 1956.

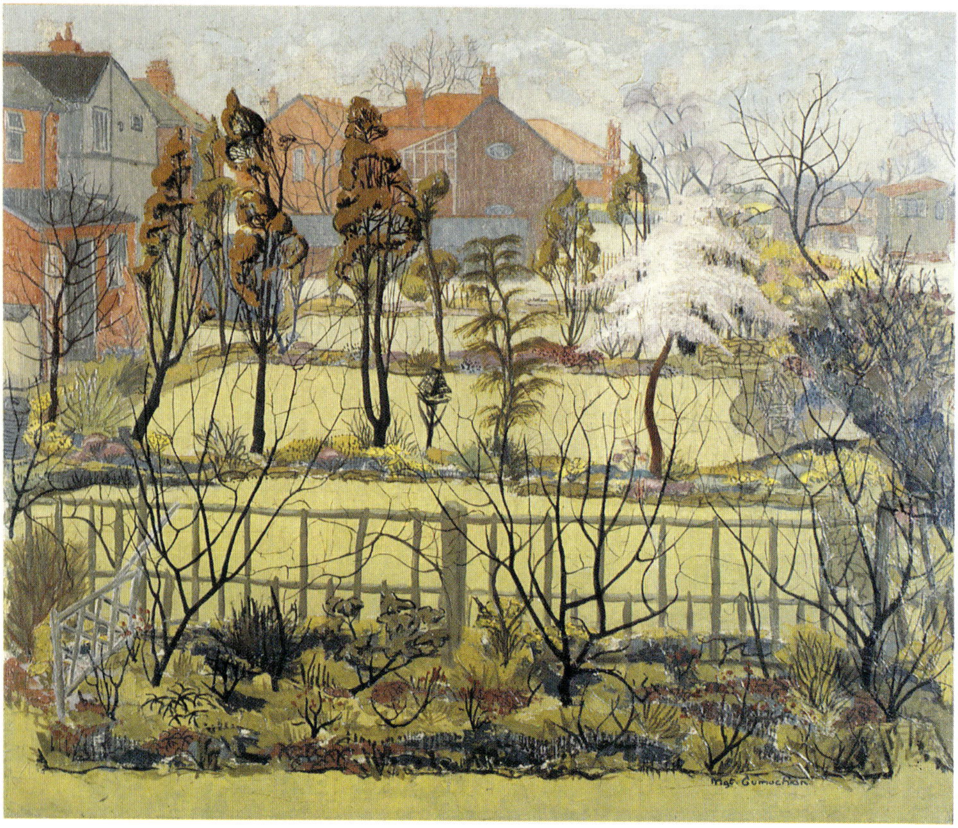

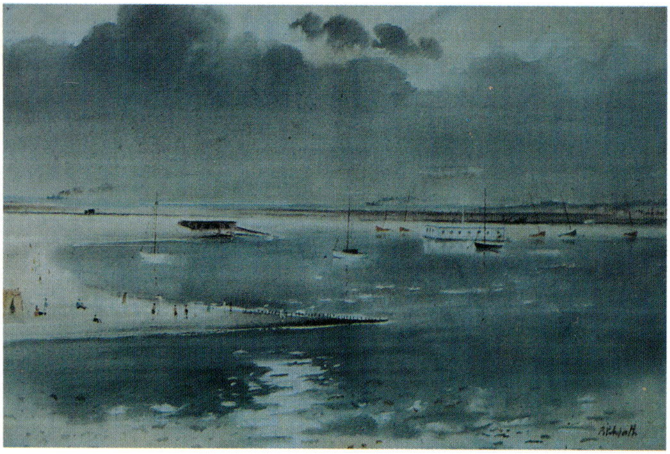

Margaret Gumuchian: Aldersgreen Gardens.

R. V. Pitchforth: Marine Lake, Southport (courtesy: Atkinson Museum, Southport).

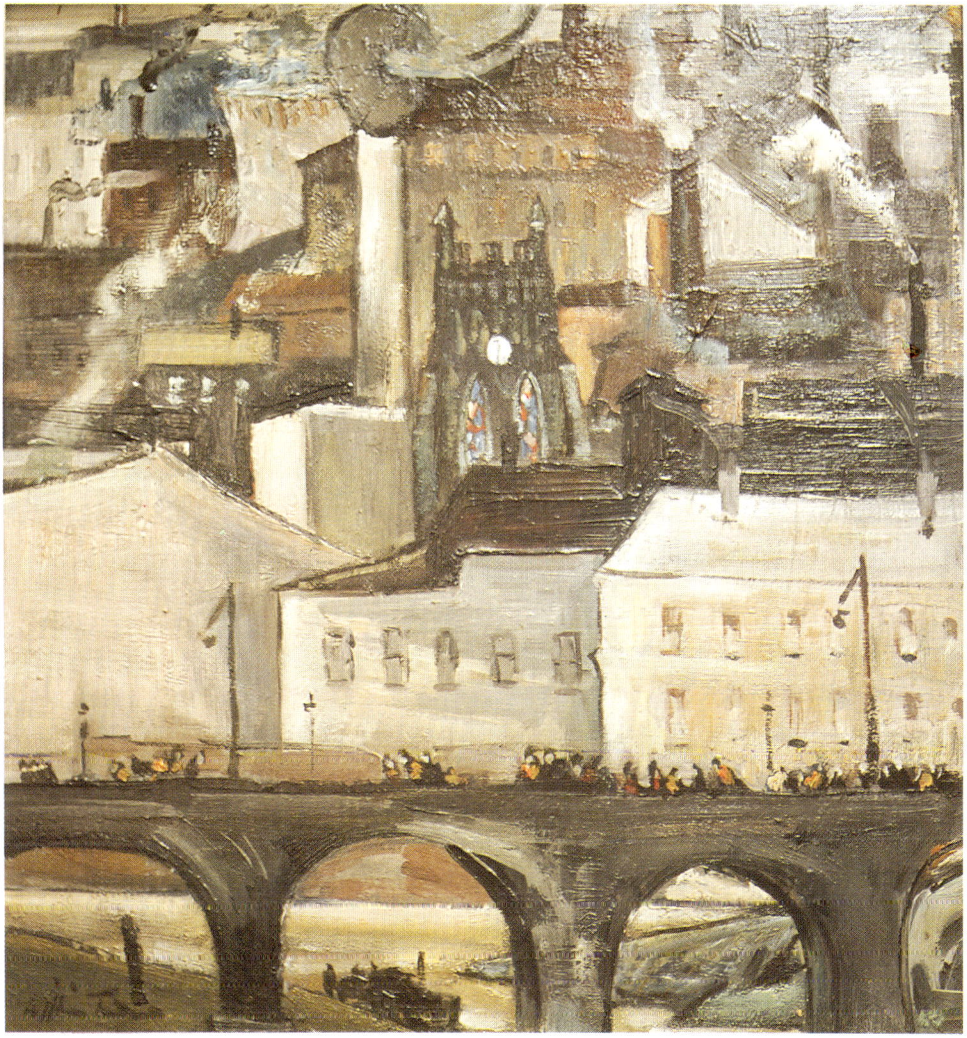

William Turner: St Mary's Stockport.

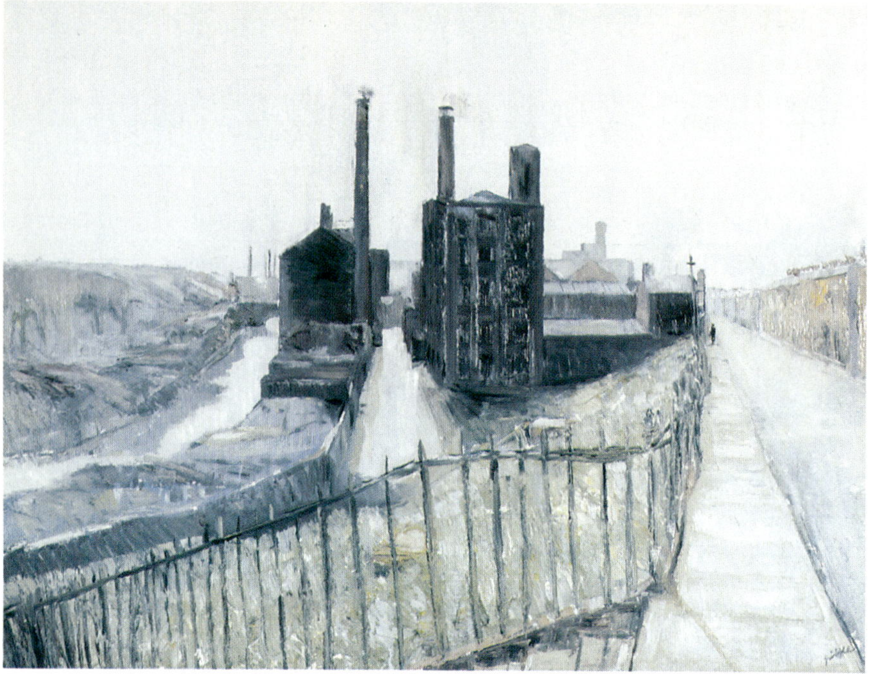

Kenneth Gribble: Park Parade, Ashton-under-Lyne (courtesy: Manchester City Art Gallery).

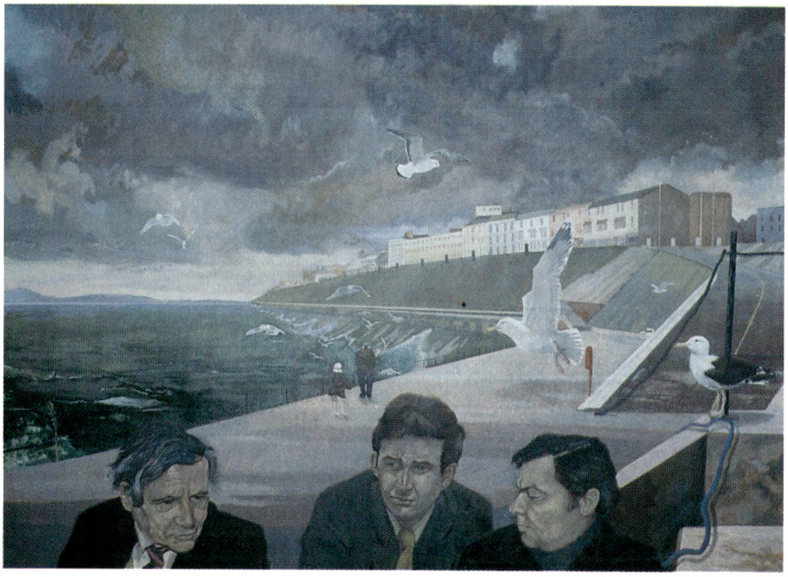

Lesley Young: Blackpool, November.

taught at a number of schools, including Withington Girls School during the late 1960's. She continues to exhibit her characteristic paintings of bare trees silhouetted against the light of an autumnal or wintry sky at Manchester Academy exhibitions. After her marriage to Ian Grant, Gumuchian had a number of two-person exhibitions with her husband, in private galleries such as Lillian Gethic's Peterloo Gallery, the Colin Jellicoe Gallery, and the Moyan Gallery.

Watercolours and drawings done on holiday visits to Cornwall, Wales, Scotland, or nearer to home, in Cheshire and Derbyshire, form the bulk of Ian Grant's landscape work done in situ; worked up into oil paintings in his Cheshire studio many of these works portray nature in a well lit, tranquil mood. Tonally well pitched to the point of telling the exact time of day, these paintings are embellished with generous quantities of paint, confidently loaded on with palette knife. Grant's art demonstrates by well structured composition and hard won skills of drawing, the ability to construct a fine picture. The subject of his demonstration is the supreme natural structure of hill, field, rock, coastline, or in the domain of human geography, street and harbour. His landscapes are often devoid of people; a composition of trees, featuring their wintry skeleton of bare branches, or the magnificent rust and bronze of autumn woods, is a familiar theme. Another is the quiet country road, closer in feel to the 1930's than to the hectic roads of the 1980's. Winter scenes feature in his work, and in some, light reflecting blankets of snow show us, in the sublime manner of his Scottish predecessor, McWhirter, that the colour of snow is never the obvious white that our mind's eye attaches to it, but rather is imbued with subtle blue, pink and orange tints. As late in his career as 1988 Ian Grant was a Vice President of the Manchester Academy, and still gave his art history lectures. These activities are testimonies to a loyal, longstanding and indefatigable member of the north west art scene.

Nine

Theodore Major

Theodore Major's immediately distinguishable work presents a disarmingly honest, angst-ridden response to the sordid, cruel circumstances of the blighted industrial environment that he grew up in. Yet a compassionate and deeply empathetic residue of feeling, using the universal symbol of an enlarged sun, brings to the anonymous streets and dark satanic mills a ray of hope. Indeed, Major has often been quick to disparage the hopeless vision of northern man that was conveyed in George Orwell's *Road to Wigan Pier*. Major's own gloomy Wigan landscapes are peopled by heroic, if somewhat passive agents of defiant survival, postured in upright stances that echo the verticals of telegraph poles or factory chimneys.

These are often the only distinguishable features within an indeterminate urban landscape, shrouded by the grey gloom of atmospheric pollution or industrial smog. Major articulates these urban scenes with an emphatic use of black and white, alleviated by a variety of toned greys to suggest distant architectural silhouette. The apocalyptic mood that such a stark palette conveys recalls the unnerving cityscapes of German artists like Meidner (who said himself: "When you paint Berlin use only white and black, a little ultramarine and ochre and a lot of umber.") Yet Major's Wigan skylines do not quiver or shake as in the German vision, but rather the block-like shapes of factories retain a geometric solidity and stability. They, no less than the people, are not about to collapse into any abyss. Since any particularised portrayal of place is rendered unlikely, if not impossible, by the enveloping atmosphere of industrial smog, Major's Wiganscapes contain that tendency of much Expressionist art to sublimate the particular towards the general. The true intention of Major's art lies in creating a universal metaphor, not only for the industrial landscape, but indeed for the human condition. The anti-establishment, anti-academic tenor of Major's art is implicit. His treatment of the industrial town readily conjures up associations with the German Expressionists, who found in the inhuman scale of modern cities ready-built metaphors for claustrophobia, agoraphobia, feelings of angst, displacement, isolation, alienation, and so on. The menacing, suffocating mist that envelops Major's streets can be read in literal terms, as pollution of everyday working environments, and also in symbolic terms of the human psyche itself. The magnified suns that manage to shine through these atmospheres, or the cloth-capped figures who retain a dignified uprightness, suggest that the liberating power of optimism, hope and perseverance - what Kandinsky referred to as the White Ray - is never far away. The utopian ray of hope tempts the onlooker to embrace a spiritual essence beyond the greed and exploitation of industrialised society.

Theodore Major was born into a poor Wigan family in 1908. His father worked in a local weaving factory. He was a devout man who became a lay reader at a church in nearby Ince. The example of the father's strong beliefs influenced the son, who adopted a more general approach to spiritual matters. This was expressed in later years in a typically terse statement: "Painting is my life and art my religion."

Theodore had one brother and four sisters. The educational prospects for any boy born into these circumstances were not great. It was intended that he should work in a local tailor's shop; a job that would prove suitable for a youth not physically strong having been affected early on by rheumatic fever. But the boy had other ideas and he chose instead to attend classes at the local Wigan Art School. Here, with other disciplines, he developed in the still life class an instinct to compose with brightly contrasted positive colours. He explored the relationship between formal components, and began to use a liberal amount of paint expressively applied with a palette knife. The young student's progress was rapid; he found himself taking classes there within a few years, and after the war was teaching every weekday evening. Major's art studies were supplemented by a day a week at Liverpool which lasted for two years. During the war he spent one day a week at Southport. The studies at Liverpool, but more especially at Southport, brought the abrasive working-class Wigan student into contact with middle-class students, who pursued art as an amateur hobby. This experience taught him to look to himself, and to a few admired exemplars. It is probable that this examination of his own origins, helped shape the course that his painting would take.

Major met his future wife at Wigan Art School. After they married in 1930, Kathleen taught at a school near Wigan and provided the family (a daughter, Mary, was born) with the basic security that enabled Theodore to pursue a serious commitment to painting. Several of Major's early portraits, of children painted in the 1940's, were painted from a discarded photograph of pupils at the school where Kathleen Major taught. The innocence, vision and imagination of children became a prime motif for an artist who maintained these qualities would soon be rooted out of the young. Many years later he wrote, in typically bombastic terms, "I see modern education as the destroyer of children's sensibilities. I believe that every child is an artist until he is educated." The world of children represented to Major's romantic, if abrasive, temperament the perfect antidote to an adult world where the primacy of intellect, calculation and materialism predominate.

The Major family lived in plain accommodation in the centre of Wigan. A large, single room within the house was all that was available in which to live, paint and raise a small child. In 1950 they moved to Appley Bridge, a small, pleasant village a couple of miles outside Wigan. For a time the new environment affected his subject and a number of semi-rural landscapes appeared. Major's post-war involvement with the Manchester art scene, in particular with Margo Ingham's Midday Studios Group, and with the Manchester Academy, has been cited in another chapter. For a time, it gave him group involvement of a kind that promoted his work and brought him modest fame as a distinctive painter of remarkable promise. Through this Manchester milieu, Major struck up a network of friendships and acquaintances. Among the better known was Lowry, who paid more than one visit to Major's Appley Bridge studio. Lowry was impressed by what he saw: a studio containing a number of masterpieces. Direct links, as well as divergences, between the work of Lowry and Major is a subject worthy of an independent essay, and will be examined shortly. John Berger, too, visited Appley Bridge, and after staying with Major for a week, wrote that Major's paintings, "rank among the best English paintings of our time." It is not difficult to see what it was in Major's work that appealed so compellingly to Berger.

Theodore Major's personal yet symbolic vision of a northern industrial town fulfilled John Berger's aesthetic and philosophical criteria for post war realism. In the early fifties Berger, then a Marxist, believed art should record the conditions of working class life with its social struggle and serve in the wider struggle for social emancipation. In this way Theodore Major's specific references to local life represented the general conditions of the industrial world. Although John Berger's ideals of the early 1950's have since been modified away from kitchen sink art and drab social realism in general, it is doubtful whether he would today disclaim the importance he once attached to Major's vision.

For a short time Major's work seemed to represent to Berger the best of English painting. David Sylvester, the art-critic, in the early 50's looked for a symbolic realism, best seen in such artists as Middleditch and Bacon. Both Major and Lowry, however, could also be regarded as symbolic realists. This is by the use of heightened anonymity and fantasy in their contrived urban settings: Lowry using a composite reconstruction from memory of a variety of places; Major de-localising specific place through the screening agencies of smogs and hazes.

Since Major's involvement with the post-war Manchester art scene, he has become increasingly a recluse. He has continued to paint on a daily basis, producing a prolific *oeuvre.* The private existence of Major denotes, however, a dissillusionment with the art world, whose power brokers (the dealers, galleries, critics and promotional magazines) are swayed by fashion or commerce. The house is always open for visitors at weekends, or during spells of inactivity in the studio, and is crammed with paintings, almost all of them oil on board. The vociferous artist answers questions in terms that express his deep convictions about the equation of truth with beauty, and the identification of beauty with what the squeamish or small-minded might consider ugly.

However much the symbolic content and expressive gesture have developed in Major's painting, early 20th century Wigan was formative visually. Major described the dark streets, morning vistas, the yellow light of the sun (he has identified yellow as being the spiritual colour of the soul) and "red flames of open blast furnaces on wet pavements" as the early visual influences that shaped his pictorial imagery.

Mervyn Levy described a quality in Major's landscape work as a "spiritual harmony which exists between man and the destiny of his surroundings." A rare family holiday to Llandudno, yielded a number of lonely seascapes holding a solitary ship. The theme of a lonely ship at sea is one for which Lowry is well known, although he developed it considerably later than Major. Similarly Major's dark grey and black factory landscapes, populated with odd, anonymous, taut figures, recall Lowry's famous views of Manchester mills with their armies of 'matchstickmen.' Yet Lowry viewed humanity as if from a hill, a psychological and literal distance separating the onlooker from the subjects of his pictures. Major's observations, like the otherwise very different work of Alan Lowndes, come down to the ground and close up to the streets and people depicted. The constitution of Lowry's work was a sound performance of academic draughtsmanship, conventional, classical composition and a mastery of naturalistic tone and colour. Lowry is the wry and cold observer. Major's painting is far more expressionistic; in technique, tenor, and meaning. A more insistent humanitarian symbolism, an indulgence into the Kafka-esque realm of the self's vulnerability to harsh external circumstances, is apparent in Major's more emotive and emotionally charged work. Lowry's vision of loneliness, conveyed in the images of empty houses, ships at sea, or in the early grotesquerie of red-eyed tramp portraits is essentially autobiographical. Major comments more

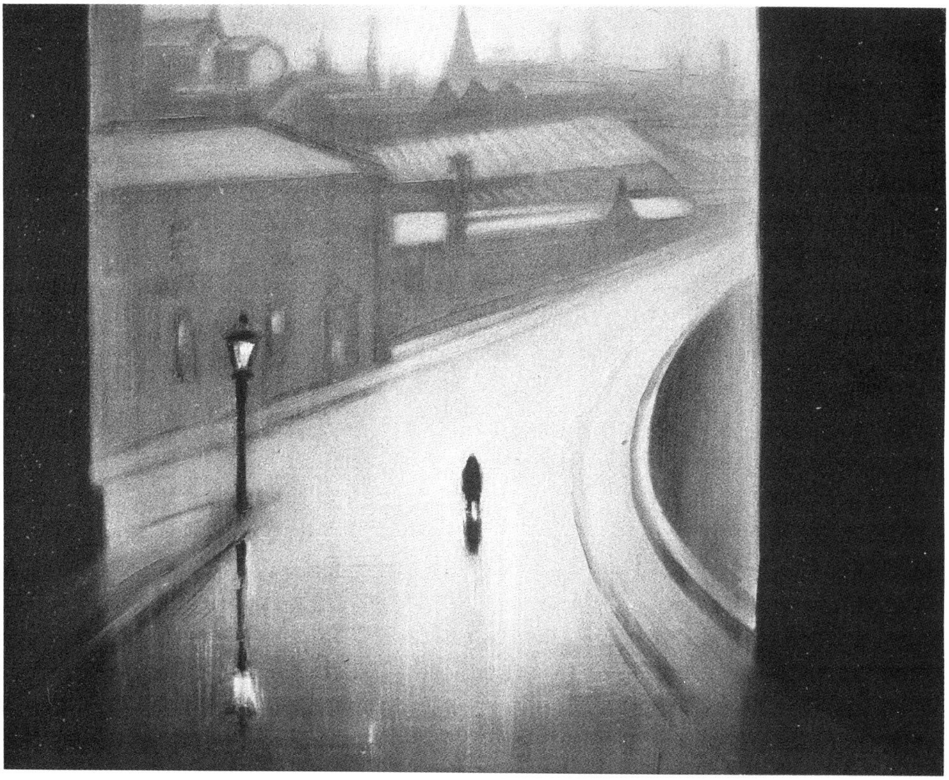

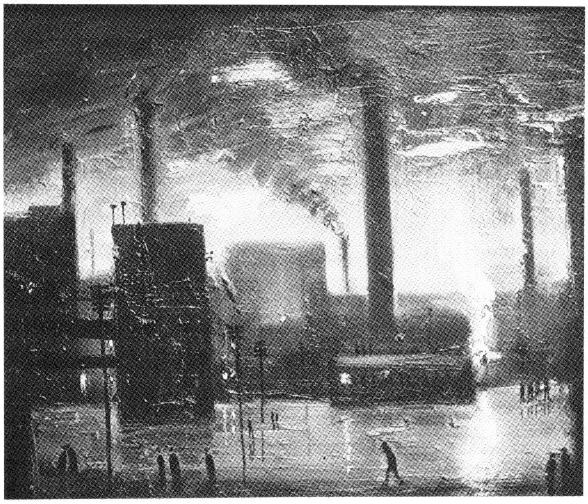

Theodore Major: Wigan Streets and Wigan Factories.

generally on the realities of the human condition in his sterile, polluted environments, with solitary figures appearing as phantoms from smogs of uncertainty. Neither artist reaches the extremity of Edvard Munch's *The Scream*. In Major it is not the figures who seek release from an oppressive ambience, rather it is the magnified sun struggling to break through the smog, that offers redemption. The artist summarised his intention "I wish to disturb and extend consciousness in the mind of the viewer. I wish to shock into 'awareness' the sensibility of people: to attack accepted standards; to awaken the mind to spiritual values."

Armed with the belief that art "portrays his longings, his sufferings, his ideals and his fears," Major began to vary the tenor of his industrial landscapes. The suns became increasingly magnified, the telegraph poles loomed larger as markers of the foreground and became crucifixes; and the pictures became more stringently ordered with more insistent horizontal and vertical axes. Skeletons populated the surrounding landscape which Major described as "terrified symbols of humanity, crawling, running." The skeletons sometimes wore halos becoming "figures of hope amid scenes of utter destruction." He has taken the desecration of the environment to its ultimate conclusion. He resurrects the death of humanity by using the grotesque image of an active skeleton. It is a strange metaphor for the survival of the spirit amidst the most terrible holocaust. Similarly he campaigns against the imposition of impersonal, modern architecture in Wigan. It is doubtful, however, that his sentimental attachment to the old would have made him resistant to the Clean Air Act. All these themes and concerns are integral to the skeleton motif, the "describing by symbolism and imagination the events and possible consequences of man's desecration and pollution of his natural environment."

The role of colour has become uppermost in Major's work since the 1960's. His admiration for the generous sensibility and glowing warmth of Fauve art is evident in a long series of variations on the nude. At first, the Matisse-like nude danced rhythmically in front of a vaguely defined European-looking city. Then gradually, the nude became the sole pictorial entity, geometrically stylised with thick dark outlines, and broken into bright zones of pure unmodified colour. In the simplified palette knife rendition of *Wigan Girl-Looking*, a portrait which uses an elongated format, Major comes close to the work of Bernard Buffet. The robust treatment in *Head of Christ* is reminiscent of Rouault. In 1960 Bill Grundy described in the *Listener* Major's portraits as "old people with terrible faces, skulls that are etched with the misery and squalor . . . but in their struggle with filth their faces have become beautiful."

Does the artist's inherently provincial point of reference, limited to a time rapidly passing, relegate him to the status of a talented but ultimately minor English eccentric? Perhaps Major's industrial skylines, with their mercurial but lurid atmospheres, are but plastic distortions of a definite place; the artist's Wigan. I believe not. In the final analysis Major does not illustrate Wigan, or even his feelings toward Wigan. Rather he finds a plastic equivalent, a purely artistic metaphor, for the contingent realities wrought by a previous generation's industrialisation of a typical northern town. For this he deserves to be ranked, as John Berger once claimed, among artists of significance of our own tumultuous time.

Ten

Alan Lowndes

The turbulent but colourful career of the Stockport-born painter Alan Lowndes (1921-1978) falls into three distinct categories. The artist's early work - and arguably the best - portrayed in rigorous and colourful terms, the streets, buildings and general visage of the mill and railway town of Stockport. The second phase of his work, coinciding with the middle years of this prolific painter's career, spanned the period between the middle 1950's and 1970 when he worked in the Cornish fishing port and famous artist's colony of St Ives. The third and final phase, from 1970 to his death from liver failure at Gloucester hospital in October 1978, focused on rural Gloucestershire.

There is no mystery about the influences that these three enormously different environments exerted on his work, which was, however, always characterised by a direct and uncomplicated commentary on the daily life and customs of the localities where he lived. As so often with painters, the early work is sometimes the most sought after and valued, and it is certainly the case that the Stockport of Lowndes' youth never left him. The dark red mills, famous viaduct, and terraced streets of his native town were imprinted on his soul. In later years, long after he had left the north, images of industrial Stockport recurred in pictures painted from memory in his sunny studio in sub-Mediterranean St Ives or in the lush green surroundings of his Gloucestershire home.

Thus we find prime Stockport subjects cropping up in pictures painted during the 1960's in Cornwall. Examples here are provided by *Mealhouse Brow* (1961), *Stockport Snow Scene* (1962), and the large *The Park, Stockport Panorama* from the year 1964. A few years later in 1970 the artist painted an anecdotal scene of a fish and chip shop *Love Lane Corner*, while as late as 1975 he produced, in Gloucestershire, a masterpiece, *Old Stockport Fair*, a late variation on the perennial theme of his home town. The exotic machinery of fairground helter-skelter and dodgem is silhouetted against the more permanent, and altogether more mundane and functional architecture of cooling tower, gasometer and beetroot coloured mill. Lowndes here reaches the soul of northern street life, rather than offering any precise topographical record or scientific reference to the decline of the industrial age. In addition, he produced a spate of clearly northern pictures though with unidentified settings, conveying amusing, sentimental or sympathetic anecdotes of street life. Thus came about images of the organ grinder, ice cream man or flower seller. Meanwhile the artist's empathy with the imaginative world of children became evident with street scenes full of children playing football, cricket or hopscotch. Old customs, like Stockport's traditional processions, the annual visit of the circus and fair, the life of the local variety theatre or cinema or pub, also appealed and provided the artist with rich source material.

Wherever he went Lowndes never failed to respond to the inherent character and idiosyncrasies of a given place. In pictures like *Great Howard Street, Liverpool* (1960) and *Warrington Back Alley* or *Hazy Morning, Huddersfield* (both 1966) Lowndes showed us he could look beyond the familiar perimeters of Stockport in his northern *oeuvre*. It is likely that annual visits back to see his family in Stockport, or to his wife Valerie's family in Yorkshire provided the specific pretexts and inspiration for the continued occurrence of such northern views in the work of an artist who had 'gone Cornish' and joined the St Ives colony. He was, therefore, in the very first instance, a painter of town skylines and streets. He was not an academically trained fine artist, and but for post-war evening classes at Stockport under the portrait painter Emmanual Levy, was largely self taught. He relied on a robust and natural talent. The use of strong, uninhibited colour and painterly surfaces notable for a variety of impastoes, scrapings and scratchings, were the hallmarks of Alan Lowndes' style.

A particularly important element in the rise of Alan Lowndes to fame and commercial success is the career of the dealer Andreas Kalman, the Hungarian émigré who soon after the war became his friend, champion, promoter and dealer. From 1950 Lowndes enjoyed regular exhibitions with Kalman, first in Manchester, at Kalman's first gallery and then after 1956 at the dealer's new gallery in London's prestigious Brompton Road. The association with Kalman gave Lowndes access to a generation of up-and-coming northern playwrights, actors and writers who grew up in similar working class circumstances, and were to love their chosen painter's rendition of the reality they all shared. Michael Parkinson, Willis Hall, Keith Waterhouse, Richard Attenborough, Albert Finney, Bill Naughton and John Osborne were some of the many celebrities from the world of arts and entertainment who invested in the pictures of Alan Lowndes.

Although I never knew Alan Lowndes, I became very well acquainted with his family. The many affectionate stories that one hears about his eccentric and at times wild life, match the tenor of the artist's work. He was by all accounts a difficult man, of often obstinate and unyielding beliefs. Argumentative sometimes to the point of being a bombast, Lowndes animated many a bar room with lively banter. He was, though, a middle-of-the-road working class socialist. Never seditious or subversive, he possessed many conventional traits. Once married he settled into a kind of bourgeois provincial lifestyle. His few concessions to unorthodox or bohemian habits were membership of a renowned artists' colony and the sometimes precarious financial predicament caused by his stubborn refusal to teach painting in the art schools. Teaching would have mitigated the need to sell his paintings to eke out a modest living for himself and his young family. Many of Lowndes' closest friends, painters like Terry Frost in Cornwall and Nicholas Horsfield in Liverpool, did just that in order to sustain themselves.

Lowndes was the epitome of the northern working class lad with a natural skill. It is debatable whether his early decision to become a painter, made at the end of the war, would have become translated into a sustained effort had he not climbed out of the grinding poverty of those early post-war days, when the young, self-styled painter set up studio in a room in a building (now demolished) opposite the picturesque indoor market at St Petersgate, Stockport. In order to appreciate the colourful nature of the man himself it is helpful to look at the career of Alan Lowndes in biographical terms. Alan Lowndes' artistic temperament was highly inventive and individualistic. He was very sociable; he painted in a direct and primitive way, yet he was well aware of the great painters of the past, and could more than hold his own in intellectual discussion. His gift lay in cutting through the superficialities of appearance to reveal the essential character of a given scene. Without needing recourse to extraneous and irrelevant topographical detailing, Lowndes' earthy painting gained an unusual and uncompromising directness. He looked hard at the ordinary, mundane things most of us take for granted, and extracted an added poetry. Despite the raw yet sensitively worked and nuanced surfaces of his paintings, Lowndes' expressionism never indulged in distortion or exaggeration for its own sake. Later in his career, when the vogue for 'pure' abstract painting and hard edge abstraction held sway, he stuck firmly to his belief in the basic representational values of painting. His work exuded a gently observed wit and quiet humour, as well as a certain nostalgia for old places and the time-honoured customs of everyday life. The buildings and streets of Stockport became Lowndes' arcadia. The magnificent viaduct of his native town sometimes ran across his pictures with an expressive clarity and boldness that highlighted the importance of the world's largest red brick viaduct to the life of Stockport.

As already noted, Lowndes was a self-taught artist. He did, though, study art at a Florentine art school at the end of the War, and later on attended the Stockport art school as a part-time evening student. Having mastered the essential practical skills of his craft learnt from the unlikely, but no less valid angle of a full knowledge and experience of the painting and decorating trade, Lowndes turned his lack of formal art training into one of his greater strengths. For Alan Lowndes was born with a sensibility and directness of vision that cannot be taught; his art was natural rather than nurtured. He was born on February 23rd 1921, one of five children of a Stockport railway clerk, Mrs Lowndes was the daughter of a blacksmith whose family originated from Kilmarnock. His paternal grandfather was a farm bailiff who lived in a pleasant cottage with garden and trees in an area of Wilmslow called Lacey Green. Alan had vague memories of him. "Even then I could tell he was a simmered down 'character'. . .and could lift a full beer barrel with teeth." He was one of seven children and he in turn had seven children through his schoolteacher wife. Only two of these had survived - Alan's father Sam, and Alan's Uncle George, whom Alan never met. Alan later remembered his grandfather as displaying 'a fondly dignified' attitude to his grandchildren. Alan's father Sam moved from Wilmslow to Stockport, having obtained a job at Heaton Chapel Station.

In the early 1920's, when Alan Lowndes was born, Stockport was still a busy manufacturing town with cobbled streets and quaint alleyways with sharply rising steps between the mills and warehouses. Stockport's main products, such as hats and clothes, were based on the cotton spinning and weaving industries which had been responsible for Stockport's growth during the eighteenth and nineteenth centuries.

In 1924 Mrs Lowndes died after giving birth to Christine, the last of the five children. This tragedy greatly added to the difficulties of an impoverished family of young children. Alan was only three when his mother died, and he later wrote: "I can hardly remember my mother. I was the youngest boy and had a bad stammer. This I was told dated from around the time my mother died. I have only one memory of her. She was in the kitchen looking lovely and in tears. On the piano in the front room my dad was playing 'Ye banks and braes o' bonnie doon.' Her soft looking auburn hair I remember most vividly." After Jenny's death, the burden of looking after the five children fell chiefly on Sam Lowndes, who needed much help from a succession of housekeepers. Jenny, the eldest girl, looked after the younger children after she left school in 1930, at the age of 14. Alan was then nine, and already showing an interest in drawing, which he

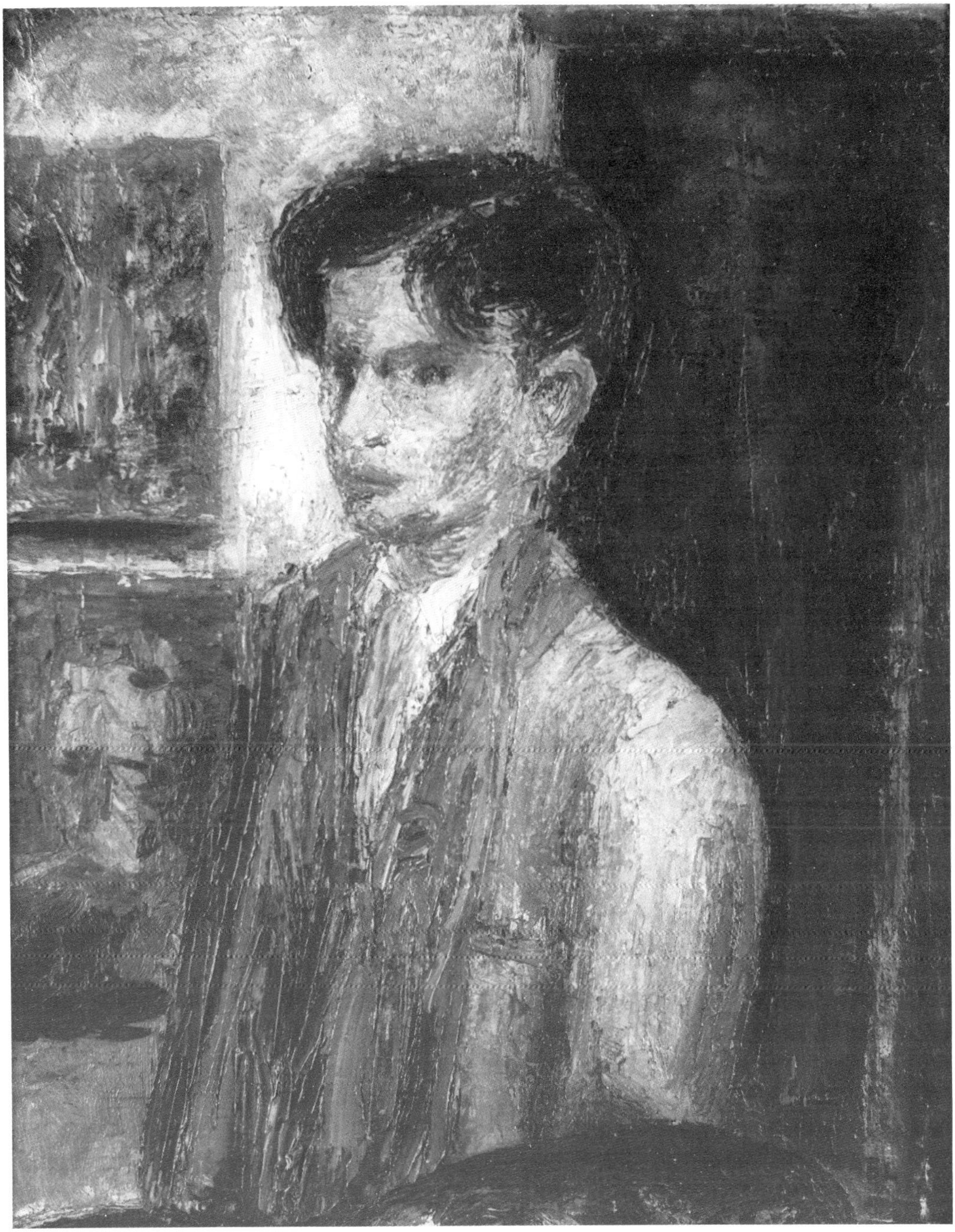

Alan Lowndes: Portrait of the Artist, *oil 1948 (courtesy: Crane Kalman Gallery).*

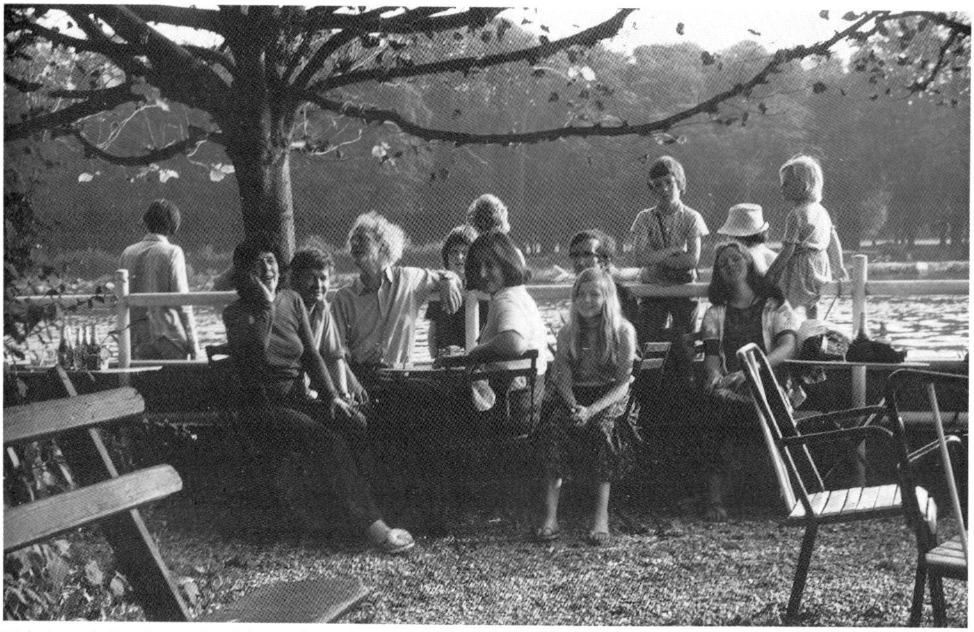

Valerie and Alan Lowndes, John and Ann Willett, Nicholas Horsfield on holiday in France in the 1960s.

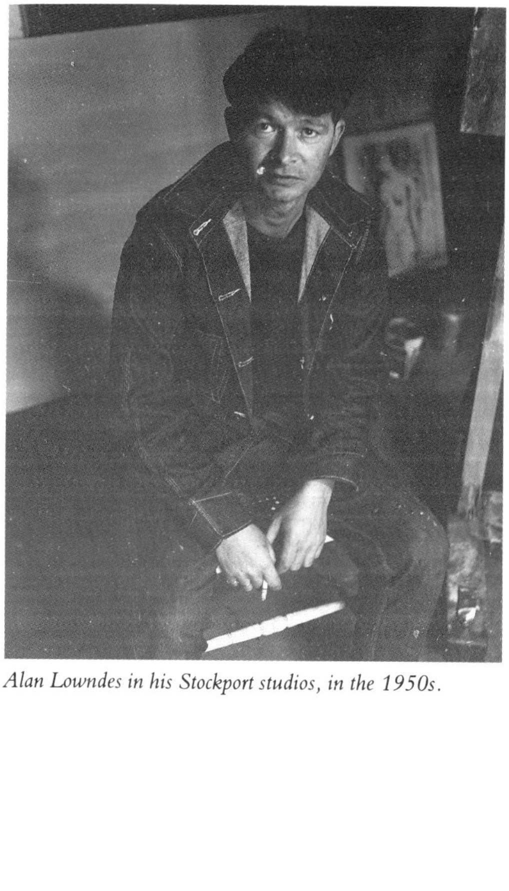

Alan Lowndes in his Stockport studios, in the 1950s.

practised on bits of fish and chip wrapping paper. Alan later wrote: "We all drew a lot in drawing books. Mostly battles of Normans and Saxons and Germans and English. Cowboys and Indians came later and with 'The Pictures.' This drawing all took place on the kitchen table, in fact everything mostly took place in the kitchen." Mr Lowndes encouraged Alan's early flair for sketching, and tried to give some help, although his own talent lay in music. Alan was an imaginative child and drew his own cartoons. He started school in 1926 at Christ Church, Heaton Norris, which was attended by all the Lowndes children. He started at the Infants where his habitual stammer did not matter. Alan never displayed any interest or talent for sport, which may in retrospect seem surprising in that street football and cricket provide the subjects of several mature paintings. Such sporting subjects were, though, more a portrayal of working-class children or urchins at play than an expression of interest in sports.

The Scottish painter Joan Eardley was an exact contemporary and there is a resemblance between her now highly esteemed paintings of Glasgow street urchins and Alan's pictures of Stockport children at play in the streets. The best examples of these are: *Boy on Street Corner* (1956), *The Goalkeeper* (1960), *Hop and Skip* (1968) and *Backyard Cricket* (1961). A large picture of 1970, *Football Match*, is of a well attended Burnden Park, home of Bolton Wanderers. Since the same subject occurs in Lowry we may cite this as a possible link, if not influence, between the older and younger artist.

He started an apprenticeship as painter and decorator with H. Pearson of Hazel Grove, Stockport. He learned much about the chemistry and behaviour of paint and went to night school at Stockport technical college to learn signwriting. One of the most immediate and arresting qualities of Alan's best work is the thick application of generous layers of palette knifed paint, one complementary colour applied on top of the next to create powerful contrasts. These textures form an uncanny resemblance to plastered walls or brick facades. Alan found that decorating the homes of the middle-classes was not an activity much to his liking. He never related socially or culturally to the poshly-spoken suburban middle-classes of the Cheshire dormitories, and the work involved an early start, transporting heavy materials through all kinds of weather, followed by a long, arduous, working day. Alan wrote that "while putting on their nauseating paper I used to draw on the lovely plain plaster underneath."

In the summer of 1939 Alan, aged 18, was an experienced Rover Scout and visited the Isle of Man with the Boy Scouts. It was a glorious summer but the threat of war was widely felt. "In 1939 a grim relief spread about. I was frankly delighted as it meant escape from the decorating - a job I've loathed ever since. I suppose this was partly why I jumped to my brother's suggestion made outside the Stockport Municipal Baths on September 1st. I left my trade with as little regret as I had left school." The story of how Alan joined the army is an amusing one which highlights the kind of mishaps which influenced the happy-go-lucky course of his life. Alan went with his brother Colin and their friend Fred Lord to Stockport baths early one evening. The baths were closed because of a swimming gala, and out of a mixture of disaffection, confusion and boredom, Alan followed Colin's advice and went straight away to the local army recruiting office to join up. In fact Colin had been in the Territorial Army since 1938. Within a day or two of joining up, this normally placid Rover Scout found himself unwittingly in the front line for service in the newly declared war against Hitler's Germany. Colin and Alan were parted soon after and did not see one another again until the war ended nearly six years later.

Alan's active war service first saw him shipped out to the Middle East. Getting there meant a circuitous journey around the horn of Africa to avoid German U-boats in the Mediterranean. It took a couple of months. The ship made its way slowly up the east coast of Africa and reached Cairo via the Red Sea. In the north African campaign leading up to and including El Alamein, Alan saw front line action with the Vickers machine gun crew, and suffered shell shock. After that battle, he fell prone to a number of diseases, including one that did permanent damage to his liver. After a few weeks recovering, he was sent to the map making unit.

With his artistic flair he was transferred to the photo interpretation unit as a draughtsman. This was part of the Royal Army Service Corps based in Italy at the New Zealand Divisional Headquarters. Alan's job was to draw the results of photographic information onto a map. Roderick Bisson, later to become a reputable Liverpool painter of surrealist and abstract compositions, was engaged on similar activities alongside him. The travel in Italy and the Middle East greatly broadened Lowndes' horizons, and in Italy he made his first serious wash drawings. Towards the war's end he sent home some of these competent sketches of tranquil camp site scenes, and quiet hillside villages. Alan reflected: "I don't know how war artists worked, but sitting up in a slit trench in the middle of a battle was definitely not for me." None of these drawings portrayed soldiers. His two sisters Jenny and Christine were able to take them along to show Emmanuel Levy at Stockport School of Art. Levy was immediately impressed and wanted to see Alan when he returned from Italy. Through his service in the map making unit, Alan was allowed to attend courses at Florence University. These were arranged as educational, therapeutic and rehabilitation exercises for war weary troops, in order to prepare them for civilian life. The experience of formal lessons in Florence clinched a half hatched ambition to become an artist. For the first time he drew from the nude model. The art treasures of Renaissance Florence, the frescoes and wall murals, particularly the work of Michelangelo and Giotto, "hit me like a brick." Of Italian frescoes and wall murals, he later wrote: "Because of my early contacts with the building trade I knew a lot about plastering, floating and skimming. I could see where bits had been chipped out and done again."

The prime paintings of Lowndes' early career were full of feeling for place - the *genius loci* - but were also expressive of a certain era. This is what makes them unique, and what distances them from Lowry's more generalised, composite and imagined industrial visions. Alan Lowndes' inbuilt aversion to institutions and organisations - a common enough attitude in artistic bohemia - stemmed from his early life. It explains why later, as a relatively successful and well-known artist he never taught in the art schools, when the supplementary income would have helped smooth out the vagaries of having to rely solely on the sale of one's work.

After the war, Alan's determination to become an artist was the paramount force in his life. He later wrote, "after nearly six years I'd had enough of war, armies, etc for a lifetime." It was not easy for a young working-class man coming out of the army to get the necessary backing, although various schemes had started to help with the education of ex-servicemen; and he had already attended the Florence art school. Levy at Stockport Art School had been much impressed by Alan's wartime sketches, and the young man duly enrolled there as a part-timer at evening classes.

Lowndes found a studio at the top of Bamford House, Churchgate, an elevated position opposite the market and church. It had views down to the cooling towers and mills. The studio had two rooms, for which Alan paid £30 a year. The studio is portrayed in *Stockport Market* (1949), the painting used to illustrate the catalogue cover of Alan's large 1972 retrospective exhibition at Stockport. Alan would spend some nights in his studio, others at home or with Jenny, who often was the sole source of nourishment for this "student of the draught Guinness." A great deal of time was of course spent in the Stockport inns, where an already damaged liver was exacerbated by habitual drinking on an empty stomach.

By the early 1950's, Stockport's immediate post-war boom was coming to an end. With the onset of the Korean war, the textile industry collapsed because of the escalating price of copper for engraving. The dress trade never really recovered for designers. By this time the King Cotton market

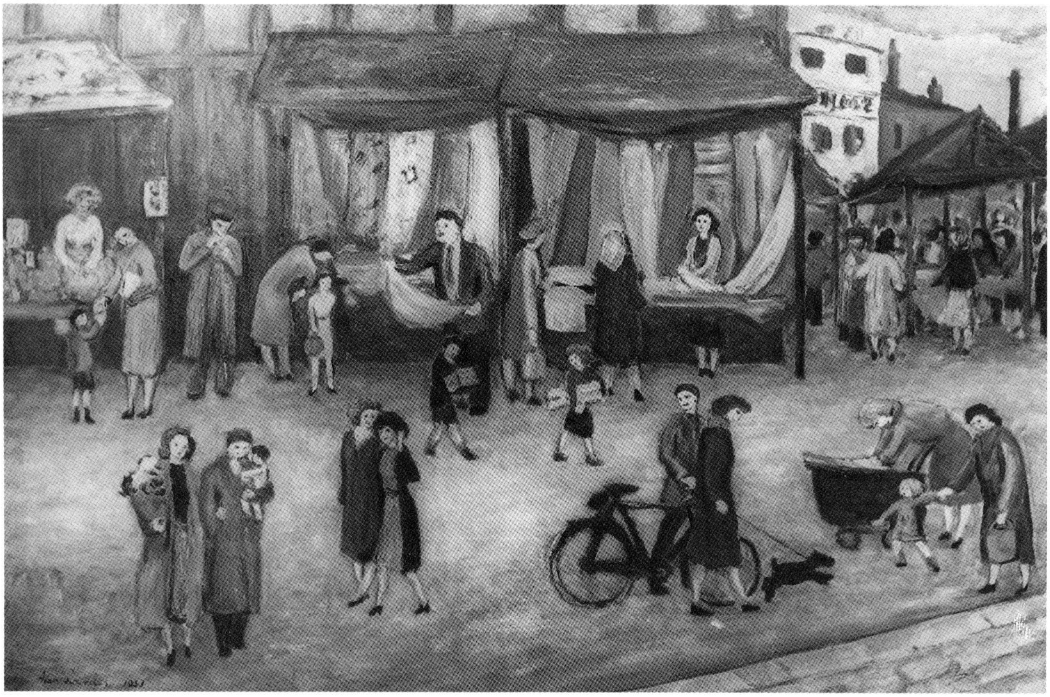

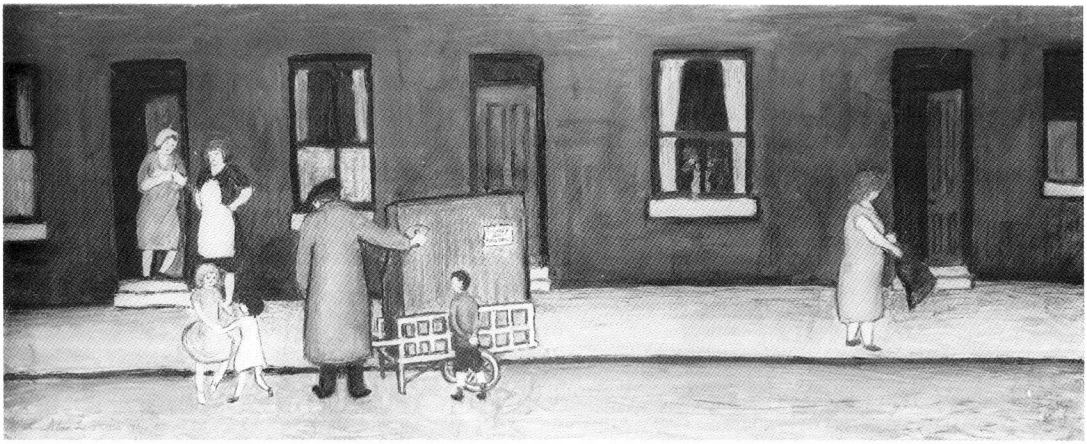

Alan Lowndes: Street Market, *oil 1953. Below* The Organ Grinder, *oil (both illustrations courtesy: Crane Kalman Gallery).*

to India had largely disappeared, although artists were still doing designs for sale to the natives in Africa. At one stage in the 19th century, when the cotton industry had reached its peak, as much as three quarters of British exports had been cotton goods. Not long after the war, and coinciding with his evening life drawing classes under Levy at Stockport Art School, Alan started working on textile designs. He worked for Julian Frank, a German Jew from Berlin. Frank had served in the German army during the Great War and was conscripted to do illustration work. He later became a quasi-cubist painter in Paris, but moved to London in 1933, the year of Hitler's rise to power in Germany. The textile design studios that Frank opened in Manchester's Oxford Street were to become the best creative studios in Britain. Interestingly, Julian Frank was one of the earliest buyers of Lowry. Work at Frank's was varied and on one occasion Alan was shipped out to Belfast with his girlfriend Frieda Clowes to do some preparatory designs. The textile designing experience went hand in hand with the earlier painting and decorating jobs as useful spurs to the development of his pictorial skill. Their influence, no less than wartime travel to Renaissance Florence, cannot be overestimated as factors in his development as a largely self-taught painter.

His eight month trip to Belfast consolidated his aim to become a full-time professional painter. On his return, Alan Lowndes' association with the newly opened Crane Gallery in South King Street was the long awaited opportunity. It was not a cut-and-dried, dealer-and-artist business relationship so much as a friendship and co-operative endeavour, although Kalman's horizons lay way beyond Alan Lowndes'. The long term aims of Kalman's enterprise soon became apparent with exhibitions of leading British artists like Sutherland and Nicholson, and European artists like Vlaminck and Bonnard.

The first exhibition at the Crane Gallery, February 1950, featured the work of Craxton, Freud and Lowndes. It included 36 Alan Lowndes paintings, ranging in price from nine to 32 guineas for the two largest, *The Power and Glory* and *The Arches*. Included in this exhibition were portraits such as *Pam* and *Miss Audrey Freeman*; industrial landscapes like the impastoed, brightly coloured *Halifax*; and pictures preoccupied with people, their activities and quirky habits. Good examples included *Cleaning Steps*, *Betting Yard* or *In the Cake Shop*. The 1949 canvas, labelled simply *Pam* in the early Crane catalogue, was purchased by Rod Steiger, who, with Mai Zetterling, became one of the earliest patrons of the Kalman Gallery. The portrait is flamboyantly coloured and remarkable for its vigorous handling. It is expressionistic in feel. The sitter was a student from Manchester University. Alan visited the

University on several occasions and attempts were made to get him to teach there, but he had a built-in reluctance to teaching, despite the financial relief this would have offered. The students sometimes made visits - 'pilgrimages' of a kind - to Alan's studio, and often bought him a meal. *Halifax* is remarkable for its depth of colour and thickly applied paint, contradicting the subject's apparent drabness. The picture was painted from drawings made on the spot which were then worked up in his Stockport studio. He visited Halifax because Thomas Crabtree, an early supporter and patron, lived there. Crabtree ran a mill factory in Halifax, and later retired to Hebden Bridge. In his warmly engaging introductory note for the catalogue, Andreas Kalman called Alan Lowndes "a rare, real and searching painter." Kalman drew a distinction between the 'soul-less,' purely technical painters and those of Alan's ilk; Alan Lowndes' expressive work rang true with its home-spun feelings and empathies, and with its unpretentious 'realism.' Kalman completed his note, which for all its hesitancy, did well at striking to the very core the kind of arguments that were thrown at Alan's paintings by the more narrow-minded, dilettante and 'smart-slick' gallery-goers. "Lowndes extracts latent beauty - the unconventional, unheroic beauty of the commonplace - from what is unsavoury only to the squeamish or the snob."

Life in Manchester - freewheeling and socialising, and making the kind of influential contacts that were to last the rest of his life - was one thing, but life back in Stockport was quite another. Alan's confidence must have grown not a little through exposure to a lively Manchester cultural milieu. It offered him the encouragement to counter family scepticism.

At the end of 1950, Alan met Nicholas Horsfield at Kalman's gallery. Horsfield worked from 1948 to 1956 as assistant regional director of visual arts at the Arts Council in Manchester, although he was a painter in his own right and later went on to teach at Liverpool School of Art. Among those he taught there were John Lennon and Stu Sutcliffe. Although Sutcliffe was later taught by Paolozzi in Hamburg, where he developed a 'tachist' abstract style, Sutcliffe's figurative work - like his superb Van Gogh-inspired self portrait of 1959 - displayed the kind of raw, expressively handled paint that was so characteristic of Alan Lowndes' work. Horsfield's association with Alan Lowndes was to be longstanding, and Alan stayed at Horsfield's Crosby home twice in the last twelve months of his life. In the 1950's their friendship grew slowly through chance meetings around Manchester. Horsfield never went to Alan's Stockport studio, but they would drink at the *Bodega* or at the *Carlton*. Although Margot Ingham's Midday Studios was a comprehensive exhibiting channel for local artists, acting as a social as well as artistic centre, Horsfield was to become acquainted with Alan more through the John Willett and Andreas Kalman circle. During the 1950's, Lowndes obtained commissions, mainly through Andreas Kalman, and he was able to work on a more ambitious scale. *Lunchtime from the Mill* (1953) is a good example. Two years later he painted *The Baker's Vault*, a solitary and detached 'Lowry-esque' building which was one of Alan's drinking places. It was primitive, with barrels used as tables, and a landlord's dog that frequently bit the patrons. During the early 1950's, the Stockport of his youth was changing. Clean air legislation had a big effect on the mill town.

By 1952 Alan was aware of the art colony at St Ives in Cornwall but was not yet warm to the idea of going there. He had an aversion to the acquired image of the fishing town as a romantic and picturesque colony for soft artists. Once Kalman had built up connections though, especially after moving to London, Alan's attitude moderated. He met several artists who had spent time there, and finally decided to make a visit. This decision was helped by John Milne, the Eccles-born sculptor, who had studied at Salford School of Art before attending classes at the Grande Chaumière in Paris. He finally moved to St Ives, working for a time as an assistant to Barbara Hepworth. In the late 1950's Alan worked at the Belle Vue Circus which came to Hyde Road in Manchester once a year, usually near Christmas. He got to know the circus people and did many sketches of animals and clowns, which led to some fully worked up paintings, including *The Tightrope Walker* (1961). He painted a large mural on the four walls of a room in the County Hotel in Stockport, based on the circus and fairground subjects which fascinated him. The hotel was demolished in the summer of 1984, and the loss of the mural created a front page news story in the *Stockport Messenger.* After 1952, Alan Lowndes made frequent visits to St Ives gradually winning a place among the artistic community. But by 1959 when, newly married, he settled there, the colony was losing some of its glamour. Sven Berlin left in 1953, Ben Nicholson in 1958, and many of the 'middle generation' painters were now ruthlessly embarked on their own careers. Yet Alan Lowndes extracted much from a still fertile and extremely lively art colony. The Cornish period is largely irrelevant to any assessment of Alan Lowndes' contribution to northern painting, but for the fact that many paintings of native Stockport were produced in his Cornish studio. By the early 1960's, Lowndes produced landscapes of the St Ives area that showed real feeling for the colouring, movement and life of the sea. He also revealed, in the manner of his early Stockport work, unselfconscious and virtuoso skills when portraying the industry of the local seafolk. Painting figures successfully into a landscape has always been a stumbling block for artists, and the sign of a good artist has often been measured in terms of his or her mastery of this difficult genre. Alan was one of the first artists since Christopher Wood to incorporate the life of the fishing community into his St Ives landscapes. He quickly gained a meaningful empathy with the Cornish fishing community. Smeaton's pier became his Cornish viaduct, and the large fishing vessels that ploughed the agitated seas, became akin to his north country railway convoys. Alan drew out the working class element of St Ives, and his Cornish work was at its best when representing the idiosyncrasies of fishing life.

It was Alan's habit to visit Stockport once a year, often in August, though these trips became less frequent in later years. He would make on-the-spot drawings which were later used as preparations for Stockport paintings executed in his Cornish studio. In a sense, therefore, Alan's Stockport period never ended, although some may point to the later Stockport paintings, with their 'déjà vu' street themes, as being the 'potboilers' of his career. But Kalman was justified in requesting north country pictures. Such subjects would always remain Alan's trademark, and his empathy with the native brickwork his most recognisable quality as a painter. Kalman knew that they sold best. The shrewd dealer was often critical of a new batch of pictures from Lowndes' atelier; he could discern the wheat from the chaff, and by no means liked every picture that Alan offered. Kalman was probably least enamoured of the portraits, although the self-portraits from the early 1948 self-portrait, right up to those of the 1970's, were haunting, arresting and very impressionable glances into the mirror. The sensitivity revealed in these self-portraits is one more instance of his versatility. He produced landscape, seascape, street scenes; he painted social genre pictures, townscapes - ranging from the heavily industrial to the more rural - and he was adept at portraiture, still lifes and interiors.

The trips made every year to Stockport through the 1960's broke Alan's heart. With the Clean Air Act, and the shift in the local industrial economy, much of the Stockport of his youth had disappeared. Many of the old buildings, streets, and areas of the past were gone, prey to the bulldozer of 'progress' and the cold logic of developer's economics. Even so, some particularly strong pictures were painted of the Stockport scene during the 1960's, produced perhaps with a measure of grief and nostalgia.

Eleven

Kenneth Gribble

The various phases into which Kenneth Gribble's work as a painter can be divided have been determined by a peripatetic teaching career that took him to many different parts of the country. Since the subject matter and thematic content of his work has always responded to his immediate environment the Lancashire industrial paintings are restricted to the period between 1955 and 1960 when he lived in, and taught art at Ashton-under-Lyne. Yet his own youth, spent in particularly industrialised regions of the West Midlands, gave him a natural empathy and feeling for the urban waste-ground and industrial architecture he chose to paint while living in Ashton. The industrial scene therefore was a formative influence, if not inspiration, in a painter who eventually embraced rural themes. So fine is the quality of his work that he ranks as one of the foremost practitioners of industrial landscape painting in Manchester in the late 1950's. He was an artist nurtured in the relatively cosmopolitan atmosphere of post-war Camberwell and Slade Schools of Art, who dug deep into the very different environment of the north west.

Kenneth Gribble was born in 1925 at Sparkbrook in Birmingham. He grew up in industrial Birmingham, and before leaving the city at the age of 14, remembered the fiery inferno created by enemy bombing of industrial locations. It was a spectacle that later provided the inspiration for several fiery furnace and factory-at-night subjects. One recalls the fascination that the flames of internal combustion held for the early locomotive draughtsmen. The early Coalbrookdale artists, and an array of watercolourists from Cotman and George Robertson to Graham Sutherland (all of whom painted fiery furnaces), also appreciated the grip that this highly emotive and enduring subject held on the artistic imagination.

The bombing led to the Gribble family's evacuation to the quieter location of Hinckley in Leicestershire. In 1943 they were once again moved, this time to Harrow in Middlesex. Kenneth's father became District Goods Manager at London's Broad Street station, a job that prompted the move south. At Harrow County School for Boys Gribble obtained the highest grades for art, and John Platt, Principal of Harrow School of Art, accepted him as a student. Kenneth Gribble was 18 years of age in 1943, and the final two years of the war saw him engaged on war service duties in a mining area of South Wales. He was occupied as a collier's helper at Blackwood, in Gwent, but was invalided out due to an allergy to dust. His wartime drawings used Blackwood and Harrow subjects - two worlds poles apart yet both faced with the same threat - and the results impressed Heber Thompson, the Hampstead-based engraver who taught part-time at the Harrow School of Art. Heber Thompson gave Gribble important letters of introduction to help him obtain a place at the Slade. Gribble went to see Randolph Schwabe at the renowned art school. Schwabe responded favourably to the young artist's Blackwood and Harrow drawings, remarking that he was an authentic talent to whom a place at the college was the appropriate reward. The Slade seemed endowed with wonderful studio spaces, though the teaching at the end of the war was, in Kenneth Gribble's own term, 'moribund'. Schwabe sent Gribble down to Camberwell for a year. Between the summers of 1946 and 1947 he benefitted from the lively Camberwell milieu that was composed of a heavy Euston Road lobby on the staff and a new intake of worldly wise and war-hardened ex-servicemen.

The year Gribble spent at Camberwell witnessed a great expansion that transformed a quiet traditional south London college into a vibrant colony of young artists. Mention is made in Humphrey Lyttleton's autobiography of a restaurant called 'Charlies' on Peckham Road, much frequented by Gribble's Camberwell contemporaries. William Johnstone, in his book *Points in Time* speaks of "a tremendously exciting time which could never be recreated" at Camberwell. Kenneth Gribble was taught stone lithography at Camberwell by John Minton, a leading light in art circles after the war. Gribble found Minton an inspiration, as a person, instructor and practising artist. Minton, however, with his own highly stylised concoction of spiky linearity, cubist paraphrases of form, and English 'neo romanticism', found the sincere but old masterish drawings that Gribble had produced during the war a touch too sober and prosaic to appeal to his own mercurial energies. Camberwell was held together at this time by a post-war camaraderie; a zest of enthusiasm swept through the place with the new class of intake. That school was held together by a competent teacher, William Johnstone. Facilities were limited, and even the building had the look of dereliction with the as yet unrepaired war damage. It was very different to the well equipped modern departments enjoyed by art students during the 1960's and beyond, yet the early post-war privations and austerities created an ambiance that prevented students like Kenneth Gribble from indulgence, complacency or pretentiousness. Gribble soon began a relentless search into the difficult techniques of traditional oil painting.

Already competent at drawing, he wanted to learn much more about the chemistry and nature of paint than could be offered by the thin-paint-and-turps brigade. The Euston Road painters on the staff at Camberwell were also caught up with dingy, drab earth colours that effectively prevented them imparting principles of positive colour. Instead Gribble learnt a great deal about paint from looking closely at the rich surfaces of the old masters at the National Gallery. He also learnt much more about what he termed the ability to 'sling' paint from a Slade 'old boy' David Bomberg, who at that time was sadly neglected by the stiff English art establishment. John Minton's use of copal varnish medium to obtain thick surfaces also interested Gribble. Experiments were made in a series of encaustic paintings using paints which Gribble made up by mixing linseed oil and beeswax with pigments purchased from Corniellsons. Gribble looked to the grand Venetian masters such as Veronese and Titian for the incentive to muster some kind of understanding of the composition and technique of oil paint. A contemporary beacon that also pointed the way was an exhibition of work by the Polish immigrant Henry Gottlib at the Redfern Gallery. His pictures were of a pearly, irridescent model with red hair who had posed for Gribble and his contemporaries at Camberwell. This model's striking features and voluptuous figure had unsettled Coldstream, who looked to a more skinny, bony frame and anaemic complexion for his own kind of understated tonal painting.

A Camberwell tutor, Colin McInnes, helped confirm the virtuousness of Gribble's intention to avoid the tonally dull, chromatically drab and thin surfaces of Euston Road painting. McInnes, an Australian, taught art history and the methods and materials of painting. He pointed out that the dilute, muted technique of the Euston Road artists, and their limited range of posed still-life or studio figure subjects needed to be bettered. The dull, colourless subjects Gribble found in the northern industrial landscape required a suitably dark and grey palette, but the fact remains that he found the example of the Euston Road painters uninspiring in many key areas. During a final Camberwell term spent in Switzerland, a great deal of time was spent in the museums. Then he returned to his parents' home in Matlock, Derbyshire where he started to draw the forceful Derbyshire landscape and learned landscape painting in oil through a tortuous process of trial and error. During the next three years at the Slade he continued the Derbyshire landscape experiments. These lessons, allied to a growing interest in Impressionism and in Chevreul's well known colour theories, did much to mould him into a skilful *plein air* painter of one-day landscape statements.

Gribble started at the Slade in 1947. Randolph Schwabe was still professor, heading a sedentary, not to say conservative staff. They included the former army officer Allan Gwynne-Jones who was overwhelmed by the new intake of ex-servicemen and young men who, in the following cold-war decade, become increasingly angry. The Euston Road artists, led by William Coldstream, were waiting in the wings ready to replace Schwabe at the Slade. Kenneth Gribble, in his capacity as Treasurer and Secretary of the Slade Society, attended Schwabe's funeral at St Pancras church. It was a rainy day and he was late arriving, but recalled seeing Gowing, Rogers, Townsend, Pasmore and Coldstream. These were prime members of the Euston Road Group who had taught at Camberwell. The appointment of Coldstream was a formality. Coldstream and his Euston Road colleague of pre-war days, Graham Bell, both painted northern industrial views, anticipating the work that Gribble would soon be doing himself. Bell was killed during the war, but anyone familiar with his superb pictures of industrial Bolton will see that the best of the Euston Road style could easily be adapted to the urban topography of Lancashire. In a similar northern, though different thematic vein, Claude Rogers, another founding member of the north London group, painted views of Southport promenade as seen through the upper windows of the hospital in which he was convalescing during the war. Such overlap between Euston Road and Lancashire shows that Gribble's Slade education was not without its uses in his eventual development of a northern industrial realism.

William Coldstream brought to the Slade a new breed of influential pundits including Kenneth Clark, Anthony Blunt and Douglas Cooper. Coldstream was also responsible for staff changes that saw the loss of the competent engraver Norman Janes who was an active member of the Manchester Academy. Gribble once asked why Janes' disappearance was not followed by that of Allan Gwynne-Jones. Coldstream answered that the latter had too many powerful friends. But a radical painter like Graham Sutherland did come in, albeit as an external assessor. He saw Gribble's drawings of Cricklewood locomotives (where the young man had worked as a railway shunter) and of mining subjects imbued with the same honest hallmark of direct experience. The works clearly affected Sutherland who had also been an apprentice railway draughtsman. Sutherland's familiarity with Gribble's subjects led to his criticism that the work was too factual and mundane as a representation of railway machinery.

The teaching at the Slade proved to be of questionable value and usefulness to the strong-minded Kenneth Gribble. He was a man of unusual maturity and discernment, whose development was enhanced by a number of traditional books. Le Coq de Boisbordran had written a treatise on drawing from memory. This technique was used as early as 1910, when students had to draw blindfold at Birmingham School of Art. One of Gribble's early art tutors at the Saltly Grammar School in Birmingham had shown him a book of the 1910 drawings. Vernon Blake's *Art and Craft of Drawing* was a standard text book used at the Slade between the wars, which extolled the all important Slade principal of measurement in drawing. Gribble was in fact already familiar with this book during his days at Harrow School of Art. Another influence was Eugene Wolf's *Anatomy for the Artist*, illustrated by George Charlton, senior drawing master under Schwabe at the Slade. Such publications gave Gribble and his Slade colleagues access to independent channels of thought on the craft of painting, adding to what was already a competitive, even challenging spirit among Slade students.

The students set the pace, criticising one another's work in preference to waiting for a tutor. Contemporaries included Richard Hamilton, the first English 'Pop' artist, Anthony Caro, and Bernard and Harold Cohen, each of whom were to become contributors to the innovative era of the sixties.

The Slade had no facilities for print making, however, and this made it necessary for Gribble to make twice weekly visits to evening lithography sessions at the Central School. He was asked to produce posters for the Young Contemporaries exhibition of 1948. Permission was granted by Coldstream for a trip to the Royal College print making facilities. Robin Darwin welcomed Gribble at Exhibition Road, and a series of lithographs produced there for his Diploma won him offers of teaching at the Central School and at the Hastings School of Art. He opted instead for a teaching job at the Constantine Technical College School of Art in Middlesbrough where, between 1950 and 1955, he taught drawing, painting, history of art, and methods and materials; all to National Diploma level. In 1951 he married an art student he had met at Harrow School of Art, and a son was born in 1953. Family responsibilities and the need to make a living kept him in teaching positions thereafter. His success in having students from Middlesbrough accepted at the major London colleges for the first time, indicated his effectiveness as a teacher. While on Teeside he produced a spate of pictures on industrial themes that would point to those he was to do in Lancashire a few years later. Teeside subjects included the docks at night, views of the steelworks, the transporter bridge, and a superb 1953 picture, *Four p.m. West Street*. This picture illustrates the frenzied rush of figures, eager to get home to a cup of tea, spilling out of factories in the

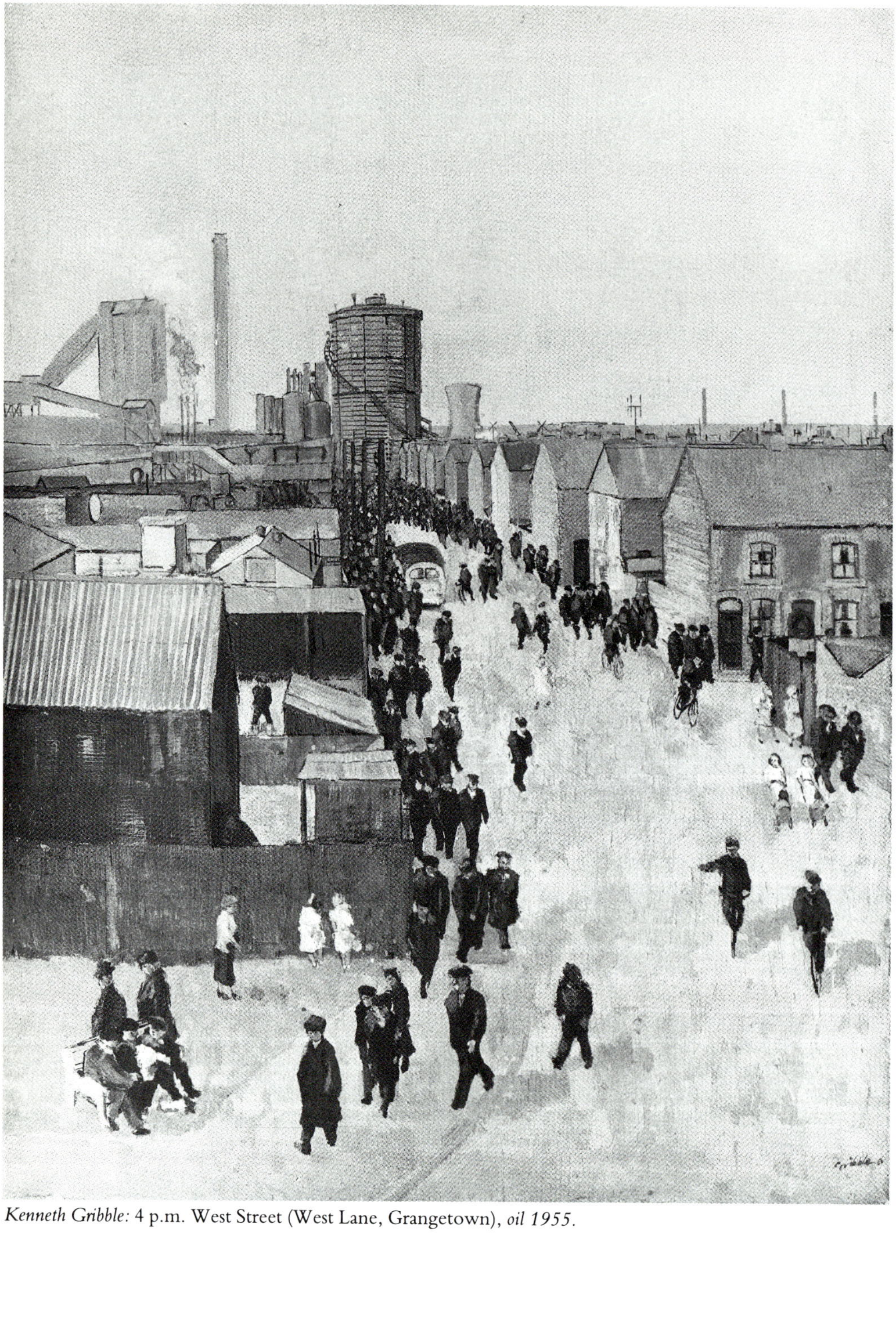

Kenneth Gribble: 4 p.m. West Street (West Lane, Grangetown), *oil 1955.*

Grangetown area of Middlesbrough.

In 1955, Gribble applied for the job of principal at the Heginbottam Art School, Ashton-under-Lyne. This was one of the 110 art schools founded in the 1860's as a response to Queen Victoria's and Prince Albert's interest in art and design and as a necessary accompaniment to expanding commercial activities. He started there in 1956 and despite a temporary threat of closure, Gribble built up Ashton, nearly doubling the number of full-time students to 50 and maintaining a healthy part-time following. He taught the principles of his own artistic education, and encouraged students to indulge in his passion for outdoor painting excursions that took in local views. He also appointed the Bolton artist Brian Bradshaw, who taught etching. Bradshaw was appreciated at the college for his free spirit, northern directness and strong political views. Another fruitful collaboration was with the portrait painter Leo Soloman, who ran a small school at Barrow before he left to run Rochdale Art School. Soloman, an early Lowry collector, was a keen fisherman and this provided the pretext for Gribble's occasional painting excursions to the banks of rivers.

Kenneth Gribble remained at Ashton until 1960, and during the second half of the 50's produced some of his finest work, including views of Park Parade, Ashton-under-Lyne, Moseley, the Snipe Pit at Audenshaw, the canals at Fairfield, Staleybridge and Audenshaw. In many of these works, Gribble brought a rich painterliness and a fresh spontaneity to an honest and direct recording of bland or derelict urban subjects. His *Park Parade, Ashton* (1958: Manchester City Art Gallery) is a powerful study in perspective, in which street, pavement, and two canals are marshalled in diminishing parallel lines from the prominent foreground railings towards the horizon line. The middle distance and centre are comprised of coloured mills, while the surrounding wasteground to the factory's left, and the empty streets to the right, evoke a desolate mood of stagnation and inertia. The formal secret of Gribble's success in this and other paintings lies in his mastery of handling - an opalescent quality resulted when the grisaille underpainting of black, white and grey was overlaid with the positive colours of mill reds and grass greens in one alla prima sweep. The sheer sophistication and panache of this underrated artist's technique is belied by the apparently bland, infertile subject matter that would prove anathema to many lesser artists.

Another Gribble painting, *Moseley* (1957: Collection the author, ex collection Sir Trenchard Cox) had the same direct spontaneity of working greyed paint wet into wet. The aerial perspective employed in this topographical view of Moseley, set against the foothills of the Pennines, is common in much of Gribble's work. Even in a much later series of tame

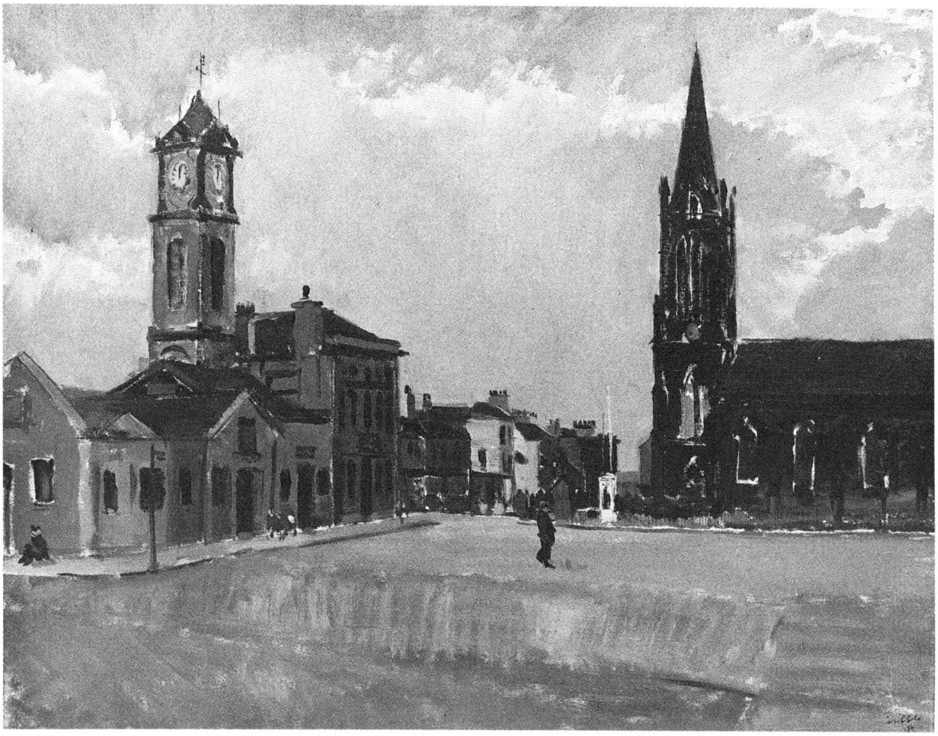

Kenneth Gribble: Market Street, Middlesbrough Yorkshire, *oil 1953.*

Kenneth Gribble: Jane, *oil 1953.*

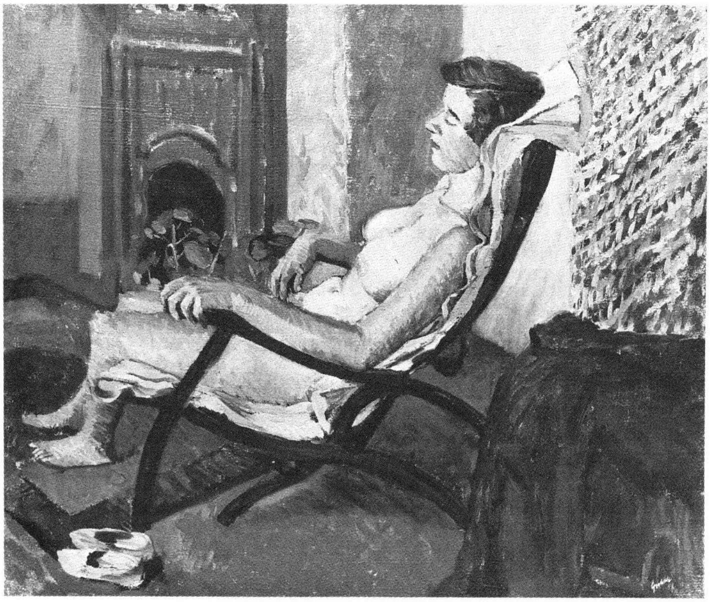

rural vistas where fields recede in the distance, a tilted or elevated perspective is often chosen. Gribble may have been inspired by Turner in his desire to paint, in impossibly palpable terms, the void that stands between us, the onlookers, and the limitless and timeless beyond. The void beyond the artist, looking down over Moseley, could be rendered in terms of atmospheric haze, fog, sunrays, or any other atmospheric device.

Kenneth Gribble's value to Lancashire art during the second half of the 1950's was due to the rejuvenating effect of his reign on the Hegginbottam School of Art. This achievement was accompanied by an output of prime industrial pictures notable for qualitative rather than quantitive excellence. He was too late to have been involved with the post-war art boom in Manchester, though he did become a full member of the Manchester Academy. Five canvases by Gribble were included in the Academy's Centenary exhibition held at the Manchester City Art Gallery in the spring of 1959. Gribble designed the menu for a well attended dinner held at the Great Hall of the Manchester Town Hall to celebrate the Centenary. Kenneth Gribble, Harry Rutherford, and Wilfred Wood hung the exhibition, while Gribble's colleagues like Ian Grant, John Bold and Harry Rutherford served ably on the selection committee. The importance of the occasion was reflected in the fact that Sir Philip Hendry, Director of the National Gallery, and Sir Trenchard Cox, director of the V&A Museum, were both present. Gribble's painting *Park Parade Ashton* was sold from the exhibition and entered the Rutherston Collection at the Manchester City Art Gallery.This represented the pinnacle of Gribble's involvement with the Manchester Art scene. His role as head of the art school at Ashton, his family responsibilities, and his early sophisticated Slade roots, all prevented him from becoming too closely identified as a fully fledged Lancashire artist. His own origins in a different albeit similarly industrial part of the country, did however predispose him to painting urban Lancashire with empathy, objectivity and perceptive clarity; the best of Gribble's Lancashire pictures fall naturally into a 'northern school' style.

In September 1957 in an article by Dick Pomfret, the *Evening Chronicle* critic, Kenneth Gribble was quoted as declaring that "I like to paint scenes within a radius of a few miles of where I live. It takes at least a year to get the 'feel' of a place, but I think I've 'got' Ashton now."

Gribble met Lowry through his former tutor, William Coldstream. The well known Lancashire artist subsequently visited Gribble both at Ashton and at Gribble's flat above the post office on Station View, Fairfield, which is in the Droylesden district of Manchester. Gribble mistrusted Lowry's taste in pictures,which seemed to be partly conditioned by the quirky nature of Lowry's character. Lowry was quietly accepting of the undeniable quality of Gribble's drawing and sophisticated use of paint, but nevertheless is likely to have found the elegant sophistication something that rankled and ran counter to his own, more idiosyncratic, and certainly less tutored style. It was this kind of apprehension towards the high manner that once prompted Lowry to say another Slade trained artist, Harold Riley, that it would take a lifetime's endeavour of painting the industrial north to effectively unravel the over refined southern style of the Slade-trained artist. What made Gribble doubt the seriousness of Lowry's judgement was not the lack of refined cosmopolitan consciousness but rather an almost perverse desire to seek out bad painting for the sheer fun of it. Lowry was egalitarian in his assessment of other people's pictures; he would hold back his true feelings and would tease with the intellectual seriousness that an artist like Gribble would bring to a discussion of painting.

It was expedient for Kenneth Gribble to maintain contact with Coldstream throughout his years at Ashton, and he called in at the Slade whenever he had the opportunity. Lowry's own visits to the Slade - which apparently he did not find congenial - resulted in Coldstream advising him to visit the Ashton art college that Gribble was running. Lowry subsequently made several conscientious visits to see the work of Gribble's students, and purchased a plaster figure by a local Ashton student, Cynthia Pellow. Links such as these helped to interest the Slade in Ashton students. Julia Bagnall, daughter of a local headmaster, became the first Ashton student to enter the Slade school. Gribble's own Slade teacher, Claude Rogers, also visited Ashton. Gribble kept up a life long friendship with Rogers, who stayed with Gribble in Middlesbrough on a Carnegie Trust painting weekend. One summer in the late 1950's Rogers wanted to meet Lowry, and was driven over to the artist's home in Gribble's old Ford 8 motor (The Ford motor formed the subject of a picture Gribble sent into the 98th annual exhibition of the Manchester Academy in 1957) The occasion was marked by humorous haggling over the purchase of a Lowry drawing that Rogers wanted. The prolonged, though good natured, haggling suggested that Lowry took well to his visitor. Afterwards Gribble drove a contented Claude Rogers back to the railway station for a journey back to London.It was the only meeting between Lowry and Rogers.

Kenneth Gribble moved to Lincoln in 1960 and between 1960 and 1966 was Principal of Lincoln Art School. He became secretary and treasurer of the Lincolnshire Artist's Society. In 1966 , after 6 contented years spent working on Lincoln subjects, he moved to Taunton where he tried to build up an art school; an impossible job in a hostile environment where the local authority wanted to run down the existing art school. In 1972 he became senior art advisor to Somerset County Council Education Department, and, after campaigning for several years on the need for Taunton to have an art gallery, had the first exhibition, of watercolour work, at the Brewhouse Arts Centre which opened in 1977. From 1980 until his retirement in 1984 he taught at Maidstone Art College, and has since continued to paint in the West Country.

Twelve

Roger Hampson

Roger Hampson was born in the spring of 1925 at Union Street, Bolton. He was the youngest of three boys. Three months after Roger's birth, the family moved the short distance to Johnson Street, where the artist was to live intermittently for the next 40 years. Union Street was a damp area near the Calet Wright Cotton Spinning Mill. The dampness may have suited cotton spinning but created much arthritis among the local population, and it must have been a relief when the family moved to a larger, drier house. The father died during the war, though mother lived on at Johnson Street for many years. Roger returned to live there after his war service, and again later after his post-war career had been punctuated by a spell in Hereford, the city to which he was eventually to return after retiring from teaching in 1978.

Hampson attended Leigh Grammar School, cycling across fields from Johnson Street to get there. After school he joined the navy and saw active service on destroyers during the war. In 1946, as an ex-serviceman, he attended Manchester School of Art, whose Principal, John Holmes, encouraged the new intake of students in a rigorous two years of study towards the Intermediate. A whole range of skills, among them anatomy, perspective and pictorial composition, were individually instilled into the students. This gave them a command of the basic grammar of art that the more experimental or conceptual framework of later post-Thubron art school training could not provide. The intermediate training, which followed traditional guidelines, did much to set Hampson on his path of fastidious craftsmanship. His work has always drawn on a frankly recorded and honestly observed industrial realism using the source material of the artist's native environment. At Manchester, Hampson joined the illustration school under Paul Keene where he did a full two years towards his N.D.D. While there, he won the Royal Manchester Institute Silver Medal - the Heywood Medal - indicating the successful application of talent and conscientious study in the illustration school. A contemporary student, Norman Jaques, also won the medal. Jaques later became another bona fide printmaker, and was to follow Hampson in the post of President of the Manchester Academy. In 1950 Hampson won the Proctor Memorial

Travelling Scholarship enabling him to study peasant life in the small mountain country of Andorra in its pre-tourism days (an uncanny anticipation of interests that were to motivate the critic John Berger years later). A year's training towards a teaching certificate upon his return to Manchester led, in 1951, to the start of his teaching career at the recently opened Bolton Secondary Technical School. Two years later, in 1953, he moved south to teach printmaking at Hereford School of Art. Kenneth Craddock, recently appointed as Principal at Hereford, had taught Hampson in Manchester. Although, many years later, Hampson retired to Hereford, he was not happy teaching there, missing above all the vitality and atmosphere of the North, from which he was always to draw his subject matter. The more sedate students he encountered during the year he taught at Hereford did not possess the same drive as the ex-servicemen students of the northern colleges.

Nevertheless, Hampson's work continued to express the northern working class themes so vividly imprinted on his consciousness in his formative years. From the Tyldesley years of his youth, Hampson retained vivid recollections of miners with blackened skin, or of cotton girls returning home with cotton fibres in their hair. The close knit community spirit gave life there compensating qualities of social cohesion that shone through the apparent gloom.

Politically the area of his youth was Labour, and as a young boy he witnessed hunger marches through Tyldesley, and saw cattle being taken down Johnson Street to the slaughterhouse. It therefore comes as no surprise that Roger Hampson continued to paint the vivid red brick terraces and collieries of Bolton; even when his teaching career, first at Hereford, and then at Loughborough and finally after the permanent move from the North with retirement to Hereford, took him away from his native town. Hampson's lino cuts of the mining town of Tyldesley are superb graphic statements of the industrial architecture, dominated by the iron towers of collieries which stand in appropriate cathedral-like postures. The recurrence of northern subjects in Hampson's work long after his remove is also echoed in the work of the Stockport painter, Alan Lowndes. Lowndes, after leaving his native Cheshire viaduct town, lived in the very different environments of first St Ives (mid-1950's to 1970) then Gloucestershire (1970 to his death in 1978).

Hampson moved back to the family home at Johnson Street, Tyldesley, with his wife and small child. Hampson's mother moved to a small house nearby. From 1954 until 1961 he used his illustration talents in the world of advertising: in Manchester he worked for Stowe and Bowden, then at Bert

Wilson advertising, and finally at the larger Artell Studios. Hampson found design work challenging and stimulating: little time was left for self-indulgence, and the functional drawing produced for advertising imagery undoubtedly had some bearing on his own private fine art work, giving his own work a greater range of communication skills, a kind of extra, pithy edge to the illustration of the street miner and colliery subjects that were occupying him. He continued to produce his own work at home, with exhibitions at Manchester's Gibb's Bookshop, the Tibb Lane Gallery, and at the annual Academy exhibitions. Hampson first showed at the Academy in 1954; two years later he exhibited in a one-man show at Gibb's Bookshop. *The Manchester Guardian* (7.5.56) applauded Hampson's first display of work at Gibb's Bookshop, and the "unusual and commendable versatility" of work based on strong design. Yet, the reviewer discerned that it was less technical polish than what was termed "the artist's gift of grasping essential human character and of exploiting the drama of strong light and dark" which it deemed resulted in "a rich expressive human sympathy which justifies the means."

The artist's first show at Tibb Lane came in 1963. Ten years later, in September 1973, Merete Bates commented in the *Guardian* that Hampson's small paintings at Tibb Lane "have a brown modesty that draws affection." However, Bates went on to declare that although the small pictures "catch a particular atmosphere or light" this was achieved at the expense of a "harder, more penetrating analysis of the industrial scene and just what it means in human terms." She rightly commented that Hampson's work did not concern itself with any direct social, political or philosophical meanings; however, what Hampson does extract from the industrial scene is a disarming realism, fortified by an unusually fine level of dexterity. He achieved the presidency of the Manchester Academy largely through the successful resolution of the classical and formal problems of the craft of painting itself. Bates finished by stating that unlike his industrial scenes Hampson's treatment of people "verges on the sentimental".

Participation in group exhibitions at Salford Art Gallery in the early 1960's, at Bolton Art Gallery every couple of years throughout the 1960's and 1970's, and in the Spring show at Southport also during the sixties, showed that Hampson was a willing contributor to a wide range of local exhibitions.

During the second half of the 1960's Roger Hampson enjoyed a number of one-man exhibitions in London and across the country. During 1966 he held an exhibition of recent monoprints both at the Tibb Lane Gallery and at the Plymouth Arts Centre. The following year he exhibited two dozen

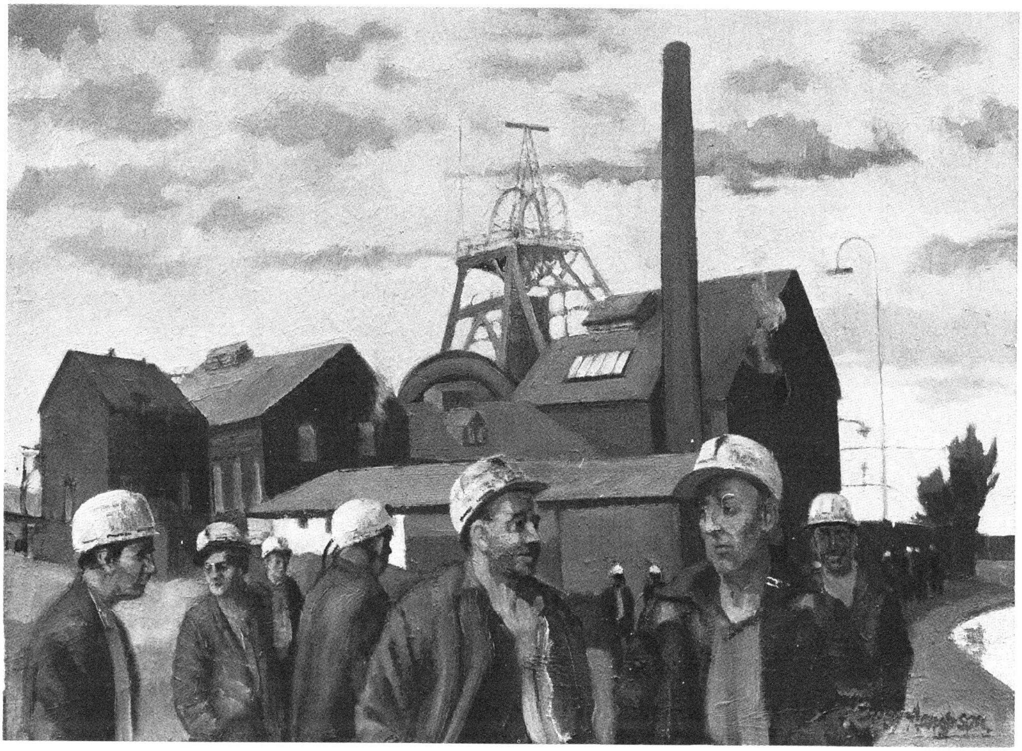

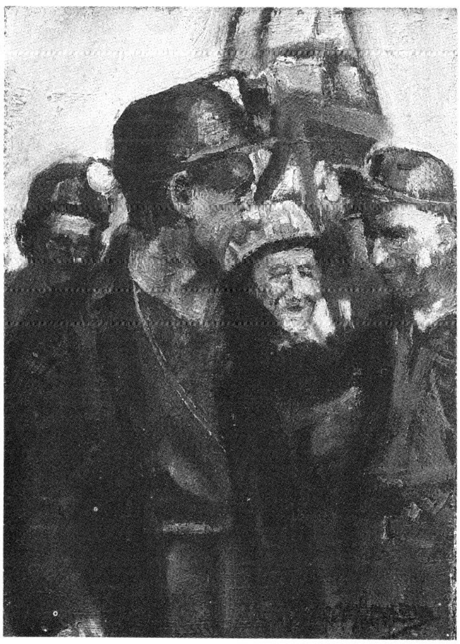

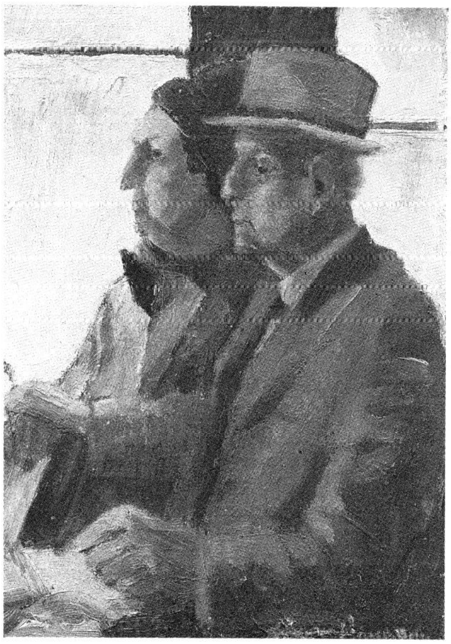

Roger Hampson: Miners Chanters Colliery, Laughing Miners I *and* Travellers, *oil*.

works at the Beaford Arts Centre in Devon, and later that summer at the Bury Art Gallery. In November, 1970 he held an exhibition at the Octagon Gallery in his native Bolton. By the late 1980's Hampson had produced nearly 150 monoprints, over 100 linocuts, over 20 litho or aquatints, and approaching 400 oil paintings. In 1957 Hampson suggested to the Tyldesley public library that the main reading room walls be used for exhibitions by local artists. Hampson displayed his own work there for ten years, at first monthly, then every three months. All the exhibits were on Tyldesley themes but, sadly, the interest was not reciprocated by the members of this nose-to-the-grindstone community. No one bought. Hampson wanted to curate the displays to help introduce the public to these true evocations of the local scene. He need not have troubled himself. The last thing people wanted to see were images of the drab environment in which they lived. Instead, they liked Trechikov's green lady, or far-away subjects of waves on a beach. Perhaps this same psychological mechanism was at work when the Manchester Gallery-goers would not invest in Lowry's pictures of the industrial scene (despite their obvious formal qualities) until their commercial and cultural value had been firmly fixed on the London art scene.

Between 1960 and 1976, Roger Hampson, together with Norman Jaques, was a member of the 'Lancashire Group of Artists'. Colin Hilton, a modest Bolton artist, founded and ran this group, whose expressed aim was to organise touring exhibitions which included about four works by each of two dozen exhibitors.

Hilton's 'Lancashire Group' was formed in 1952 and drew its members from as wide an area of the county as possible. A diversity of styles was encouraged. The Group showed in many of the fine municipal galleries of Lancashire, and as a later exhibition of members showed (the 20th exhibition in 1971), the variety of artists had been achieved. That exhibition included, in addition to Hampson: John Blockley, John Bold, John Bowes, Harold Hemingway (then the Group's chairman), Morgan Hewinson, Colin Hilton, Walter Hirsch, Norman Jaques, Robert Mann, Peter Shaw, Donald Stanier, Robert Tuson, Stanley Warburton, Derek Wilkinson, and José Christopherson. Through the Group's penultimate exhibition in 1975 Hampson sold a painting to Salford Art Gallery, and a monoprint of a miner to Blackburn Art Gallery.

It was teaching, however, that provided Roger Hampson with the support to continue practising as a painter. He had taught part-time at Bolton and Manchester, and in 1961, thanks to the Principal, John Nicholson, Hampson successfully obtained the Vice-Principal's job at

Bolton School of Art. In 1967 he became Principal, and moved from the family Tyldesley home into Bolton itself. Hampson was Principal until 1978, when he moved on to Loughborough. He developed foundation courses in fine art and in vocational design (graphics, textiles, fashion). The years in charge at Bolton coincided with his being first Treasurer, then President of the Manchester Academy. He took this position over from Harry Rutherford, the Sickert-inspired artist (Rutherford was bequeathed Sickert's Manchester class) who was forced to stand down on health grounds. Hampson was assisted as President by an efficient secretary, Donald Rayner, an urbane and popular water-colour artist. The Academy was enjoying a heyday; annual dinners were still held, as tradition decreed, in the plush upstairs galleries of the Manchester Art Gallery. Luminaries like Hugh Casson, Lord Rhodes, Lord Lever, and Lord Hughton, came as chief guests. The Mayor attended, emphasising civic pride in the historic Manchester Academy's annual exhibition. At one packed Academy dinner in January, 1972, the Bishop of Manchester delivered a speech criticising the Minister of the Arts, Lord Eccles, for proposing entrance charges to museums.

Among the innovations introduced by Hampson to improve the effectiveness of the Academy within the art scene of the north west, was a scheme for Academy members to be shown at the Southport Art Gallery after the Academy Spring Show. One such exhibition was a pictorial and photographic history of the academy to celebrate its centenary. Another was Hampson's invitation to Terry Frost to exhibit his large abstract pictures at the Manchester Academy exhibitions. Hampson had also invited Frost to do some teaching at Bolton. Despite the marked differences in Hampson's and Frost's work Hampson no doubt valued Frost's large-hearted empirical approach to picture making as being instructive to his Bolton students. To inspire an enthusiasm in young art students for experiments with colour and abstract harmonies was one thing, but to successfully press Terry Frost's occasionally flamboyant work on older academy stalwarts like Hal Yates was quite another. Yates, in particular, was a very dogged character opposed to abstract art which he commonly termed 'monkey' painting. Yates was belligerent towards non-academic and non-representational art, and he resented what he felt was an undemocratic invitation to an outsider like Frost to exhibit with academy members.

Roger Hampson was in a good position to foster links between the Academy and the local art schools. He encouraged the best artists in the locality to send in their work in a clear effort to revolve the wheels of this still tradition-bound institution. One particularly prominent example of

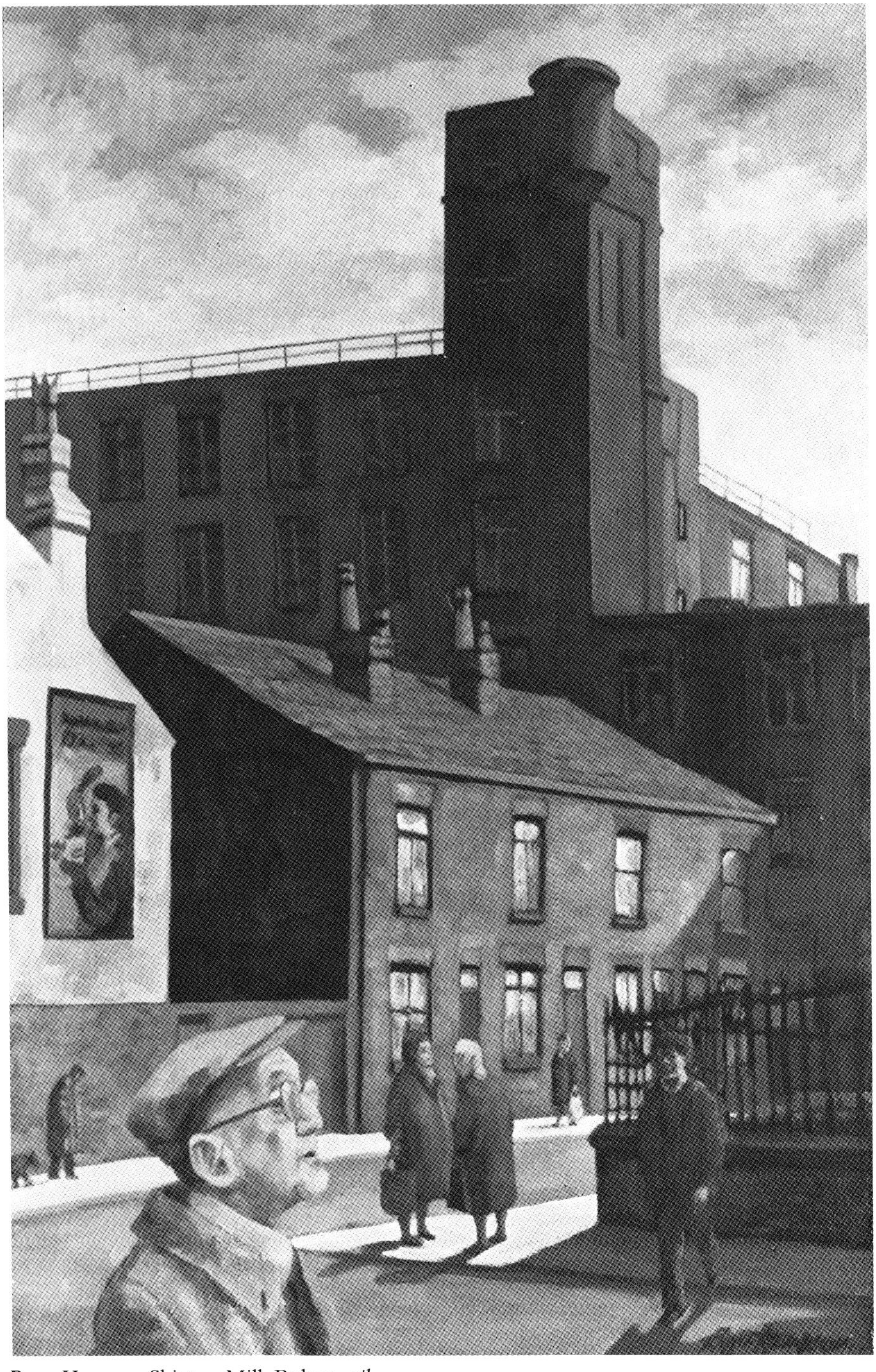

Roger Hampson: Shipton Mill, Bolton, *oil*.

Hampson's success in widening Academy exhibitions came with the submission of work by Norman Adams, whose large scale, brightly coloured watercolours of natural subjects would certainly have added sunshine to Academy shows. Adams was then Head of Painting at Manchester Polytechnic, and his introduction into Academy exhibitions also attracted several colleagues in the painting department. In 1978, Hampson left for a teaching post at Loughborough, leaving Keith Godwin as Academy President. Roger Hampson's personal modesty is reflected in the unpretentious realist work of an artist who never employs fashionable tricks, or plays the power game of the art market. An integrated vision of the industrial region of his formative years continues to mould his painting. His career as a practising artist has been buttressed by the many activities of service, to widen the competent practice and appreciation of the finest qualities of painting. Hampson declined an assured niche in Royal Academy summer exhibitions when on one occasion he sent in a couple of works which were accepted, but hung unsatisfactorily in an overcrowded setting. Hugh Casson subsequently made strong overtures for him to send work to Burlington House, but Hampson declined. The artist has preferred exhibiting in less grand surroundings, as the list of his many group exhibitions around Lancashire reveals.

Hampson's integrity and single minded approach was not lost on Lowry, who liked his work and bought several of his paintings from exhibitions at the Salford Art Gallery. A prolonged exchange of views on artistic matters was not possible with Lowry because of his dislike of 'talking shop' with fellow professionals, but Hampson and Lowry did spend time together. On one occasion, sitting on a selection panel of an open exhibition at Stockport Art Gallery, they ran across a number of clichéd galleon and kitten-in-a-basket pictures. This prompted a surprisingly favourable response from an artist of Lowry's level of achievement. For Lowry there was no such thing as bad art. So-called bad art would be sure to appeal to someone. Hampson knew that Lowry's often tongue-in-cheek comments were sometimes tailored to fit the occasion, though in this instance there is a clear sense of Lowry's very democratic (though uncritical) regard for all forms of art, however crude or simple.

Thirteen

Harold Riley and William Turner

The painter Harold Riley was born in Salford in 1934, a home grown talent who was to enjoy a varied career, bringing him into contact with the rich and the famous. Riley's artistic identity and reputation is today curiously divided. On the one hand, he followed in the footsteps of Lowry and recorded the industrial suburbs of his native Salford; on the other, he pursued the life of an international portraitist. It is a duality hard to unify. What Riley probably took from Lowry was the habit of looking at humanity as if from the outside. This detached observation in both artists' work - sometimes tempered with wry humour - proved to be the link between the humble Salford subjects and the glittering glamour of the commissioned work. In spite of considerable differences between Lowry and Riley - differences of generation, class, style and educational background - there was a great kinship between them for a time.

Riley's father was a jazz pianist who made a living by dealing in pianos. His mother encouraged Harold's early interest in art. Riley attended the local grammar school where the arts in general, but theatre in particular, were greatly encouraged. Among Riley's contemporaries at Salford Grammar were Albert Finney and Shelagh Delaney. Riley thus found himself in a sympathetic environment. His early talent for drawing came to the attention of his drawing teachers, Eric Satchwell, Ernest Goodman and Harry Stevens, designer of the early 'Guinness' posters. Inevitably, one of Riley's earliest visitors at the school was Lowry, who was curious enough about his work to seek out a meeting with Riley's parents. At the age of eleven, Harold Riley would have been hard pressed to understand the unlikely figure of the artist as an unromantic and drably dressed man straight off the back streets of Salford. Riley soon after joined the Salford Arts Club, founded by Ernest Goodman shortly after the war. The group met on a Friday evening for criticism and debate on artistic matters.

In 1953, aged 19, Riley entered the Slade on the strength of a folio of drawings done in a particularly unpromising area that surrounded the Manchester to Liverpool railway line. The work impressed Coldstream and Monnington, the Slade tutors who were to exert most influence on Riley between 1953 and 1957. Lucian Freud and Claude Rogers also took an interest in Harold Riley's work. Lowry visited and, as he had done ten years before, looked with interest at the young man's work. In 1958, Riley went on to study art history at the Courtauld Institute and won the Rome Abbey Scholarship. This gave him the opportunity to live and paint at the British School in Rome. He also spent some time in Florence. On his return from Italy he hoped to avoid National Service by spending a year in Castile, Spain. Unfortunately, Riley was eventually obliged to do his two year National Service stint in the army. In 1960 he returned to Salford, able at last to pursue his two chief talents, drawing and football.

Before attending the Slade, Harold Riley had shown outstanding promise as a footballer. Louis Rocca, then chief scout of Manchester United, had Riley playing in the Manchester United junior team alongside young players like Duncan Edwards and Eddie Coleman. Edwards, who died following the Munich air disaster, was the outstanding talent of his generation. Riley learnt from playing alongside players like Edwards that he would never be able to compete at the very highest level. Nevertheless, had he not decided to turn his back on a football career, it is likely he would have made the grade as an average first division or good second division player.

During 1954, Riley returned to Manchester from his studies in London. He had lunch one day with Ted Frape, director of the Salford Art Gallery, and Lowry. Frape courted Jack Goldberg, an influential member on the arts committee of the council, and, with Goldberg's help, was able to purchase Lowrys for the Salford collection. Lowry may possibly have seen Riley as a kind of protégé. He hoped Riley would continue to record the changing face of Salford during the second half of the 20th century. But whereas Lowry always painted to the north of Salford, Harold Riley would concentrate his drawing studies on the area to the south.

John Minton, who also admired Harold Riley's flair for drawing, was a useful contact. He invited Riley to his home in Kensington for a week and together they visited all the principal London galleries. During his first year at the Slade drawing studies were followed by graduation to life drawing classes. His personal tutor Tom Monnington was particularly interested in the young man's drawing and a friendship developed. Indeed, Monnington stopped off in Salford every summer to see Riley while on his way to fishing holidays in Scotland. Another Slade teacher, Ceri Richards, taught Riley lithography. A further influence was the Bloomsbury area to the south of the school's Gower Street location. Topographical drawings of the area's richly endowed roof and street perspectives showed a Euston Road school flavour. Riley discovered the buildings that challenged him in London were bigger and tighter versions of those he was used to in the North. The

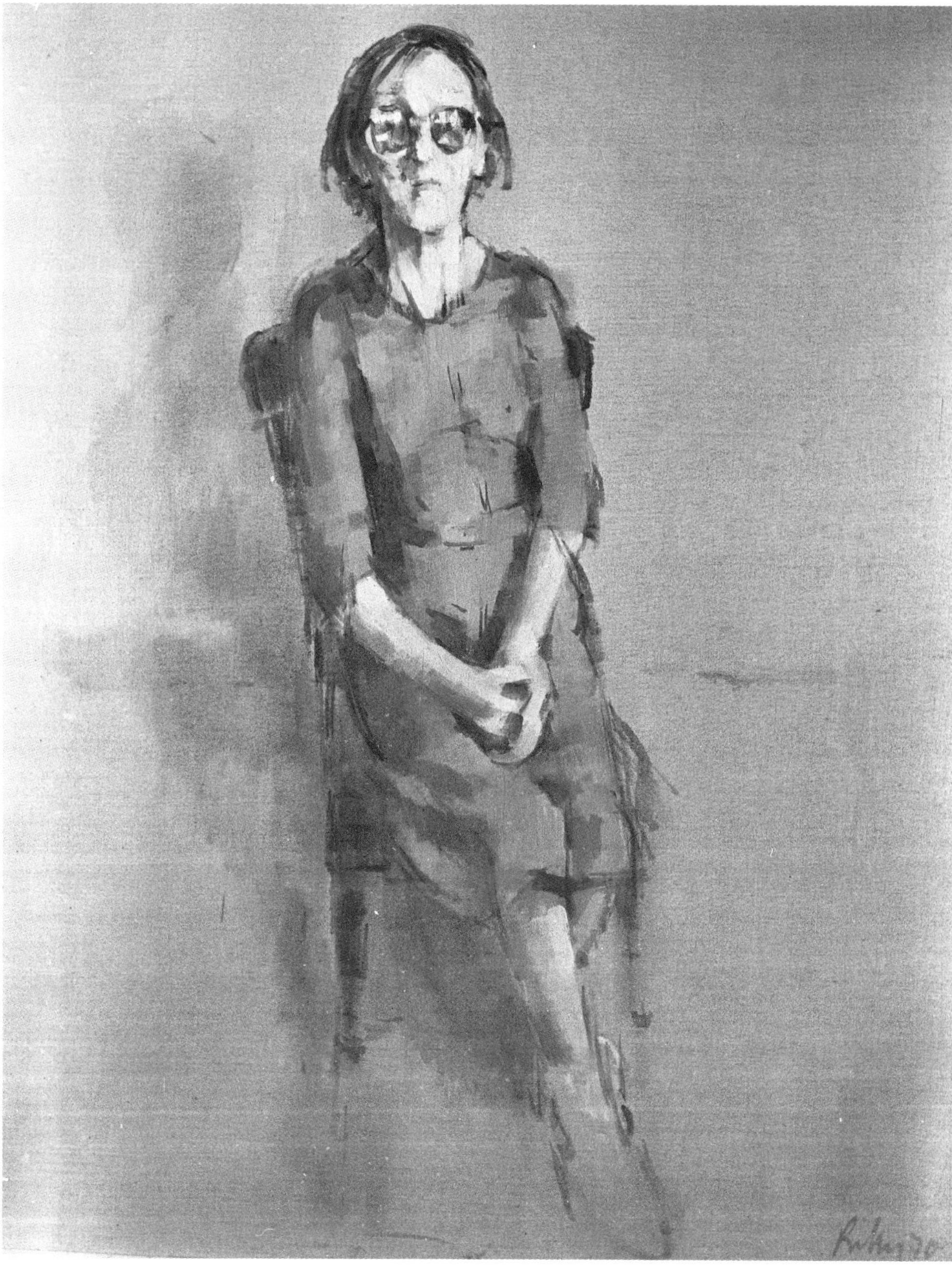

Harold Riley: Portrait of Alice Fairweather, *oil.*

Slade years, above all else, gave Riley the sophisticated style that enabled him to pursue the career of a society portrait painter.

Riley's interest in football resulted in a spate of portraits of some of the game's great figures. As well as painting Edwards and Coleman, Riley produced portraits of George Best, Denis Law and Bobby Charlton, key players in the great championship and European Cup side of the late sixties. Later, in 1984, Riley was commissioned by a businessman, Ernie Kearns, to paint a portrait of Sir Matt Busby. Another football commission came from Tony Stratton-Smith, journalist and art collector, who required a portrait of Denis Law for an article he was writing for the *Daily Mail.* The newspaper did not like the unconventional back view portrait and declined to use it. Riley was granted permission by Les Olive, Club Secretary, to sit on the touchline at important Old Trafford games. From here he made quick sketches or took photographs to use for the painting of football scenes in his studio. Riley found the sporting occasion a fitting subject for art. The colours, atmosphere, high drama and liveliness of packed Old Trafford matches impressed themselves on an artist alive to it all, and bent on distilling the moment of athletic confrontation and the split-second posture of animated contest.

Football subjects occur in the work of several prominent British painters, notably Claude Rogers, Charles Cundall, Lowry and Alan Lowndes. Ironically, one former Manchester United manager, Dave Sexton, when collecting a large number of Harold Riley's works, concentrated on non-football subjects.

During the second half of the 1950's, Harold Riley began exhibiting work at the Manchester Academy spring show. He remembered, and admired, T.C. Dugdale's fine and stately portraits and knew one of the Academy's oldest figures, Francis Dodd, who was so supportive of younger painters. Kenneth Slater purchased many of Riley's contributions to local Manchester exhibitions, and later on began dealing in them. Riley conversed a great deal with the watercolourist, Terry McGlynn, an Academy stalwart by this time. At the end of 1960, Harold Riley, by then living in the Pendleton district of Salford, had a successful exhibition at the library in Manchester. It was an ideal homecoming for the young painter. The exhibition was a sell-out, and among the buyers were Albert Finney Shelagh Delaney, and the local Salford Art Gallery. Another exhibition at Gibb's Bookshop also proved a big seller. The bookshop owner was the brother-in-law of Harry Stevens, one of Riley's earliest art masters at Salford Grammar. With money from these exhibitions, he acquired at a low rent an old coach house studio on Lancaster Road in Salford. Riley held the studio from 1961 to 1976.

From 1961, Riley immersed himself in the topographical recording of Salford but found he could not keep up with the rate of demolition. A sadness at the loss of old places went hand-in-hand with an interest in things that were in the process of becoming. Photographs were taken and paintings were made recording these changes. Salford Art Gallery gave him exhibitions every two years and purchased many of his works. So did private collectors such as industrialist Kenneth Slater. Riley saw Lowry frequently during the 1960's. One meeting, in the summer of 1965, resulted in Riley publishing a pamphlet, reproducing many of his working portrait drawings of Lowry. These led to a superb and vivid evocation of Lowry in a tempera portrait used to illustrate the pamphlet cover. The two had lunch together about once a month. Riley was probably no more successful than anyone else in piercing the outer armour of the great introvert. The two kept a respectable distance and maintained a mutual respect for one another's work, though occasionally Lowry was goaded into passion when opinions differed sufficiently. Obvious differences suggest themselves in the work of these two artists. Riley was more interested in people, even in the landscapes and street views. Lowry concentrated on places and his industrial scenes were backdrops to a theatre that was largely devoid of human emotion. The famous matchstick clones who tramp disconsolately across his canvases are painted in afterwards, as mere props to the greater preoccupation with architectural location. Harold Riley was emphatically interested in people, and part of his unusual talent for portraiture was based on a keen interest in reaching people's innermost character. This is very clear in his portrait of Lowry. It is a very human but real portrait, Lowry squinting in the full force of daylight, and showing the shrewd and humorous side of his personality through a very prominent and revealing mouth. Riley's great interest in character is what ultimately makes him a reliable portrait painter. Lowry, of course, seldom painted portraits though those of his mother, father, or of himself, are alternatively tender or unnerving. Lowry's views on art tell us more about the sensibility lurking behind his vision. He found Rembrandt and Titian - two of the greatest conveyors of the innermost secrets of their sitters - totally foreign to him. He found Canaletto very wooden, yet he liked the Pre-Raphaelite painters Rossetti and Burne-Jones. Harold Riley once took Lowry on motor car excursions to the Queen's Park Art Gallery where Pre-Raphaelite pictures could be seen. The Rossetti drawings that Lowry owned - depicting the 'femme fatale' beauty - are part of the Lowry legend. The younger artist even took him to London. In spite of Riley's formal, classical Slade

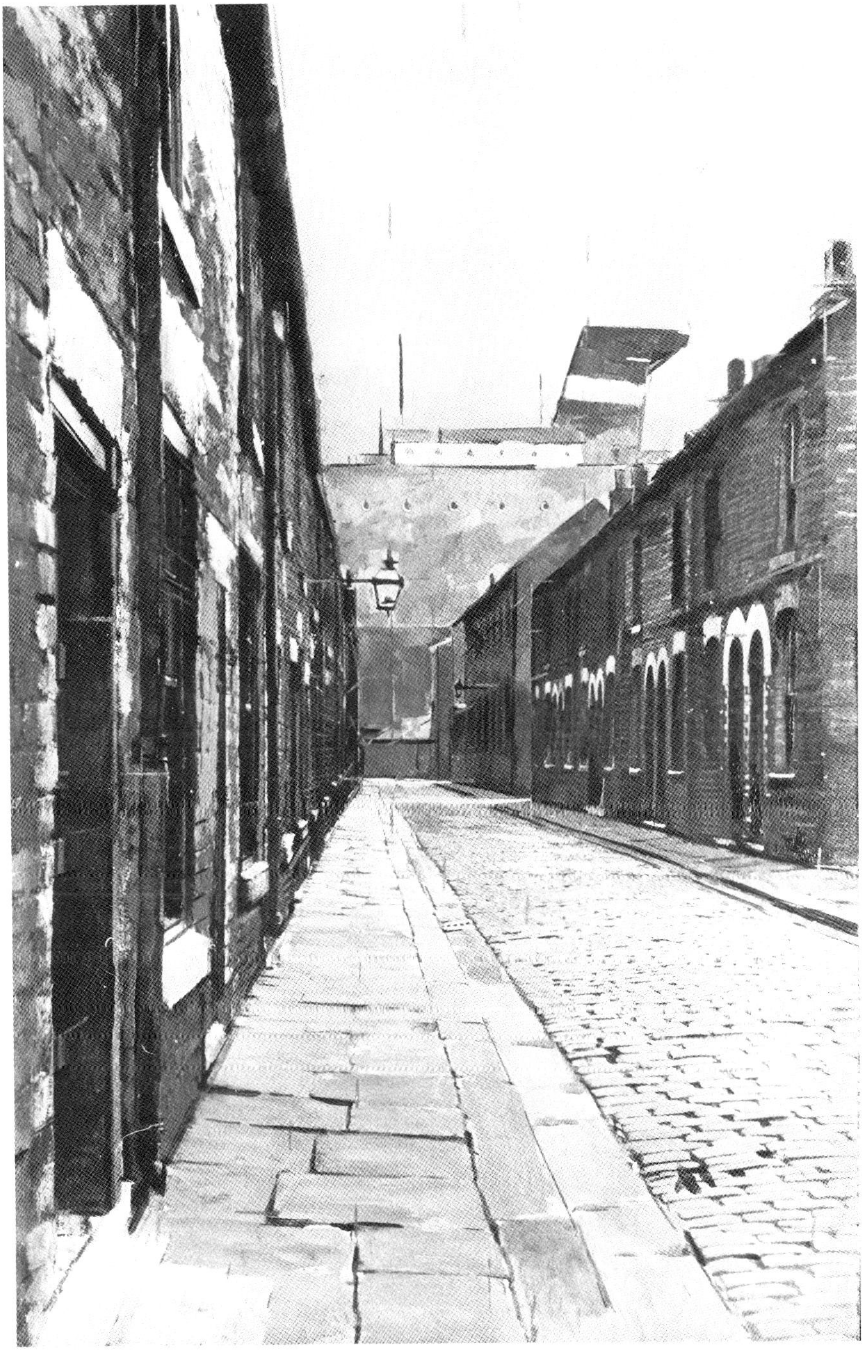

Harold Riley: Street by the Docks, Salford, *oil (courtesy: University of Salford).*

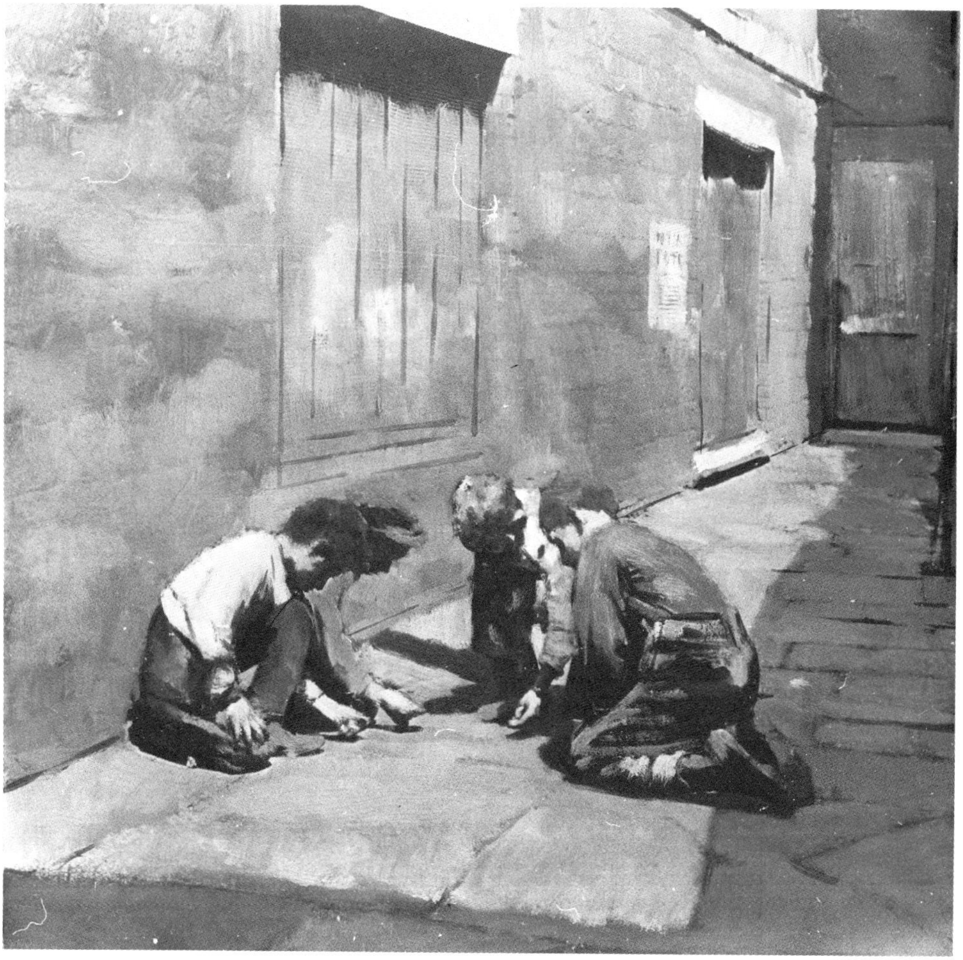

Harold Riley: Marbles, *oil 1963*.

training, he is an artist driven by the conviction that the message and meaning of a painting is of greater significance than the means used to create it; a point of view that would have been congenial to the older man.

A major turning point in Harold Riley's career came in 1970. He was commissioned to paint the portrait of the Duke of Edinburgh in his position as Vice-Chancellor of the University of Salford. The picture, which shows the duke in profile wearing academic dress, was subsequently displayed at both the Royal Academy and the Manchester Academy. Many people were not impressed, which is surprising since it is honest in its realism, and technically admirable. Nevertheless Riley was approached by Chicago publisher, John Schaeffer, who commissioned him to make two portraits a year, usually of well known dignitaries or statesmen, in return for an annual fee. The result was that for 15 years Harold Riley made enough money from a few commissioned portraits to avoid full-time teaching. Among the many notable portraits that Riley painted were: Richard Nixon, Paul Getty, Barbarolli, Maria Callas, Popes John 23 and Paul 6, and a number of powerful bankers. The sitting was usually formal and businesslike, and Riley had little opportunity to get to know the people he was painting. Riley's Slade professor, William Coldstream, once told him that the exhilarating challenge of successful portrait painting lay in being confronted with someone never seen before, so that a cold, impartial study of physiognomy and character could be conducted. Schaeffer also commissioned the Italian sculptor, Manzu, the fifties French realist Bernard Buffet, and the American painter, Jasper Johns, to produce regular work, and Riley had the opportunity to meet these artists in Chicago.

In the 1970's Harold Riley experimented with different graphic media which would help him discover a relationship between painting and photography. Although he continued to record the changing face of Salford he did so with new methods of paint application which included spraying paints over photographs, and using the photograph as a means of arresting the split-second movement of a city street. The series done on sporting themes provided one source for his fascinating study into movement. He published a number of pamphlets and books. These included an interview with Matt Busby, illustrated with working drawings that Riley made of Old Trafford's legendary figure, leading to the portrait. A similar production was of a typical day spent with Lowry in 1965, also illustrated with working pencil drawings of Lowry that led to the tempera portrait. A book, *Street Dogs*, recorded drawings that Riley had been making from 1951 to 1985 and echoes somewhat the humour implicit in the fascination that Lowry had for cripples. Shelley Rhode, in her biography of Lowry, refers to one trip that Lowry made with Riley to the centre of Manchester where the older man was positively delighted to have found cripples or partially deformed people. By focussing his attention on the much-loved English pet, the dog, Riley was recreating in humorous terms a feature of street life that was less disturbing. The Riley dog drawings are mainly rapid pen and ink characterisations and display a pronounced use of crosshatching. One or two earlier drawings of dogs are also reproduced, drawn with the more delicate and elaborate grace afforded by a pencil. These are classic dog drawings, using a variety of smudged, shaded or hatched chiaroscuro techniques. In the 1980's Riley has returned to traditional small scale easel painting with an emphasis on still life.

William Turner was born in Chorlton-in-Medlock in 1920. He began his education at a local school in Gorton, and went on to study part-time at Derby School of Art. These studies were only possible through release from the Royal Ordnance Corps, in which he served from 1940 to 1946. The spasmodic life drawing studies, snatched at every opportunity during the war years, perhaps explain the development of a natural style of painting, notable for its directness, apparent ease of execution, and avoidance of academic stodginess. He may have become bogged down in the technical and structural aspects of painting had he taken up his enrolment at Manchester School of Art after the war. Instead, he decided to pursue a job in Cheetham Hill hand colouring photographs for Progress Ltd. When William Turner arrived at the firm in 1946, both Emmanuel Levy and his wife Ursula had only recently left. Turner was happy in this art-related occupation until 1956, when he began teaching life drawing and painting at an Adult Education College in Mosley Street. Among his many students was Marion Maxwell Reekie, daughter of the well known Manchester Academy painter. He also taught at Hulme Hall School.

William Turner never lacked confidence. Despite his limited training his paintings are characterised by energy and vitality. He exhibited early, showing his work with impunity among the chief artists of Manchester. He first showed at the Manchester Academy in 1949, and continued to make contributions on many occasions thereafter. During the second half of the 1950's he exhibited at Gibb's bookshop, followed in 1958 with an exhibition at the Tibb Lane Gallery and a one-man showing at Salford Art Gallery. The Salford exhibition announced the arrival of a fully-fledged Manchester painter, unafraid of bringing painterly spontaneity and lyrical energy to local subject matter. One of his most individual qualities has been the ability to paint Manchester's most drab industrial areas with a palette and

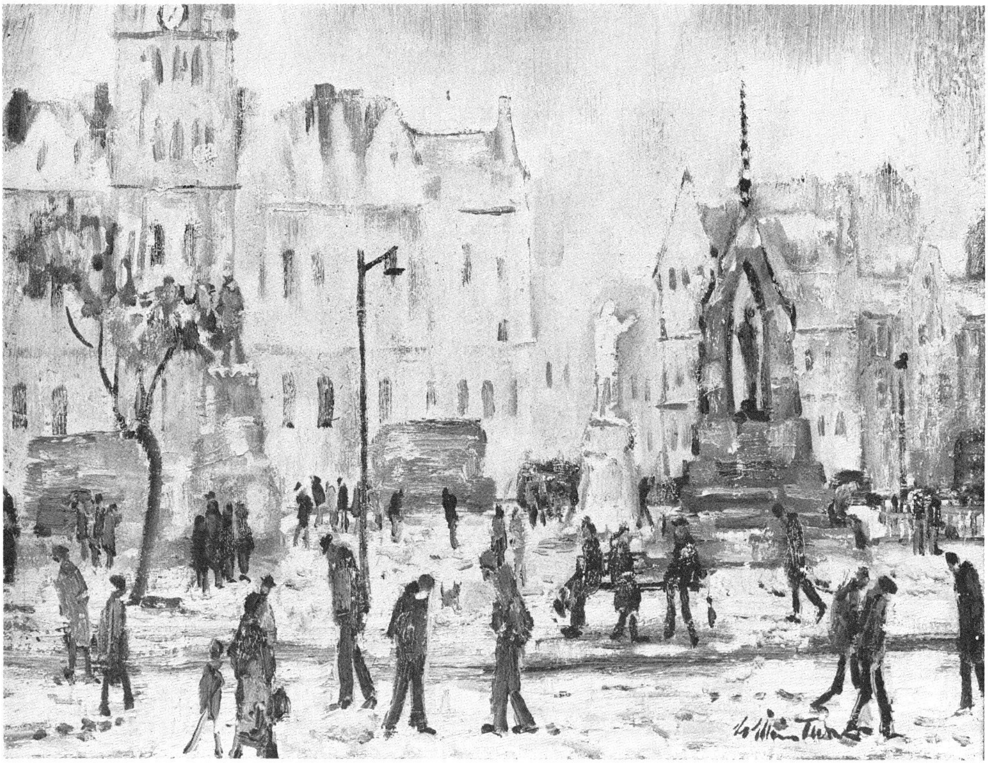

William Turner: Albert Square, Manchester in February, *oil.*

Reddish Lane, *oil.*

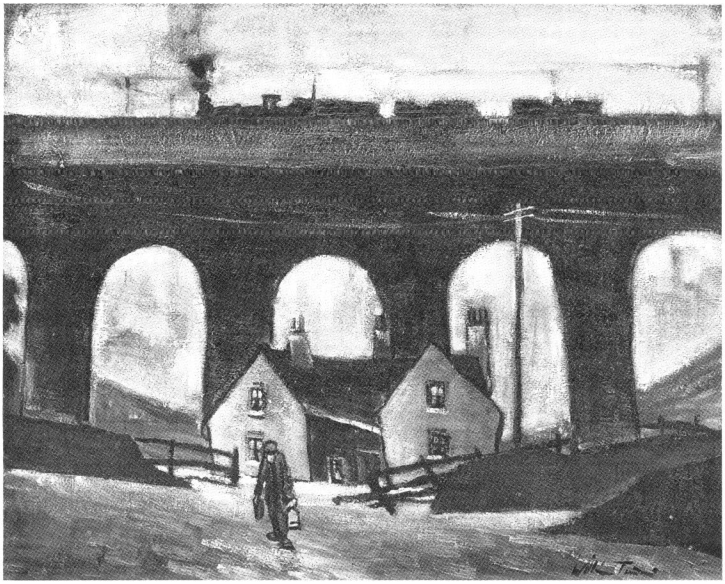

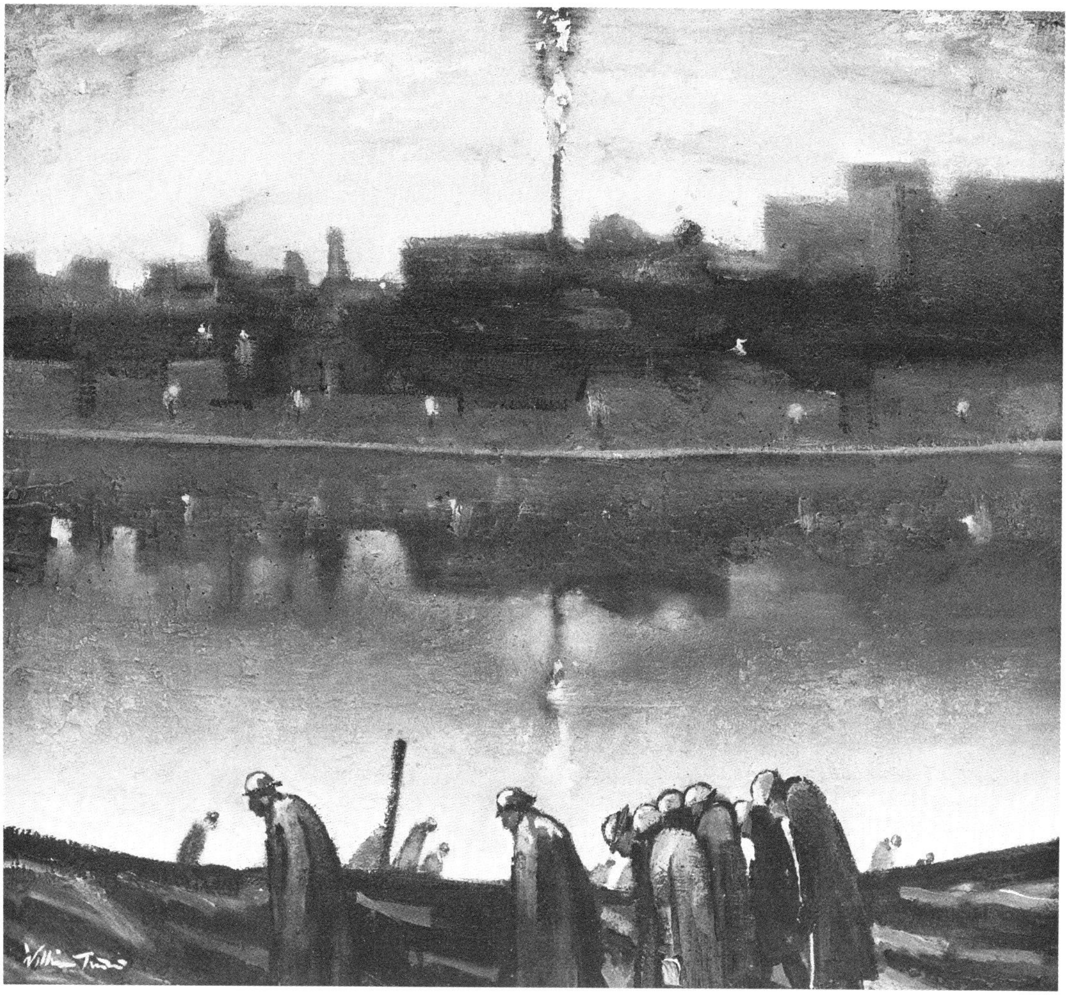

William Turner: The Men from Bromborough, *oil*.

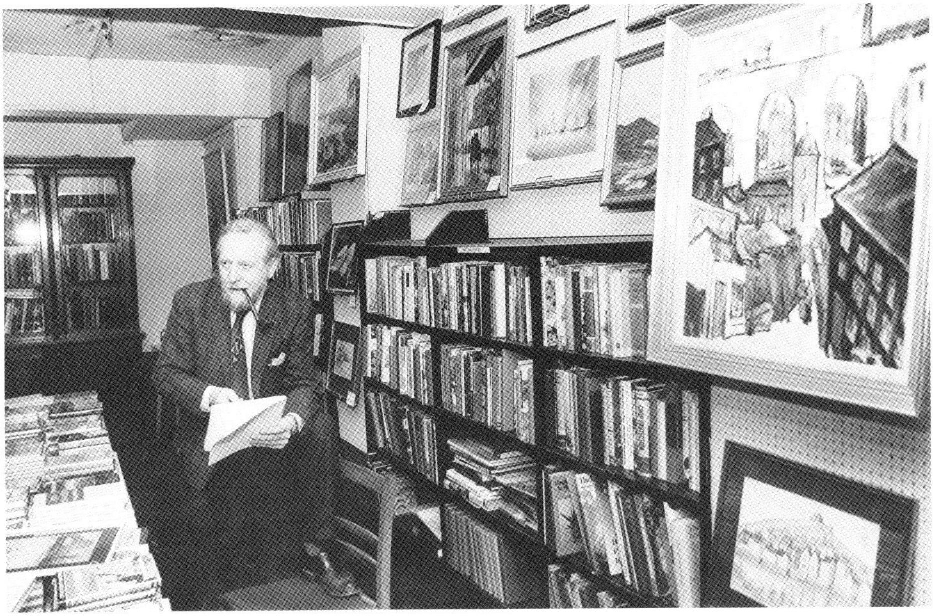

William Turner with his exhibition at the Gibbs bookshop 1979.

handling of pigment associated with the Parisian paintings of Utrillo, Vlaminck, and other *petits maîtres*. Whilst retaining classic elements of *la belle peinture* Turner's paintings remain true to the atmosphere, light and visual incidents of the northern industrial scene.

One clue to the brisk confidence in Turner's style has been his habit of painting mainly from memory. An avid cyclist, he collected memories of places experienced as transitory impressions. Such fleeting images, stored by a sharp memory, could then be expressed through the hand of a naturally fluent painter, and through an eye unwilling to retain excessive topographical detail. The composite view which often resulted was also a feature of Lowry's work, and Lowry was particularly influential in Turner's development. Turner's natural sense of colour also drew him towards the paintings of Lowry's own teacher, Adolphe Valette, with his impressionistic and sometimes monochromatic views of Manchester canals or warehouses. Additional influences were Beckmann's powerful imagery, and the 'Fauve' palette and liquid paint handling of Vlaminck.

Turner's colourful interpretations of Stockport were associated with those of Alan Lowndes, whom Turner had first met through Andreas Kalman's Crane Gallery. Turner fitted in well with this South King Street milieu but Kalman was reluctant to take on Turner as the gallery could only afford to 'carry' one local artist. Even so, the paintings that Kalman was then showing by artists such as Smith or Hitchens, or by European artists like Vlaminck, Soutine, and Bonnard, made a great impact on Turner, who became a regular visitor to the exhibitions. Turner's acquaintance with Lowndes continued less formally at the Yates Winebar, during the years that Turner was living in Pendleton. They never saw one another's studios, but developed a kindred attitude towards art. Lowndes' belief that colour was the primary vehicle of artistic expression was accepted by Turner, but there were inevitably differences of opinion between these two self-willed, though complementary painters. The friendship with Lowry was a different matter. Turner first met Lowry at the Kardomah, in company with Geoffrey Green, owner of Tibb Lane Gallery. During the late 1950's and 1960's, Lowry visited Turner's exhibitions at this Gallery. Lowry refused to give specific answers to Geoffrey Green's questions about Turner's work but he did at least see Turner's exhibitions regularly thereafter. One concrete piece of advice given by Lowry to both Turner and Harold Riley was to implore them to get out and paint Manchester before it was too late. Turner's experience of Lowry was much the same as anyone else's - he seldom wanted to talk about art for long. Lowry did, however, show respect for Turner and Riley. They were invited to his home on separate occasions and allowed to sketch the artist. On Turner's first visit Lowry opened the door but would not allow him in. On a second visit with his wife he was met with hearty hospitality.

William Turner moved from Salford to Cheadle Hulme in 1955. The nearby viaduct town of Stockport had the advantage of hills as an undulating backdrop, adding further interest to the rich industrial architecture. The many Stockport pictures produced since then have often been done in a series of up to six all worked on together, then reworked, until each painting is completed. Such an open-ended approach complements the overriding impression of energy and spontaneity.

The Tibb Lane shows of the late 1950's and early 1960's won considerable critical praise. Brian Bradshaw, writing for the Bolton paper, said that "Turner's churches, mills and houses are distorted into expressive shapes: they sway, bend and twist with serpentine character."[1] Another description of a "hall of mirrors distortion of rippling walls and rubberoid faces," seemed to suggest undertones of Soutine or the Germans, though Turner's more balanced composition and subtler colouring owed more to Vlaminck. The *Manchester Guardian* reporter discerned "a rising star" and alluded to "paintings in which distortion is equally a part of the structure and of the expression."[2]

Despite some objectors such as the prickly Hal Yates, William Turner became a member of the Manchester Academy in the late 1970's. He has continued to be a distinctive exhibitor at Academy exhibitions. His work finds well deserved popularity among the art-buying public, who want authentic local realism matched by painterly spontaneity and generosity of colour.

NOTES

1 *Bolton Evening News* 14.1.60 Brian Bradshaw

2 *Manchester Guardian* 7.1.60

Illustrations

Colour

Between pages 144 and 145

Augustus John, *Two Jamaican Girls*
L.S. Lowry, *Outside the Mill*
Roger Hampson, *Bickershaw Colliery*
Theodore Major, *Wigan Scene*
Peter Hoida, *Weston*
Alan Lowndes, *Old Stockport Fair*

Between pages 176 and 177

Nicholas Horsfield, *Landscape*
Bob Crossley, *Disused Pit*
Margaret Gumuchian, *Aldersgreen Gardens*
R.V. Pitchforth, *Marine Lake, Southport*
William Turner, *St Mary's, Stockport*
Kenneth Gribble, *Park Parade, Ashton-under-Lyne*
Lesley Young, *Blackpool, November*

Black and White

J.M.Whistler, *Shipping at Liverpool* 15
George Mayer-Marton, *Shipyard, Liverpool* 21
Nicholas Horsfield, *The Large Sky* 24
Barbara Lander, *Abstract sculpture* 24
Max Blond, *Across the Mersey* 36
Sam Walsh, *Dinner Party (22 people and me)* 36
Charles Cundall, *Liverpool from the Mersey* 50
Grainger Smith, *The Enemy Raid* 50
W.C.Penn, *Sir Sidney Jones* 53
Arthur Ballard, *Non Figurative Painting* 58
Adrian Henri, *The Entry of Christ into Liverpool* 62
Donald McKinlay, *Composition D* 62
Henry Lamb, *Euphemia* 67

Henry Lamb, *Professor Horace Lamb* 68
Francis Dodd, *Henry Lamb* 70
Forrest Hewit 75
Forrest Hewit, *Northern Ballroom* 75
Fred Yates, *Stockport Viaduct* 79
L.S. Lowry and Tom Cross at the Northern Young Artists Exhibition 82
Julian Trevelyan, *The Potteries* 89
Brian Bradshaw, *Bolton* 89
Georg Eisler, *Whitworth Street* 90
Manchester Academy in early 1930s 98
Malcolm Milne, *Bowl of Flowers* 104
Harry Rutherford, *Penzance* 104
Charles Holmes, *Near Greenwood Mill* 107
James Chettle, *War Memorial, Manchester* 122
Harold Workman, *Printing camouflage cloth* 122
Emmanuel Levy, *Loading the Pictures, Aberystwyth* 124
Frank Dodman, *Manchester Dock* 131
Norman Jaques, *Three Trees* 131
John Milne, *Gnathos* 137
Norman Janes, Two wood engravings 141
L.S. Lowry, *Ancoats Hospital, Outpatients Department* 142
L.S. Lowry, *Excavations at Manchester* 142
Ian Grant, *Midday Studios, Manchester* 152
Margo Ingham discussing a pastel by Ian Grant 152
Ned Owens hanging three Ian Grant paintings 153
John Bold, *Kilronan Arran* 153
Richard Weisbrod, *Lancashire Landscape* 159
Terry McGlynn, *Ashes Farm Kinder* 159
Ian Grant, *Cheshire Mill* 173
Margaret Gumuchian, *Beach Scene, Blackpool* 175
Theodore Major, *Wigan Streets* 182
Theodore Major, *Wigan Factories* 182
Alan Lowndes, *Portrait of the Artist* 189
Valerie and Alan Lowndes, John and Ann Willett, Nicholas Horsfield on holiday 190
Alan Lowndes in his Stockport studios 190
Alan Lowndes, *Street Market* 194
Kenneth Gribble, *4 p.m. West Street* 204
Kenneth Gribble, *Market Street, Middlesbrough* 206
Kenneth Gribble, *Jane* 206

Roger Hampson, *Miners Chanters Colliery* 213
Roger Hampson, *Laughing Miners* 213
Roger Hampson, *Travellers* 213
Roger Hampson, *Shipton Mill, Bolton* 216
Harold Riley, *Portrait of Alice Fairweather* 220
Harold Riley, *Street by the Docks* 223
Harold Riley, *Marbles* 224
William Turner, *Albert Square, Manchester in February* 227
William Turner, *Reddish Lane* 227
William Turner, *The Men from Bromborough* 228
William Turner with his exhibition at the Gibbs bookshop 229

Index

A
Adams, Norman. 217
Adshead, M. 46
Allan, Ronald. 94, 117, 155, 158
Allen, Charles. 17
Allen, Fred. 48
Allsop, George. 176
Almond, Dorothy. 84
Andrews, Joseph. 46
Ardizzone, Edward. 121
Auerbach, Frank. 25
Ayres, Gillian. 37
Ayrton Millicent. 59, 61

B
Bacon, Francis. 145, 180
Bagnall, Julia. 208
Ballard, Arthur. 6, 13, 22, 26, 35, 59, 61, 63
Barry, Sir Charles. 93, 148
Baskerville, R. 6, 157, 158, 160, 161
Baynes, Keith. 26
Bayes, Walter. 93
Bell, Graham. 23, 202
Bell, Vanessa. 86
Bell, Martin. 7, 26, 46, 47, 49, 52, 55, 56, 57, 59, 60, 61
Bell, Robert Anning. 17,
Bennett, Mary. 61
Berlin, Sven. 11, 151, 156, 157
Bertram, Neville. 61
Birch, Charles Bell. 20
Bisson, Roderick. 7, 9, 51, 54
Blackadder, Elizabeth. 82
Blake, Vernon. 203
Block, Martin. 116
Blockley, John. 214
Blond, Jonathan. 11, 20, 35
Blond, Leslie. 34, 37
Blond, Max. 10, 11, 34, 35
Bold, John. 48, 123, 125, 130, 157, 160, 161, 163, 207, 214
Bomberg, David. 25, 201
Bone, Muirhead. 66, 132
Bowes, John. 61, 117, 123, 133, 155, 158, 161, 162, 214
Boyd, Graham. 41
Bradley, Helen. 13
Bradshaw, Brian. 60, 61, 82, 123, 128, 130, 139, 144-7, 205, 230
Bratby, John. 61, 147
Braque, George. 27, 38, 60
Brockhurst, Gerald. 95, 129
Brooks, Marjorie. 46
Brown, Ford Madox. 127
Brown, Ralph. 31
Buffet, Bernard. 147, 183, 225
Bulley, Margaret. 7
Burne-Jones. 222

C
Cameron, D. Y. 94
Caro, Anthony. 43, 88, 203
Carr, David. 144
Carr, Henry. 31
Carter-Preston, Edward. 47, 49
Cassidy, John. 119
Casson, Hugh. 215, 217
Charlton, George. 203
Chettle, James. 46, 71, 93, 94, 96, 103, 105, 106, 108, 109, 110, 115, 117, 119, 121
Chowne, Gerard. 17, 18
Christopherson, José. 84, 144, 158, 161, 163, 214
Clausen, George. 132
Coburn-Witherop, J. 19, 22, 46, 48, 54, 55, 80
Cockrill, Maurice. 7, 13
Cohen, Bernard. 203
Cohen, Harold. 203
Coldstream, William. 26, 201, 202, 207, 218, 225
Connard, Phillip. 49
Cooper, Byron. 98, 99, 101, 103
Cooper, Heaton. 135

Copley, John. 101, 123, 134
Copnall, Frank. 47, 48, 51
Copnall, Teresa. 52, 54
Corser, Trevor. 80
Corbridge, John. 81
Crabtree, Trevor. 42
Craddock, Kenneth. 130, 135, 211
Craxton, John. 162, 195
Cross, Tom. 80-82
Crossley, Bob. 28, 139, 143, 144
Cundall, Charles. 94, 96, 100, 103, 105, 110, 117, 120, 123, 126, 129, 132, 221

D
Dacre, Isabel. 96, 102, 132
Dali, Salvador. 163
Dalwood, Hubert. 21
Darwin, Robin. 170, 203
Davies, Austin. 35, 56, 57, 59, 60
Davies, Glenys. 64
Davies, John. 132
Deane, Fred. 145
Denvir, Bernard. 13, 166
Dodd, Albert. 171
Dodd, Francis. 66, 93, 94, 96, 98, 100, 101, 109, 110, 111, 115, 126, 127, 132, 221
Dodman, Frank. 11, 19, 130
Dooley, Arthur. 7, 20, 31
Drey, Agnes. 117
Drummond, Malcolm. 74
Dugdale, Tom. 74, 95, 98, 103, 105, 106, 117, 123, 130, 134, 140
Durrant, Jennifer. 43, 87

E
Eardley, Joan. 191
Edkins, John. 7, 22
Elliff, Brian. 25, 26
Eisler, Georg. 7, 12
Epstein, Jacob. 20, 31, 132, 165
Etty, William. 61

F
Fairclough, Bernard. 158, 163, 166
Fairhurst, H. 76
Feather, Yankel. 61
Fell, Sheila. 13
Fergusson, J. D. 116
Fisher, Pamela. 123
Fishwick, Clifford. 22
Fitton, James. 69, 147
Foster, John. 42, 43
Fothergill, Ian. 81
Frampton, Meredith. 95
Frank, Julian. 195
Frankenthaler, Helen. 43
Fraser, R. 47
Frost, Terry. 187, 215
Fry, Roger. 18, 108
Fuller, Leonard. 100

G
Gabain, Ethel. 126, 133, 134
Garland, Molly. 54
Gardiner, Reg. 84
Garside, John. 119
Garside, Oswald, 48, 52, 125
Gauld, John. 117, 120, 127, 129, 130
Gear, William. 139
George, Patrick. 34
Giacometti, Alberto. 146
Goddard, Michael. 86
Godwin, Keith. 42, 217
Goldsworthy, Andy. 88
Gordon, Brian. 22
Gottlib, Henryk. 201
Gouk, Alan. 40
Grant, Ian. 11, 46, 49, 62, 71, 81, 91, 119, 120, 150, 154, 156, 160, 161, 162, 167, 169-177
Greaves, D. 109
Gribble, Ken. 11, 145, 199-209
Grieffenhagen, Maurice. 169
Grimmond, William. 105, 120, 126, 129, 134, 139
Grimshaw, Trevor. 87
Gross, Anthony. 121
Grosvenor, Edgar. 52
Gumuchian, Margaret. 82, 91, 176, 177

H
Haffar, Leila. 123, 158, 160
Hallam, Marilyn. 88
Hamilton, Richard. 64, 87, 203

Hampson, Roger. 11, 91, 92, 128, 130, 135, 139, 145, 210-217
Hammersley, J. 93
Hargreaves, Joan. 157, 160, 161
Harrison, Claude. 84
Hart, John. 7, 60, 61
Hartas, Philip. 61
Hartley, Mooney. 76, 95, 101, 111
Harvey, Harold. 129
Haward, Laurence. 73, 119, 120, 125, 126, 127, 134, 144, 148, 149
Hayward, Arthur. 80, 118
Hemingway, Harold. 6, 105, 109, 112, 123, 125, 128, 130, 214
Hemm, Gordon. 171
Henri, Adrian. 8, 63, 64
Hepworth, Barbara. 61, 137, 197
Heron, Patrick. 64
Hertford, Irvine. 47
Hewinson, Morgan. 214
Hewit, Forrest. 72, 74, 76, 77, 78, 108, 111, 114, 115, 117, 120, 123, 134, 147
Hilton, Arthur. 117, 123, 156, 157, 160
Hilton, Colin. 214
Hilton, Roger. 40, 63
Hinchcliffe, Richard. 46, 48, 52
Hirsch, Walter. 214
Hitchens, Ivon. 83, 230
Hockney, David. 64
Hodgkin, Howard. 34
Hodgkins, Frances. 78, 99, 158
Hoffman, Hans. 38, 42
Hoida, Peter. 11, 39-40
Hollow, Geoff. 43, 88
Holmes, Charles. 93, 100, 102, 108, 109, 112
Holmes, John. 81, 210
Hopkins, Clyde. 88
Horsfield, Nicholas. 6, 9, 11, 22-29, 45, 59, 61, 63, 82, 187, 196
Horton, Percy. 25
Hoyland, John. 39, 64, 88
Huggill, Henry. 19, 52
Hughes, Malcolm. 145
Hughes, Margaret. 59
Humphreys, Winifred. 51

I
Ingham, Bryan. 80
Ingham, Margo. 10, 26, 33-4, 82, 84, 130, 150-51, 154, 156, 160, 162-3, 166, 171-2, 174-5, 196.
Irvin, Albert. 39

J
Janes, Norman. 120, 129, 133, 134
Jardine, George. 6,7, 37
Jaques, Norman. 91, 92, 144, 210, 214
Jellicoe, Colin. 177
John, Augustus. 17, 18, 66, 102, 135, 165
Johnston, Colin. 80
Johnston, William. 200
Jowett, Percy. 25
Johnson, Audrey. 84

K
Kalman, Andreas. 20, 83, 86, 164-5, 186, 195-98, 229
Kandinsky, Wassily. 179
Keen, Jeff. 7
Keene, Paul. 91, 171, 210
Kershaw, Walter. 86-87
Kirchherr, Astrid. 10
Kirk, Janet. 96, 110, 123
Knight, Joseph. 66, 132

L
La Dell, Edwin. 176
Lamb, Henry. 65-69, 93, 101, 103, 110, 111, 125, 129, 134 5.
Lamb, Horace. 65, 66, 69
Lancaster, Percy. 47, 54-5, 96, 117, 120, 132, 133-5, 155, 170
Lander, Barbara. 11, 40-1, 43
Lander, Richard. 40
Lanyon, Peter. 38
Lavery, Sir John. 95
Le Breton. 6
Lennon, John. 37, 196
Lessore, Thérèse. 74
Levy, Emmanuel. 6, 10, 26, 74, 96, 98, 100-2, 119, 123, 125, 135, 145, 148, 186, 192, 193, 195.
Lewis, Kevin. 11, 91

Lewis, Stephen. 11, 40-43, 88
Lhote, André. 170
Lightfoot, Maxwell Gordon. 16
Lindner, Moffat. 99
Lloyd, Pamela. 82
Lothian, Murdock. 64
Lowe, Jeff. 88
Lowe, Vera. 91
Lowndes, Alan. 6, 10, 22, 28, 83-4, 86, 128, 133-4, 145, 157, 162, 165, 167, 181, 185-198, 211, 221, 229
Lowry, L. S. 6, 26, 27, 33, 82, 83, 84, 86, 102, 106, 109, 111, 112, 114-16, 120, 121, 123, 132, 140, 148, 156, 157, 162, 164, 167, 180-81, 195, 207-8, 217-18, 221-2, 225, 229, 230
Lutyens, Sir Edwin. 52
Lynch, Donald. 51
Lyons, Mike. 42

M
Mackarell, Peter. 7
Madox Brown, Ford. 127, 134
Magnus, Emma. 108
Major, Theodore. 6, 11, 86, 123, 128, 130, 133, 135, 139, 145, 151, 155, 157, 158, 160, 161, 162, 163, 164, 165, 167, 178-184
Mann, James. 17, 48, 54
Mann, Robert. 214
Marples, George. 55
Martin, Alison. 46
Martin, Hannah. 171
Mason, Mike. 42
Massey, Delia. 140
Matisse, Henri. 170, 172, 183
Mayer-Marton, George. 7, 21, 56, 57, 59, 60.
McBryde, Robert. 133, 138, 162
McCarthy, John. 20
MacColl, D.S. 17
McEvoy, Ambrose. 102
McGill, J. 40
McGlynn, Terry. 125, 130, 134, 139, 143, 144, 148, 156, 157, 158, 160, 163, 221,
McInnes, Colin. 201
Mackarell, Peter. 63
McKinlay, Donald. 11, 37, 60
McNair, Herbert. 17, 18
McNay, M. G. 63
McWhirter. 177
Meidner. 178
Merek, Jeremy. 86
Messent, Charles. 156, 158, 160, 166
Michaelangelo. 39, 193
Middleditch, Edward. 109, 128, 147, 180
Milne, John. 136
Milne, Malcolm. 96, 100, 102, 103, 117, 120, 197
Minton, John. 133, 162, 200, 201, 219
Mitchell, William. 21
Monaco, Lorenzo. 108
Monet, Claude. 18, 29, 72, 100
Moore, Henry. 21, 31, 83
Monnington, Tom. 170, 218, 219
Mooney, Hartley. 76, 95, 101, 109, 111
Morris, Cedric. 78
Mostyn, Margery. 99, 100, 119
Mostyn, Tom. 71, 73, 99
Munch, Edvard. 183
Mundy, Henry. 34, 37, 38, 64
Munnings, Alfred. 106, 144

N
Nash, Paul. 111, 120, 165
Newcomb, Mary. 86
Nevinson, Christopher. 17, 111, 120
Newton, Eric. 103, 116, 123, 157
Nicholls, Bertram. 93, 94, 97, 98, 101, 103, 143
Nicholson, Ben. 83, 84, 138, 156, 165, 195, 197
Nicholson, Winifred. 86
Noland, Ken. 42, 43

O
Oliver, Charles. 49
Olsson, Julius. 49, 99
O'Brien, Peter. 171
O'Malley, Tony. 88
Oppenheimer, Charles. 71, 72, 95, 96, 98,. 100, 106
Orpen, William. 48, 93, 95, 102, 140
Owens, Ned. 130, 148, 150, 151, 154, 156-158, 160, 162, 164, 166, 167, 171, 172

P
Park, John. 80, 94, 96, 100, 101, 106, 109, 110, 111, 118, 156
Pasmore, Victor, 202
Paton, Hugh. 71
Paolozzi, Eduardo. 21
Pellow, Cynthia. 208
Penn, William. 22, 37, 46-49, 51, 52, 54, 55, 56
Percival, Robert. 59, 61
Picasso, Pablo. 127, 170
Pilkington, Margaret. 108, 155
Piper, John. 165
Pissarro, Camille. 102
Pitchforth, Vivian. 25, 29-32, 121, 128, 135
Platt, John. 199
Pollard, George. 111, 112
Pollock, Jackson, 40
Poons, Larry. 43
Platts, Stella. 130
Preston, Edward Carter. 47
Proctor, Dod. 118

R
Rabin, Sam. 10
Ratcliffe, Henry. 30, 31, 32, 33
Rathbone, Richard. 17
Rayner, Donald. 215
Reade, Vincent. 105, 109
Reed, Stanley. 46, 51, 54-57, 59, 118, 145
Reekie, Marion Maxwell. 11, 106
Reekie, William Maxwell. 46, 69, 71, 72, 73, 74, 76, 105, 110, 111, 116, 120, 125, 129, 130, 143, 154
Rembrandt. 222
Reilly, C. 96
Richards, Ceri. 219
Richier, G. 21
Ricketts, Charles. 102, 108
Riding, Harold. 139
Rigden, Geoff. 88
Riley, Harold. 11, 13, 145, 151, 208, 218-231
Riley, Robin. 7, 20, 22, 35, 36
Ritchie, Hannah. 76, 78
Rivel, John. 170
Roberts, William. 160
Robertson George. 199
Rodin, A. 136
Rogers, Claude. 23, 32, 202, 208, 218
Roocroft, Ted. 91
Rosoman, Leonard. 21
Rossetti, G. 14, 222
Rothenstein, William. 23, 170
Royle, Herbert. 94
Rushbury, Henry. 126
Rutherford, Harry. 6, 26, 76, 80, 92, 103, 106, 110, 111, 134, 140, 145, 207, 215

S
Satchwell, Eric. 218
Saunders, Kay. 42, 43
Saunders, Jane. 78
Schwabe, Randolph. 132, 202, 203
Scrutton, Hugh. 6, 59, 82, 157, 158, 161
Senior, Derek. 97, 120, 121, 123, 125, 127, 128, 130, 138, 139, 143, 156
Severini. 172
Sewter, Alan. 143, 144, 145, 146, 147, 148
Sewter, Charles. 56, 57, 59, 60, 61, 81, 97, 174
Sharpe, Charles. 48, 51, 52, 54, 55
Shaw, Peter. 214
Shemelt, Mary. 88
Sickert, Walter. 23, 28, 29, 72, 74, 76, 77, 78, 103, 114, 115, 116, 147, 165, 215
Simpson, Alex. 86
Simpson, June. 86
Smart, Borlase. 99, 106
Smart, Rowley. 102
Smith, David. 38
Smith, Grainger. 49, 51, 52, 54
Smith, Herbert Tyson. 20, 49
Smith, Jack. 64
Smith, Matthew. 83, 97, 164
Solomon, Leo. 205
Sorrel, Alan. 26
Soutine, C. 20, 83, 230
Spear, Ruskin. 25, 40, 69
Spence, Basil. 20
Spencer, Gilbert. 25
Spencer, Stanley. 17, 25, 110, 120, 158
Stafford, Carolyn. 13

Stanier, Donald. 214
Steer, Philip Wilson. 37
Steinthal, Egbert. 71
Stevens, Harry. 218, 221
Stevenson, W.L. 60
Stubbs. G. 39
Summer, Roger. 158, 160
Sutcliffe, Stuart. 7, 22, 196
Sutherland, Graham. 84, 121, 165, 195, 199, 202
Sweet, David. 88, 91
Swynnerton, Annie. 102
Swynnerton, Joseph. 102
Sylvester, David. 180

T
Tankard, Allan. 19, 54, 57, 60
Taylor, Arnold. 134
Taylor, Doris. 91
Taylor, Françoise. 6
Taylor, Ray. 158, 160, 166
Thearle, Herbert. 54
Thompson, Heber. 200
Thornton, Les. 40
Tippin-Moreton, Bertha. 51
Titian. 222
Tonkin, Paul. 88
Tonks. 17
Townsend, William. 202
Trevelyan, Julian. 23
Tucker, Anthony. 62, 63
Tunnicliffe, Charles. 84, 97, 100, 117, 120, 129
Turner, William. 11, 91, 226-231
Tuson, Robert. 214
Tyson-Smith, Herbert. 51, 55

U
Uglow Euan. 64
Underwood, Hazel. 82
Utrillo, Maurice. 57, 229

V
Van Gogh, Vincent. 39, 102, 164
Vaughan, Keith. 147, 162
Velasquez. 14
Vlaminck, Maurice. 20, 123, 164, 195, 229, 230
Valette, Adolphe. 10, 23, 65, 101, 229
Vitofski, Henry. 55

W
Wadsworth, Edward. 17
Walker, John. 64
Walsh, Sam. 7, 22, 37, 63
Warburton, Stanley. 214
Warden, William. 54
Warhol, Andy. 8
Watt, Tom. 88
Watkinson, Ray. 162
Wedgewood, Geoffrey. 26, 52, 54, 56
Weight, Carel. 86, 138
Weisbrod, Richard. 84, 114, 123, 125, 146, 156, 158, 160, 161, 162, 163, 168
Whistler, James McNeill. 14, 66, 132
Whittle, Stephen, 44
Wildman, William. 100
Wilkinson, Derek. 214
Willett, John. 11, 18, 22, 27, 29, 34, 37, 97, 133-35, 138, 139, 143, 163, 164, 197
Williams, Terrick. 45, 93, 102, 106
Williamson, Harold. 116, 143
Willcock, Jack. 91
Wilson, Richard. 39
Wilson, Scottie. 84
Windsor, Alan. 81
Wood, Christopher. 78, 110, 198
Wood, Grant. 19
Wood, Wilfred. 140, 207
Workman, Harold. 105, 111, 126, 139
Wragg, Gary. 88
Wright, Gertrude. 101
Wynter, Brian. 147

Y
Yates, Fred. 11, 22, 80, 130, 134
Yates, Hal. 73, 114, 129, 138, 139, 143, 144, 148, 156, 158, 160, 166, 215, 230
Young, Lesley. 11, 87
Young, Richard. 60, 61, 63
Youngerman, Nan. 147

Z
Zadkine, Ossip. 136